LAND RIGHTS NOV

Land rights for Indigenous Peoples are a global phenomenon and have become an important part of the liberal democratic state. But despite their promise of restoring "Land Back," most land justice frameworks have largely preserved the status quo. In this work, William Nikolakis draws from the diverse experiences of Indigenous and non-Indigenous scholars and legal practitioners from across the world. This book documents both the persistent barriers to "Land Back" as well as the opportunities for moving forward with land justice. By bringing these diverse voices together, Nikolakis seeks to share lessons from land justice movements, with the goal of advancing land rights for Indigenous Peoples across the world. This title is also available as open access on Cambridge Core.

For more than two decades, NIKOLAKIS has worked with Indigenous Peoples to secure their rights to lands and resources. He is a professor at the University of British Columbia, where he was instrumental in developing the Bachelor of Indigenous Land Stewardship. He has published more than sixty peer-reviewed publications and four edited books. Nikolakis is also a practicing lawyer in British Columbia and works closely with First Nations to revitalize the stewardship of their lands.

LAND RIGHTS NOW

Global Voices on Indigenous Peoples and Land Justice

Edited by

WILLIAM NIKOLAKIS
University of British Columbia

CAMBRIDGE
UNIVERSITY PRESS

CAMBRIDGE
UNIVERSITY PRESS

Shaftesbury Road, Cambridge CB2 8EA, United Kingdom

One Liberty Plaza, 20th Floor, New York, NY 10006, USA

477 Williamstown Road, Port Melbourne, VIC 3207, Australia

314–321, 3rd Floor, Plot 3, Splendor Forum, Jasola District Centre, New Delhi – 110025, India

103 Penang Road, #05-06/07, Visioncrest Commercial, Singapore 238467

Cambridge University Press is part of Cambridge University Press & Assessment,
a department of the University of Cambridge.

We share the University's mission to contribute to society through the pursuit of
education, learning and research at the highest international levels of excellence.

www.cambridge.org
Information on this title: www.cambridge.org/9781009521543

DOI: 10.1017/9781009521581

First published 2025

A catalogue record for this publication is available from the British Library

Library of Congress Cataloging-in-Publication Data
Names: Nikolakis, William, editor.
Title: Land rights now : global voices on indigenous peoples and land justice / edited by William Nikolakis,
University of British Columbia, Vancouver.
Description: Cambridge, United Kingdom ; New York, NY : Cambridge University Press, 2025. |
Includes bibliographical references and index.
Identifiers: LCCN 2025000099 (print) | LCCN 2025000100 (ebook) | ISBN 9781009521543 (hardback) |
ISBN 9781009521574 (paperback) | ISBN 9781009521581 (epub)
Subjects: LCSH: Indigenous peoples–Land tenure–Law and legislation. | Indigenous peoples–Claims. |
Indigenous peoples (International law)
Classification: LCC KI352 .L36 2025 (print) | LCC KI352 (ebook) | DDC 346.04/32089–dc23/eng/20250114
LC record available at https://lccn.loc.gov/2025000099
LC ebook record available at https://lccn.loc.gov/2025000100

ISBN 978-1-009-52154-3 Hardback
ISBN 978-1-009-52157-4 Paperback

CONTENTS

ACKNOWLEDGMENTS

The journey for publishing this book took more than 5 years. Many people provided important contributions, both personal and intellectual. I would first like to thank the contributors for sharing their experiences and insights. I would like to thank Justin O'Brien for his wisdom and guidance early on in the development of this book.

My deepest gratitude to the reviewers, to Julie McGonegal for her proficient editing and indexing, and to the University of British Columbia Open Access Fund for making this book more accessible.

Finally, my love and gratitude to my family, Aimee Nygaard, and Ava and Mila Nikolakis – this could not have happened without your support.

CONTRIBUTORS

JAGANNATH AMBAGUDIA is Professor and Dean, School of Social Sciences and Humanities, and Deputy Director, Tata Institute of Social Sciences, Guwahati Campus, Assam, India.

IAN G. BAIRD is a Professor, Department of Geography, University of Wisconsin-Madison, United States.

AHMED BENDELLA is Amazigh, a researcher with the Global Diversity Foundation, and LADSIS Hassan II University of Casablanca.

OMAIRA BOLAÑOS CÁRDENAS is Director, Latin America and Gender Justice Programs, Rights and Resources Initiative, Washington D. C., United States.

RICARDO CAMILO NIÑO IZQUIERDO is Indigenous Arhuaco, and Coordinator for the Indigenous Secretariat of the National Commission of Indigenous Territories, (CNTI), Colombia.

MARI CARMEN ROMERA is a researcher with the Anthropology and History of the Construction of Social and Political Identities (AHCISP) and Laboratori d'Anàlisi de Sistemes Socio-Ecològics en la Globalització (LASEG) Universitat Autònoma de Barcelona (ICTA-UAB).

EMILY CARUSO is a researcher with the Global Diversity Foundation.

JOEL E. CORREIA is an Assistant Professor in the Human Dimensions of Natural Resources Department at Colorado State University in Fort Collins, Colorado, United States.

SANDRA CORTÉS ACOSTA is an Environmental Economist, EnviroStrat, Auckland, Aotearoa/New Zealand.

UGO D'AMBROSIO is a researcher with the Global Diversity Foundation.

DANIEL DIAMOND is a member of the Opaskwayak Cree Nation and an Assistant Professor at the Faculty of Law, University of Manitoba, Canada.

PABLO DOMINGUEZ is a researcher with GEODE/Éco-anthropologie, Centre National de la Recherche Scientifique, the Global Diversity Foundation and the Anthropology and History of the Construction of Social and Political Identities (AHCISP) and Laboratori d'Anàlisi de Sistemes Socio-Ecològics en la Globalització (LASEG) Universitat Autònoma de Barcelona (ICTA-UAB).

FERNANDA FRIZZO BRAGATO is a Professor of Law, Universidade do Vale do Rios do Sinos (Unisinos) Law School, Brazil.

JOCELYN GETGEN KESTENBAUM is a Professor of Law, Benjamin N. Cardozo School of Law, Yeshiva University, United States.

MARCOS GLAUSER is a researcher with Tierraviva and PRONII-CONACYT, Paraguay.

ROBERT K. HITCHCOCK is a Professor, University of New Mexico, Alberquque. United States.

CARWYN JONES is Ngāti Kahungunu and Pūkenga Matua (Head Lecturer) for the Ahunga Tikanga Programme (Māori Laws and Philosophy) at the Te Wānanga o Raukawa, Aotearoa/New Zealand.

LASSANA KONÉ is a lawyer with the Forest Peoples Programme, Abidjan, Côte d'Ivoire.

OULA-ANTTI LABBA is Sámi from Eanodat / Enontekiö, Sápmi, and currently works in the Ministry of Justice, Finland.

SOUFIANE M'SOU is Amazigh and a researcher with the Global Diversity Foundation.

FRANCIS MARKHAM is a Research Fellow, Centre for Aboriginal Economic Policy Research (CAEPR) at the Australian National University.

GARY MARTIN is a researcher with the Global Diversity Foundation.

SMITH MOETI is *G//ana San* from Metsiamong and a member of the Central Kalahari Residents Committee.

WILLIAM NIKOLAKIS is an Assistant Professor, University of British Columbia, Canada.

HEIDI NORMAN is a member of the Gomeroi Nation and Professor at the University of New South Wales, Australia.

DOUGLAS SANDERSON (AMO BINASHII) is a member of the Opaskwayak Cree Nation, and the Prichard Wilson Chair in Law & Public Policy, and Decanal Advisor on Indigenous Issues, University of Toronto, Canada.

MARIA SAPIGNOLI is an Associate Professor, University of Milan, Italy.

YOGESWARAN SUBRAMANIAM is Advocate and Solicitor, Associate Member, Centre for Malaysian Indigenous Studies, University of Malaya, Malaysia.

ALEXANDRA TOMASELLI is a senior researcher at the Institute for Minority Rights of the European Academy of Bozen-Bolzano, Eurac Research, Italy.

RODRIGO VILLAGRA-CARRON is a Professor, Federal University of Latin American Integration, Brazil, and researcher associated with Tierraviva.

ROBERT A. WILLIAMS JR. Member of the Lumbee Tribe, North Carolina is the Regents Professor, E. Thomas Sullivan Professor of Law and Faculty Co-Chair of the University of Arizona Indigenous Peoples Law and Policy Program, James E. Rogers College of Law, University of Arizona, United States.

FOREWORD

In his 1973 book, *God Is Red: A Native View of Religion*, Vine Deloria Jr., the Standing Rock Sioux author and activist who back then was what we would call today the pre-eminent American Indian "influencer" of the twentieth century, fashioned a dramatic call to action:

> Who will find peace with the lands? The future of humankind lies waiting for those who will come to understand their lives and take up their responsibilities to all living things. Who will listen to the trees, the animals and birds, the voices of the places of the land? As the long-forgotten peoples of the respective continents rise and begin to reclaim their ancient heritage, they will discover the meaning of the lands of their ancestors.

Now, precisely a half-century later, those "long-forgotten peoples," the Indigenous Peoples of the Americas, Asia, Africa, the Pacific, and Sápmi, as Deloria foretold, have indeed taken this call to action to heart, rising up, and, as the chapters in this book show, asserting and advancing their demands for land justice and Land Back as they seek to reclaim their ancestral homelands stolen by their European colonizers and the successor post-colonial governments put in their place.

The experiences and struggles of Indigenous Peoples in demanding land justice and Land Back from their governments in each of the countries described are all uniquely shaped and driven by different and varying national laws, policies, prejudices, and degrees of repression, intimidation, and violence aimed at Indigenous Peoples who seek to reclaim their ancestral lands. But it must always be remembered that those distinctive experiences and stories of dispossession and spoliation are all the distilled by-products over centuries of a singular and still vibrant legal principle, the Doctrine of Discovery, adhered to by the colonizing nations of Europe in varying forms, and unquestioningly embraced by their successor post-colonial governments. The Doctrine recognized a superior sovereignty and title in the European nation claiming "discovery" rights over the Indigenous Peoples and lands it intended to bring under its exclusive control. The Doctrine vested in the "discovering" European nation the unquestioned power to unilaterally extinguish or deny competing title or rights claimed by the Indigenous Peoples who had occupied and managed their ancestral homelands since time immemorial.

Today, the Doctrine continues to do its work in providing a legal basis, policy justification, and launching pad for the human rights violations, crimes, and abuses perpetuated against Indigenous Peoples demanding land justice and land back. The irony, of course, is that as the world confronts the twin global crises of climate change and mass species extinction, it is becoming increasingly recognized that the Indigenous Peoples of the world possess the knowledge and ability necessary to successfully conserve and manage biodiverse ecosystems, "carbon sinks," and protected conservation areas far more effectively than governments or conservation organizations can. And importantly, they can do it at a fraction of the cost, particularly where their rights are recognized, respected, and supported.

As this book shows, in country after country examined and analyzed, having those rights recognized, respected, and supported is no easy task for Indigenous Peoples anywhere in the world, even in the most so-called progressive states, such as Canada, Australia, New Zealand, and the Nordic countries. Yet, Indigenous-based conservation and control over ancestral Indigenous lands and resources is the most effective, efficient, and equitable path forward to safeguarding the planet. We know that the protection of the ecological integrity of critical ecosystems and positive conservation outcomes are strongly correlated with engaged and empowered Indigenous community-based management that recognizes Indigenous Peoples' human rights, including their rights to self-determination, consultation, and free, prior, and informed consent. Addressing the immense global challenges of climate change and species extinction through legal recognition of Indigenous land rights and Indigenous-led management and control of those lands and resources creates unprecedented opportunities for the world and for Indigenous Peoples to expand Indigenous stewardship and knowledge for the benefit of all humanity. As this book clearly demonstrates, however, our international and domestic laws, regulations, and institutions have yet to fully appreciate or seize upon these opportunities. They have been far too slow to recognize that the odds of successfully addressing these global challenges are much higher without land justice and Land Back for

Indigenous Peoples, who stand ready and are uniquely able to "take up their responsibilities to all living things." Indigenous Peoples and their knowledge and stories have much to offer the world, teaching the rest of us "the meaning of the lands of their ancestors."

Robert A. Williams, Jr.
Lumbee Tribe of North Carolina
Regents Professor and Faculty Chair
The University of Arizona, Indigenous
Peoples Law and Policy Program

"Land Back"

Indigenous Peoples and Land Rights

WILLIAM NIKOLAKIS

Introduction

Across the globe, Indigenous Peoples continue their struggle for land rights. Too often, few gains are made. Despite this, Indigenous Peoples maintain their resistance and advocacy to get their "Land Back," often in the face of violence and discrimination. This book brings together voices from across the globe on land rights. Many of these voices are from countries where little has been published. The chapters examine the patterns that form land rights: from dispossession to the state-driven processes for recognition and reclamation of land rights, and the strategies and barriers to securing land rights. The book then details the opportunities that exist for Indigenous Peoples to get their Land Back.

The ownership, use, and enjoyment of lands is fundamental to the survival of Indigenous Peoples. Evidence also shows that Indigenous lands (and stewardship) are critical to tackling the climate and biodiversity crisis (Blackman & Veit, 2018; Blackman et al., 2017; Fa et al., 2020; Garnett et al., 2018; Russell-Smith et al., 2013; Schuster et al., 2019). Land rights also create dilemmas. In most cases, the state establishes the tests for who gets "land rights" (recognition) and what they get (reclamation), and typically the state can infringe on these rights to authorize resource extraction (with or without consent). Too often the lands returned are marginal and a fraction of the claimants' traditional territories. Winning back land rights is typically time, resource, and emotionally intensive, with claimants having to "prove" their rights in arduous legal processes that often take decades to settle. Importantly, land rights can mire Indigenous Peoples within the labyrinth of the state's bureaucracy, and there may be considerable restrictions on how these lands can be used.

Land rights do, however, offer some tenure security for landowners, and where these rights are justiciable and enforceable, they can create a layer of protection against encroachment. As an academic and activist shared with me, for Indigenous Peoples in colonized countries, "The only thing worse than having land rights is not having them." Drawing from the experiences of twelve countries, the aim of this book is to identify what is working and what is not, with the ambition to support land rights in practice.

The Land Rights Story: Insights from Yirrkala

Dispossession and Strategies to Safeguard Land Rights

Across the world there are countless stories of dispossession. This chapter focuses on the experience of the Yolngu (or Yolŋu) people of Yirrkala to illuminate this pattern of dispossession, the strategies used to protect and reclaim lands, and the processes set in place by the state for recognizing and reclaiming land rights.

For tens of thousands of years, Yolŋu people have lived at Yirrkala, by the rich Arafura Sea, and today it is part of the Northern Territory of Australia. Indigenous Peoples, like the Yolŋu, have occupied the Australian continent for at least 65,000 years, reflected in archaeological evidence, the ongoing cultural practices, and the profound Indigenous connection with "country" (Clarkson et al., 2017).[1] For generations, the Yolŋu traded *trepang* (sea cucumber) and other items to Macassan seafarers, who came south each trading season from Sulawesi. The arrival of Europeans to Yolŋu territory in the 1870s, however, was different from their contact with the Macassans. Britain had asserted sovereignty to parts of southern Australia in 1788, and colonization, like elsewhere, was marked by violence, denial of Aboriginal rights to land, and the coercion of "natives" by the state. The settlers brought with them an insatiable hunger for land and resources to feed ambitions of social and economic mobility.

The newly drafted Australian Constitution, formed at federation in 1901, made no mention of the country's first peoples' laws and their land

---

[1] Legal decisions have coined this as "time immemorial," but it is argued that this term is vague and frames Indigenous Peoples' occupation of their lands as something that occurred in antiquity (Weir, 2013).

ownership systems, like that of the Yolŋu.[2] In 1931, Yirrkala became part of the Arnhem Land Aboriginal reserve – an area for exclusive occupation by Indigenous Peoples and their use. At around 90,000 square kilometers in size, the Arnhem Land reserve included hundreds of clan groups, including the Yolŋu. In 1934, a Methodist mission was established at Yirrkala, following a lethal confrontation between the Yolŋu and Japanese pearlers (Morphy, 2008). Growing violence meant the mission station became a safe place for Yolŋu (Morphy, 2005). In 1963, the Yolŋu and the missionaries received word that the federal government in Canberra, located more than 4,000 kilometers south, had granted a mining lease to over 360 square kilometers of Yolŋu land near Yirrkala.

To stop the development of a bauxite mine in their homelands, the Yolŋu rallied and petitioned the government to recognize their land ownership at Yirrkala. The petition, written in Yolŋu Matha and English on bark, known as the "Bark Petition," was tabled before the House of Representatives in August 1963.[3] A parliamentary committee of inquiry considered the issue of Yolŋu land ownership at Yirrkala, but the mine lease was granted anyway. The Yolŋu then commenced an action in the Northern Territory Supreme Court, claiming proprietary native title rights to the mine site. In their claim, the Yolŋu sought declarations to occupy and use these lands free from outside interference. This was Australia's first native title or land rights case.

The decision in *Milirrpum v. Nabalco Pty. Ltd.*[4] was handed down by Justice Blackburn in 1971. Blackburn reasoned that when British settlers arrived, Australia was *terra nullius* or "nobody's land."[5] Under British colonial constitutional law, the absence of prior possession meant the Crown gained absolute title to the land and English law applied (to the Yolŋu as well, despite them not being recognized as British citizens). British law effectively filled a legal vacuum across Australia. This legal concept of *terra nullius* was applied in other parts of the world, from

---

[2] The Australian Constitution, 1901, had two provisions on Aboriginal Australians: section 51 (xxvi), that the Commonwealth had power to make laws with respect to people of any race, except Aboriginal peoples (this power was left to the states); and section 127, that Aboriginal peoples were not to be counted in any population census. The wording relating to Aboriginal peoples was removed from both provisions in a 1967 referendum.

[3] The Bark Petition is on public display at Australia's Parliament House in Canberra.

[4] (1971) FLR 141.

[5] The doctrine (or fiction) of *terra nullius* was overturned in Australia in 1992, in the High Court decision of *Mabo v. Queensland (No. 2),* 1992 175 CLR 1.

western Canada to the Democratic Republic of Congo (DRC), to legitimate the transfer of land to colonial governments and to settlers.

While Justice Blackburn acknowledged Yolŋu evidence of an elaborate
system of rules and customs related to land, he characterized these rules
and customs as spiritual or religious, rather than proprietary. The Yolŋu,
he concluded, belonged to the land, but the land did not belong to them.
He wrote: "On the foundation of New South Wales, therefore, and of
South Australia, every square inch of the territory in the Colony became
the property of the Crown."[6] There was no Yolŋu right to land, and the
mine could proceed.[7]

Recognition and Reclamation

The winds of political and social change swept across much of the world
during the 1960s and 1970s. Indigenous Peoples and ethnic minorities
protested and advocated for basic citizenship rights, which were previously denied to them (Anaya & Williams, 2001). Against a backdrop of
Indigenous resistance to historical and ongoing dispossession, the settler-
colonial governments commenced (and in some cases recommenced) the
project of "settling" with Indigenous Peoples in the 1970s. Across the
globe, different pathways were developed for the recognition of
Indigenous Peoples and their land rights and processes for the reclamation of their land. For example, in the United States, the *Alaska Native
Claims Settlement Act* 1971 provided title to lands for Alaskan Native
corporations.[8] As well, the modern treaty process commenced in Canada

---

[6] (1971) FLR 141 at 245.

[7] This decision was not appealed to the High Court of Australia – a conservative bench
meant the risk for squashing land rights was high – but the time for change was nearing
(Woodward, 2005). However, recently, Australia's Federal Court ruled in favor of the
Gumatj traditional landowner's claims for up to $700 million (Australian dollars) in
compensation for the acquisition of the Gove mine site in 1969, without the just terms
required by section 51 (xxxi) of the Australian Constitution, 1911. The Australian
Government has sought leave to appeal this decision. See http://bit.ly/3HnODx7. The
High Court of Australia granted special leave to the Commonwealth Government to
appeal this decision on October 19, 2023. The decision of the Federal Court, if affirmed
by the High Court, could have wide-ranging implications for native title holders across
the country. This appeal was dismissed by the High Court of Australia on the March 12
2025, in the decision of Commonwealth of *Australia* v. *Yunupingu* [2025] HCA 6.

[8] Similar trends, for example, were followed in Brazil, with constitutional recognition of
Indigenous Peoples and their land rights in 1988; in Colombia with the creation of the
National Political Constitution, 1991, recognizing Indigenous Peoples and their collective
rights; and Paraguay in 1981, with the Statute of Indigenous Communities.

in 1973, after the Supreme Court of Canada's decision in *Calder v. British Columbia*, recognizing that Aboriginal title had likely survived the British Crown's assertion of sovereignty.[9]

Spurred on by *l'esprit du temps*, the failure of the Yolŋu's land rights case (*Milirrpum*), and the Gurindji people's "walk off" at the Wave Hill pastoral station in the Northern Territory, a report into recognizing Aboriginal land rights was commissioned by the Australian government in 1973. The Aboriginal Land Rights Commission, headed by the Yolŋu's counsel in *Milirrpum*, Edward Woodward, recommended a statutory land rights scheme for the Northern Territory. This scheme became federal legislation applying only to the Northern Territory, the *Aboriginal Land Rights (Northern Territory) Act* 1976, and remains the high-water mark for land rights in Australia. This statute provides a real property right to exclusive ownership and use of lands for successful claimants, with consent required for any state encroachments. Lands are governed through statutory land trusts, reflecting in part, Indigenous modes of social organization, and were designed in the spirit of "self-administration" (Neate, 1989).[10] According to Labour Party powerbroker H. C. "Nugget" Coombs, this land rights legislation was critical for ensuring Indigenous Peoples in the Northern Territory did not become a "dependent, landless proletariat with no other options" (1993, p. 3). Ironically, the *Aboriginal Land Rights Act* took effect on January 26, 1977, or Australia Day, the day marking the anniversary of British settlement in the country – a day referred to as Invasion Day or Survival Day by Indigenous Peoples and their allies.

Later efforts to have a national land rights framework across Australia were thwarted, though the existence (or survival) of native title (customary land rights) was recognized by the High Court of Australia in the 1992 *Mabo* decision, which Dorsett and McVeigh argued became the "site of engagement of Australian common law and jurisprudence with Indigenous law and jurisprudence" (2012, p. 471); this decision opened the door for further native claims across the continent. However, this ruling was codified with the passing of the *Native Title Act* 1993, where subsequent amendments to this statute and jurisprudence have restricted

---

[9] In Canada, the James Bay and Northern Quebec Agreement was the first modern treaty signed in 1975. Since then, twenty-six modern treaties have been concluded across the country, providing title to more than 600,000 square kilometers of land (Government of Canada, 2020).

[10] A federal policy to develop a national land rights scheme was abandoned by Prime Minister Bob Hawke in 1986.

the breadth and scope of Indigenous laws to preserve Crown sovereignty, and with it the recognition and reclamation of land rights (Foley & Anderson, 2006).

Recognition: Who Are Indigenous Peoples?

Indigenous Peoples have played a foundational role in the growth of "rights" dialogue, both at domestic and at international scales, advocating for rights to self-determination and a recognition of their land rights (among other rights) (Anaya & Williams, 2001; Xanthaki, 2007). Gaining momentum in the 1960s and 1970s, Indigenous Peoples advocated for their "continued survival as distinct communities with historically based cultures, political institutions, and entitlements to land" (Anaya & Williams, 2001, p. 34). While there is no single universal definition of Indigenous Peoples, at the international level, Jose Martinez Cobo (1986–7) developed a working definition, taken up by the United Nations, as those peoples "having a historical continuity with pre-invasion and pre-colonial societies that developed on their territories, [and] consider themselves distinct from other sectors of the societies now prevailing on those territories ... They ... are determined to preserve, develop and transmit to future generations their ancestral territories and, their identity."

Adding to this, Erica-Irene Daes (1996) described that Indigenous Peoples have an experience of subjugation, marginalization, dispossession, exclusion, or discrimination. On every inhabited continent there are Indigenous Peoples, who are often treated by the state as unique political and individual entities (Tully, 2000). It is typical for the state to establish the processes for the recognition of Indigenous Peoples, the nature and scope of any rights (such as land rights, rights to hunt and fish), and safeguards on these rights from encroachment.[11] For example, the common law-settler states of Canada, Australia, New Zealand, and the United States (the CANZUS states) established "corporate rights vested to historically continuous indigenous groups" (Gover, 2015, p. 345), which are held by these collectives in perpetuity. Povinelli (2002) described this phenomenon as the "cunning of recognition," where the state establishes

---

[11] See, for example, *Haida Nation v. British Columbia (Minister of Forests)*, [2004] 3 S.C.R. In *Haida Nation*, it was ruled that the state has a "duty to consult" where there is a potential violation of Aboriginal rights, even where these rights have not been formally recognized (para. 32). This is a duty to consult only, and is not a duty to get consent from Indigenous Peoples for any proposed encroachment (para. 31).

"authenticity tests" for recognizing Indigenous Peoples and their rights, assessing and validating claims to Indigeneity and to land rights through the executive and the courts. Coulthard connects this phenomenon to the "structural and psychoaffective facets of colonial domination" (2014, p. 49), "where colonial rule does not depend solely on the exercise of state violence, its reproduction instead rests on the ability to entice Indigenous Peoples to identify, either implicitly or explicitly, with the profoundly asymmetrical and nonreciprocal forms of recognition either imposed on or granted to them by the settler state and society" (2014, p. 25).

In any case, rights by themselves are insufficient, being "only effective to the extent that they are morally and institutionally enforceable" (Ivison, 2003, p. 338). Peoples must also have the capabilities to exercise these rights, or the freedoms, agency, health and wellbeing, and the opportunities to put these rights into practice (Sen, 1981).

Land Rights: Recognition and Reclamation Processes

Land rights to me has always been there. I've always practiced my rights. So, them telling us we now have title never meant nothing to me, because to me we've always owned it.[12]

Indigenous Peoples have and continue to be dispossessed of their lands, displaced, and discriminated against. Despite this, they continue with their advocacy and action for redress and protection against further transgression. Gilbert defined land rights as rights to "occupy, enjoy and use land and resources; restrict or exclude others from land; transfer, sell, purchase, grant or loan; inherit and bequeath; develop or improve; rent or sublet; and benefit from improved land values or rental income" (2013, p. 115). Land rights are foundational for basic human rights, for without land rights the basic human rights to food, housing, security, and religion or culture cannot be fully achieved (Gilbert, 2013). Land rights, according to Ivison, flow to Indigenous Peoples not as racial or cultural entities, but as "political, or perhaps more precisely, as constitutional ones" (2003, p. 334), reflecting the pre-existing laws of Indigenous Peoples and their systems of land ownership.

---

[12] Personal communication, Member, Xeni Gwet'in First Nation, 2021 (title-holding group, from Tsilhqot'in Nation, the first declaration of Aboriginal title by the Supreme Court of Canada in 2014).

There are generally three parts to Indigenous land rights: (1) they are typically a collective and perpetual right held by an Indigenous collective, who have a pre-existing legal connection to a territory, for members to exclusively occupy, possess, and use the land. Once reclaimed, often under state-defined processes, this land is typically inalienable, unless transferred or sold to the state, and the state typically has powers to encroach upon land rights in special circumstances with or without the consent of the landowners; (2) the landholding group determines membership to the collective, and while there are collective rules and norms that determine membership, the state also often establishes (or at least affirms) membership (Gover, 2010; Nikolakis et al., 2016); and (3) there is a right to be self-determining – in the sense that landowners can govern their land in their own ways, putting this land to use for collective and individual benefit, and typically with responsibilities and duties to maintain the land for future generations.[13]

While there has been considerable discussion around land rights at the international level, there is "strictly speaking . . . no human right to land under international law" (Gilbert, 2013, p. 115).[14] Thus, there is a considerable degree of variability across the world for how land rights are recognized, the processes for reclamation, and the protections and safeguards on land rights. The chapters in this book demonstrate a number of approaches for recognition and reclamation of Indigenous land rights: (1) constitutional provisions; (2) statutes; (3) customary, common, civil, or Islamic laws; (4) policies, decrees, or other orders; and (5) treaties and self-government agreements.

1. Constitutional approaches for recognizing Indigenous Peoples and their land rights exist across diverse jurisdictions, from Canada to the Democratic Republic of Congo (DRC), to Brazil and Colombia (among

---

[13] For example, in Canada in *Tsilhqot'in Nation* the court ruled that Aboriginal title confers ownership rights akin to fee simple title, including a right to decide how land is used, to generate economic benefits, and to proactively use and manage land (para. 73). Aboriginal title is an exclusive right to use land, but the use must be consistent with the "group nature of the interest and the enjoyment of the land by future generations" (para. 88).

[14] Gilbert (2013) documents human rights instruments affirming Indigenous Peoples' land and self-determination rights: The General Comments on the International Covenant on Civil and Political Rights (ICCPR), the International Convention on the Elimination of All Forms of Racial Discrimination (ICERD) and Human Rights Committee's jurisprudence of article 27 of ICCPR. The Indigenous and Tribal Peoples Convention (No. 169) of the International Labour Organization also provides for Indigenous land rights.

others). As constitutions are the supreme law in many jurisdictions, and typically require public referenda to be changed, constitutional provisions offer the most secure and powerful mechanism for recognizing and protecting land rights (Nikolakis & Hotte, 2020). However, enforcing these provisions on the ground has typically proven challenging, as documented in the chapter on the DRC by Lassana Koné (this volume), where the "legal dualism" in the constitution recognizing customary and state land rights is not given effect in practice – which perpetuates tenure insecurity for Indigenous Peoples, and suggests a robust institutional framework must be built around constitutional provisions to make these effective.

2. Statutes are the most common approach for recognizing and restoring land rights; for example, New Zealand codified and restricted customary or native title in the *Te Ture Whenua Māori/Māori Land Act* 1993 (TTWM), and later in the *Marine and Coastal Area Act* 2011. Australia has the federal *Native Title Act* 1993, as well as state and territory land rights statutes like the *Aboriginal Land Rights (Northern Territory) Act* 1976; India has the *Forest Rights Act* 2006; Norway has the *Finnmark Act* 2005; and other examples include Botswana, Chile, Honduras, and Colombia. Statutes are binding and instrumental, and they are more secure than policies or jurisprudence. However, statutes can be repealed or amended like the situation in Australia or New Zealand, or simply ignored by government or other actors, or interpreted differently than their intent by courts (Nikolakis & Hotte, 2020), and there are numerous examples across the world of statutes stripping away or diluting land rights (for example, the United States' American Indian treaties).

3. Customary, common, civil, or Islamic laws are legal principles defined or developed by a collective's authorized institutions. Customary laws are the laws, practices, and customs developed by Indigenous societies that give expression to land ownership and use. Common law is developed by judges. The decisions or case law offer precedential authority; however, this authority can be overruled by a superior court, distinguished, or codified by the legislature like the Australian *Native Title Act* that codified the doctrine of native title in the *Mabo* decision. Civil law countries have codified laws around property and land rights, while Islamic laws are those interpreted from scriptures and other legal sources by jurists (muftis) and are typically drawn from codes today. In pluralistic legal systems, different approaches may operate in parallel; for instance, customary law may be incorporated into the common, civil or Islamic law in a form of legal dualism,

with examples from the DRC and Morocco in this book. There are instances where the courts are taking a more expansive view on incorporating customary Indigenous law in Aboriginal or native title cases, such as in Canada and Australia (what Roughan, 2009, described as a form of "legal association").

4. Policies, decrees, and other orders are those developed by the executive arm of government. These policies may be substantive, such as establishing a land tenure and land titling policy, or they may be symbolic, like recognizing Indigenous prior occupation, without implementing land rights. Policies and decrees are not binding in the same way the constitution, statute, and precedent are, but they can reshape norms and practices, which may be a preliminary step towards creating law.

5. Written treaties set out the terms of settlement between Indigenous nations and settler-colonial governments, the most well-known perhaps being the American Indian treaties recognizing the US tribes as "domestic dependent nations," concluded up until 1871. In Canada and New Zealand, historic treaties were signed (and typically not honored), and modern treaty processes have been established that provide for a distribution of lands, compensation, and self-governance powers (Borrows, 2006). There has also been growing public attention on treaties more recently in Australia. Canada has concluded self-government agreements, such as with the Westbank First Nation, and a Sechelt First Nation self-government agreement was legislated in 1986. Both these agreements in British Columbia set out the terms of the governing powers of the First Nations and redistribute lands back to the First Nations.

Many countries are a hybrid of the different mechanisms listed above; for example, Canada and Malaysia have constitutional provisions, engage in treaties or self-government agreements with Indigenous Peoples, and have common-law recognition of land rights. Regardless of the approach, it is typically the claimants who have to prove their rights through procedures laid out and heard by the state – and their struggles too often yield isolated, poorly resourced, and meagre gains. Typically, the customary laws and institutions of Indigenous Peoples are not reflected in land rights regimes.

A Framework for Conceptualizing Land Rights

The experience of the Yolŋu of Yirrkala is shared across the world. Indigenous Peoples have been dispossessed and displaced, but their resistance and advocacy in many cases has led to their recognition as distinct peoples with unique rights and land ownership. The people of Yirrkala had their title to land "confirmed" in 1980 under the 1976 *Aboriginal Land Rights (Northern Territory) Act*, a federal statute creating legal processes for traditional lands that had not been alienated as Crown land, to be returned to "traditional owners" (Neate, 1989). These lands were returned as inalienable and collectively held Aboriginal freehold land.

In the global picture, the Yolŋu's reclamation of their traditional lands is an anomaly. A Rights and Resources Initiative (2015) report found that while more than 50 percent of the world's lands are the territories of Indigenous Peoples, only 10 percent of these are legally recognized as such (covering around 1,176 million hectares). Most of the "recognized" lands were in five countries: China, Canada, Brazil, Australia, and Mexico. The rights accorded in these jurisdictions vary greatly. Noteworthy from the study is that forty of the sixty-four countries analyzed did not have any land rights mechanisms in place. In a follow-up study the Rights and Resources Initiative (2023) analyzed seventy-three countries that covered 85 percent of the global estate, and found an increase in Indigenous and local community land tenures to 1,264 million hectares in 2020 (up 1.4 percent from 2015). It is important to note that 61.4 percent of these Indigenous lands were in the five countries listed above. The bulk of the countries analyzed in the Rights and Resources Initiative studies did not have any land rights mechanisms in place.

Those peoples without recognized and secure land rights are at continued risk of further dispossession and displacement by settlers and state-backed energy, mining, agricultural, and forestry interests. Garnett et al. (2018) identified that 37 percent of the Earth's remaining "natural lands" are within the territories of Indigenous Peoples. These lands tend to have lower intensity land uses, and they are the remotest and least populated areas on Earth. Because of this, they are at heightened risk from dispossession. Where Indigenous lands are titled, offering some form of legal protection, these areas are shown to reduce deforestation compared to other areas (Benzeev et al., 2023; Baragwanath & Bayi, 2020; Blackman et al., 2017; Sze et al., 2022) and thus store more carbon (Blackman & Veit, 2018; Walker et al., 2014).

A Conceptual Model for Land Rights

The chapters in this book reveal patterns of dispossession; strategies to reclaim lands; processes for recognition and reclamation, most often driven by the state; the barriers to reclaiming lands; and the opportunities available to Indigenous Peoples for advancing and safeguarding their land rights. Taken together, each of these dimensions form a conceptual model for understanding the development of land rights (see Figure 1.1).

- *Dispossession* – To dispossess is to deprive people of their lands, their property, and their livelihoods. The chapters in this book focus on the historical and ongoing processes and tools for dispossession. There remain significant dispossession pressures on Indigenous Peoples, with or without secure title to their lands.
- *Strategies* – Indigenous Peoples have applied various strategies to secure and safeguard their land rights. These strategies are dynamic as land rights are at constant threat of derogation or dispossession (even with an "enforceable" title). These strategies include activism, direct action and advocacy, litigation and negotiation at local and at international scales. Whyte (2011) documented that the success of these strategies is dependent on the power of Indigenous Peoples vis-à-vis the state, and their capacity and resources to effectively engage with, and contest, the state.
- *Recognition and reclamation* – There are legal, administrative, and political processes to recognize Indigenous Peoples and their land rights, and to restore full land rights to those dispossessed (in some cases these are simply access rights). Often the state determines the parameters of these recognition and reclamation processes, which have important consequences for Indigenous Peoples and their land rights.
- *Barriers* – There are structural and cultural factors that enable dispossession. These include power relations, which affirm the state's sovereignty and land grabs, supported by the state, as documented across the chapters. Lobbying and advocacy by the agricultural and natural resources sectors frustrate recognition and reclamation processes and undermine land rights.
- *Opportunities* – There are pathways that have been developed by Indigenous Peoples to advance and safeguard their land rights in ways consistent with their goals and values. These opportunities can reshape (and potentially transform) the institutional and political framework to create the space to reclaim and safeguard land rights.

Figure 1.1 illustrates the interaction of these dimensions, starting at point A, **Dispossession**, which has catalyzed **Strategies** by Indigenous Peoples to secure and safeguard land rights (point B). These strategies have

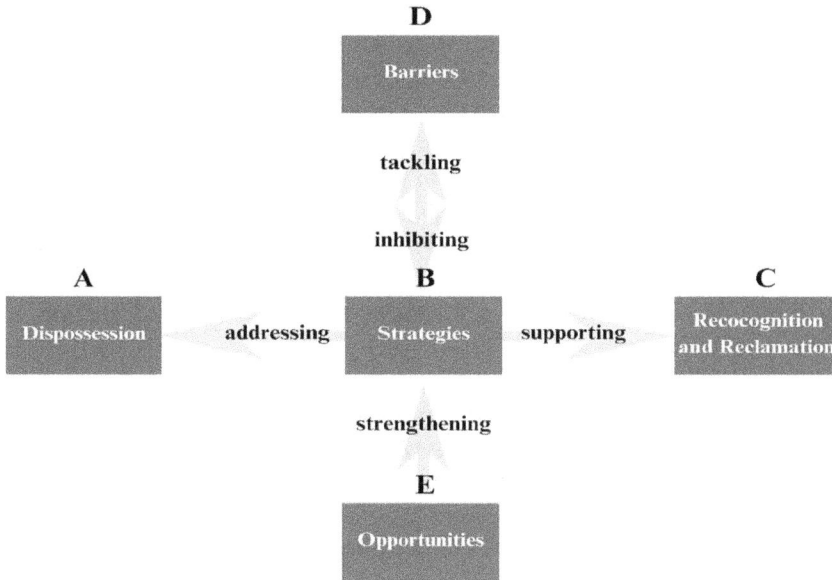

Figure 1.1   Land rights recognition and reclamation conceptual framework

activated **Recognition and Reclamation** processes (point C). There are **Barriers** (point D) to securing land rights, such as power dynamics and populist politics, which can restrict this transition to **Recognition and Reclamation**. The **Strategies** applied can directly address the **Barriers** that prevent land rights (reflected in a two-way arrow between these dimensions), and counter-strategies can be employed by those threatened by land rights (such as the natural resource and agriculture sectors). The **Opportunities** (point E) are those pathways to strengthen **Strategies** and **Recognition and Reclamation** processes, and to mitigate **Dispossession**.

Overview of the Collection

The book is organized into three sections to reflect the "common ground" between jurisdictions: Latin America; Australia, Canada, and New Zealand; and Africa and Asia.

Latin America

The Latin American countries typically recognize Indigenous Peoples and their customary land ownership in constitutions. *The Elusive*

Promise of Indigenous Land Rights in Paraguay: Achievements, Challenges, and Current Trends, by Joel E. Correia, Rodrigo Villagra-Carron and Marcos Glauser, traces the country's major legal achievements on land rights. They note that despite these protections, 2021 saw record violent dispossessions of Indigenous Peoples in the country. The authors develop the term "pendulum policies" to trace the shifts in state-Indigenous relations from "violation" to "justice" and then back to "violation," highlighting a persistent "implementation gap" in land rights laws. The role of international law and strategic litigation has pushed the pendulum towards "justice," yet serious threats, from land renting to direct violence, remain.

Article 231 of Brazil's constitution guarantees Indigenous Peoples the collective right to return to and occupy their traditional lands, consistent with international obligations. Professors Fernanda Frizzo Bragato and Jocelyn Getgen Kestenbaum write in *Recognizing and Reclaiming Indigenous Peoples' Constitutional Land Rights in Brazil: Challenges and Opportunities* that despite this constitutional guarantee, there has been an active campaign of land grabs and violence that has undermined the country's land rights framework. Indigenous Peoples have litigated to reclaim and protect their lands, but the courts have applied a "temporal framework doctrine" ("*tese do marco temporal*") to deny Indigenous People their rights to ancestral lands if they did not occupy and control those lands at the creation of the 1988 Brazilian Constitution. A new political administration may reverse this trend.

In the chapter *Indigenous Peoples and Territorial Rights in Colombia: Advances, Challenges, and Setbacks in Implementation,* Omaira Bolaños and Ricardo Camilo Niño (Arhuaco) describe how the country's 1991 National Political Constitution (NPC) recognized Indigenous Peoples and their collective rights. However, most of the 33 million hectares of collectively held lands in Colombia occurred prior to 1991. A persistent internal armed conflict stalled land justice in the post-1991 period, fueled by land conflict. A 2016 Peace Accord sought to resolve land ownership disputes and maintain civil stability. The authors explore the legal framework and historical context that sustains land injustice in Colombia.

Chile does not have constitutional recognition of Indigenous Peoples – a situation that two recent constitutional reforms and referenda sought to remedy. Both of these referenda failed, and Indigenous Peoples and their land rights continue to be governed by the Indigenous Law of 1993. This statute has been slow to deliver land justice for Indigenous Peoples in

Chile. Against this background, Alexandra Tomaselli's chapter, *Indigenous Land Rights in Chile: Dispossession, Misrecognition and Litigation*, details how litigation, combined with direct action, has been an important and sometimes effective strategy for safeguarding Indigenous lands from development pressures.

Australia, Canada, and New Zealand

Australia, Canada, and New Zealand are among the common-law settler countries that have sought to reconcile with Indigenous Peoples and integrate them into their constitutional orders. In the chapter *Aboriginal Land Rights in Australia: Neither National nor Uniform*, Dr Francis Markham and Professor Heidi Norman (Gamilaroi Nation) argue that the return of an Aboriginal presence across all Australian landscapes since the 1960s is a significant transformation in the colonial geographic imagination and the dominant narratives of absence, erasure and denial. The chapter weaves together the fragmented approaches and innovations for recognizing and reclaiming Indigenous land rights across the country.

In *Dispossession by Treaty, Dispossession by Statute: Indigenous Title in Eastern and Western Canada*, Professors Daniel Diamond and Douglas Sanderson, both from the Opaskwayak Cree Nation in Canada, document how the Torrens land titling system, developed in Australia and adopted in British Columbia, was used to dismantle Aboriginal title, and enhance the fungibility of land to settlers. Most of the valuable land was appropriated through the Torrens system in British Columbia, where it has remained ineligible up to this point in time for Aboriginal title claims.

In *Māori Land Law in Aotearoa New Zealand: Recognising Land as tāonga tuku iho*, Carwyn Jones (*Ngāti Kahungunu*) and Sandra Cortés Acosta document a "legislative" approach to Māori land rights, which narrows their scope and leaves these rights vulnerable to changing political whims. They examine the development of the *Te Ture Whenua Māori/ Māori Land Act* 1993 and the *Marine and Coastal Area (Takutai Moana) Act* 2011, which restricts customary or native title (focusing on recognition rather than reclamation), and thus are inconsistent with Māori relationships to *whenua* (land) and *tikanga* (law, values and practices). Jones and Cortés Acosta argue that a constitutional approach for recognizing and safeguarding land rights is critical for nurturing Māori relationships to land characterized as *tāonga tuku iho* (a treasure that connects current generations with their ancestors and future generations).

Africa and Asia

The concept of Indigeneity is contested across much of Africa and Asia. However, Indigenous Peoples across these continents are advocating for recognition as distinct peoples and for the return or protection of their lands. In his chapter *Land Rights of Indigenous Peoples in the Democratic Republic of Congo: "First Come, Last Served,"* Lassana Koné writes that the Democratic Republic of Congo's (DRCs) constitution enshrines a "legal dualism" that recognizes both state and customary laws to land ownership. Yet, land laws continue to deny Indigenous Peoples a registered and indefeasible title to their lands, meaning they remain vulnerable to dispossession. Without secure tenure, several *Batwa* communities have procured community forest concession licences, which while only an incremental step towards land justice, offer some form of jurisdiction and standing over their territories. But accessing these concessions can be complex, limiting the effectiveness of this strategy for many Indigenous communities across the DRC. In 2022, the Law on the Protection and Promotion of the Rights of Indigenous Pygmy Peoples was passed, which aims to strengthen the land rights of Baka, Bambuti, and Batwa peoples. This law took effect in 2023, and while it is too soon to evaluate its performance, experience suggests implementation will be problematic.

In *San Land Rights in Botswana: A Critical Analysis*, Robert Hitchcock, Maria Sapignoli and Smith Moeti (*G//ana San*) document that the country's 60,000 San peoples continue to hold fragile land and resources rights. While they are not legally recognized as Indigenous Peoples in Botswana, some lands have been set aside for the San people, like the remote area settlements. These communal lands are inalienable, though there are no guarantees to safeguard them. San have actively organized to strengthen their land rights through non-government organizations, lobbying for their rights nationally and internationally, and litigated in the High Court, where some cases have been successful. The Central Kalahari San legal decisions have in fact set international precedents for human rights to water. However, the Botswana government has not honored many of the High Court judgments, leaving San in a precarious position.

The *Amazigh* Peoples of Morocco's High Atlas region are considered as the Indigenous Peoples of the region. Over millennia they have maintained their cultural identity as well as the *agdal* customary system, which governs their lands, pasture, water, and forests in an unforgiving climate. In the chapter by Ahmed Bendella (*Amazigh*) and colleagues, entitled *Rights over Land among Amazigh Peoples in Morocco: The Case of the High Atlas*, the authors examine the oral-based *agdal* system, which is embedded in a deep "socio-ecological" interdependency, and guided by the *j'maa* (local community assemblies) and customary law. They provide insight around the resilience of the *agdal* system in the face of shifting social, political, cultural and ecological forces.

The Indian constitution recognizes *Adivasis*, or India's Indigenous Peoples. However, drawing from land tenure evidence, Professor Jagannath Ambagudia, in *Adivasis and Land Rights in India: Dispossession and the "Implementation Gap,"* shows the landholding patterns of *Adivasis* have been altered across the country, and land alienation has accelerated, leading to *Adivasi* insurgencies. To address this, Professor Ambagudia calls for a strengthened land rights framework in India, grounded in customary institutions and in the principle and process of free prior and informed consent.

In *Legal Privileges and the Effective Recognition of Indigenous Land Rights: Lessons from Malaysia*, Yogeswaran Subramaniam documents the diversity in constitutional privileges afforded to the Peninsular Malaysia Orang Asli, and the natives of Sabah and of Sarawak. While Malaysia's courts have guarded the rights of these three recognized Indigenous Peoples, they have also been reluctant to expand these rights to reflect changing international Indigenous norms, such as free prior and informed consent, with implications for land rights. Subramaniam argues that a full implementation of land rights laws, combined with free prior and informed consent, is critical to protecting land rights in Malaysia.

In Cambodia and Thailand, Indigenous Peoples have used the political system to build support for their recognition and to assert collective land rights. But, according to Ian Baird in *Indigenous Peoples and Electoral Politics in Thailand and Cambodia: One Strategy to Secure Land Rights in Contested Spaces,* there has been mixed success through this strategy – though it appears to be the most effective option in contexts where Indigeneity is a contested concept.

A concluding chapter entitled *Reclaiming Land Rights Under the Pressure of Nation States – Insights and Future Directions from Sápmi*, written by Sámi lawyer Oula-Antti Labba, weaves together the key themes throughout the book, drawing on the Sámi experience. The conclusion traces the shared histories and modern realities of dispossession, processes for recognition and reclamation, strategies to reclaim lands, and persistent barriers to land rights, reflected in an "implementation gap." The conclusion also offers directions for practice and future research on land rights.

Looking Ahead

Indigenous Peoples living with stronger forms of tenure security, such as on the Northern Territory's Aboriginal freehold lands, and who are actively stewarding their lands in their own ways, show reductions in lifestyle-related and chronic diseases (Burgess et al., 2005; Garnett et al., 2009; McDermott et al., 1998), and are better able to maintain their language and culture (Biddle & Swee, 2012).[15] However, powerful voices continue to assert that Indigenous land rights are divisive and stymie resource development (Kirkwood et al., 2005; Aiken & Leigh, 2011; Nikolakis et al., 2014). This situation has been playing out in Brazil, where safeguards to protect Indigenous lands have been reduced, leading to conflict, violence and deforestation (Begotti & Peres, 2019; Ferrante & Fearnside, 2019).

Those Indigenous Peoples who can secure land rights are not, in many instances, resourced to fully implement them, and the challenges for leveraging economic benefits from collective and inalienable lands are well documented (Altman, 2004; Nikolakis, 2008, 2010; Nikolakis et al., 2016). Further, despite the enormous wealth generated from Indigenous-held lands – particularly the minerals and energy sectors – many Indigenous communities live below the poverty line (Cornell, 2005; Langton & Longbottom, 2012; Stavenhagen, 2006). Because of this, it is common that Indigenous Peoples living on their lands remain dependent on the state in many ways (Alfred & Corntassel, 2005). Yolŋu elder Galuwruy Yunupingu, who was a young man during the signing of the Bark Petition at Yirrkala in 1963, was quoted in 2013 as saying "We have looked forward to the land rights giving us something . . . The land rights is for Aboriginal people but the land ownership and use of land . . . is not for Aboriginal people, it's for mining companies. For white fellas" (Laughland, 2013).

The next phase for many Indigenous Peoples after reclaiming their lands is to revitalize and strengthen their governance, and to take control of their lands and their futures, which can be equally as big a challenge as winning Land Back (Nikolakis and Nelson, 2019). This challenge is

---

[15] It must be acknowledged that despite a coordinated "whole-of-government" focus, there has been little progress made in Australia in "closing the gap" between Indigenous and non-Indigenous populations on life expectancy and child mortality. The gap is widest in remote and very remote communities, where Indigenous Peoples more often than not live on their own lands (Australian Government, 2020). Despite decades of attention, the most recent Closing the Gap report in 2023 showed that only four of fifteen targets to close the gap on Indigenous socio-economic disadvantage, which included life expectancy, adult imprisonment, housing, early childhood development and language retention (among others), were on track to be met (Productivity Commission, 2023).

reflected in the words of a member of the Tsilhqot'in Nation from British Columbia, Canada: "Because now that we have proven land rights, now the next step is, what do we do with title? And I think that's the big question now, where do we go with it? And what does that mean?" (personal communication, 2021).

While land rights alone are insufficient to address the deep-seated challenges Indigenous Peoples face, they are foundational, a first step. In designing land rights, the space must be created for Indigenous Peoples to be themselves, or what Leanne Simpson refers to as *biskaabiiyang* in *Anishinaabemowin*, or the act of "returning to ourselves" (Simpson, 2017, p. 17). Without this space, any land rights framework will simply replicate the colonial project of dispossession.

References

Aiken, S. R., & Leigh, C. H. (2011). Seeking redress in the courts: Indigenous land rights and judicial decisions in Malaysia. *Modern Asian Studies*, 45(4), 825–875.

Alfred, T., & Corntassel, J. (2005). Being Indigenous: Resurgences against contemporary colonialism. *Government and Opposition*, 40(4), 597–614.

Altman, J. (2004). *Sustainable development options on Aboriginal land: The hybrid economy in the twenty-first century*. Canberra: Centre for Aboriginal Economic and Policy Research, Australian Natural University.

Anaya, S., & Williams, R. (2001). The protection of Indigenous Peoples' rights over lands and natural resources under the Inter-American Human Rights System. *Harvard Human Rights Journal*, 14, 33–86.

Australian Government. (2020). Closing the gap report 2020. Canberra: National Indigenous Australians Agency. https://ctgreport.niaa.gov.au/sites/default/files/pdf/closing-the-gap-report-2020.pdf

Baragwanath, K., & Bayi, E. (2020). Collective property rights reduce deforestation in the Brazilian Amazon. *Proceedings of the National Academy of Sciences*, 117(34), 20495–20502.

Barume, A. K. (2010). *Land rights of indigenous peoples in Africa*. Copenhagen: IWGIA.

Begotti, R. A., & Peres, C. A. (2019). Brazil's indigenous lands under threat. *Science*, 363(6427), 592.

Benzeev, R., Zhang, S., Rauber, M. A., Vance, E. A., & Newton, P. (2023). Formalizing tenure of Indigenous lands improved forest outcomes in the Atlantic Forest of Brazil. *PNAS nexus*, 2(1), 287.

Biddle, N., & Swee, H. (2012). The relationship between wellbeing and Indigenous land, language and culture in Australia. *Australian Geographer*, 43(3), 215–232.

Blackman, A., Corral, L., Lima, E. S., & Asner, G. P. (2017). Titling indigenous communities protects forests in the Peruvian Amazon. *Proceedings of the National Academy of Sciences*, 114(16), 4123–4128.

Blackman, A., & Veit, P. (2018). Titled Amazon indigenous communities cut forest carbon emissions. *Ecological Economics*, 153, 56–67.

Borrows, J. (2006). Ground-rules: Indigenous treaties in Canada and New Zealand. *New Zealand Universities Law Review Journal*, 22(2): 188–212.

Burgess, C. P., Johnston, F. H., Bowman, D. M., & Whitehead, P. J. (2005). Healthy country: Healthy people? Exploring the health benefits of Indigenous natural resource management. *Australian and New Zealand Journal of Public Health*, 29(2), 117–122.

Clarkson, C., Jacobs, Z., Marwick, B., Fullagar, R., Wallis, L., Smith, M., Roberts, R. G., Hayes, E., Lowe, K., Carah, X., Florin, S. A., McNeil, J., Cox, D., Arnold, L. J. Hua, Q., Huntley, J., Brand, H. E. A., Manne, T., Fairbairn, A., Shulmeister, J., Lyle, L., Salinas, M., Page, M., Connell, K., Park, G., Norman, K., Murphy, T., & Pardoe, C. (2017). Human occupation of northern Australia by 65,000 years ago. *Nature*, 547, 306–310.

Coombs, H. C. (1993). *Issues in dispute, Aborigines working for autonomy*. Darwin: Australian National University, North Australia Research Unit.

Cornell, S. (2005). Indigenous peoples, poverty and self-determination in Australia, New Zealand, Canada and the United States. In R. Eversole, J-A. McNeish, & A. D. Cimadamore (eds.), *Indigenous peoples and poverty: An international perspective* (pp. 199–225). London: Zed Books.

Coulthard, G. S. (2014). *Red skin, white masks: Rejecting the colonial politics of recognition*. Minneapolis, MN: University of Minnesota Press.

Daes, E. I. A. (1996). *Working paper on the concept of indigenous peoples* (UN doc. E/CN. 4/Sub. 2/AC. 4/1996/2). New York: United Nations.

Dorsett, S., & McVeigh, S. (2012). Conduct of laws: Native title, responsibility, and some limits of jurisdictional thinking. *Melbourne University Law Review*, 36(2), 470–493.

Fa, J. E., Watson, J. E., Leiper, I., Potapov, P., Evans, T. D., Burgess, N. D., . . ., & Garnett, S. T. (2020). Importance of Indigenous Peoples' lands for the conservation of intact forest landscapes. *Frontiers in Ecology and the Environment*, 18(3), 135–140.

Ferrante, L., & Fearnside, P. M. (2019). Brazil's new president and 'ruralists' threaten Amazonia's environment, traditional peoples and the global climate. *Environmental Conservation*, 46(4), 261–263.

Foley, G. & Anderson, T. (2006). Land rights and Aboriginal voices. *Australian Journal of Human Rights*, 12(1), 83–108.

Garnett, S. T., Burgess, N. D., Fa, J. E., Fernández-Llamazares, Á., Molnár, Z., Robinson, C. J., Watson, J. E. M., Zander, K. K., Austin, B., Brondizio, E. S., Collier, N. F., Duncan, T., Ellis, E., Geyle, H., Jackson, M. V., Jonas, H.,

Malmer, P., McGowan, B., Sivongxay, A., & Leiper, I. (2018). A spatial overview of the global importance of Indigenous lands for conservation. *Nature Sustainability*, 1(7), 369.

Garnett, S. T., Sithole, B., Whitehead, P. J., Burgess, C. P., Johnston, F. H., & Lea, T. (2009). Healthy country, healthy people: Policy implications of links between Indigenous human health and environmental condition in tropical Australia. *Australian Journal of Public Administration*, 68(1), 53–66.

Gilbert, J. (2013). Land rights as human rights: The case for a specific right to land. *SUR: International Journal on Human Rights*, 10(18), 115–135.

Gover, K. (2010). Comparative tribal constitutionalism: Membership governance in Australia, Canada, New Zealand, and the United States. *Law & Social Inquiry*, 35(3), 689–762.

(2015). Settler–state political theory, 'CANZUS' and the UN declaration on the rights of indigenous peoples. *European Journal of International Law*, 26(2), 345–373.

Government of Canada. (2020). Treaties and agreements, Ottawa, Canada. www .rcaanc-cirnac.gc.ca/eng/1100100028574/1529354437231

Ivison, D. (2003). The logic of Aboriginal rights. *Ethnicities*, 3(3): 321–344.

Kirkwood, S., Liu, J. H., & Weatherall, A. (2005). Challenging the standard story of indigenous rights in Aotearoa/New Zealand. *Journal of Community & Applied Social Psychology*, 15(6), 493–505.

Langton, M., & Longbottom, J. (eds.). (2012). *Community futures, legal architecture: Foundations for Indigenous peoples in the global mining book*. Oxon: Routledge.

Larsen, P. B., & Gilbert, J. (2020). Indigenous rights and ILO Convention 169: Learning from the past and challenging the future. *The International Journal of Human Rights*, 24(2–3), 83–93.

Laughland, O. (2013, July 10). Land rights are empty, Yolngu elder tells Rudd on bark petition anniversary. The Guardian. www.theguardian.com/world/2013/jul/10/land-rights-empty-yolngu-rudd

Martinez Cobo, J. (1986–87). *Study of the problem of discrimination against indigenous populations*. New York: United Nations. www.un.org/development/desa/indigenouspeoples/publications/martinez-cobo-study.html

McDermott, R., O'Dea, K., Rowley, K., Knight, S., & Burgess, P. (1998). Beneficial impact of the Homelands Movement on health outcomes in central Australian Aborigines. *Australian and New Zealand Journal of Public Health*, 22(6), 653–658.

Morphy, F. (2008). Enacting sovereignty in a colonized space: The Yolngu of Blue Mud Bay meet the native title process. In D. Fay and D. James (eds.), *The rights and wrongs of land restitution: 'Restoring what was ours'* (pp. 99–122). New York: Routledge-Cavendish.

Morphy, H. (2005). Mutual conversion? The Methodist church and the Yolngu, with particular reference to Yirrkala. *Humanities Research*, 12(1), 41–53.

Morris, M., Garavito, C. R., Salinas, N. O., & Buriticá, P. (2009). *La consulta previa a pueblos indígenas: Los estándares del derecho internacional.* Bogota: Universidad de los Andes.

Neate, G. (1989). *Aboriginal land rights law in the Northern Territory.* Sydney: Alternative Publishing Co-operative.

Nikolakis, W. D. (2008). *Determinants of success among Indigenous enterprise in the Northern Territory of Australia* (Doctoral dissertation, University of South Australia).

Nikolakis, W. (2010). Barriers to indigenous enterprise development on communally owned land. *Global Business and Economics Review*, 12(1–2), 85–99.

Nikolakis, W., Akter, S., & Nelson, H. (2016). The effect of communication on individual preferences for common property resources: A case study of two Canadian First Nations. *Land Use Policy*, 58, 70–82.

Nikolakis, W., & Hotte, N. (2020). How law shapes collaborative forest governance: A focus on indigenous peoples in Canada and India. *Society & Natural Resources*, 33(1), 46–64.

Nikolakis, W., & Nelson, H. W. (2019). Trust, institutions and Indigenous self-governance: An exploratory study. *Governance*, 32(2), 331–347.

Nikolakis, W., Nelson, H. W., & Cohen, D. H. (2014). Who pays attention to indigenous peoples in sustainable development and why? Evidence from socially responsible investment mutual funds in North America. *Organization & Environment*, 27(4), 368–382.

Povinelli, E. A. (2002). *The cunning of recognition.* Durham, NC: Duke University Press.

Productivity Commission. (2023). Closing the gap. Annual Data Compilation Report July 2023. Australian Government, Canberra. www.pc.gov.au/closing-the-gap-data/annual-data-report

Rights and Resources Initiative. (2015). *Who owns the world's land? A global baseline of formally recognized indigenous and community land rights.* Washington, DC: RRI.

   (2023). *Who owns the world's land? Global state of Indigenous, Afro-descendant, and local community land rights recognition from 2015–2020*, 2nd edition. Washington, DC: RRI.

Roughan, N. (2009). The association of state and indigenous law: A case study in 'Legal Association.' *University of Toronto Law Journal*, 59(2), 135–178.

Russell-Smith, J., Cook, G. D., Cooke, P. M., Edwards, A. C., Lendrum, M., Meyer, C. P., & Whitehead, P. J. (2013). Managing fire regimes in north Australian savannas: Applying Aboriginal approaches to contemporary global problems. *Frontiers in Ecology and the Environment*, 11(s1), e55–e63.

Schuster, R., Germain, R. R., Bennett, J. R., Reo, N. J., Arcese, P. (2019). Vertebrate biodiversity on indigenous-managed lands in Australia, Brazil, and Canada equals that in protected areas. *Environmental Science & Policy*, 101, 1–6.

Sen, A. (1981). Rights and agency. *Philosophy & Public Affairs*, 11(1), 3–39.

Sieder, R. (2016). Indigenous peoples' rights and the law in Latin America. In D. Short & C. Lennox (eds.), *Handbook of indigenous peoples' rights* (pp. 414–423). New York: Routledge.

Sikkink, K. (2005). The transnational dimension of the judicialization of politics in Latin America. In R. Sieder, L. Schjolden, & A. Angell, A. (eds.), *The judicialization of politics in Latin America* (pp. 263–292). New York: Palgrave.

Simpson, L. B. (2017). *As we have always done: Indigenous freedom through radical resistance*. Minneapolis, MN: University of Minnesota Press.

Soley, X., & Steininger, S. (2018). Parting ways or lashing back? Withdrawals, backlash and the Inter-American Court of Human Rights. *International Journal of Law in Context*, 14(2), 237–257.

Stavenhagen, R. (2006). Indigenous peoples, land and territory. In P. Rosset, R. Patel, & M. Courville (eds.) *Promised land: Competing visions of agrarian reform* (pp. 208–219). Oakland, CA: Food First Books.

Sze, J. S., Carrasco, L. R., Childs, D., & Edwards, D. P. (2022). Reduced deforestation and degradation in Indigenous Lands pan-tropically. *Nature Sustainability*, 5(2), 123–130.

Tully, J. (2000). The struggles of indigenous peoples for and of freedom. In D. Ivison, P. Patton, & W. Sanders (eds.), *Political theory and the rights of indigenous peoples* (pp. 36–59). Cambridge: Cambridge University Press.

Walker, W., Baccini, A., Schwartzman, S., Ríos, S., Oliveira-Miranda, M. A., Augusto, C., Ruiz, M. R., Arrasco, C. S., Ricardo, B., Smith, R., Meyer, C., Jintiach, J. C., & Campos, E. V. (2014). Forest carbon in Amazonia: The unrecognized contribution of indigenous territories and protected natural areas. *Carbon Management*, 5(5–6), 479–485.

Weir, L. (2013). "Time immemorial" and Indigenous rights: A genealogy and three case studies (Calder, Van der Peet, Tsilhqot'in) from British Columbia. *Journal of Historical Sociology*, 26(3), 383–411.

Whyte, K. P. (2011). The recognition dimensions of environmental justice in Indian country. *Environmental Justice*, 4(4), 199–205.

Woodward, E. (2005). *One brief interval: A memoir*. Melbourne: Melbourne University Publishing.

Xanthaki, A. (2007). *Indigenous rights and United Nations standards: Self-determination, culture and land* (Vol. 52). Cambridge: Cambridge University Press.

PART I

Latin America

Indigenous Peoples across *Latin America* range from being significant parts of the overall population in Bolivia and Guatemala, to minorities in Argentina and Uruguay. However, the Latin American countries have some of the most comprehensive Indigenous land rights laws across the globe. Most nations across Latin America have adopted the International Labor Organization (ILO) 169, Indigenous and Tribal Peoples Convention. Larsen and Gilbert (2020) identified the ILO 169 as the "only international binding treaty on indigenous peoples' rights" (p. 83). ILO 169 establishes duties on states to protect and promote the rights of Indigenous Peoples, which it argued produced across the Latin American region a "'norms cascade' whereby elected democratic governments ratified numerous international human rights instruments as a means of staking their global democratic credentials" (Sieder, 2016, p. 416).

Yet popularism (Soley & Steininger, 2018), together with globalization and commodity extraction, has seen land and resource grabs across the region, with flagrant and often violent transgressions against Indigenous Peoples and their land rights (despite the legal protections) (Begotti & Peres, 2019; Ferrante & Fearnside, 2019). Indigenous Peoples have responded with three key general strategies to protect and advance their land rights across Latin America: mobilizing through social movements to advocate for land rights; litigating for and judicializing Indigenous rights in the courts, such as in Chile and parts of Colombia (Morris et al., 2009); and, where there has been a lack of success in domestic courts (and enforcing judgments), sometimes exploring extranational legal fora, such as the Inter-American Commission and Court to support their rights (Sieder, 2016; Sikkink, 2005). Since the early 2000s, the Inter-American Court of Human Rights has developed a body of jurisprudence around the collective rights of Indigenous Peoples in parts of Latin America, and established duties on state members to protect these rights (Morris et al., 2009). There has been a defining tension within states around accepting and implementing these decisions (Soley & Steininger, 2018).

2

The Elusive Promise of Indigenous Land Rights in Paraguay

Achievements, Challenges, and Current Trends

JOEL E. CORREIA, RODRIGO VILLAGRA-CARRON, AND MARCOS GLAUSER

Introduction

News headlines in 2021 revealed a troubling trend in Paraguay: "Indigenous communities are violently dispossessed in pandemic times" (La Nación, 2021); "For the second time in one year they have dispossessed the Indigenous community Cerrito from Arroyo Guazú" (UltimaHora, 2021); and "Paraguay: A violent wave of dispossessions batter Indigenous communities" (Movimiento Regional por la Tierra, 2021). Each headline – and there are many more like them – documented a violent conflict in an increasingly challenging context where long-standing land tenure inequality and socio-economic marginalization stoke a heated debate about the elusive promise of Indigenous land rights in Paraguay.[1] Although the politics of Indigenous land rights have been contentious for decades, the shocking number of violent conflicts in 2021 cast a new light on the fraught and delicate status of these rights. Across the country, and particularly in areas of extensive soybean production, producers of agro-export commodities, often with state support, forcibly removed Indigenous Peoples from lands they claimed, or they threatened those already titled with displacement (Barrios, 2021). Such events are marked by the burning and razing of homes, direct violence or the threat of it, and the criminalization of land claimants.

The current trends illustrate two related processes evaluated in this chapter. A historical analysis of key moments for Indigenous land rights

---

[1] Here, we are indebted to Engle's (2010) work on "the elusive promise of Indigenous rights."

within Paraguay demonstrates what we call "pendulum policies," where state actions move from *violations* of land rights toward the codification and protection of land and territorial rights (*justice*), and then back to *violations* again. It is worth noting here that Paraguay has a robust Indigenous rights framework that includes constitutional guarantees, regulatory policy and law, and the ratification of major international mechanisms like the International Labor Organization (ILO) Convention 169 and endorsement of the United Nations Declaration on the Rights of Indigenous Peoples (UNDRIP). This brings us to the second trend we evaluate: the implementation gap. Put simply, the "pendulum policy" pattern illustrates not merely state negligence, but a persistent gap between the juridical and discursive guarantee of *de jure* rights and the normalized violation of rights through *de facto* acts that erode Indigenous Peoples' rights and threaten their wellbeing. We ground these observations in an analysis of the role that international human rights mechanisms have played in supporting domestic struggles for land rights and of the current threats to Indigenous communities that result from acts that undermine territorial integrity, such as direct dispossession and land renting.

This chapter provides a grounding in Paraguay's historical and current socio-political dynamics. We base our work on literature, an assessment of Inter-American System actions, and consideration of current violent dispossessions. Moreover, we draw from our deep experience and commitment, sharing over forty years of experience working on Indigenous land rights in Paraguay from academic research, direct involvement in strategic litigation before the Inter-American Court, extensive advocacy and activism with Indigenous communities across the country, and the co-production of strategies to support Indigenous autonomy.

History and Evolution of Indigenous Land Rights

Nineteen different Indigenous Peoples, among five distinct linguistic families, have lived, and continue to live, across Paraguay: the Guaraní (Aché, Avá Guaraní, Mbya, Pai Tavytera, Guaraní Ñandeva, Guaraní Occidental), Maskoy (Toba Maskoy, Enlhet North, Enxet South, Sanapaná, Angaité, Guaná), Mataco Mataguayo (Nivaclé, Maká, Manjui), Zamuco (Ayoreo, Yvytoso, Tomáraho), and Guaicurú (Qom). Historically they practiced different forms of a mobile lifestyle from hunting and gathering to small-scale cultivation practices. The rich cultural diversity of Indigenous Peoples remains present today, but many groups and languages are highly threatened due to extensive deforestation and pressures from expanding agricultural and ranching frontiers across the country, in both the Atlantic Forest to the east and Chaco Forest to the west. Due to persistent discrimination and racist policies, Indigenous Peoples are the most marginalized social group in the country; however, they maintain their resistance, demanding land rights and political inclusion despite the multitude of contemporary and historical barriers we discuss in this chapter.

Like the swing of a pendulum, the history of Indigenous territorial rights since Paraguay's independence from Spanish colonization is one of advances and setbacks. The relationship of exploitation, territorial alienation and genocide of the "colonial Indian" (Bonfil Batalla, 1972) is the birthmark of the Paraguayan nation-state that continues to the present, which can be understood as a type of habitus, or what Bourdieu (1992) might call "a structuring structure." Despite the dynamic events that created the structure of unequal socio-economic relations in Paraguay, these forces remain stubbornly persistent and stable. Broadly speaking, inequality has long marked two prevailing sectors of society: wealthy Spanish *encomenderos and colonists* on the one hand, and marginalized Indigenous communities on the other, from Guaraní settled on Jesuit missions to those in the Chaco whom colonists long fought. Surprisingly similar social and economic relations continue to be reproduced in Paraguay today and are plain to see in the politics of Indigenous land rights.

Today, large landowners, ranchers, soybean farmers, and transnational agro-commodities companies largely comprise the elite and upper class of Paraguayan society. The inequity is illustrated by the fact that 4.3 percent of existing landowners control 90 percent of the land in Paraguay, or roughly 29,500,000 hectares of land (Güereña & Rojas Villagra, 2016). Meanwhile, the nineteen different Indigenous Peoples across Paraguay have collectively secured 1,143,945 hectares of land (i.e., returned for possession and occupation or in the process of being titled but still in the name of another entity). To be clear, this is the total amount of land currently recognized as under Indigenous possession, which is twenty-five to thirty times less than the total area that corresponds with the ancestral and traditional territories of Paraguay's Indigenous Peoples (Villagra, 2021).

Indigenous-State Relations and Land in the Nineteenth Century

In the nineteenth century, four key events impacted Indigenous territories that have enduring importance on land rights today. First, several early leaders of Paraguay, following independence from Spain, employed a "pendulum policy" toward Indigenous Peoples, where some protections for land rights were granted but state policy also shifted to violent ends to repress and dispossess Indigenous Peoples. We briefly outline several moments that mark important shifts in state actions toward Indigenous Peoples. First, the peace treaty between the dictator, Rodríguez de Francia (1814–1940), and the Cacique Mbaya Calapa-mi of 1821 recognized Calapa-mi's territory (Ribeiro, 2009) and nudged the pendulum toward incipient Indigenous land tenure before the state. Although the treaty was not the only one of its kind, Francia spared no effort to combat the Indigenous Peoples in the country's border region to ensure the country's territorial integrity, a policy followed by subsequent President Carlos Antonio López (1842–1862) and his son Francisco Solano (1862–1870) (Velázquez, 2003). Second, in 1825 Francia decreed that all lands within Paraguay without existing title would become state property. The decree included the autonomous Indigenous territories technically within the state's borders, but effectively outside the realm of the state due to little contact or knowledge of Paraguayan laws (Miranda, 1982). Third, President Antonio López issued the decree of 1848 that dissolved the twenty-one Guaraní "Indian villages" previously established by the Spanish colony. The decree made Guaraní "free citizens" of the state's "communal" regime, yet stripped them of their community lands (Velázquez, 2003). Finally, after the War of the Triple Alliance (1865–1870), Paraguay enacted laws between 1883 and 1885 to sell vast areas of public lands to finance war debts (Pastore, 2008), which resulted in the sale of Indigenous territories without the consent of Indigenous Peoples. Thus, by the end of the nineteenth century, the measures taken by both Francia and López had clearly shifted the pendulum in an oppressive direction, by first stripping Indigenous Peoples of their territories through law, then materially when selling Indigenous lands to finance state debts.

Emergent Indigenous Land Rights in the Twentieth Century: A Land Rights Framework

Indigenous-state relations changed over the course of the twentieth century from total tutelage to multicultural democracy. The 1904 Colonization Law coupled with the 1909 "Law of the conversion of Indians to Christianity and civilization" established concessions up to 7,500 hectares to create Indigenous reductions (akin to reservations) entrusted to religious missions, persons, or societies. Though the laws did not differ much from previous state approaches, they ratified state-led Indigenous tutelage, confinement, and Christianization in new ways (Velázquez, 2003). In 1936, Presidential Decree 7389 established a "National Board of Indigenous People" that gave the military powers to oversee Indigenous affairs in addition to Christian churches already charged with doing so. A new national constitution enacted in 1940 omitted Indigenous Peoples and their territorial rights, while the Agrarian Statute of the same year maintained colonial-era communal land for Indigenous communities and set a maximum surface parameter based on the Indigenous demography (Velázquez, 2003). The Statute also defined an agricultural purpose for Indigenous lands like those required of peasant colonies, a bias of interpretation and application of Indigenous territorial rights that survives today.

The Alfredo Stroessner dictatorship (1954–1989) further exemplified the state's "pendulum policy," creating a Department of Indigenous Affairs within the Ministry of National Defense in 1958, with the explicit objective of assimilating and settling Indigenous Peoples, and the implicit goal of controlling "internal subversion" and the borders (Horst, 2007). The military role in Indigenous affairs, coupled with an expansion of the agricultural frontier promoted by the 1940 statute, resulted in genocide against the Aché people during the 1960s and 1970s (Münzel, 1973), shifting the pendulum to brutal direct violence. Aché were not the only peoples subject to violence and egregious human rights violations, so too, among others, were the Enenlhet de Casanillo. In the mid-1970s, international pressure over the Aché case, together with the rise of pro-Indigenous activists and the incipient Indigenous movement promoted by the Marandú Project (Chase Sardi & Susnik, 1995), impelled the state to promulgate the 1981 Law 904/81 "Statute of Indigenous Communities" that created the Paraguayan Institute of the Indigenous (INDI).

In short, Law 904/81 is the starting point for contemporary processes of recognition and restitution of Indigenous lands, but also, and frustratingly so, a source of juridical stagnation. Law 904/81 recognizes the pre-existence of Indigenous communities before the creation of the Paraguayan state, ensures the legal representation of elected or named community leaders, and gives qualifying communities legal personhood. Legal personhood is the process through which Indigenous communities receive state recognition and thereby the right to claim land as collective property owned by the community. The recognition process establishes strict requisites about what constitutes a community and how communities interface with the state. For example, to obtain recognition, a community must comprise at least twenty families, elect or name specific leaders to represent the community to state agencies, and report such processes to INDI for adjudication and approval. Recognition creates the opportunity to claim collective rights while also tacitly ensuring the state arbitrates the extent of those rights. Beyond recognition, the law ensures that Indigenous communities have the right to communal titling of the lands they currently or traditionally own. Indigenous communities can claim land restitution through an administrative process before INDI and/or the National Institute of Rural Development and Lands (INDERT).[2]

Paraguay established a new constitution with the democratic transition that began in 1989 when Stroessner was forced from power. Importantly, Chapter V of this constitution codifies several principles as inalienable Indigenous rights, such as the pre-existence of Indigenous Peoples before the state and the right to communal property in sufficient extension and quality (exceeding the basic parameter established by Law 904/81), and guarantees a non-encumbrance, lease, or alienation of these lands. Indigenous and pro-Indigenous activists participated decisively in this legal achievement (Melià & Telesca, 1997) that was complemented by the 1993 passage of Law 234 that ratifies Convention 169 of the International Labour Organization (ILO), the endorsement of both the 2007 UNDRIP and the 2016 Organization of American States Declaration on the Rights of Indigenous Peoples (OASDRIPS). Together, the 1992 Constitution, Law 234, and affirmation of UNDRIP and OASDRIPS create a robust *de jure* framework to ensure Indigenous land rights and processes to title lands to Indigenous Peoples.

Limits to Indigenous Land Rights

There are significant limitations to Indigenous People's land rights in Paraguay, starting with the fact that INDI is the only government entity responsible for the restitution of Indigenous land claims. If, for example, an agreement is reached between Indigenous communities and private landowners, INDI must acquire the claimed lands with the budget allocated to it by Parliament and title them on behalf of the community. Such amicable

---

[2] INDERT was formerly called the Institute of Rural Wellbeing (IBR), which was created and regulated by the 1963 laws 852 and 854, later repealed after the fall of Stroessner with the 2002 Law 1863.

agreements between Indigenous Peoples and private landowners are unlikely, given the general resistance to selling lands to Indigenous Peoples. What typically works for driving land restitution is Indigenous community advocacy and protest for land claims, accompanied by pressure and legal support from NGOs and Indigenous organizations, as well as international attention (Griffiths, 2015).

To protect claims while they are being processed, precautionary measures must be granted by state judges under Law 43/1989. However, these measures are usually insufficient, even when they are granted, due to the lack of sanctions on landowners who often disregard restrictions through actions like subdividing and selling the land or deforesting it. Furthermore, if there is no agreement between landowners and INDI for the purchase of land, the process advances to Parliament for expropriation. Yet, the past two decades show that Parliament routinely rejects expropriation based on four tired arguments: (1) lands are used for agricultural production and therefore rationally exploited, (2) lands are protected as a private forest reserve, (3) INDI is allegedly corrupt, an observation that could be extended to many state entities, and (4) Indigenous people lack the ability or conditions to care for land, a racist assertion that is sometimes used (Ramírez, 2002).

The Paraguayan state's record in securing lands for Indigenous Peoples is thus quite fraught. From passage of Law 904/81 to the present, state agencies have only acquired 47 percent of land currently secured to Indigenous communities, and often return less land than is guaranteed in the law. To clarify, under the law, communities in the Chaco are entitled to a *minimum* of 100 hectares per family and in the southern region of Paraguay the *minimum* is 20 hectares per family. Differences are based on the diverse ecological factors in both regions, though these minimums are contested as insufficient and dictated by a bias toward agrarian production rather than Indigenous lifeways. Most land purchases have been made through INDI, though the Ministry of Public Works and Communication has also been a source for land restitution when lands are titled as mitigation for infrastructure development impacts.

In summary, several factors align to undermine *de facto* Indigenous land rights. Contemporary trends, influenced by the historical processes and laws we have noted, manifest today as ineffective administrative processes, the inability of INDI to effectively carry out its role due to the constraints or misappropriation of its budget, the insufficient protection and judicial guarantee of Indigenous claims and titled lands, as well as the predominant political will of Parliament and the executive power to defend the privileges of landowners (Griffiths, 2015; Villagra, 2018). Taken together, these factors clearly show the limits of the institutions and powers of the state to protect Indigenous territorial rights (Villagra, 2021). Recent history has shown that the only way to push the "pendulum" toward justice is through the synergies formed via organized community resistance, which includes alliances between civil society organizations and NGOs that help create international pressure through advocacy and strategic litigation. In terms of litigation, the decisions from the Inter-American System and Universal Human Rights Systems have proven vitally important in Paraguay (Inter-American Court of Human Rights, 2005, 2006, 2010; Inter-American Commission on Human Rights, 1999, 2007, 2020; United Nations Human Rights Committee, 2021). We now turn to discuss the effects of such pressure campaigns and international legal bodies.

Implementation Gaps for Rights and the Role of International Human Rights Mechanisms

Indigenous land rights in Paraguay are tenuous despite a well-established legal framework that has failed due to little institutional support that undermines the effective protections of the law (Villagra, 2021). Reporting on his work across the Americas, former United Nations (UN) Special Rapporteur on the Rights of Indigenous Peoples, Stavenhagen (2006), noted that challenges to Indigenous rights like those in Paraguay can be described as an "implementation gap," where states fail to ensure that *de jure* rights to land and other protections are enforced in practice (see also Rodriguez & Kauffman, 2015). In fact, the gap between *de jure* and *de facto* Indigenous rights is widespread in the Americas (Wright & Tomaselli, 2019). This dynamic is plain to see in Paraguay when viewed through the lens of Indigenous efforts to reclaim portions of their ancestral territories (Ayala & Cabello, 2006).

Numerous studies show that Indigenous communities with *de jure* land rights in Paraguay experience *de facto* land dispossession (Ayala, 2013; Villagra, 2018). Several factors contribute to this: deforestation driven by expanding agricultural industries (Glauser, 2018), exploitative land renting schemes that undermine the Indigenous tenure (Bogado et al., 2016), state refusal to enforce Indigenous land rights after restitution (Correia, 2019a), and myriad forms of violence from direct physical harm (Correia, 2019b; Cabello Alonso & Ayala Amarilla, 2020) to exposure to agrochemicals associated with soybean production

(Ezquerro-Cañete, 2016; Hetherington, 2020), among others. Given the overwhelming influence of export commodity crops on the national economy and history of land tenure, state institutions seem more inclined to uphold private property rights for agribusiness producers, like soybean farmers and cattle ranchers, than to restore lands to Indigenous Peoples (Barrios, 2021 Schvartzman & Oviedo, 2019). The effects of such *de facto* policy choices are discriminatory along clearly racial lines, whereas Indigenous Peoples are regularly subject to harms of ineffectual policy or direct state actions against them in ways that large-scale non-Indigenous landholders rarely, if ever, experience.

Discrimination against Indigenous Peoples in Paraguay manifests in many ways that intersect with land rights (Quiroga & Ayala, 2014; Glauser, 2018). Lack of secure land rights generates myriad challenges that can be seen across many aspects of Indigenous People's daily life: from sanitation and basic health care to access to formal and traditional education and the ability to create meaningful livelihoods and maintain cultural practices. Land tenure insecurity coupled with compromised living conditions due to dispossession perpetuates marginalization – trends evidenced by the fact that Indigenous Peoples experience the highest rates of infant mortality and official unemployment, as well as the lowest levels of access to formal education and health services in Paraguay (DEEGC, 2012; United Nations Human Rights Council, 2015). These conditions persist regardless of more than thirty years of policy and legal framing to support Indigenous rights. Thus, the denial of land rights – both through resisting restitution and the enforcement of land rights after restitution – is a site where discrimination, racism, and human rights violations are clear to see (Mendieta, 2018; Correia, 2019a; Glauser & Villagra, 2021).

When policies aim to support non-Indigenous landholders and consistently create challenges for Indigenous Peoples seeking formal land rights, such policies perpetuate discrimination. Paraguayan rights organizations have recorded and denounced the Paraguayan state for not acting on the issue of structural discrimination, exploitation, forced labor, and racism against Indigenous Peoples in Paraguay historically and in the present day (International Working Group on Indigenous Affairs, 2008; Iniciativa Amotocodie, 2009; Tierraviva a los Pueblos Indígenas del Chaco, 2013; BASE IS, 2018; Tierra Libre, 2021). The prevalence of discrimination against Indigenous Peoples in general and the racialized enforcement of land rights in specific raises many questions. What happens when the state denies its rights-bearing citizens the benefit of their rights? What recourse do people have in those instances and where do they turn?

After exhausting all domestic legal options, often the only choice left is to scale up struggles for rights by appealing to international solidarity organizations and human rights organizations with the goal that international pressure will drive local change (Keck & Sikkink, 1998). International human rights organizations have played an important role in shaping the terrain of Indigenous land rights in Paraguay. Numerous international NGOs, like El Centro por la Justicia y el Derecho Internacional (CEJIL), the International Working Group on Indigenous Affairs and Amnesty International, have advocated for Indigenous land rights in collaboration with local Paraguayan organizations. However, we only highlight work by the United Nations (UN) and the Inter-American System in this chapter due to space constraints.

International Human Rights Mechanisms in Support of Indigenous Peoples

The UN human rights monitoring and the Rapporteur for the Rights of Indigenous Peoples have provided vital external reports based on rigorous, impartial investigations that detail ongoing human rights violations against many Indigenous communities in Paraguay (Tauli-Corpuz, 2015; Bhoola, 2018; United Nations Human Rights Committee, 2021). Such reporting shows an enduring pattern of state failure to safeguard Indigenous land rights, which ultimately generates other challenges that undermine wellbeing and result in rights violations beyond, but related to, land (Correia, 2021). The UN reporting has unfortunately done little to shape on-the-ground realities for Indigenous Peoples by changing dynamics of land control and enjoyment of rights, despite being a valuable source and external validation of the work done by national human rights organizations, like Tierraviva a los Pueblos Indígenas del Chaco, the Federación por la Autodeterminación de los Pueblos Indígenas (2015), and the Coordinadora de Derechos Humanos Paraguay.

To be clear, we want to underscore that work by the UN, both via the Rapporteur for the Rights of Indigenous Peoples and standards created by the UNDRIP, has been important for creating political pressure and offering a tool to advocate for legislative change. But the lack of enforcement mechanisms or ability to drive specific actions beyond reprimands and recommendations leaves any action on improving land rights to state political will characterized by an implementation gap (Stavenhagen, 2006; Rodriguez & Kauffman, 2015; Correia, 2018a). However, a landmark decision by the UN Human Rights Committee in October 2021 found that Paraguay failed to prevent the toxic contamination of the traditional lands of the Ava Guarani community Campo Agua'ē by a commercial farmer, and thus violated their right and sense of "home" (United Nations Human Rights Committee, 2021). How the Paraguayan authorities receive and comply with the recommendations and reparations dictated by the UN Human Rights Committee is yet to be seen.

The Inter-American System, however, has been a more effective international mechanism that Indigenous Peoples and their allies have used to meaningfully reshape the politics of land rights across the country. The Inter-American System, composed of the Inter-American Commission on Human Rights (IACHR) and the Inter-American Court of Human Rights (IACtHR), is a legal mechanism under the auspices of the Organization of American States used to ensure human rights of member state citizens when states abrogate their responsibilities to protect citizen rights. The IACHR and IACtHR have played a vital role in Indigenous land rights in Paraguay – both by bringing attention to the egregious human rights violations related to Indigenous land dispossession and by creating a juridical wedge that Indigenous activists and their allies can use to push the Paraguayan state to make meaningful material changes in the form of land restitution and related acts.

Procedurally, victims of human rights abuses must first exhaust all domestic legal remedies – that is, in the case of land claims, the administrative process and/or expropriation project – before petitioning the IACHR to adjudicate a case. If the IACHR accepts the case, it works as an intermediary between victims and states to negotiate a friendly settlement. Failure to reach a settlement means the case can be advanced to the IACtHR, which then proceeds as a trial with both sides presenting evidence. The Inter-American System has been used numerous times to adjudicate cases related to Indigenous land rights in Paraguay, though not always with success as evidenced in the 1977 petition for Aché rights abuses resulting from land dispossession and state refusal to uphold their basic rights (Inter-American Commission on Human Rights, 1977). Unfortunately, in that 1977 case, the IACHR only reprimanded the state for its actions but did not move further for Aché land restitution given tenuous tenure laws under the Alfredo Stroessner dictatorship (1954–1989) at the time the case was heard. Beyond the Aché case, the IACHR has issued precautionary measures related to several Indigenous land rights matters, including but not limited to the following communities: Kelyenmagategma, Yakye Axa, Sawhoyamaxa, Xákmok Kásek, and Ayoreo Totobiegosode peoples living in voluntary isolation.

IACHR Land Rights Settlements

To date, the IACHR has facilitated three land restitution settlements and issued several precautionary measures regarding land rights in Paraguay. The first settlement involved two Enxet and Sanapaná communities – Lamenxay and Kayleyphapopyet – who sought land restitution for ancestral territories that had been sold in the late 1800s without their knowledge or permission. Both communities had filed claims for land restitution per Law 904/81 and the national constitution; however, the responsible state institutions never resolved the land claim. The IACHR facilitated a friendly settlement that returned 21,844.44 hectares of land to the communities in 1999 (Inter-American Commission on Human Rights, 1999).

The second settlement involved the Enxet community of Kelyenmagategma. Like Lamenxay and Kayleyphapopyet, Kelyenmagategma lands were sold without community permission, though community members had remained on the lands to work as ranch hands, often for little or no pay. After petitioning the Paraguayan state for land restitution in accord with the law, relations with the Algarrobo SA ranch administrators soured to the point that multiple violent dispossessions occurred under the watch of Paraguayan police where ranching staff burned houses, threatened community members with direct violence, and because of the ensuing melee, one elderly woman from the community, Teresa Gaona, died (Inter-American Commission on Human Rights, 2007). The state's failure to facilitate land restitution and the role of police during multiple violent attacks impelled the IACHR to facilitate a friendly settlement that was reached in 2011 with the return of 8,748 hectares of land to Kelyenmagategma.

The IACHR adjudicated the third and most recent friendly settlement regarding the Mbya community of Y'aká Marangatu. Like the two settlements that preceded it, the state refused to adjudicate Y'aká Marangatu land restitution petitions, effectively forcing the community in a decades-long conflict with soybean farmers who sought the community's lands (Inter-American Commission on Human Rights, 2020). However, in 2020 the state agreed to restitute the 219 hectares in question to the community. In each friendly settlement, land restitution underpins community claims – though it is also worth noting that the process has resulted in other material gains for communities, such as indemnity payments or environmental impact monitoring.

IACtHR Land Rights Judgments

The IACtHR has issued three judgments regarding Indigenous land rights in Paraguay to date: the Enxet community Yakye Axa (Inter-American Court of Human Rights, 2005), the Enxet community Sawhoyamaxa (Inter-American Court of Human Rights, 2006), and the Sanapaná and Enxet community Xákmok Kásek (Inter-American Court of Human Rights, 2010). While each case is distinct, they share some common themes. All are in Paraguay's western Chaco region, where lands were sold without Indigenous consultation and converted to extensive cattle ranching. The Paraguayan state repeatedly failed to adjudicate each community's respective land claims, thus aggravating their dispossession and related human rights abuses. Each community confronted fierce resistance from landowners who refused to negotiate for the return of their core ancestral territories. Although the state has returned at least part of the land each community claims, the restitution to each community following IACtHR judgments has been excruciatingly slow – over a decade in each instance and in one case nearly twenty years.

In summary, the Inter-American System has played an important role in facilitating land restitution and enforcing Paraguay's land rights framework. The ability of Indigenous communities to regain portions of their ancestral territories through friendly settlements and strategic litigation before the IACtHR effectively advances Indigenous land rights. In turning to international human rights bodies, Indigenous Peoples and their allies have secured important legal victories with meaningful material changes for many communities, including state institutional reforms and the establishment of monitoring mechanisms (Villagra, 2021). Yet such advances also make clear the persistence of the "implementation gap" that haunts contemporary land rights dynamics in Paraguay and thus international pressure seems necessary to force the state to ensure its rights framework. Once at the vanguard of Latin America or land rights in the early 1990s, the country's judicial mechanisms to support Indigenous land rights run up against state resistance for the return of lands because of disruptions to agribusiness interests, something that has clear discriminatory effects on Indigenous Peoples.

Barriers and Threats to Indigenous Land Rights

The current situation of Indigenous Peoples in Paraguay illustrates a systematic violation of their rights and shows an implementation gap in the recognition and enforcement of land rights. The policy pendulum has swung from *justice* back to *violation*. Given the historic and contemporary trends we traced earlier, Indigenous Peoples continue to be excluded from an economic model that privileges agrarian sectors, which have become increasingly violent and humiliating for Indigenous Peoples (Cabello Alonso & Ayala Amarilla, 2020, p. 50). The dispossession and the prevailing economic model not only impact Indigenous wellbeing in many ways but also result in a profound socio-economic inequality, where 65 percent of Indigenous Peoples now live in poverty and more than 30 percent in extreme poverty (DGEEC, 2017). As Imas et al. (2020) show, 97.9 percent of Indigenous Peoples in Paraguay have at least one unmet basic need, like adequate water access, health care, or sanitation. Foundational to these needs is land tenure. In this section, we illustrate the land inequity in Paraguay, with those lands already secured for Indigenous Peoples being patently insufficient. In addition to titling, demarcation and delimitation delays, we suggest that land leasing and evictions are among the most important challenges to Indigenous land rights today.

There is a clear discrepancy between the amount of land that the constitution guarantees to Indigenous Peoples and that which Indigenous Peoples actually possess or claim because state officials ascribe to the strict limits outlined in Law 904/81 instead of the constitutional view of land rights. The exact quantity of land under Indigenous control is difficult to ascertain because there is no consolidated registry of such data, despite improved land registries at the state and private levels. According to the first official national population census conducted in 1981, 38,703 people were identified as Indigenous. Of the three main peoples in the Eastern Region – the Paĩ-Tavyterã, the Mbya Guaraní, and the Ava Guaraní – 20, 80, and 30 percent respectively had nowhere to settle because of land reforms and historic dispossessions (Brunn et al., 1990, p. 14). However, some ten years later the state registered 471,655 hectares of land to 254 recognized communities throughout the country (Brunn et al., 1990) with an Indigenous population that totaled 49,487 (Melià & Telesca, 1997). The 2002 census provided a more comprehensive count through a participatory methodology and estimated 87,099 Indigenous Peoples among 414 Indigenous communities (see Table 2.1).

Table 2.1 Statistics on Indigenous Peoples and land tenure 1981–2020

Year	Total Indigenous population in the country	Total Indigenous lands guaranteed	Total Indigenous communities in the country	Total number of communities renting	Percentage renting of the total
1981	No data	38,703	No data	No data	No data
1992	471,655	49,487	254	No data	No data
2002	717,952	87,099	415	120	29%
2012	963,953	117,150	493	182	37%
2020	1,143,945	125,227	521	192	37%

This survey also included land conflicts and tenure data (DGEEC, 2003) that showed deforestation impacted 120 of the identified communities and 185 (44.7 percent) had no land of their own (Kretschmer & Rehnfeldt, 2005, pp. 44–46). In 2006, Indigenous organizations estimated that a total of 717,952 hectares were now guaranteed across the whole country (Ayala & Cabello, 2006, pp. 362–363). The most recent census in 2012 recorded 493 communities where 357 had land title and 134 did not; two communities did not report data (DGEEC, 2015) (see Table 2.1). According to Villagra (2018), there are currently some 521 communities, plus 272 villages and neighborhoods and 47 family groupings across Asunción and the Metropolitan Area of the Central Department – that is, 840 groups or collective units.

As discussed earlier, while some land has been returned to Indigenous communities, the returned lands are insufficient even in light of the minimum baseline established by the now outdated Law 904/81. Indigenous land rights outlined in Law 904/81 are clearly influenced by agrarian reforms intended for non-Indigenous *campesino* families because the law states that each Indigenous family within a recognized community is entitled to twenty hectares of land in the eastern region of Paraguay and 100 hectares of land in the Chaco region. That baseline calculus used to determine land restitution ignores Indigenous territorial relations and reduces them to property relations. However, when using that baseline as a standard to measure state compliance with Indigenous land restitution, the total amount of land returned to Indigenous communities in the eastern region nearly meets the legal requirements. By the same measure, the state has returned less than 50 percent of lands eligible to Indigenous communities in the Chaco. In addition, there are now claims that transcend individual communities and refer to *peoples* who are seeking to recover and manage their own contiguous *territories* (Casaccia, 2009; Inter-American Commission on Human Rights, 2016). And yet the Executive branch has just reduced the 2021 budget for land purchases by 381 percent compared to 2020. The tensions present in the dynamics of land restitution illustrate that policy shifts regarding land restitution are akin to a *pendulum*, pushed back and forth from the direction of *justice* through organized resistance for specific cases, or in the direction of *violations* for repressive acts by prevailing political and economic interests centered on the control of land.

The delay in titling, demarcation, and delimitation is proportional to the pace of progress and expansion of agribusiness, which continues to put pressure on Indigenous territories. Thus, communities that do not have leaders and lawyers to navigate the land restitution procedures end up losing hope of recovering part of their territory, often dispersing in other communities, in urban centers, or roadsides (Tierraviva a los Pueblos Indígenas del Chaco, 2013). Yet these delays continue even after land restitution because it commonly takes years to title land on behalf of communities and to carry out necessary legal requirements. The irregular titling process, coupled with the lack of a reliable cadaster, threatens the legal security of Indigenous communities and hinders the implementation of development projects from both the private and public sectors. Moreover, the common practice of granting environmental licenses that allows the deforestation of areas used by Indigenous Peoples, without a mechanism to review or challenge the issuance of such licenses, runs counter to IACHR's statements about the implementation of development plans and projects without first fully identifying and guaranteeing communal property rights through titling, delimitation, and demarcation (Inter-American Court, 2006).

The lease and rental of Indigenous lands to third parties is frequently practiced and constitute one of the greatest *de facto* threats to Indigenous land rights in Paraguay. The rental of Indigenous lands flagrantly violates the guarantees of Constitution Article 64 that prohibits the lease of Indigenous lands. Many Indigenous communities are effectively forced into renting portions of their lands for cattle pasture, soybean cultivation, and timber extraction because few economic opportunities exist outside of the predominant agro-export development model. Land renting is both a consequence of structural economic and social inequalities as well as a practice that reproduces extreme poverty among Indigenous populations because lands are often severely degraded by agricultural activities with few economic outcomes for community members. Studies also point to other serious effects because renting is often endorsed, if not directly carried out and protected using public force by municipal authorities, corrupt INDI officials, local politicians, prosecutors and police (Villagra, 2018). Such outcomes reveal not only the challenges Indigenous Peoples face to access justice, but also the partiality of government officials.

Finally, forced evictions and the criminalization of Indigenous leaders have become the main threat and a tool for agribusiness to advance its interests in Indigenous territories. While violence has long been associated with the antagonistic relationships between the agribusiness sector and many Indigenous communities in Paraguay (Correia, 2019b; Quiroga & Ayala, 2014; Tauli-Corpuz, 2015; Tusing, 2021), an alarming spark in direct violence marks a re-emergence in the undermining of Indigenous land tenure in times of the pandemic. Between May and November 2021 alone, at least eight Indigenous communities were violently expelled from their territory, as noted in Table 2.2. By forced eviction we mean the permanent or temporary removal of individuals, families, and/or communities from the homes and/or lands they occupy,

Table 2.2 Indigenous communities dispossessed of land in 2021. Data derived from Barrios (2021)

Date	Community/People	District/Department	Number of families
May 13, 2021	Cerrito/Ava Guarani	Minga Porá/Alto Parana	85
June 1, 2021	Yvy Porá/Ava Guarani	Santa Rosa del Aguaray/San Pedro	80
June 6, 2021	Acaraymí/Ava Guarani	Itakyry/Alto Parana	150
June 16, 2021	Ka'a Poty/Ava Guarani	Itakyry/Alto Parana	Unknown
July 7, 2021	Cristo Rey/Ava Guarani	Yvyrarovana/ Canindeyú	100
July 8, 2021	Tekoha Ka'avusu/ Ava Guarani	Itakyry/Alto Paraná	60
November 18, 2021	Hugua Po´i/Mbya	Raúl Arsenio Oviedo/ Caaguazú	70
November 29, 2021	Cerrito/Ava Guarani	Minga Pora/Alto Paraná	80

without appropriate means of legal or other protection, or access to such means (ESC Committee, 1997). The increasingly common use of armed non-state agents in the execution of illegal evictions must also be added to this list (Cabello & Ayala, 2020).

Conclusions: Recognition and the Road Ahead

Reflecting on the swinging policy pendulum of land rights in Paraguay – from *violation* to *justice*, and then back to *violation* – the new era of land dispossession marks a new period of violations against Indigenous Peoples in the country. The politics and practice of Indigenous land rights in Paraguay reveal the limits of the country's current policy framework, despite major legal victories like passage of Law 904/81, the adoption of Chapter V of the 1992 Constitution, and ratification of ILO 169 that promised more equality. The IACtHR called into question these limits in each of its three rulings against Paraguay (Inter-American Court of Human Rights, 2005, 2006, 2010), and recommended necessary legal and institutional reforms that the state has yet to comply with. More than a matter of creating new laws and mechanisms to support land rights, our work here suggests that the longstanding influence of land-extensive agricultural commodity production has been a key driver of socio-economic inequality and racial marginalization that undermines Indigenous wellbeing.

Despite having a clear process to recognize Indigenous communities and adjudicate land restitution – as indicated in the national constitution and Law 904 – the actual process of returning lands and securing them after restitution is riddled with problems. Those problems often emerge when communities that have gained legal personhood in accordance with the law demand restitution of lands that are privately held and often used for agricultural production by non-Indigenous Peoples. Given the Paraguayan state's strict interpretation that "rationally exploited" land cannot be expropriated or returned to Indigenous communities without voluntary landowner permission (Correia, 2018b; Inter-American Court of Human Rights, 2006), the political economy of agricultural commodity production effectively takes precedence over Indigenous rights and the minimum guarantee of land restitution that recognition should ensure. Given this situation, looking forward, the most important safeguard of Indigenous land rights in Paraguay will be robust cross-sector alliances, led by Indigenous communities in collaboration with local rights-focused NGOs and international advocacy organizations; these alliances will have to work with sympathetic lawmakers to advance and safeguard land rights and, if necessary, appeal to international human rights bodies to bring further pressure on the state to act consistently with the law.

The chapter highlights that legal recognition has been used to appeal to international human rights bodies where violations of due process have been addressed in IACtHR judgments, IACHR friendly settlements, and a recent UN Human Rights Committee decision. In this regard, strategic alliances between Paraguayan NGOs, advocacy organizations, and Indigenous communities have used recognition to bridge the gap between *de jure* and *de facto* rights in specific cases discussed earlier. Although it is undeniable that implementing the Inter-American System recommendations and judgments has been challenging (Correia, 2021; Open Society Justice Initiative, 2017), Indigenous Peoples and their allies use strategic litigation, advocacy, negotiation, and direct actions to push the pendulum further in the direction of *justice*. The road ahead is uncertain, as new legislative initiatives further threaten to undermine Indigenous land rights and the current wave of violent dispossessions continues unabated. However, our Indigenous collaborators and inter-locutors have not lost faith in the promise of land rights and their ability to recover and rebuild their relations with their ancestral territories. We too maintain that the struggle for Indigenous land rights in Paraguay must continue until each community has its land back and is able to determine the path of its own future.

References

Ayala, Ó. (2013). El derecho al desagravio como forma del derecho a un espacio propio y autónomo. In P. Dobreé (ed.), *La tierra en el Paraguay: De la desigualdad al ejercicio de derechos* (pp. 63–77). Asunción: Programa Democratización y Construcción de la Paz.

Ayala, Ó., & Cabello, M. J. (2006). Entre la realidad y los avances de la justicia internacional. In Ó. Ayala (ed.), *Derechos Humanos en Paraguay 2006* (pp. 359–370). Asunción: Codehupy. Coordinadora del Derechos Humanos de Paraguay. Asunción, Paraguay.

Barrios, C. M. (2021). Un año de violencia, exclusión y desalojos contra comuni-dades indígenas. Derechos de los pueblos indígenas. In *Derechos Humanos Paraguay 2021* Asunción: CODEHUPY.

BASE IS. (2018). Denuncian atropellos contra pueblos indígenas. www.baseis.org .py/denuncian-atropellos-contra-pueblos-indigenas

Bhoola, U. (2018). *Report of the Special Rapporteur on contemporary forms of slavery, including its causes and consequences on her mission to Paraguay.* United Nations Human Rights Council.

Bogado, M., Portillo, R., Villagra, R. (2016). Alquiler de tierras y territorios indígenas en el Paraguay. *Cuadernos de Lepaarq*, 13(26), 106–123.

Bonfil Batalla, G. (1972). El concepto de indio en América: una categoría de la situación colonial. *Anales de Antropología*, 9, 105–124.

Bourdieu, P. (1992). *The logic of practice* (R. Nice, trans.). California: Stanford University Press.

Brunn, A., Chase Sardi, M., & Ángel Enciso, M. (1990). *Situación sociocultural, económica, jurídico-política actual de las comunidades indígenas en el Paraguay.* Asunción: Centro Interdisciplinario de Derecho Social y Economía Política, Universidad Católica.

Cabello Alonso, J., & Ayala Amarilla, Ó. (2020). Desamparo, crisis alimentaria, desalojos: Rastros de la violencia hacia pueblos indígenas. In C. Paraguay (ed.), *Derechos Humanos Paraguay 2020* (pp. 47–60). Asunción: Codehupy.

Casaccia, G. M. (2009). El reclamo territorial Ayoreo Totobeigosode. *Avá Revista de Antropología*, 14, 1–19.

Chase Sardi, M., & Susnik, B. (1995). *Los indios del Paraguay.* Madrid: MAPFRE.

Comité DESC. (1997). Observación General N° 7 El derecho a una vivienda adecuada: Los desalojos forzosos. www.escr-net.org/es/recursos/observacion-general-no-7-derecho-una-vivienda-adecuada

Correia, J. (2018a). Adjudication and its aftereffects in three Inter-American Court cases brought against Paraguay: Indigenous land rights. *Erasmus Law Review*, 1, 43–56.

(2018b). Indigenous rights at a crossroads: Territorial struggles, the Inter-American Court of Human Rights, and legal geographies of liminality. *Geoforum*, 97, 78–83.

(2019a). Unsettling territory: Indigenous mobilizations, the territorial turn, and the limits of land rights in the Paraguay-Brazil borderlands. *Journal of Latin American Geography*, 18(1), 11–37.

(2019b). Soy states: Resource politics, violent environments and soybean territorialization in Paraguay. *The Journal of Peasant Studies*, 46(2), 316–336.

(2021). Reworking recognition: Indigeneity, land rights, and the dialectics of disruption in Paraguay's Chaco. *Geoforum*, 119, 227–237.

DEEGC (Direccioìn General de Estadiìstica, Ecuestas y Censos). (2012). Pueblos indiìgenas en el Paraguay: Resultados finales de poblacioìn y viviendas. www.ine.gov.py/Publicaciones/Biblioteca/indigena2012/Pueblos%20indigenas%20en%20el%20Paraguay%20Resultados%20Finales%20de%20Poblacion%20y%20Viviendas%202012.pdf

Engle, K. (2010). *The elusive promise of indigenous development: Rights, culture, strategy.* Durham: Duke University Press.

Ezquerro-Cañete, A. (2016). Poisoned, dispossessed and excluded: A critique of the neoliberal soy regime in Paraguay. *Journal of Agrarian Change*, 16, 702–710.

Federación por la Autodeterminación de los Pueblos Indígenas. (2015). Situación territorial de los pueblos indígenas de Paraguay. https://fapi.org.py/wp-con tent/uploads/2015/11/Libro-Tom-Final.pdf

General Directorate for Statistics, Survey and Census (DGEEC). (2003). Pueblos Indígenas del Paraguay. Resultados Finales Censo 2002. Fernando de la Mora: DGEEC.

(2015). Censo de Comunidades de los Pueblos Indígenas. Resultados Finales 2012. Fernando de la Mora: DGEEC.

(2017). Encuesta Permanente de Hogares 2016: Principales Resultados. Fernando de la Mora: DGEEC.

Glauser, M. (2018). Entendiendo las respuestas de un pueblo indígena del Chaco Paraguayo a la desposesión territorial. *Gestión y Ambiente*, 21(2), 86–94.

Glauser, M., & Villagra, R. (2021). Procesos de Despojo y re-territorialización Contemporáneos de los Pueblos Ava Guaraní, Mbya Guaraní y los Paĩ Tavyterã de la Región. *Revista de Estudios & Pesquisas Sobre as Américas*, 14(3), 103–140.

Griffiths, T. (2015). *Situación Territorial de los Pueblos Indígenas del Paraguay*. Asunción-Oxford: FAPI-Forest Peoples Programme.

Güereña, A., & Rojas Villagra, L. (2016). *Yvy Jára: Los dueños de la tierra en Paraguay*. Asunción, Oxfam en Paraguay.

Hetherington, K. (2020). *The government of beans: Regulating life in the age of monocrops*. Durham: Duke University Press.

Horst, René H. (2007). *The Stroessner regime and the Indigenous resistance*. Gainsville: Florida University Press.

Imas, V., Serafini, V., & Zavattiero, C. (2020). La política de protección social en el Paraguay. Superación de la pobreza y el hambre. Asunción: Codehupy.

Iniciativa Amotocodie. (2009). The case of the Ayoreo. *IWGIA Report*. www.iniciativa-amotocodie.org/wp-content/uploads/2019/08/The-case-of-the-ayoreo.pdf

Inter-American Commission on Human Rights. (1977). "Ache" Indians v. Para., Case 1802, Inter-Am. C.H.R., OEA/Ser.L/V/II.43, doc. 21, corr. 1.

(1999). Caso No 11.713. Comunidad Enxet Lamenxay Informe de Solución Amistosa No 90/99.

(2007). Informe No 55/07 Petición 987-04. Admisibilidad. Comunidad Indígena Kelyenmagategma del Pueblo Enxet-Lengua y Sus Miembros, Paraguay.

(2016). Medida Cautelar No. 54-13 Asunto comunidades en aislamiento voluntario del Pueblo Ayoreo Totobeigosode respeto de Paraguay 3 de febrero de. www.oas.org/es/cidh/decisiones/pdf/2016/MC54-13-Es.pdf

(2020). Informe No. 256/20 Petición 745-05. Informe de Solución Amistosa Comunidad Indígena Yaka Marangatu Pueblo Mbya, Paraguay.

Inter-American Court of Human Rights. (2005). Case of the Yakye Axa Indigenous community v. Paraguay judgment of June 17, 2005, merits, reparations, and costs.
   (2006). Case of the Sawhoyamaxa Indigenous Community v. Paraguay judgment of March 29, 2006, merits, reparations, and costs.
   (2010). Case of the Xákmok Kásek Indigenous community v. Paraguay judgment of August 24, 2010, merits, reparations, and costs.
International Working Group on Indigenous Affairs. (2008). *Los Aché del Paraguay: Discusión de un genocidio*. Denmark: Copenhagen.
Keck, M. E., & Sikkink, K. (1998). *Activists beyond borders: Advocacy networks in international politics*. Ithaca: Cornell University Press.
Kretschmer, R., & Rehnfeldt, M. (2005). *Población Indígena*. Fernando de la Mora: DGEEC.
La Nación. (2021, July 12). Violentos desalojos a comunidades indígenas en pandemia.
Melià, B., & Telesca, I. (1997). Los pueblos indígenas en el Paraguay: conquistas legales y problemas de tierra. *Horizontes Antropológicos*, 3(6), 85–110.
Mendieta, M. (2018). El principio de igualdad y no discriminación. Aproximaciones a la descriminación estructural del estado paraguayo hacia los pueblos indígenas. *Derecho Global: Estudios Sobre Derecho y Justicia*, 4(10), 153–180.
Miranda, A. (1982). *Desarrollo y pobreza en el Paraguay*. Rosslyn, VA: Inter-American Foundation; Asunción: Comité de Iglesias para Ayudas de Emergencia.
Movimiento Regional por la Tierra. (2021, July 14). Paraguay: Violenta oleada de desalojos golpea acomunidades indígenas.
Münzel, M. (1973). *El pueblo Aché: Genocido en Paraguay*. Copenhague: IWGIA.
Open Society Justice Initiative. (2017). *Strategic litigation impacts: Indigenous people's land rights*. New York: Open Society Foundations.
Pastore, C. (2008). *La lucha por la tierra en el Paraguay*. Asunción: Interconental Editora. (Original work published 1972)
Quiroga, L., & Ayala, Ó. (2014). Violencia e impunidad hacia el pueblo Pãi Tavyterã-Kaiowa: Aproximación a la Situación de violaciones de derechos humanos en la frontera paraguayo-brasileña. Asunción: Tierraviva a los Pueblos Indígenas del Chaco.
Ramírez, A. (2002). Derechos de los Pueblos Indígenas: Denegación Estructural de Derechos a los Pueblos Indígenas. In M. V. González, M. Palau, H. Valiente, S. Villagra, and V. Villalba (eds.) *Derechos Humanos en Paraguay 2002* (pp. 417–440). Asunción: Coordinadora de Derechos Humanos del Paraguay.
Ribeiro, A. (2009). Los indios (en) (y) la independencia paraguaya. *Studia Historica*, 27, 279–308.
Rodriguez, C. G., & Kauffman, C. (2015). De las órdenes a la práctica: Análisis y estrategias para el cumplimiento del Sistema Interamericano de Derechos Humanos. In M. Rojas (ed.), *Desafios del sistema interamericano de derechos humanos: Nuevos tiempos, viejos retos* (pp. 276–317). Bogotá: DeJusticia.

Schvartzman Muñoz, L., & Oviedo, S. (2019). Nueva ola del agronegocio avanza sobre tierras indígenas: Desalojos irregulares de comunidades del pueblo Avá Guaraní. In M. Palau (ed.), *Con la Soja al Cuello 2019* (pp. 84–87). Asunción: Base Investigaciones Sociales.

Stavenhagen, R. (2006). *Report of the Special Rapporteur on the situation of human rights and fundamental freedoms of Indigenous peoples*. United Nations Economic and Social Council, New York.

Tauli-Corpuz, V. (2015). *Report of the Special Rapporteur on the rights of Indigenous Peoples: The situation in Paraguay*. United Nations Human Rights Council, Geneva.

Tierra libre. (2021). El pueblo Manjui sufriendo una limpieza étnica silenciosa. https://tierralibre.org.py/index.php/2021/08/11/el-pueblo-manjui-sufriendo-una-limpieza-etnica-silenciosa

Tierraviva a los Pueblos Indígenas del Chaco. (2013). *Situación de los derechos a la tierra y al territorio de los pueblos indígenas en el Paraguay*. Asunción: Tierraviva.

Tusing, C. (2021). The new Guarani reductions: Aftermaths of collective titling in Northern Paraguay. *The Journal of Peasant Studies*, 50(1), 391–410.

UltimaHora. (2021, November 30). Desalojan por segunda vez en el año a comunidad indígena Cerrito de Arroyo Guazú.

United Nations Human Rights Committee. (2021). *Dictamen aprobado por el Comité a tenor de artículo 5, párrafo del Protoclo Facultativo, respeto de la comunicación Núm*. New York: United Nations.

United Nations Human Rights Council. (2015). Report of the Special Rapporteur on the rights of Indigenous peoples: The situation of Indigenous peoples in Paraguay. https://un.arizona.edu/search-database/situation-indigenous-peoples-paraguay

Velázquez Seiferhel, D. (2003). Condición Jurídica de los indígenas en el Paraguay entre 1811 y 1870. El problema de los pueblos indígenas como entidades colectivas. El problema de la ciudadanía. In L. L. Claude, R.E. Di Martino Ortiz, R.S. Geoghegan, Y.L. Simon Sosa, M.V. Huerta (eds.) *Digesto Normativo sobre Pueblos Indígenas del Paraguay*. (pp. 8-63). Asunción: Corte Suprema de Justicia, División de Investigación, Legislación y Publicaciones - IWGIA - Tierraviva.

Villagra, R. (2018). Diagnóstico socio-jurídico de tierras y territorios indígenas en Paraguay. *Suplemento Antropológico*, 53(1), 129–182.

(2021). The situation of Indigenous peoples in Paraguay. In A. Chirif (ed.), *Towards the conquest of self-determination: 50 Years since the Barbados Declaration* (pp. 277–296). Copenhagen: International Working Group on Indigenous Affairs.

Wright, C., & Tomaselli, A. (2019). *The prior consultation of Indigenous peoples in Latin America: Inside the implementation gap*. London: Routledge.

3

Recognizing and Reclaiming Indigenous Peoples' Constitutional Land Rights in Brazil

Challenges and Opportunities

FERNANDA FRIZZO BRAGATO AND JOCELYN GETGEN
KESTENBAUM

Introduction

Today, some 1.7 million Indigenous Peoples, belonging to 305 tribes (*povos*), and speaking 274 different languages, have broad national and international legal protections in Brazil (United Nations, 2014).[1] According to Brazil's international and domestic legal obligations, Indigenous Peoples are descendants of peoples that pre-existed invasion and colonization in their territory; that fully or partially preserved their social, political, cultural, legal, or other institutions; that self-identify as Indigenous; and that are recognized by their communities as members (following the Cobo definition of Indigenous Peoples).[2]

In addition to being subjects of nationally and internationally recognized human rights, equally and without discrimination, Indigenous Peoples in Brazil are entitled to certain collective rights based on the right to conserve and maintain their own territories, cultures, traditions, and customs. These rights include: the right to occupy their traditional

---

[1] In the 2022 Census, the Brazilian Institute of Geography and Statistics (IBGE) found the Indigenous population had reached 1.693 million people, which represents 0.83 percent of the total population. The 2010 Census counted 896,917 Indigenous Peoples in the country. The increase in the Indigenous population was 88.82 percent in twelve years, while the growth of the total population in the same period was 6.5 percent. FUNAI (2023), https://abre.ai/funainotice.

[2] This definition also coincides with Article 1 (b) of International Labour Organization (ILO) Indigenous and Tribal Peoples Convention No. 169, 1989, ratified by the Brazilian State on April 19, 2004, through Decree 5,051.

lands;[3] the right to self-determination;[4] and the right to free, prior, and informed consultation[5] or consent, on measures that may affect their territories or ways of life.[6]

The 1988 Constitution represents the first and most powerful recognition of Indigenous Peoples' territorial and cultural rights in Brazil's history. Since its enactment, Indigenous Peoples not only have had the right to occupy their traditional lands, but also have had the right to the exclusive use and enjoyment in ways consistent with their traditional and distinct ways of life.[7] Additionally, the state generally is prohibited from removing Indigenous Peoples from their traditional lands and must seek Congressional authorization before extracting resources or carrying out any infrastructure projects on Indigenous lands.[8] In all cases, Indigenous communities must be consulted in good faith with the aim of obtaining consent when state or private actions may affect their rights, including and especially land rights.

Before 1988, Brazil's official policies toward Indigenous Peoples aimed to integrate and assimilate Indigenous communities into what the legislation called "national communion,"[9] representing an erasure of many groups' distinct cultures and practices. While the post-1988 constitutional provisions included broader legal protections for Indigenous Peoples, as Benatti et al. (2015) emphasizes, Brazil has consistently failed to implement and enforce these rights in practice – an experience shared across most of the chapters in this book. Recent power shifts have led to Brazil partially reversing the trend toward dismantling Indigenous Peoples' rights. However, Brazil's executive and judicial branches have intentionally curtailed many of these constitutional guarantees, or have impeded the full enjoyment of these rights in recent years. Brazil's

---

[3] 1988 Brazilian Constitution Article 231, § 1; United Nations Declaration on the Rights of Indigenous Peoples (UNDRIP), Article 26; ILO No. 169, Article 13 and 14; Organization of American States (OAS), Declaration on the Rights of Indigenous Peoples, Article XXV, 2.

[4] UNDRIP, Article 3; OAS Declaration Article III and XXI.

[5] ILO 169, Article 6; 1988 Brazilian Constitution Article 231, § 3º.

[6] ILO 169, Article 6, 2; UNDRIP, Articles 19 and 32, 2; OAS Declaration, Articles XXIII, 2, XXVIII, 3, and XXIX, 4.

[7] Brazilian Constitution Article 231, § 2º.

[8] Brazilian Constitution Article 231, § 3º and 5º.

[9] For example, Article 1 of Brazilian Law 6.001 / 1973 (Indian Statute) states, "This Law regulates the legal status of Indians and indigenous communities, with the purpose of preserving their culture and integrating them progressively and harmoniously into national communion." See www.planalto.gov.br/ccivil_03/Leis/L6001.htm.

legislative branch has attempted several times to pass legislation to restrict rights guaranteed under the 1988 Constitution (de Souza Filho, 1992). Indeed, from 2011 to 2022, the emancipatory potential of Indigenous Peoples' rights was threatened by legal, political, economic, and social restraints rooted in the country's deeply embedded colonial structures, especially within those Brazilian institutions charged with realizing Indigenous rights (Beltrão & Oliveira, 2014).

This chapter analyzes the achievements of 1988: successes resulting from an intense process of political mobilization by Indigenous Peoples and their civil society allies, combined with a theoretical shift away from colonialist conceptions of the inferiority of Indigenous epistemologies and worldviews. This chapter next examines barriers that Indigenous Peoples face in enforcing their constitutional and international human rights, as well as the opportunities created since the change in government in January 2023. It concludes by proposing recommendations to advance the implementation and full realization of Indigenous land rights in Brazil.

Pre-1988: Dispossession and Recognition

Pre-contact, Latin America's Indigenous populations had varied land tenure regimes: from extensive bureaucratic and agriculturally advanced societies, such as the Inca and Aztec empires, to more loosely structured kinship communities, such as those in the Amazon region (Angeles & Elizalde, 2017). In 1500, Portuguese conquerors wrote a letter to the king upon arriving in what is today Brazil, reporting from a distorted Western perspective on the existence of naked, vigorous, brown (*pardo*) men with whom they were unable to establish any communication (Carta de Pêro Vaz de Caminha, 1500). From their political and economic points of view, European travelers often misunderstood and mischaracterized the sophistication of Indigenous Peoples' relationship to their lands, describing them as destitute and decentralized, without formal legal systems, currency, or ways of accumulating wealth. What they did have was "a chief for every hut" and nature to provide everything they needed (Staden, 1930).

In addition to the partiality of colonizers' reports, the scarcity of archaeological remains in tropical areas prevents firmer conclusions about Indigenous ways of life in Brazil before colonial violence and dispossession. Some archaeologists have argued that Brazil's Indigenous Peoples lacked political institutions and central authority, a view that has been challenged, with the documented existence of organized political institutions, such as chiefdoms (Fausto, 2000). For many Indigenous Peoples in the Brazilian Amazon, land tenure was adapted for survival as they fled violent conquest and colonization and, consequently, assimilated practices or peoples from other traditional groups while retaining certain practices from their pre-contact societies (Le Tourneau, 2015).

On contact, an estimated 3.6 million Indigenous Peoples were living in a system of collective land ownership. Colonial settlers accelerated the decimation of the Indigenous population through war, extermination, and enslavement, as well as diseases, such as smallpox, measles, and tuberculosis (Pacheco de Oliveira, 2006). Indigenous Peoples inhabiting Brazil were never recognized as sovereign nations; throughout the colonial period, the official policy was either to integrate "friendly" Indigenous Peoples (i.e., those who did not openly resist colonial violence) into settler colonial society through marriage, religious conversion, and domestic servitude, or to kill or enslave Indigenous Peoples considered to be "enemies" (Perrone-Moisés, 1992).

Until the 1988 Constitution, Brazilian legislation did not consider Indigenous Peoples as legal subjects with full capacity to bear rights and responsibilities of citizenship – even though prior laws had granted Indigenous Peoples the right to occupy their traditional lands (Mendes Junior, 1921). As early as 1680, the Portuguese Crown guaranteed Indigenous Peoples the right to lands they occupied by granting title acknowledging occupation as an inherited right (supported by the Brazilian legal theory of *indigenato*) (Calafate, 2018). In 1845, Royal Decree 426 established guidelines for converting Indigenous Peoples to the Catholic religion; at the same time, it mentioned the possibility of the non-removal of Indigenous Peoples who wished to remain on their lands under certain requirements (Calafate, 2018). After independence from the Crown, settlers illegally claimed large swaths of Indigenous lands, converting them into private property through registration and retitling, despite Decree 1318 of 1854, which exempted Indigenous Peoples from requiring title to their lands (Calafate, 2018).

In 1918, the Brazilian central government established the Indian Protection Service (SPI), the agency charged with assimilating and "civilizing" Indigenous Peoples into national society under "tutelage." The SPI also allocated and managed Indigenous lands, creating reservations[10] in

[10] The idea of demarcation of Indigenous lands by the Union came with the creation of SPI, which demarcated about fifty-four Indigenous reserves in small areas, totaling less than 300 thousand hectares (Curi, 2010).

which the state founded schools to teach Indigenous children Portuguese and other Western subjects, while forbidding Indigenous languages. Over time, many Indigenous traditional leadership structures lost power and many communities suffered complete destruction as peoples (Brand, 1997).[11]

The SPI survived four different constitutions (1934, 1937, 1946, and 1967). Despite nearly all of them recognizing Indigenous Peoples' occupancy rights over their inhabited lands, the harmful practices of "civilization" and assimilation of Indigenous Peoples into Brazilian society guided official government policies and practices until 1988 (Almeida, 2018). The SPI was responsible for "reserve" lands, requiring the federal states to title them. The SPI aimed at preparing and training the Natives to be small farmers capable of supporting themselves (Lima, 1992). Consequently, protecting Indigenous Peoples' lives, culture, and lands was never a genuine concern of Brazilian society and government.

During the Brazilian dictatorship (from 1964 to 1985), the SPI was charged with corruption and the mistreatment of Indigenous Peoples, and was replaced by the National Indian Foundation (FUNAI). In 1973, the Brazilian state enacted the "Indian Statute" (Law 6.001), granting broader protections to Indigenous lands[12] – for example, the right to have Indigenous lands demarcated by Federal Union, according to tribal uses, customs, and traditions, and correspondent to the space where they lived or carried out activities essential to their subsistence or economic activities (Becker & Rocha, 2017). However, the law maintained the flawed logic of Indigenous Peoples' inferiority, classifying individuals according to their level of integration into the national society, which impacted the civil and political rights they were able to enjoy.

Brazilian governments have never properly enforced any land rights in practice, with systematic violations leading to the expropriation of huge portions of Indigenous lands, illegal land transfers, and land registrations to private individuals (Calafate, 2018).

---

[11] From 1900 to 1957, Brazilian anthropologist Darcy Ribeiro found that eighty-seven Indigenous Peoples were extinguished in the country, representing 50 percent of the ethnic groups that were still isolated, extinguished after the first contact, and 67 percent of the ethnic groups in permanent contact with the national society (Ribeiro, 1986).

[12] Notably, however, Brazilian law has never granted to Indigenous communities an absolute ownership to land (i.e., fee simple title) all Indigenous territories are property of the Federal Union of Brazil, according to Article 20 of the 1988 Brazilian Constitution.

Birth of the Brazilian Indigenous Rights Movement

Until the 1960s, many of Brazil's Indigenous Peoples lived in isolation from each other, largely unaware of their shared oppression or rights struggles (Lacerda, 2018; Barbosa & Fagundes, 2018). Under military dictatorships, the Brazilian government became more concerned with Indigenous rights due to international pressure following widespread impacts, including violence, and from major infrastructure projects such as dams and highways (Demetrio & Kozicki, 2019). To avoid losing development project funding, especially in the Amazon, the Brazilian government not only ratified ILO Convention No. 107 in 1966, but also introduced broader protections of Indigenous lands in the 1967 Constitution and national legislation.[13]

Considered a turning point for Indigenous rights in Brazil, the 1971 Symposium on Interethnic Friction in South America, held at the University of the West Indies in Barbados and sponsored by the World Council of Churches, culminated in the Barbados Declaration (Becker & Rocha, 2017). Offering a critique of the colonial treatment of Indigenous Peoples and a way forward toward self-determination, the declaration highlighted the shared responsibilities between the state, the religious missions, and academy, for the "liberation" of Latin America's Indigenous Peoples (Barbosa & Fagundes, 2018). The Barbados Declaration[14] had a profound impact by pointing out that social scientists, religious missions, and the state must establish new relationships with Indigenous Peoples founded on respect for their worldviews and autonomy (Lacerda, 2018).

The Barbados Declaration also criticized religious institutions, transforming Indigenous-Catholic Church relations. In 1972, Catholic missionaries in Brazil created the Indigenous Missionary Council (CIMI)[15] to defend Indigenous groups in their struggles for land and self-determination (Barbosa & Fagundes, 2018) without interfering with their customs and beliefs (Lopes, 2014). At its First General Indigenous Assembly in 1975, the CIMI members drafted a final document stating they sought "by all means to return to Indigenous Peoples the right to be subjects, authors and recipients of their growth" (as cited in Barbosa &

---

[13] Brazil Const. 1967, Article 86; Indian Statute of 1973.
[14] In 1977, this time with the participation of Indigenous Peoples, there was a second meeting in Barbados that boosted their participation in the UN system.
[15] See https://cimi.org.br.

Fagundes, 2018). In this spirit, the CIMI began to support the organization of Indigenous Assemblies throughout the country, providing Indigenous activists with transportation, lodging, and food. The first Assembly of Indigenous Chiefs took place on April 19, 1975, in the city of Diamantino, in the state of Mato Grosso (Lacerda, 2018).

At the same time, civil society began to organize in support of Indigenous rights. For example, in 1974, the Ecumenical Documentation and Information Center (CEDI) was created, promoting the publication of journalistic information on Brazil's Indigenous populations. In 1977, the National Indian Support Association (ANAI) was created in the city of Porto Alegre. In 1978, journalists, anthropologists, and jurists founded the Pro-Indian Commission (CPI), which became one of the most important avenues for visibility of Indigenous leadership and advocacy during the 1988 Constituent Assembly (Barbosa & Fagundes, 2018).[16]

This process of Indigenous empowerment culminated in 1980 with the creation of the Union of Indigenous Nations (UNI), which played a central role in Indigenous advocacy in the Constitutional Assembly (Verdum, 2009) and, consequently, in the recognition of Indigenous rights in the 1988 Brazilian Constitution (Barbosa & Fagundes, 2018).

Indigenous Participation in the 1988 Constituent Assembly

The year 1985 marked the end of a decades-long brutal military dictatorship. When José Sarney assumed the Presidency, he proposed to convene a Constituent Assembly to the National Congress. The newly elected parliamentarians began to work on drafting a new constitution on February 1, 1987 (Oliveira, 1993).

The National Constituent Assembly offered an opportunity to bring Indigenous claims to the political debate and to gain important rights to redress colonial violence (Carvalho, 2000). Actively participating in the drafting of the 1988 Constitution, Indigenous leaders in Brazil mobilized, acquired voice and power, and countered powerful interests that opposed their demands (Verdum, 2009). After two unsuccessful attempts to participate directly in drafting the new constitution, the UNI mobilized

---

[16] Other organizations that promoted discussions and advocacy for the Indigenous cause were the Institute of Socioeconomic Studies (INESC), the Brazilian Association of Anthropology (ABA), which was heavily involved in the issue of "Indianness criteria" adopted by the military regime, and the Order of Lawyers from Brazil, Rio de Janeiro Section (OAB / RJ), who, in 1985, defended "indigenous representation in a special character" at the National Constituent Assembly.

Indigenous communities to refer the agenda to Congress and pressure parliamentarians to include their demands (Lacerda, 2018). Their agenda was put forward through establishing a minimum program for Indigenous rights in the Constituent Assembly, supported mainly by the CIMI, INESC, CEDI, and the Pro-Indian Commission of São Paulo (Fernandes, 2016). This program was launched in 1986 as a manifesto signed by twenty-nine organizations, and included the following claims: (1) recognition of Indigenous Peoples' territorial rights; (2) demarcation and guarantee of Indigenous lands; (3) Indigenous Peoples' exclusive enjoyment of the natural resources existing in the soil and subsoil of their territories; (4) resettlement, under decent and fair conditions, of non-Indigenous settlers on Indigenous lands; and (5) recognition of and respect for the social and cultural organizations of Indigenous Peoples. Given the absence of Indigenous parliamentarians in the National Constituent Assembly, the Indigenous movement addressed their demands in two ways: through proposals for popular amendments and by mobilizing the Indigenous movement and laws protecting Indigenous rights via subcommittees and the plenary of the National Constituent Assembly (Barbosa & Fagundes, 2018).

The most critical moment of the constitutional drafting negotiations was the vote on the chapter entitled "On Indigenous Peoples" when Indigenous delegations from various regions of the country camped out in Brasilia for three weeks of intense advocacy. Contentious recommendations during this period argued for continuing the guardianship regime, restricting land rights to present occupation, and denying constitutional protections to assimilated Indigenous Peoples. Strong and persistent pressure from Indigenous delegations resulted in the withdrawal of these recommendations (Lacerda, 2018).

Indigenous Constitutional Rights and Post-1988 Advancements

Article 231 of the 1988 Constitution protects Indigenous land rights, and specifically ensures original, inalienable, and irrevocable rights over the lands that Indigenous Peoples traditionally occupy, permanent possession of traditional lands, and the exclusive use of natural resources found on their territories (Cavalcante, 2016). The constitution defines "traditionally occupied lands" as those that Indigenous Peoples permanently inhabit, use for "productive activities,"[17] and are essential to preserving

---

[17] "Productive activities" can mean hunting, fishing, collecting fruits and seeds, small plantations [roças], handicrafts, etc.

environmental resources necessary for their wellbeing and physical and cultural reproduction.[18] These lands are then designated for Indigenous Peoples' permanent possession, exclusive use, and full enjoyment of their mineral and natural resource wealth.[19] Further, Brazil's National Congress must authorize any removal of Indigenous Peoples from their lands in the event of a natural disaster or epidemic that endangers their population, or when it is in the national interest.[20]

Communities have autonomy to govern their lands and resolve internal issues, but Brazilian legislation regulates important aspects of relations between them and non-Indigenous society. For example, given Indigenous Peoples' constitutional *original* land rights, any non-Indigenous settler occupation, economic exploitation, or possession of these lands would be considered illegal and invalid under law.[21] Further, FUNAI collaborates with Indigenous Peoples on various activities, such as supporting their development and exercising police power in their defense, but no longer performs any guardianship function.[22]

Demarcation

Scholars argue that the acknowledgement of original rights to tradition-ally occupied Indigenous lands in Article 231 of the constitution neither grants nor bestows such rights, but rather recognizes the preexisting rights of Indigenous Peoples that precede the Brazilian state (Calafate, 2018). Demarcating these lands is an obligation of the Federal Union. Demarcation consists of an administrative legal process for recognizing lands as Indigenous traditional territories under Decree 1.775, which includes: (1) identification; (2) delimitation; (3) contestation by third parties; (4) demarcation; (5) ratification; (6) issuance of presidential

---

[18] Brazil Constitution, Article 231(1).

[19] Brazil Constitution, Article 231(2). Despite these protections, the constitution also permits a carveout for the Federal Union to extract resources under certain circum-stances. See Article 231(3). Although no implementing legislation currently exists to permit and regulate mining or other natural resource extraction on Indigenous lands, bills are pending before the National Congress to effectuate this carveout provision under the constitution. See Bill 191/2020.

[20] Brazil Const., Article 231 (5).

[21] Constituição da República Federativa do Brasil. See www.planalto.gov.br/ccivil_03/consti tuicao/constituicaocompilado.htm.

[22] For more information, see FUNAI (2023), www.gov.br/funail.

Table 3.1 Indigenous lands demarcated since 1988 (*Source:* https://pib
.socioambiental.org)

President	Period	Number	Size (hectares)
Luiz Inacio Lula da Silva	Jan 2023	6	615,237
Jair Messias Bolsonaro	Jan 2019 to Dec 2022	0	0
Michel Temer	May 2016 to Dec 2018	1	19,216
Dilma Roussef	Jan 2015 to May 2016	10	1,243,549
Dilma Roussef	Jan 2011 to Dec 2014	11	2,025,406
Luiz Inacio Lula da Silva	Jan 2007 to Dec 2010	21	7,726,053
Luiz Inacio Lula da Silva	Jan 2003 to Dec 2006	66	11,059,713
Fernando Henrique Cardoso	Jan 1999 to Dec 2002	31	9,699,936
Fernando Henrique Cardoso	Jan 1995 to Dec 1998	114	31,526,966
Itamar Franco	Oct 1992 to Dec 1994	16	5,432,437
Fernando Collor	Mar 1990 to Sep 1992	112	26,405,219
José Sarney	Apr 1985 to Mar 1990	67	14,370,486

decree; and (7) registration (Curi, 2010).[23] This administrative process usually begins from an Indigenous community's request, and is carried out by FUNAI, resulting in a title for exclusive use and enjoyment for one or more different Indigenous ethnicities and ownership to the Federal Union (Brazil).

Since the adoption of the 1988 Constitution, the federal government, with the exception of the Bolsonaro administration, has completed the demarcation process for significant amounts of Indigenous lands (see Table 3.1) (Baines, 2014).[24]

Territorial and Environmental Management Plans (PGTAs)

In 2012, based on the demand and participation of several Indigenous organizations, Brazil issued an Executive Order (Decree 7747/2012) to create the National Policy for Territorial and Environmental Management of Indigenous Lands (PNGATI). This decree sets forth

---

[23] While Article 67 of the Constitutional Transitional Provisions Act of the 1988 Federal Constitution required demarcation of Indigenous lands within five years of the promulgation of the constitution, the Brazilian government has not concluded all demarcation processes.

[24] Brazil's territorial extension is 851,196,500 hectares (8,511,965 km^2), and Indigenous lands comprise 113,185,694 hectares (1,131,857 km^2) or 13.3 percent of the country's estate.

the creation of Territorial and Environmental Management Plans for Indigenous Lands (PGTAs), to be carried out by Indigenous communities with technical and financial support from the government. The PGTAs were conceived to strengthen Indigenous Peoples' decision-making systems, using their knowledge of their territories, and allowing the maintenance and transmission of such knowledge to future generations (Baveresco & Meneses, 2014).

In the wake of this policy, some Indigenous communities successfully implemented PGTAs in the Amazonian State of Acre. The NGO Acre Pro-Indian Commission provides training for Acre's Indigenous agroforestry agents (AAFIs). These agents are responsible for carrying out community surveillance; dialogues with local, state, and national authorities; and the occupation of strategic areas for the protection of territories which safeguards land rights.[25] In the northeast region, FUNAI acquired two cattle-ranching farms in 2007. The Tingui Botó people received the partially degraded land with dead springs, silted rivers, and pesticide-contaminated soil – and without riparian forest. The community produced seedlings of native species to recover the vegetation, managed to improve water quality, reestablished the fauna and flora, and strengthened family farming. The community has a factory producing manioc flour, which is consumed by families and the surplus is sold in commerce (Baveresco & Meneses, 2014). Another promising example of a PGTA success is the "Pacto das Águas" Program, set up by the Rikbaktsa, Zoró, Arara, and Gavião peoples of northwestern Mato Grosso State. The program keeps forests standing through improved forest management of Brazil nuts and natural rubber.[26]

Other Rights

The 1988 Constitution also recognizes procedural rights for Indigenous Peoples and obligates the Federal Public Prosecutor (MPF) to defend such rights and interests in all relevant judicial proceedings.[27] The constitution grants federal courts jurisdiction to adjudicate disputes over Indigenous rights.[28] Another significant advancement in Indigenous land rights in the wake of the 1988 Constitution was the 2002 ratification of

---

[25] See https://abre.ai/agroecoacre.
[26] See www.pactodasaguas.org.br.
[27] Brazil Constitution, Articles 129(V) and 232.
[28] Brazil Constitution Article 109(XI).

ILO Convention No. 169, calling for the protection of Indigenous rights, including the right to free, prior, and informed consultation and/or consent (FPIC).[29]

Article 21 of the American Convention on Human Rights (ACHR), promulgated in Brazilian law by Decree 678/1992,[30] guarantees the right to private and communal properties. Likewise, Article 8 of the ACHR establishes the right of the individual to be heard in the courts. These provisions have been interpreted by the Inter-American Court of Human Rights (IACHR) as suggesting that Indigenous Peoples should be heard on all matters involving their communal property.[31] Likewise, Article 26 of the ACHR provides for the right to progressive development, which cannot impede upon the realization of other economic and social rights provided for in the Pact of San Salvador[32] and afforded to Indigenous Peoples. Finally, the American Declaration on the Rights of Indigenous Peoples (ADRIP),[33] adopted in 2016, is a *soft law* (non-binding) instrument that grants greater cultural autonomy and diversity. Article XXV, 2 guarantees the right to lands they traditionally occupy; Articles III and XXI the right to self-determination; and Articles XXIII, 2, XXVIII, 3, and XXIX, 4 the right to be consulted before any measure that could affect them.

Current Challenges and Opportunities for Indigenous Land Rights Enforcement

Post-1988, the Indigenous movement has continued to grow and expand dialogue and deliver achievements despite resistance. In 2006, Gersem

---

[29] See www.planalto.gov.br/ccivil_03/_Ato2004-2006/2004/Decreto/D5051.htm.

[30] See www.planalto.gov.br/ccivil_03/decreto/d0678.htm.

[31] In this sense, see the IACHR decision in Community Garifuna Triunfo de la Cruz & its members v. Honduras. Merits, Reparations and Costs. Judgment of October 8, 2015. Series C No. 305; IACHR., Case of Kichwa Indigenous People of Sarayaku v. Ecuador. Merits and reparations. Judgment of June 27, 2012. Series C No. 245; IACHR., Case of the Mayagna (Sumo) Awas Tingni Community v. Nicaragua. Merits, Reparations and Costs. Judgment of August 31, 2001. Series C No. 79; IACHR., Case of the Xákmok Kásek Indigenous Community. v. Paraguay. Merits, Reparations and Costs. Judgment of August 24, 2010. Series C No. 214; IACHR., Case of the Kaliña and Lokono Peoples v. Suriname. Merits, Reparations and Costs. Judgment of November 25, 2015. Series C No. 309; IACHR., Case of the Saramaka People. v. Suriname. Preliminary Objections, Merits, Reparations, and Costs. Judgment of November 28, 2007 Series C No. 172.

[32] Report on Admissibility and Merits No. 38/09, Case 12.670; National Association of Ex-Employees of the Peruvian Social Security Institute et al. v. Perú, adopted by the Inter-American Commission on Human Rights, March 27, 2009, para. 140–147.

[33] See www.oas.org/es/council/AG/regular/46RGA/documents.asp.

Luciano, an intellectual Baniwa, in a tone of hope, stated that Brazil's Indigenous Peoples were living at an outstanding historical moment. They had been "breathing a less repressive air, resuming their ethnic and identity social projects, rescuing, revaluing, and reviving cultures and traditions, reappropriating their lands, relearning their languages, and returning to practice their rituals and ceremonies" (Luciano, 2006).

Nonetheless, Verdum (2009) comments that none of the post-1988 governments, even the most progressive, implemented significant changes in the state's political-administrative practices and structures, with a stagnation in measures recognizing the political autonomy of Indigenous Peoples, as well as the lack of demarcation of lands outside the Amazon. The PNGATI, intending to fund and propel Indigenous self-government, largely has not been implemented, despite the isolated successes, culminating with the closure of bodies to execute the policy by the Bolsonaro administration.[34] These have been supported by the current administration.[35] The former UN Special Rapporteur on the Rights of Indigenous Peoples, James Anaya, also visited Brazil in 2009 and issued a report documenting several rights violations and making recommendations for the Brazilian state to improve the conditions for their implementation (Anaya, 2009).

In 2016, during Anaya's successor Victoria Tauli-Corpuz's visit to Brazil, she noted that the situation had only worsened. In her 2016 report, Tauli-Corpuz clearly stated that "today, Indigenous Peoples face more profound risks than at any time since the adoption of the Constitution in 1988." She also observed that the concentration of economic and political powers in the hands of a small segment of Brazilian society, as well as recent political and institutional changes, have contributed to further disempowering Indigenous Peoples and promoting structural discrimination (Tauli-Corpuz, 2016).

In a 2009 landmark Supreme Federal Court (STF) ruling,[36] the demarcation of Raposa Serra do Sol lands was upheld, covering an area of roughly 1.7 million hectares. Notwithstanding, the Court also issued controversial opinions that helped to weaken Indigenous People's rights to self-determination, stating that demarcation is limited by the scope of the Federal Union's power, akin to a mere "supporting" participation, under the purview of the Federal Prosecutor. The judge's critique of

---

[34] See https://ispn.org.br/site/wp-content/uploads/2022/06/Documento10AnosPNGATI.pdf.
[35] See https://abre.ai/pngati.
[36] See Supremo Tribunal Federal [STF]. Petition. 3.338/2009.

UNDRIP in this lawsuit was also contrary to international law interpretation; the Court found that Brazil should not rely upon the self-determination clause since the Brazilian constitution is "the" only binding law for Brazilian Native peoples, preventing them from being recognized as Indigenous Peoples with self-determination rights.

At first glance, land demarcation rights in Brazil seem robust. According to FUNAI, there exist 736 Indigenous lands across the country, occupying nearly 14 percent of Brazil's national territory.[37] Most demarcated Indigenous lands (54 percent), encompassing more than 98 percent of the total area designated to Indigenous lands in Brazil (Sobrevila, 2008),[38] are in the northern regions in the Amazon rainforest.[39] Outside of the Amazon region, two-thirds of Indigenous communities live displaced and dispossessed either in small and sparse areas. Many of these areas were created by SPI between 1910 and 1967 as reservations (Oliveira, 1993). FUNAI has a backlog of approximately 490 pending requests for land demarcation and has stalled 132 Working Groups advancing demarcation claims. During the Bolsonaro administration, the government dramatically cut FUNAI's budget and staff,[40] and zero progress was made in identifying and demarcating any claimed Indigenous lands.[41]

While the juridical treatment of Indigenous territorial claims has been largely unfavorable to Indigenous communities, in September 2023 the Supreme Court finally overruled precedent that prevented Indigenous Peoples from reclaiming their lands. Although the STF had recognized the continuous demarcation of the extensive Raposa Serra do Sol land and confirmed Indigenous land rights in 2009, the Court also set forth the "timeframe doctrine" (*marco temporal*), an interpretation of the constitution requiring Indigenous presence in their claimed area on the very date of the Brazilian Constitution's promulgation: October 5, 1988.

---

[37] See *Terra Indígena: o que é*, FUNAI.
[38] According to Sobrevila, the World Bank funded Indigenous Lands Project that, in 1996, managed to complete the legalization and assistance in the protection of approximately 121 Indigenous areas in the Brazilian Amazon. At this time, only more than 250 Indigenous lands had been demarcated by FUNAI.
[39] The rest of the Indigenous lands are divided between "Domínio Mata Atlântica," with 211 (30 percent), and others, or 77 (11 percent) (IBGE, 2010).
[40] See https://abre.ai/intindios.
[41] See https://terrasindigenas.org.br. The pending request data was obtained in a petition filled by FUNAI lawyers in a lawsuit discussing demarcation. The number of the lawsuit is 5001142-89.2017.4.04.7119, before the Federal Court in Cacheira do Sul.

While the STF decided that the effects of the decision mentioned above would not extend to other cases, lower courts began to adopt indiscriminately the "timeframe doctrine" to nullify the land demarcation processes (Sartori Junior, 2018). Former UN Special Rapporteur on Indigenous Rights Victoria Tauli-Corpuz, among others, argued that the "timeframe doctrine" was in conflict with constitutional provisions by constraining Indigenous rights to lands and natural resources and by hindering valid demarcation processes (Tauli-Corpuz, 2016). Therefore, the September 2023 overruling of this doctrine, has been deemed as an advance for the protection of Indigenous lands.

However, in the National Congress, parliamentarians led by the "Ruralist caucus" (*Ruralistas*), tied to agribusiness, who had been relentlessly proposing bills considered harmful to Indigenous land rights (DHESCA, 2017), reacted negatively to the Supreme Court ruling and the approved Law 14.701/23.[42] In addition to other provisions, the new Act set forth the timeframe doctrine, requiring the presence of Indigenous communities in a claimed area since 1988, ignoring the overall context of violent evictions that motivated the overruling in the Supreme Court. Further, the powerful Ruralist caucus led a massive campaign to withdraw constitutionally and internationally recognized Indigenous rights with strong support from military and other economic sectors, such as mining.[43]

Land tenure insecurity, combined with poor socio-economic conditions inside and outside of Indigenous lands, has resulted in Indigenous Peoples' increased dependency on the state[44] and in violence from land grabbers.[45] In turn, the government uses arguments of extreme "poverty" and the absence of self-sustainability to justify economic exploitation on Indigenous lands, permitting large-scale agriculture, mining, logging, and infrastructure works, such as dams, roads, and electric lines.

Many factors explain the difficulties Indigenous Peoples have encountered since 1988 to enforce their constitutional rights. Carvalho (2000)

---

[42] See www.planalto.gov.br/ccivil_03/_ato2023-2026/2023/lei/L14701.htm#:~:text=LEI%20N%C2%BA%2014.701%2C%20DE%2020%20DE%20OUTUBRO%20DE%202023&text=Regulamenta%20o%20art.,19%20de%20dezembro%20de%201973.

[43] In the last term, there was only one Indigenous representative in the National Congress. Joenia Wapichana was the first Indigenous deputy since Mario Juruna, in 1984, and the first Indigenous woman ever to be elected to the National Congress.

[44] See https://abre.ai/notmpf.

[45] See CIMI, the several Violence Reports against Indigenous Peoples issued annually: https://cimi.org.br/observatorio-da-violencia/o-relatorio/.

writes that Brazil, unlike other Latin American countries, has not supported Indigenous involvement in political processes. The resistance of the military and many parliamentarians to the recognition of Indigenous rights, even if they voted in favor of them in the National Constituent Assembly, was a foreshadowing of the obstacles Indigenous Peoples would face in the coming years – the era of implementation, which saw a dismantling of Indigenous rights (Barbosa & Fagundes, 2018).

Post-Bolsanaro

Bolsonaro's defeat and President Lula's election in October 2022 caused yet another shift in the Brazilian government's relationship with Indigenous Peoples. At the beginning of his term, President Lula created the unprecedented Ministry of Indigenous Peoples (MPI) and appointed as minister Sonia Guajajara, an Indigenous woman who had been elected federal deputy, along with another Indigenous woman, Celia Xakriabá. To head FUNAI, the government appointed Joenia Wapichana, an Indigenous woman who had been the only Indigenous parliamentarian in the last legislature. The MPI coordinates and implements the country's Indigenous policy, including land demarcations. The Lula administration has already completed six demarcation processes, and re-enacted PNGATI bodies dissolved by the previous government.[46] Additionally, in the early days of the Lula administration, the government took several measures to remedy the humanitarian disaster facing the Yanomami, including removing miners from their lands. The government has not yet managed, however, to reverse the dismantling of FUNAI, whose budget plummeted from R$1.1 billion in 2013 to R$645 million in 2023 – a drop of 41 percent in a single decade.[47]

The most notable recent achievement of the Indigenous land rights movement was undoubtedly the STF's decision in September 2023 to reject the "timeframe doctrine." In a case that discussed the nullification of a land demarcation, on the grounds that the community was not present on their Indigenous territories in 1988, the Court unanimously decided that the date of promulgation of the Federal Constitution (October 5, 1988) cannot be used to define an Indigenous communities' traditional land occupation.[48]

---

[46] See https://abre.ai/ebcdem.
[47] See https://abre.ai/otempofunai.
[48] See https://abre.ai/stfmt.

While the decision supports Indigenous Peoples' interests, many Indigenous communities, lawyers, and allies are critical of this case because the decision also sets forth the government's obligation to compensate good faith non-Indigenous occupants, which is at odds with Article 231 of the constitution, which only allows compensation for any improvements to land by good faith occupants. Critics argue that this stipulation will be a practical obstacle for advancing demarcations, because of the potentially high monetary costs for any compensation to be paid by the government.[49]

Unfortunately, resistance to advancing the implementation of Indigenous rights has not ceased. The composition of the National Congress remains ultraconservative and loyal to economic interests, especially agribusiness interests. In a retaliatory response to this judgment, the National Congress approved Law No. 14.701, which, among other provisions that weaken the protective framework for Indigenous land rights, requires Indigenous presence on the land to be demarcated on the date of the promulgation of the constitution. As of this writing, President Lula vetoed the law, but Congress could still override his veto.

Conclusions and Recommendations

Brazil's transition from dictatorship to democracy in the 1980s resulted in positive legal changes for Indigenous Peoples, especially with the guarantees of the 1988 Constitution. The constitutional guarantee for Indigenous Peoples to occupy their traditional lands remains the primary source of Indigenous People's survival and resistance to ongoing settler colonial laws, policies, and practices throughout the country. While the 1988 Constitution remains the law of the land, the past ten years of struggles to claim Indigenous land rights have demonstrated that the support from the government is critical to the full realization of land rights. Without the Brazilian government's commitment to land rights, Indigenous Peoples will be at continued risk from dispossession and erasure as independent peoples.

Nevertheless, the political mobilization of Indigenous Peoples in the National Constituent Assembly process has provided many important lessons, and the challenging years have been a time of intense mobilization and resistance. Since President Lula took office in 2023, Indigenous

---

[49] See https://abre.ai/carns.

Peoples have already obtained several gains. The establishment of the MPI offers additional promise, especially under Indigenous leadership, toward respect for Indigenous Peoples' reciprocal and spiritual relationship with their lands. The MPI can support FUNAI to advance land demarcations, create and accomplish territorial and environmental management plans, conduct prior consultations, and strengthen health and educational policies.

The Brazilian Supreme Court must also reaffirm its standing and once more overturn the "timeframe doctrine," especially given that the National Congress may vote to override President Lula's veto to the law that established this requirement to demarcations. The Brazilian National Congress has clearly indicated that any improvements to Indigenous land rights will face strong political opposition in a divided society, particularly by the Ruralistas. Globalization and international commodity markets continue to drive encroachment and impact Indigenous communities and their land rights, and have a strong resonance in Brazilian politics.

Indigenous Peoples must continue to resist and claim political space in state structures toward realizing land rights. Despite being important for advancing the protection of some rights, conflicting interests and power asymmetries limit the possibilities of marginalized groups to make real achievements in political arenas. Driven by grassroots and national political mobilizations, Indigenous Peoples and their allies, in conjunction with global Indigenous interests, must apply constant pressure on the Brazilian state, transnational corporate actors and international investors to protect and safeguard Indigenous land rights in the country. Without this constant vigilance, land rights in Brazil will remain fragile.

References

Almeida, A. C. (2018). Aspectos das políticas indigenistas no Brasil. *Interações*, 19(3), 611–626.

Anaya, J. (2009). Report of the Special Rapporteur on the situation of human rights and fundamental freedoms of Indigenous People. www2.ohchr.org/english/bodies/hrcouncil/docs/12session/A.HRC.12.34.Add.2.pdf

Angeles, L., & Elizalde, A. (2017). Pre-colonial institutions and socioeconomic development: The case of Latin America. *Journal of Development Economics*, 124, 22–40. https://doi.org/10.1016/j.jdeveco.2016.08.006

Araújo, A. V. Wapixana, J., Pankararu, P., Kaingang, L., Guarany, V., & Anaya, S. J. (2006). *Povos Indígenas e a Lei dos "Brancos": o direito à diferença.*

Ministério da Educação, Secretaria de Educação Continuada, Alfabetização e Diversidade, LACED/Museu Nacional. http://portal.mec.gov.br/index.php?option=com_docman&view=download&alias=644-vol14povos-indigenas-pdf&category_slug=documentos-pdf&Itemid=30192

Baines, S. G. (2014). *Territórios indígenas ressignificados*. 29a Reunião Brasileira de Antropologia. www.29rba.abant.org.br/resources/anais/1/1401976123_ARQUIVO_bainesSimposioEspecial014.pdf

Barbosa, J. M. A., & Fagundes, M. G. (2018). Uma revoada de pássaros: O protagonismo indígena no processo Constituinte. *Revista Brasileira de História & Ciências Sociais*, 10(20), 175–196.

Bavaresco, A., & Meneses, M. (2014). *Entendendo a PNGATI: Política Nacional de GestãoTerritorial e Ambiental Indígenas*. GIZ/Projeto GATI/Funai.

Becker, S., & Rocha, T. P. (2017). Notas sobre a "tutela indígena" no Brasil (legal e real), com toques de particularidades do sul de Mato Grosso do Sul. *Revista da Faculdade de Direito UFPR*, 62(2), 73–105. http://revistas.ufpr.br/direito/article/view/49443

Beltrão, J. F., & Oliveira, A. C. (2014). Movimientos, pueblos y ciudadanías indígenas: Inscripciones constitucionales y derechos étnicos en latinoamerica. In J. F. Beltrão, J.C Monteiro de Brito Filho., I. Gómez, E. Pajares, F. Paredes & Y Zúñiga (eds.), *Derechos Humanos de los Grupos Vulnerables* (pp. 241–274). DHES. Red de Derechos Humanos y Educación Superior.

Benatti, J. H., Rocha, A. L. S., & Pacheco, J. S. (2015). Populações Tradicionais e o Reconhecimento de seus Territórios: Uma Luta Sem Fim. *7º Encontro da ANPPAS –Encontro Nacional da Associação Nacional de Pós Graduação e Pesquisa em Ambiente e Sociedade*. https://abre.ai/poptrad

Brand, A. J. (1997). *O impacto da perda da terra sobre a tradição kaiowá/guarani: Os difíceis caminhos da palavra*. Porto Alegre, Tese de Doutorado: Pontifícia Universidade Católica do Rio Grande do Sul.

Brasil. (2014). Comissão Nacional da Verdade [CNV]. Relatório (Vol. 2). *Texto 5 – Violações de direitos humanos dos povos indígenas*. Brasília: CNV. www.cnv.gov.br/images/pdf/relatorio/volume_2_digital.pdf

Calafate, P. (2018). The rights of the Indigenous Peoples of Brazil: Historical development and constitutional acknowledgment. *International Journal on Minority and Group Rights*, 25(2), 183–209.

Carta de Pêro Vaz de Caminha. (1500). 1 de Maio de 1500. https://abreai.link/vh744

Carvalho, G. O. (2000). The politics of Indigenous land rights in Brazil. *Bulletin of Latin American Research*, 19(4), 461–478.

Cavalcante, T. V. (2016). Terra Indígena: Aspectos históricos da construção e aplicação de um conceito jurídico. *História*, 35, e75. https://doi.org/10.1590/1980-436920160000000075

CIMI. (1987). A Verdadeira Conspiração contra os Povos Indígenas, a Igreja e o Brasil. Brasília: CNBB – CIMI. https://abreai.link/2upmu

Comission Interamericana de Derechos Humanos (CIDH). (2010). Derechos de los pueblos indígenas y tribales sobre sus tierras ancestrales y recursos naturales: Normas y jurisprudencia del sistema interamericano de derechos humanos. OEA/Ser.L/V/II. Doc. 56/09. www.oas.org/es/cidh/indigenas/docs/pdf/Tierras-Ancestrales.ESP.pdf

Cunha, M. C. (2018). Índios na Constituição. Novos Estudos Cebrap, 112, 429–443. https://doi.org/10.25091/S01013300201800030002

Curi, M. (2010). Os Direitos Indígenas e a constitutuição federal. *Consilium: Revista Eletrônica de Direito, Brasília*, 4(1), 1-17. www.unieuro.edu.br/site novo/revistas/downloads/consilium_04_03.pdf

Demetrio, A., & Kozicki, K. (2019). Transitional injustice for Indigenous Peoples from Brazil. *Rev. Direito Práx*, 10(1), 129–169. https://doi.org/10.1590/2179-8966/2017/28186

DHESCA. Direitos Humanos e Povos Indígenas no Brasil. (2017). Relatório da Relatoria de Direitos Humanos e Povos Indígenas da Plataforma de Direitos Humanos – Dhesca Brasil, Terra de Direitos. https://fianbrasil.org.br/rela torio-da-relatoria-de-direitos-humanos-e-povos-indigenas-da-plataforma-dhesca/

Fausto, C. (2000). *Os índios antes do Brasil*. Rio de Janeiro: Jorge Zahar.

Fernandes, P. (2016). Povos indígenas, segurança nacional e a Assembleia Nacional Constituinte: as Forças Armadas e o capítulo dos índios da Constituição brasileira de 1988. *Revista InSURgência*, 1(2), 142–175. https://doi.org/10 .26512/insurgncia.v1i2.18881

Instituto Brasileiro de Geografia e Estatística (IBGE). (2010). Censo Demográfico 2010: Características gerais dos indígenas. Ministério do Planejamento, Orçamento e Gestão; Instituto Brasileiro de Geografia e Estatística. Rio de Janeiro. www.ibge.gov.br/indigenas/indigena_censo2010.pdf

Instituto Brasileiro de Geografia e Estatística (IBGE). (2016). Atlas Nacional Digital do Brasil 2016. www.ibge.gov.br/apps/atlas_nacional

Instituto Socioambiental (ISA). (2022). Localização e extensão das TIs. https://pib .socioambiental.org/pt/Situação_jur%C3%ADdica_das_TIs_no_Brasil_hoje

Lacerda, R. F. (2018). *Os povos indígenas e a Constituinte (1987–1988)*. Brasília, Brasil: Conselho Indigenista Missionário-CIMI.

Le Tourneau, F. M. (2015). The sustainability challenges of indigenous territories in Brazil's Amazonia. *Current Opinion in Environmental Sustainability*, 14, 213–220. https://doi.org/10.1016/j.cosust.2015.07.017

Lima, A. C. S. (1992). O governo dos índios sob a gestão do SPI. In M. C. Cunha (ed.), *História dos Índios no Brasil* (pp. 155–174). São Paulo, Brasil: Companhia das Letras.

Lopes, D. B. (2014). O direito dos Índios no Brasil: a trajetória dos grupos indígenas nas Constituições do país. *Espaço Ameríndio*, 8(1), 83–108. https://seer.ufrgs.br/EspacoAmerindio/article/view/41524/29955

Luciano, G. J. S. (2006). *O índio brasileiro: O que você precisa saber sobre os povos indígenas no Brasil de hoje*. Ministério da Educação, Secretaria de Educação Continuada, Alfabetização e Diversidade; LACED/Museu Nacional.

Mendes Junior, J. (1921). *Os Indigenas do Brazil. Seus Direitos Individuaes e Politicos*. Sao Paulo: Typ. Hennies Irmaos. https://archive.org/details/OsIndigenasDoBrazilSeusDireitosIndividuaesEPolticos/page/n7

Oliveira, M. M. (1993). Fontes de informações sobre a Assembléia Nacional Constituinte de 1987: Quais são, onde buscá-las e como usá-las. Senado Federal, Subsecretaria de Edições Técnicas. www.senado.leg.br/publicacoes/anais/constituinte/fontes.pdf

Pacheco de Oliveira, J. (2006). *A presença indígena na formação do Brasil*. Secretaria de Educação Continuada, Alfabetização e Diversidade (Secad)/LACED/Museu Nacional.

Perrone-Moisés, B. (1992). Índios livres e índios escravos: Os princípios da legislação indigenista do período colonial (séculos XVI a XVIII). In M. Cunha (ed.), *História dos Índios no Brasil* (pp. 115–132). Companhia das Letras. São Paulo, Brazil.

Ribeiro, D. (1986). *Os índios e a civilização. A integração das populações indígenas no Brasil Moderno* (5th ed.). Vozes. Recife, Brazil.

Sartori Junior, D. (2018). Colonialidade e o marco temporal da ocupação de terras indígenas: Uma crítica à posição do Supremo Tribunal Federal. *Hendu – Revista Latino-Americana de Direitos Humanos*, 7(1) 88-100.http://dx.doi.org/10.18542/hendu.v7i1.6005

Sobrevila, C. (2008). *The role of Indigenous Peoples in biodiversity conservation: The natural but often forgotten partners*. Washington, DC: The World Bank. https://abreai.link/3mwzx

Souza Filho, C. F. M. (1998). As novas questões jurídicas nas relações dos Estados nacionais com os Índios. *Apresentação no Seminário Bases para uma nova política indigenista*. http://laced3.hospedagemdesites.ws/laced/arquivos/05-Alem-da-tutela.pdf

(1992). O direito envergonhado (O direito e os índios no Brasil). *Revista IIDH*, 15, 145–165.

Staden, H. (1930). *Viagem ao Brasil*. Rio de Janeiro, Brasil: Oficina Industrial Graphica.

Survival International. (2019). What Brazil's President, Jair Bolsonaro, has said about Brazil's Indigenous Peoples. www.survivalinternational.org/articles/3540-Bolsonaro

Tauli-Corpuz, V. (2016). Report of the Special Rapporteur on the rights of indigenous peoples on her mission to Brazil. https://digitallibrary.un.org/record/847079#record-files-collapse-heade

(2019). Jair Bolsonaro's stance on indigenous people is discriminatory and racist. https://abre.ai/vtaulicorpuz

United Nations. (2014). CEPAL. *Los pueblos indígenas en América Latina: Avances en el último decenio y retos pendientes para la garantía de sus derechos.* (United Nations Economic Commission for Latin America and the Caribbean) CEPAL-, Santiago, Chile. http://repositorio.cepal.org/bitstream/handle/11362/37222/S1420521_es.pdf?sequence=1

Verdum, R. (2009). Povos Indígenas no Brasil: o desafio da autonomia. In R. Verdum (ed.), *Povos Indígenas: Constituições e Reformas Políticas na América Latina* (pp. 91–112). São Paulo, Brazil: Instituto de Estudos socioeconômicos (INESC).

Yrigoyen Fajardo, R. Z. (2009). Aos 20 anos da Convenção 169 da OIT: Balanço e desafios da implementação dos direitos dos Povos Indígenas na América Latina. In R. Verdum (ed.), *Povos Indígenas: Constituições e reformas Políticas na américa Latina.* São Paulo, Brazil: Instituto de Estudos socioeconômicos (INESC).

4

Indigenous Peoples and Territorial Rights in Colombia

Advances and Challenges in the "Implementation Gap"

OMAIRA BOLAÑOS CÁRDENAS AND RICARDO CAMILO
NIÑO IZQUIERDO

Introduction

Colombia has some of the most robust and secure land tenure regimes in Latin America, with full rights to land ownership, access, withdrawal, management, exclusion, due process, and compensation (RRI, 2014, 2015, 2018; Velázquez Ruiz, 2018).[1] However, the recognition of Indigenous Peoples' collective land rights has advanced in a context of intense land conflict, driven by a profound inequality to land access. Colombia has the highest concentration of land ownership in the world: one percent of landowners own more than 80 percent of the land, and the remaining 99 percent own less than 20 percent (Faguet et al., 2016; Guereña, 2017).

In 1991, the Colombian National Political Constitution (NPC) recognized and protected a comprehensive set of collective rights for Indigenous Peoples: to land, culture, identity, self-government, autonomy, and political participation. The NPC ratified the collective property rights of Indigenous Peoples under the *resguardo*, an administrative

---

[1] RRI's Tenure Tracking analysis defines three typologies of tenure categories: Category 1, administered by the government (lands or forests under this category are legally claimed as exclusively belonging to the state); Category 2, designated for communities (national law recognizes communities' rights to access and withdrawal, or to exclude others, and their participation in the management of lands and/or forests); and, Category 3, ownership (lands or forests are owned communities where their rights of access, withdrawal, management, exclusion, due process, and compensation are legally recognized for an unlimited duration). Alienation rights (whether through sale, lease, or use as collateral) are not required for communities to be classified as land or forest owners under this framework.

regime for Indigenous Peoples' communal lands, born during colonial times. *Resguardo* is defined as a "legal and socio-political institution of special character, formed by one or more Indigenous communities, which with a collective property title (equivalent in guarantees to private property), own their territory, governed by an autonomous organization protected by the Indigenous jurisdiction and its own regulatory system" (Decree 2164 of 1995 compiled in Decree 1071 of 2015).

Article 7 of the NPC provides that "The State recognizes and protects the ethnic and cultural diversity of the Colombian Nation" (Corte Constitutional, 2021), a shift from the assimilationist 1886 Constitution and policies aiming to fragment and dispossess Indigenous Peoples of their collective ancestral lands (Semper, 2018). However, the promise of the NPC was hampered by a long-lasting internal armed conflict over land access and use, violence, and forced displacement of Indigenous and other rural communities. The 2016 Peace Accord sought to address land disputes. But the implementation of the Peace Accord and its promise of land justice was hampered by delays, political polarization, and several scandals over the management of public resources. In some rural areas, violence has again seen a resurgence.

This chapter details how land rights remain a contentious subject in Colombia: this issue is historically contested and rooted in enduring land disputes between state actors and Indigenous communities. The current land rights framework emerged from both the legislative actions and the socio-political mobilization of Indigenous Peoples, the latter playing a critical role in shaping land policy and achieving the restitution and recognition of their ancestral lands.

The chapter documents the legal and political strategies used by Indigenous Peoples to secure collective land rights in this contested setting. By taking a historical perspective, this chapter traces the structural factors affecting land rights implementation, and the repeating cycles of recognition, poor performance, and limitations on the enjoyment of tenure rights. Finally, the chapter explores the challenges and opportunities for land rights from the current Peace Accord.

Achieving Recognition of Indigenous Peoples' Collective Land Rights: A Historical Perspective

To understand the contradictions in Colombia's Indigenous land rights framework, one must look at the historical and political factors driving change and the structural factors that make Indigenous land rights contentious. Villa and Houghton (2004) discussed three territorial and population dynamics that have been affecting Indigenous land rights since the nineteenth century Republican era. The first dynamic began with Law 11 of 1821, which considered Indigenous Peoples as free and equal to the rest of country's population and ordered the dismantling and distribution of *resguardo* lands to other populations. This legislation displaced many Indigenous communities from their lands and turned people into day laborers and sharecroppers. The second dynamic was the expansion of the agricultural frontier and peasant colonization resulting from the civil violence in the 1950s. A third dynamic emerged during the 1970s agrarian crisis, expanding the planting of illegal crops, such as coca leaves and opium poppy, often around Indigenous territories, and catalyzing new forms of violence against Indigenous Peoples.

Muñoz Onofre (2016) argued that Colombia's land rights framework is embedded in a socio-economic model focused on the exploitation of natural resources, which ignores the existence and validity of Indigenous Peoples' territorial management perspectives, and thus leading to conflicts.

The following sections provide a chronology of major policies on Indigenous Peoples' rights to their ancestral lands from the Republican period until the late 1900s, showing the repeating cycles of recognition, poor performance, and limitations on the enjoyment of tenure rights.

The Republic Contexts

The Spanish colonial power imposed a new regime atop the social-economic, political, and communal land systems of Indigenous populations. Within this period, the *resguardo* emerged as a colonial model of social organization, administration, and control of territory, under which the colonial power assigned *resguardo* lands to Indigenous populations. The *resguardo* was a legislative initiative for the protection of subjugated Indigenous populations that encouraged their demographic recovery, but all the while liberated other lands for distribution to non-Indigenous settlers. In the *resguardo*, the community exercised full control and full domain for the use of the land and was protected against selling or leasing (Mayorga Garcia, 2004). Although Indigenous Peoples during the colonial period resisted the *resguardo* system, today the *resguardo* constitutes the strongest legal tenure regime for Indigenous Peoples in Colombia.

In the context of the New Republic after independence, liberal principles promoted the free market and the individual rights of citizens, which affected Indigenous Peoples' collective tenure systems (Semper, 2018). The clash of ideological principles between individual and communal property rights flourished in a series of contradictory statutes that, while recognizing the Indigenous populations' rights to their communal lands, equally defined mechanisms for the erosion of the communal property – such is the case of Articles 3 and 11 of Law 1821, which ordered the extinction of Indigenous Peoples' obligation to pay tributes, while promoting the distribution of *resguardo* lands to non-Indigenous individuals respectively (Morales Gomez, 1979). Table 4.1 lists the key Indigenous policies created during the New Republic that either recognized or abolished the special status of Indigenous Peoples and their collective tenure rights.

Law 89 of 1890 was an important legal antecedent for Indigenous land rights: Articles 14 to 22 enshrined Indigenous Peoples' collective ownership over the *resguardo*, and the recognition of Indigenous councils (*Cabildos*)[2] as legitimate self-governance systems (Rodriguez, 2017; Ulloa, 2010). Despite the discriminatory content of the law against Indigenous Peoples and its integrationist intention, for a long time this law was the only legal tool for the vindication of Indigenous territorial rights, ethnic identity, and autonomy and governance. In the early twentieth century, Law 89 of 1890 became the major legal precedent for Indigenous Peoples to recover usurped lands in the next century (see the later section on Indigenous resistance and mobilization). In 1996, Constitutional Court Ruling No. C-139/96 declared the unconstitutionality of several articles of Law 89 of 1890 that treated Indigenous Peoples as "savages" and minors and as subjects of cultural assimilation, although it did not question the validity of the law (Semper, 2018).

---

[2] Decree 1071 of 2015 defines Indigenous Cabildos as a "special public entity, which are recognized and elected by procedures proper to an Indigenous community, who will have the legal representation to exercise authority, abiding by the law of use, customs and regulations proper to their community." Article 246 of the 1991 NPC provides that Indigenous Peoples' representative authorities may exercise jurisdictional functions within their territories, in accordance with their own standards and procedures, ensuring they do not conflict with the constitution and laws of the Republic (www.cidh.org/countryrep/colombia93eng/chap.11.htm). Some Indigenous groups maintain forms of organization different from the Cabildo system, which has forced the government to recognize the Associations of Traditional Authorities, which is a public legal entity created by Decree 1088 of 1993 responsible for promoting and coordinating with local, regional, and national authorities the execution of health, education, and housing projects.

Table 4.1 Policy development for Indigenous Peoples during the 1800s

Regulations impacting Indigenous collective tenure rights	Regulations favoring Indigenous collective tenure rights
Decree of September 24, 1810, issued by the Supreme Government Junta of Santa Fe on the termination of the *resguardo* system, which recognized Indigenous Peoples as citizens with equal rights and duties as other citizens. These measures sought to replace collective land property with individual private property.	Simon Bolivar issued a decree on May 20, 1820, that ordered the restitution of *resguardo* lands to Indigenous communities; however, it implied the internal division of communal lands to allow the participation of Indigenous communities in the free market.
The Law of October 4 of 1821 declared legal equality, subjecting Indigenous Peoples to the common law, and ordered the distribution of *resguardos* in five years.	The Law of June 30 of 1824 promoted the distribution of vacant lands to Indigenous communities, or lands lacking a property title, and the creation of *parroquias* to integrate "wild indigenous" into the national economy.
The Law 11 of 1821 declared Indigenous Peoples as citizens of the state, promoted the integration of Indigenous lands into the market, and ordered the gradual dissolution of the *resguardo* system. It suppressed the special status and the protections of Indigenous Peoples under the premise of equality.	The Law 11 of April 27 of 1874 recognized Indigenous Peoples' authority for regulating their internal affairs.
The Law 192 of 1824 incorporated Indigenous populations from zones not integrated into the economy into the missionary and evangelization processes, and Indigenous lands were given to the church.	The Law 89 of 1890 recognized and adopted the Cabildo as Indigenous Peoples' organizational structure and self-governance system, and their right to their collective territories guaranteed them a special status.
The laws of March 6, 1832, and June 2, 1834, are complementary, facilitating the division of *resguardo* into individual parcels.	
The Law of June 22, 1850, ordered the free distribution and alienation of the *resguardos* and allocation of individual property titles to Indigenous Peoples, just like any other citizens.	

The Turn of the Twentieth Century

The early twentieth century was characterized by the government seeking to gain more control over Indigenous lands, while Indigenous land rights struggles emerged in the south of the Colombian Andean region. The government established a series of *concordats* with the Catholic Church in 1903, 1920, and 1973 to exercise administrative, judicial, and educational control over Indigenous Peoples, including through conversion to Catholicism and assimilation into the wider society. The Christian missions settling Indigenous lands were a driving force for the dismantling of Indigenous cultures and territories. According to Boza Villarreal (2013), until the late 1970s Catholic missions comprised 77 percent of the country's territory. However, by the 1980s, their power and control was reduced. As shown in Table 4.2, in the first half of the twentieth century, the government passed a series of laws promoting the dissolution of the *resguardo* system. For instance, Law 200 of 1936 regulated the dissolution of Indigenous lands lacking legal titles. In the second half of the century, a new structure for the legal collective tenure regime started forming, with new laws and decrees, including the enactment of the 1991 NPC, which established major changes in the state's relationship with Indigenous Peoples.

The social agrarian reform under Law 135 of 1961 was created against a backdrop of increasing political tensions and the re-emergence of internal armed conflict that displaced rural populations. The reform aimed to democratize rural property, including abolishing the division of Indigenous lands, and promoted the formalization of *resguardo* (Figueroa, 2016; Semper, 2018). The law created the Colombian Institute of Agrarian Reform[3] (INCORA in Spanish) to manage agrarian issues, and to acquire, redistribute, and provide lands to the landless, including the creation of *resguardo* lands (Balcazar et al., 2001).

Additionally, Decree 2117 of 1969, which partially regulated Law 135 of 1961, created the "Indigenous reservation"[4] tenure regime system, considered a regressive measure as it eliminated Indigenous Peoples' ownership rights over their territories, granting only usufruct rights. After advocacy by Indigenous Peoples, the government issued Decree

---

[3] The national agency in charge of land formalization has been dissolved on several occasions, passing functions from one institution to another and changing the scope of its role. The first agency was INCORA followed by The Colombian Institute of Rural Development (INCODER), and currently the National Land Agency (ANT).

[4] Decree 2117 of 1969 (www.suin-juriscol.gov.co/viewDocument.asp?id=1759090).

Table 4.2 Policy development on Indigenous Peoples' land tenure rights during the 1900s

Regulations impacting Indigenous collective tenure rights	Regulations favoring Indigenous collective tenure rights
Law 55 of 1095 recognized the private property rights of non-Indigenous individuals over areas of *resguardos*. Article 2 made legal the dispossession and dissolution of the *resguardo* system.	Law 135 of 1961 created the Colombian Institute of Agrarian Reform – INCORA, in charge of establishing new *resguardos*. It safeguarded vacant lands occupied by Indigenous communities from seizure by private individuals.
Law 51 of 1911 extinguished collective lands in the Valle of Sibundoy.	Law 31 of 1967 ratified the ILO Convention 1957.
Law 104 of 1919 extinguished *resguardos* with less than 200 people and judicialized Indigenous communities resisting land closure.	Regulatory Decree 2001 of 1988 of Law 31 of 1967 defined the legal procedure for the creation of *resguardos* on vacant lands and ordered the conversion of Indigenous reserves (created under Decree 2117 of 1969) into *resguardos*, returning the collective property rights of Indigenous Peoples to their ancestral lands.
Law 19 of 1927 created a special commission to divide and distribute Indigenous communal lands to new settlers.	Law 30 of 1988 (which reformed Law 200 of 1936) ordered the creation of new *resguardos*, restituted *resguardos* previously dissolved, and established that vacant lands occupied by Indigenous Peoples could only be used for the constitution of *resguardos*.
Law 111 of 1931 empowered the judicial and administrative authorities to order the division of *resguardos*.	National Political Constitution of 1991 ratified the collective property of Indigenous Peoples over the *resguardo*.
Law 200 of 1936, known as Statuto of Land, regulated the dissolution of Indigenous lands without titles, and granted these lands to new settlers.	Law 21 of 1991 ratified the ILO Convention 169 of 1989. This affirmed Indigenous Peoples' rights to self-determination, autonomy, territorial and socio-cultural integrity. There are also recognized rights to enjoy natural resources, health, education, political participation, and the right to be consulted about state's administrative actions that can affect these rights.

Table 4.2 (*cont.*)

Regulations impacting Indigenous collective tenure rights	Regulations favoring Indigenous collective tenure rights
Law 100 of 1944 (*Aparceria* or sharecropping Law) strengthened large-scale private landholdings and promoted unjust systems between landless peasants and landlords.	Law 60 of 1993 defined the allocation of financial resources to *resguardos*, outlining norms and competences according to Articles 151 and 288 of the NPC.
Law 81 of 1958 promoted agrarian development on Indigenous lands, required Indigenous communities to prove colonial titles to their lands, and declared lands without titles vacant lands of the nation.	Law 160 of 1994, chapter XIV, defined *resguardo* and its socio-environmental functions. Resguardos, as "indigenous reserves," were linked to Article 63 of the NPC that defined Indigenous territories as inalienable, imprescriptible, and not subject to seizure.
Decree 2117 of 1969 created a new tenure regime, "the Indigenous reserves," limiting Indigenous tenure rights to mere usufruct rights and restraining the collective property ownership of Indigenous Peoples over their lands.	Decree 2164 of 1995 regulated Law 160 of 1994, regarding the procedure for the creation, titling, extension of land area, and formalization of Indigenous lands.
	Decree 1397 of 1996 created a Permanent Table of Consensus of Indigenous Peoples (MPC) and the National Commission of Indigenous Territories (CNTI). Decree 1396 of 1996 created the Commission of Indigenous Peoples' Human Rights.
	Law 387 of 1997 enacted the protection of internally forced displaced peoples, with an ethnic perspective.

2001 of 1988 regulating Law 135 of 1961 in relation to the constitution of *resguardo* and compelled the conversion of Indigenous reservations back into *resguardos*.[5]

---

[5] Decree 2001 of 1988 (www.suin-juriscol.gov.co/viewDocument.asp?id=1755876).

Throughout the evolving legal framework, Indigenous socio-political mobilization played a critical role in the restitution and recovery of their ancestral lands, while reshaping the country's Indigenous rights policies and resisting statutory actions to rollback their rights.

Indigenous Social and Political Mobilization

The first and second half of the twentieth century saw a series of Indigenous uprisings. First, in the southern provinces of Cauca, Huila, and Tolima, where the Indigenous movement resisted increasing dispossession pressures, the renowned Nasa Indigenous leader, Manuel Quintín Lame, organized an ethnic political movement to advance Indigenous communities' territorial rights by using the existing legal framework, in particular Law 89 of 1890 (Vasco Uribe, 2008). Through a process of reinterpreting the laws, Quintín Lame created a rights-based plan: the restitution and expansion of the *resguardo* lands; the strengthening of the *Cabildo* governance system; abolition of the *terraje*;[6] compliance with laws favorable to Indigenous Peoples' rights, such as Law 89 of 1890; and protection of Indigenous history, language, and traditions, among others (Sanchez Gutierrez & Molina Echeverri, 2014).

Quintin Lame's struggle influenced contemporary Indigenous movements in the 1970s and 1980s, with his political theory published in 1971, entitled *The Thought of the Indio Educated in the Jungle*, becoming a manifesto of the Indigenous movement after his death. In the same year, the Regional Indigenous Council of Cauca (CRIC) was founded on Lame's political ideology of land restitution and actions to recover thousands of hectares of lands (Benavides, 2009). The CRIC inspired the formation of a broader Indigenous movement: in 1982 the National Indigenous Organization of Colombia (ONIC) emerged, and a pan-ethnic Indigenous movement expanded, with organizations advocating for autonomy, control of territories, and the assertion of their distinctive ethnic identities, positioning Indigenous rights as a national public issue (Muñoz Onofre, 2016; Ulloa, 2010). These changes reshaped the political

---

[6] *Terraje* was a feudal and servile relationship, by which any Indigenous person paid with free labor had a right to live in and use a small plot of land within the hacienda of a landlord, normally located in the same lands taken from Indigenous *resguardos*. The *terraje* persisted until the 1970s when it was swept away by the Indigenous rights struggle that began in that decade (Vasco Uribe, 2008).

context and opened up opportunities for Indigenous political participation and representation.

In the 1980s, the Misak peoples led symbolic actions for ancestral land recovery[7] under the principles of "greater right" and "reclaiming the land to recover everything," and regained the *resguardo* Guambia in the State of Cauca. First, on July 19, 1980, the Misak recovered the Mercedes hacienda located at the core of their ancestral territory, under the control of political and economic elites, through a collective action involving the Misak community in solidarity with other Indigenous communities (CINEP, 2022; Tunubala Yalanda, 2016). This strategy of reclaiming land led to the legal recognition of *Cabildos* as public law entities with the administration function over their territories. The *Cabildo* of Guambía was the first to receive land restitution with autonomy according to their uses and customs (Velasco Alvarez, n.d.).[8]

Customary Laws and Governance

Despite assimilation pressures, Indigenous traditional forms of authority and governance continue. Each Indigenous group has its way of seeing the world and understanding the universe; this cosmo-vision is the foundation of traditional laws and self-governance. Some of the diverse concepts of traditional laws and self-government are the Law of Origin (from creation), Natural Law (laws of the natural world, earth, the spirits, and mythology since the beginning of time), Overarching Right (the law of the first inhabitants of America, passed down by elders and from the ancestors, who show the ways to act, and the rules that must be obeyed), and the Own Law (part of the cultures of Indigenous Peoples, their ways of living, thinking, and practicing justice).

The Law of Origin is the highest expression of the Arhuaco people's laws (from the Caribbean coast in the Sierra Nevada de Santa Marta), where all the obligations and rights of community members and all people are defined. Helmer Torres Solis, an anthropologist from the Arhuaco people (2004, p. 15), asserted that the Law of Origin integrates the rules of conduct and knowledge and guidelines of relationships with nature that the creator father *Serankua* left to the four brother peoples of

---

[7] Recovery is the term used by Indigenous Peoples to describe "the act of reclaiming territories by occupying usurped land" (Rappaport, 2005, p. 29).

[8] The recovery of the Guambia *resguardo* continued throughout the 1980s and 1990s. During this period, twenty-five Indigenous lands were recovered in the municipality of Silvia, in the Cauca State (Tunubala Yalanda, 2016).

the Sierra (Arhuaco, Kogui, Wiwa, and Kankuamo). These laws create balance, and from their spiritual obligations maintain the balance of both the Sierra Nevada (the mother) and the rest of the universe for the benefit not only of the Sierra peoples, the "older brothers," but also the other peoples of the earth or "younger brothers."

The laws of Indigenous Peoples are oral, including the cultural foundations and forms of exercising justice (Defensoria del Pueblo, 2018). These traditional laws are protected by Decree 4633 of 2011, and in accordance with section 11 of Article 8 and Article 150 of the NPC, which recognize the coexistence of Indigenous norms and laws with those of the state. Among Indigenous Peoples, traditional and spiritual authorities are Taitas, Iachas, Mamus, Payes, Jaibanas, Abuelos, Abuelas, Brujos shamans, wise men, wise women, and traditional healers. There are traditional Indigenous Guards, such as Chaskis, Wasikamas, Cuiracuas, Kiwe, Thegnas, and Samaneros. Also, Indigenous Peoples have political-administrative authorities such as governors, captains, mayors, chiefs, and *Thuthenas* (councillors) among other denominations and their structures of government, such as Cabildos, Association of Cabildos, Association of Traditional Indigenous Authorities, and Indigenous Councils (Defensoria del Pueblo, 2018).

The *Cabildo* governance structure emerged during the colonial era. Republican Law 89 of 1890, Articles 4–6, defined the functions of the *Cabildo*, which has the role of administering and governing Indigenous communities. Decree 4633 recognizes the *Cabildos* and traditional Indigenous authorities as unique public law entities. Decree 1088 of 1993 regulates the creation of Indigenous *Cabildos* and the association of traditional authorities as public entities with legal personality, and with their own assets and administrative autonomy.

Legal Frameworks for Recognizing Indigenous Peoples' Collective Tenure Rights

In the early 1990s, the Constitutional Assembly developed during a political crisis, with a weak state besieged by the consolidation of a drug trafficking economy into the state's political structures (Diaz Uribe, 2021). The participation of Indigenous Peoples in the Constitutional Assembly positioned them not only as members of Colombian society, but as national political actors who could shape the Indigenous rights framework established in the 1991 NPC. Muñoz Onofre (2016) wrote that Indigenous participation in the Constitutional Assembly was a reconciliation process with the entire country, which reaffirmed the rights of Indigenous Peoples. The 1991 NPC safeguarded collective ownership, land use planning, and the autonomy and self-governing systems of Indigenous and Afro-descendant communities in relation to their collective territories (Bolaños Cardenas et al., 2021).

Muyuy (1998, cited in Herreño Hernandez, 2004, p. 259) identified six groups of rights recognized in the NPC.

1. *Cultural identity*: protections for ethnic and cultural diversity; Indigenous languages and bilingual education; cultural heritage; cultural equality and dignity as a fundamental basis for citizenship; and the right to exercise Indigenous justice systems (Articles 2, 7, 10e, 11, 12, 68n5, 70, 72, 246).
2. *Territorial autonomy*: recognizing *resguardo* and Indigenous territories as part of the nation's administrative-territorial entities, with autonomy for Indigenous Peoples to exercise their own governance system and self-development through their customary systems (*Cabildos*). *Resguardo* are inalienable, imprescriptible, and guaranteed against seizure (Articles 63, 286 and 287).
3. *Political and social autonomy and participation*: the right to political participation and representation in the Senate and House of Representatives. Article 171 establishes that there will be two seats in the Senate for Indigenous Peoples, via the Special Indigenous Constituency, but this does not preclude the possibility of participating in elections in the National Constituency or regional elections through political parties. There is recognition of double citizenship for Indigenous Peoples in frontier areas (Articles 176, 96c).
4. *Environmental and natural resources rights*: rights to prior consultation on projects within Indigenous territories (Articles 79 and 80).
5. *Economic rights*: the *resguardo* lands are interpreted as municipalities for managing national funds (Article 357). Article 329 recognizes the conformation of Indigenous territorial entities, although these are subject to creating the Comprehensive Law of Territorial Planning.
6. *Custom and tradition*: Article 330 recognizes the right of Indigenous Peoples to govern and regulate their territories according to their customs and traditions, and states that the exploitation of natural resources in Indigenous territories shall be done without harming the cultural, social and economic integrity of Indigenous communities. The government shall encourage the participation of Indigenous representatives in any natural resource decisions.

Additionally, Article 86 defines the legal mechanism of immediate action (known as *tutela* in Spanish), where any Colombian citizen can demand the protection of their fundamental constitutional rights. The Constitutional Court, the highest tribunal in judicial matters, ensures compliance with, and safeguards the integrity and supremacy of, the Constitution (Corte Constitutional, 2021). The courts are crucial for claiming rights and justice, and Indigenous organizations have embraced a litigation strategy and the *tutela* as a central legal tool to assert, defend, and pressure the government to fulfill its constitutional responsibilities for protecting ancestral territories. For example, the Indigenous Secretariat of the National Commission of Indigenous Territories (CNTI) won a *tutela* against the National Land Agency (ANT) for administrative due process, the protection of ethnic and cultural diversity, and the safeguarding of the Embera Katio people's collective property in northern Colombia. The Embera Katio people had to wait for more than four decades for the recognition of their collective lands (CNTI, 2021c), and the ruling paved the way for other Indigenous communities to resolve their long-unresolved land claims.

The Colombian government had also ratified the ILO Convention on Indigenous and Tribal Peoples 169 (1989) through Law 21 of 1991. With this ratification, prior consultation became a fundamental right of Indigenous Peoples to have their voices heard and considered in decisions that impact them in both formalized and non-formalized Indigenous territories.[9] The Constitutional Court ruling SU-039 of 1997 defined the objectives of prior consultation for natural resources activity on Indigenous territories: the community shall have comprehensive knowledge of the project planned in their territories and the mechanisms and procedures to implement them; the community shall be informed of the potential impacts on their subsistence, their social cohesion and their

---

[9] Rodriguez Garavito and Orduz Salinas discussed the legal dilemmas of prior consultation rights in Colombia, pointing out that "Prior consultation is defined in a dispersed manner by international and Colombian norms and jurisprudence, which in turn have different levels of obligatory nature. In addition to the normative dispersion, prior consultation is defined with very general parameters, but the procedural details have not been developed by legal norms." The Constitutional Court has established rules for cases in which the consent of the peoples is necessary (Court Ruling C-208 of 2007), and has specified the scope of consent as measures "whose magnitude [has] the potential to disfigure or disappear their ways of life" and "represent a high social, cultural and environmental impact on an ethnic community, cultural and environmental impact on an ethnic community, which could put its existence at risk" (Court Ruling T-19 of 2011, 2012, p. 7, 9).

cultural, political and economic practices; and the community shall debate among its members and representatives the advantages and disadvantages of the project, and freely express their interests and concerns around the viability of the project (Rodriguez, 2017).

The Implementation of the 1991 NPC

Following the 1991 NPC, new legislation and reforms were issued to recognize or amend existing laws on the collective rights of Indigenous Peoples. Moreover, Indigenous Peoples acquired rights to propose new or amend existing legislation in order to materialize their territorial rights. However, as the implementation of the collective rights achieved under the NPC were limited, the discontent among Indigenous organizations increased, motivating a sequence of mobilizations that combined direct actions and the strategic use of the courts to pressure the Colombian State to respect their unique and constitutional rights. In 1996, Indigenous leaders started forty-three days of peaceful takeover of the Episcopal Conference to protest the government's non-compliance with the constitutional provisions for Indigenous rights and the lack of state action to counteract the increasing violence against Indigenous leaders (El Tiempo, 1996). The protest was resolved with the creation of three high-level commissions for official direct dialogue between the national government and Indigenous Peoples to resolve issues related to human rights, territorial rights, and prior consultation rights. These tables were the National Commission of Indigenous Peoples Human Rights (CDDHHPI) (Decree 1396 of 1996), the National Commission of Indigenous Territories (CNTI), and the Permanent Table of Consultation with Indigenous Peoples (MPC) (Decree 1397 of 1996) (CNTI, 2019).

Tutela Legal Instrument Recognized by the 1991 NPC

With the spread of constitutional reforms in the Latin American region since the 1990s, the courts have become crucial for rights and justice. Colombian Indigenous organizations have extensively and strategically used the *tutela* legal instrument and the Constitutional Court to resolve or clarify legal gaps for the protection of their collective rights. Some of the current legislation originated from Constitutional Court rulings, such as Decree 2333 of 2014 on the special protection of Indigenous ancestral and customary collective lands as fundamental to the preservation of

Indigenous Peoples' culture, identity, and social and economic systems. The decree defines the principles for recognition and respect of Indigenous self-governance and legal systems, institutions, norms, and procedures (Ulloa, 2010).

These political cycles of recognition, dispossession, and Indigenous mobilization intersect with the Colombian fifty-year internal armed conflict that exacerbated violence against Indigenous communities. Indigenous Peoples were significantly impacted by this violence, and it altered their land ownership and autonomy, and disrupted their livelihood and use systems, their gardens, rivers, and forest resources (CNMH, 2013).

Advances on the Titling of Indigenous Collective Lands

Although Indigenous Peoples have secured ownership rights to over 35.6 million hectares of *resguardo* lands (see Figure 4.1), most of these collective lands were titled before the 1991 NPC (Muñoz Onofre, 2016, p. 65; Ortega-Roldan, 1993). CNTI reported that 1,450 Indigenous land formalization claims sat before the ANT, some of which have been waiting for more than two decades to be resolved (CNTI, 2019).

Scholars have analyzed the intrinsic contradictions of the 1991 NPC, which on one hand creates a protection framework, while on the other promotes an extractive economic model that affects Indigenous territories (Muñoz Onofre, 2016; Valencia Hernández et al., 2017). This contradiction is reflected in the case of four Indigenous groups of the Sierra Nevada de Santa Marta: Kogui, Arhuaco, Wiwa, and Kankuamo, whom in 1973 obtained recognition by the Colombian government of a ring of sacred sites extending around the base of the mountain range, known as the "Linea Negra" or "Black Line."

In 1995, resolution 837 was issued to guarantee their fundamental right to prior consultation and to participate in any legislative measure affecting their ancestral territory.[10] Despite these protections, a series of political negotiations and legal battles around the demarcation of the

---

[10] Resolution 002 of January 4, 1973. In 2018, Decree 1500 redefined the ancestral territory of the Arhuaco, Kogui, Wiwa, and Kankuamo peoples of the Sierra Nevada de Santa Marta, expressed in the system of sacred spaces of the "Black Line" as a traditional area of special protection and spiritual, cultural, and environmental value, according to the principles and foundations of the Law of Origin, Law 21 of 1991, and other provisions enacted. The decree considers 348 sacred sites.

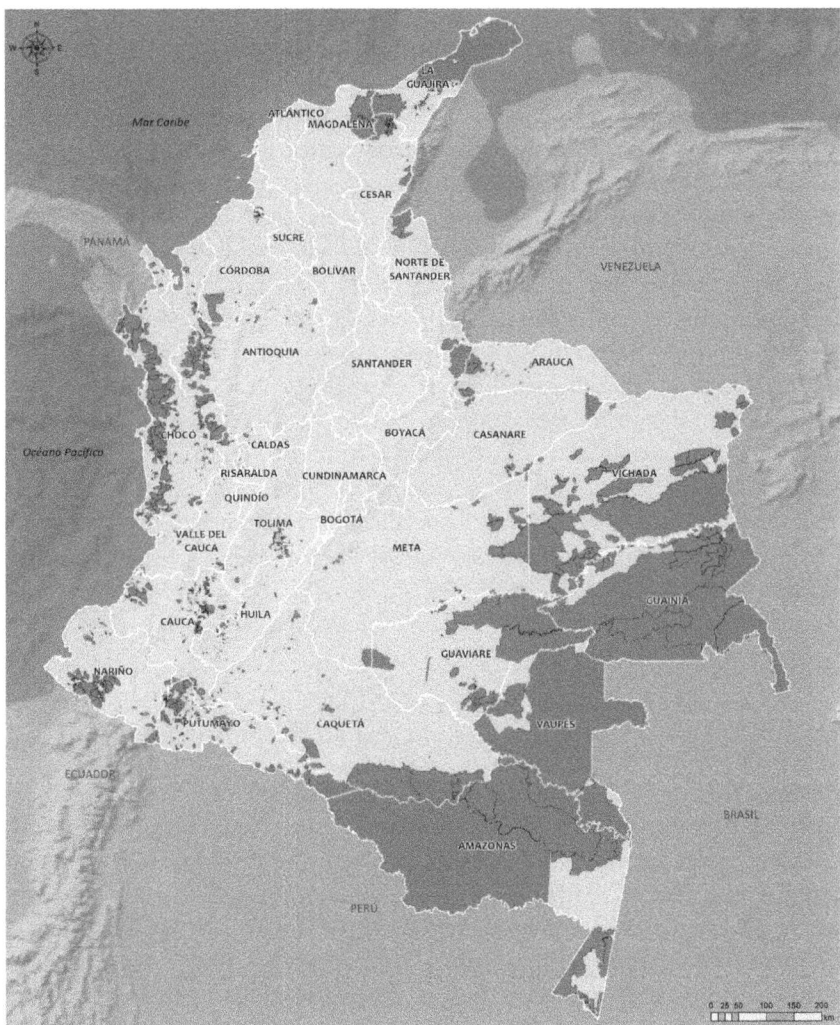

Figure 4.1   Map of formalized Indigenous Territories (authors' own creation based on data from ANT and CNTI)

Linea Negra have taken place. An increasing interest in the minerals around the Linea Negra have resulted in the approval of 132 mining concessions (another 200 mining requests are pending approval) (Mongabay, 2020).

With the signing of the 2016 Peace Agreement between the Colombian government and the guerrillas FARC, the country hoped to leave behind a chronic situation of violence, injustice, and profound inequality regarding land access. The Peace Agreement recognized the inequality of land ownership as the root cause of this conflict. The Comprehensive Rural Reform (RRI in Spanish) of the Peace Agreement aimed to address land inequality by promoting the formalization of land ownership and land restitution, with particular emphasis on women's rights and vulnerable rural populations (Acuerdo Final de Paz, 2017). The Peace Agreement included an Ethnic Chapter, which established the principles of "no regression" and safeguards considerations to guarantee the respect of ethnic peoples' collective rights, such as prior consultation rights, and respect for the collective land rights accrued under national and international legislation, among others (Comisión Étnica, 2018).

However, the implementation of the Peace Agreement was delayed under the government of former President Duque (2018–2022), impacting land justice initiatives. During Duque's tenure, violence, exclusion, and the systematic killing of social leaders escalated, igniting a series of protests by Indigenous Peoples across Colombia, called the "National Ethnic, and Popular Minga" (MINGA) (BBC News Mundo, 2020; Romero Peñuela & Granados, 2021; Paz Cardona, 2020).[11]

Indigenous People's Land Rights in the Peace Agreement Context

Between 2012 and 2016, historic peace negotiations between the government and the guerrillas FARC concluded with the Peace Agreement, entitled the "Conclusion of the Conflict and the Construction of Stable and Lasting Peace." Although praised for promoting inclusion and citizenship participation and selected delegates (Mendes, 2020; Zambrano & Gomez, 2013), Indigenous and Afro-descendant Peoples, as distinct ethnic groups, only gained access to the negotiations in the final month because of international pressure to include them. By working together under an autonomous initiative called the Ethnic Commission, they achieved the addition of an Ethnic Chapter to the Peace Agreement, which defined the principles of non-regression of their collective land rights (Bolaños Cardenas et al., 2021; Comisión Étnica, 2018).

---

[11] The "Minga" is a civil and non-violence resistance strategy emerging from the Indigenous movement in the Cauca region and became a symbol for collective action in the defense of their rights. Minga manifestations have taken place in 2013, 2015, 2016, 2017, 2019, 2020, and 2021.

Both the peace negotiation process and the post-agreement outcomes evolved in a context of increasing discontent and protest by ethnic groups and the agrarian social movements against economic development programs directly affecting their land rights and local economies. Moreover, the failure to implement the Peace Agreement and the Ethnic Chapter exacerbated violence, generating a humanitarian crisis, and increased massive protests across the country. The 2019 *Minga* protest mobilized more than 20,000 people nationwide, and pressured the government to include an investment plan to solve the tenure rights problems in the National Development Plan 2018–22 – a plan that remains stubbornly unresolved (DNP, 2019).

The Law of Victims and Land Restitution (Law 1448 of 2011)[12] preceded the signing of the Peace Agreement and provided official recognition of the victims of Colombia's armed conflict[13] and the dramatic long-lasting land conflict that accounted for an estimated 6 million hectares of land being forcibly abandoned or usurped by different actors (Restrepo & Bernal, 2014). Decree 4633 of 2011 defined measures for the integral reparation of Indigenous Peoples' collective rights and the restitution of their territories, and recognized Indigenous territories as victims of the conflict based on the integral conception, the cosmovision, and the special relationship between Indigenous Peoples and their lands. However, there are limited advances on integral compensation and land restitution for victims of the conflict due to government opposition.

In 2019, the Ombudsman asserted that of the 121,462 total claims for land restitution (individual and collective), 64 percent were denied based on assessments that violated the law (Defensoria del Pueblo, 2019), while the Colombian Commission of Jurists (Comision Colombiana de Juristas, 2019) documented that only fourteen claims for collective land restitution were ordered by specialized judges, of which nine overlapped with mining concessions granted by the government, violating the prior

---

[12] Law 1448 of 2011 establishes the principles for the integral restoration of the victims' rights to access the truth, justice, and just compensation, while defining the mechanism to redress the victims' experiences of dispossession. The law adheres to an international framework on the protection of war victims and recognizes the disproportionate impacts and forced displacement suffered by Indigenous communities and other ethnic groups. Law 2078 of 2021 reformed Law 1448 of 2011 and Decree 4633 of 2011 and extended its term until June 10, 2031.

[13] During the presidential periods of Alvaro Uribe (2002–2008), the armed conflict and violation of human rights increased while a categorical denial persisted around the existence of the victims of the internal conflict (Martinez, 2013).

consultation rights of Indigenous communities. Analysis by the CNTI (2021b) showed that by February 2021, there were 573 requests for the restitution of Indigenous territories filed before the Land Restitution Unit, but only 2.9 percent of this total have received a court ruling.

The Comprehensive Rural Reform

The Comprehensive Rural Reform (RRI in Spanish) defined the pathways for land justice by promoting the formalization of land ownership and the implementation of restitution for victims and the land restitution law. The RRI targeted 10 million hectares for land redistribution, of which 3 million hectares constituted the so-called Land Fund for free distribution to rural populations, and 7 million for a massive formalization of rural property, including a multi-cadastre process aimed at updating and expanding current national cadastre data to better inform decisions on land rights formalization (Acuerdo Final de Paz, 2017).

Some authors argued that Decree 902 of 2017, for the implementation of the RRI, undermined the core problem of the conflict: the persistent private land concentration among cattle and agricultural interests, which impeded a fair distribution of land to poor rural populations (Chavarro cited in Chavez, 2018). Chavez (2018) explained that after a failed referendum to approve the 2016 Peace Agreement, the terms of the Peace Agreement were renegotiated, and substantial modifications were made to the RRI. These modifications limited the scope of the RRI and positioned it as a mechanism for rural development through agroindustry expansion. This created inequitable dynamics between poor peasants and large-scale producers, via Law 1776 of 2016 for areas of economic and social rural development interest (known as the ZIDRES law).

Thus, the changes to the Peace Agreement and the RRI, and the implementation decree, ignored historic power relations, inequality, and corruption, and made large-scale landowners the beneficiaries of the land formalization process (Chavez, 2018).

Another adjustment to the RRI was the modality for rural land allocation. The ANT implements the RRI under a "supply model" of land administration to accelerate the access and formalization procedures for rural land tenure. Espinosa et al. (2020) argued that the "supply model" is an innovative and effective approach, coherent with the territorial approach of the RRI, and "suggests a change in the dynamics of the state in relation to the citizens, as it privileges the guarantee of rights of those who reside in the rural areas" (2020, p. 12). This new model of land administration contrasts with the "demand model" based on requests currently practiced under land Law 160 of 1996. Questions remain unresolved about the implications for the long-standing claims of Indigenous communities and the historical debt of the state.

Of the municipalities affected by the armed conflict, 79 percent lack basic cadastre information, and of these, around sixty municipalities in the provinces of Choco, Amazonas, Vaupes, Guainía, and Nariño are home to 81 percent of the Indigenous *resguardos* and collective lands of Afro-descendant communities (Comision Etnica, 2018). The CNTI argued that the implementation of the multi-cadastre process has ignored their constitutional rights and the terms of the Peace Agreement, generated segregation and exclusion, promoted and exacerbated conflicts in the territories, and violated their prior consultation rights (CNTI, 2021a). The current multi-cadastre implementation process is only implemented in areas where *resguardo* lands are legally recognized, thus impacting those Indigenous Peoples without *resguardo* rights (CINEP/CERAC, 2021). Using the *tutela,* the Indigenous MPC and CNTI pressured the government to define a road map for FPIC implementation and the integration of the territorial perspective in the multi-cadastre process (CNTI, 2021a). If the multi-cadastre process addresses the legal rights of all Indigenous Peoples of Colombia, it could be a mechanism to resolve pending land claims and persistent conflicts.

Development Plans with a Territorial Focus (PDET in Spanish) is the planning and management instrument created by Decree 893 of 2017 to implement the RRI in the most vulnerable regions of the country. There are 16 subregions of the country embracing 170 municipalities, representing 36 percent of the national territory prioritized, based on the following criteria: a high level of poverty, a high degree of impact from the internal armed conflict, institutional weaknesses, illicit crop cultivation, and illegal economies. Within the total areas prioritized, there are 452 *resguardos* (Comision Etnica, 2018).

However, these instruments have yet to resolve land inequality. The advances and results claimed by the national government on formalization of *resguardo* lands under the RRI do not coincide with Indigenous Peoples' evaluations. For instance, according to CINEP/CERAC report, "the progress reported by the National Land Agency in relation to formalization of *resguardos* under the RRI are in fact, backlogs for collective land titles of former land agencies, INCORA and INCODER" (CINEP/CERAC, 2021, p. 18). In this sense, the ANT has not complied with the commitments of the RRI and Ethnic Chapter to secure collective land rights under the Land Fund.

The lack of compliance with the terms of the RRI and Ethnic Chapter have serious implications due to a lag in the formalization of Indigenous Peoples' territorial rights. Indigenous Peoples continue to pressure and influence the national government to comply with the constitutional framework protecting their rights. Indigenous political advocacy and litigation have compelled the government to issue Decree 1824 of 2020, which clarified the legal validity of the *resguardo* land titles of colonial or republic origin, and their protection during implementation of the RRI, as these will not be counted as available lands for distribution. The decree also established that requests for clarification of such titles, for their restructuring or extension, may be made by traditional authorities, *Cabildos* or Indigenous organizations through their prior consent (CINEP/CERAC, 2021).

Concluding Remarks and Recommendations

Although the 1991 NPC is the legal basis for advancing Indigenous Peoples' rights in Colombia, it has not resulted in the full restitution and protection of their collective lands. One of the major real positive impacts has been the use of the *tutela* legal mechanism for enforcing rights and the rulings of the Constitutional Court, which has strengthened the constitutional rights of Indigenous Peoples.

While there have been significant legal advances for land rights, there are still challenges as tension persists in the implementation of these laws. There are deep-seated barriers to advancing land rights in practice. However, the resilience of Indigenous Peoples to consistently organize and defend their rights through political mobilization and litigation, and to recover their ancestral lands, has been a driving force for policy and constitutional reforms, even as internal conflict has intensified.

In the current post-conflict context, Indigenous Peoples have contributed to the realization and implementation of the Peace Agreement. The integral implementation of the Ethnic Chapter and Decree 902 of 2017, which adopt measures to facilitate the implementation of the RRI in land matters, specifically in procedures for access and formalization, and the Land Fund, is crucial in this phase of peace reconstruction. Looking ahead, the government must guarantee the effective operation of the Land Fund and regulate the sub-account for Indigenous communities' access to collective lands, as established by Article 18 (12) of Decree

902 of 2017. It is imperative that the government clarifies the percentage of land allocated to Indigenous communities from the 3 million hectares of land the government plans to purchase under the RRI. Equally, it is crucial to define the percentage of lands for Indigenous communities among the 7 million hectares the government plans to formalize nationwide.

Moreover, the government needs to allocate the funds required for these land purchases, while improving coordination among institutions involved in land tenure rights and simplifying the administrative procedures for the formalization of Indigenous collective tenure rights. In this way, the government can ensure Indigenous Peoples are in fact recognized as rightsholders in the Comprehensive Rural Reform of the Peace Accord.

References

Acuerdo Final de Paz. ("Final Agreement to end the Armed Conflict and Build a Stable and Lasting Peace"). (2017). *Acuerdo final para la terminación del conflicto y la construcción de una paz estable y duradera.* Government of Colombia Bogotá.

Balcazar, A., Lopez N., Orozco M., & Vega M. (2001). Colombia: Alcances y lecciones de su experiencia en reforma agraria. *CEPAL, United Nations.* Santiago, Chile. www.cepal.org/sites/default/files/publication/files/4493/S019751_es.pdf

BBC News Mundo. (2020, October 21). Redacción. Protestas en Colombia: Qué es la minga indígena y qué papel juega en las manifestaciones. *BBC News Mundo.* www.bbc.com/mundo/noticias-america-latina-54625586

Benavides, F. (2009). La movilización de los pueblos indígenas y la luchas por sus derechos en Colombia. *International Catalan Institute for Peace, working paper #8*, Barcelona.

Bolaños Cardenas, O. Arango, J.H., Lovera C.G., Molina, E.H.. (2021). Bridging research and practice to influence national policy: Afro-Colombian territorial rights, from stagnation to implementation. *Bulletin of Latin American Research*, 41 (3): 387–403. https://doi.org/10.1111/blar.13248

Boza Villarreal, A. (2013). Negotiating indigenous autonomy: Politics, land, and religion in Tierradentro (Colombia), 1905–1950 [Doctoral Dissertation]. The Dietrich School of Arts and Science, University of Pittsburgh.

Centro Nacional de Memoria Histórica [CNMH]. (2013). !Basta ya! Colombia: memorias de Guerra y dignidad. www.centrodememoriahistorica.gov.co/descargas/informes2013/bastaYa/basta-ya-colombia-memorias-de-guerra-y-dignidad-2016.pdf

Chavez, D. (2018). Avances y dificultades en la implementación de la Reforma Rural Integral: Una deuda pendiente con el campo colombiano. *Revista Colombiana de Sociología* 41 (1)(Suplemento), 81–103.

CINEP. (2022). Proceso de Resistencia del pueblo Misak "recuperar la tierra para recuperarlo todo." *Planetapaz.* www.consorcio.org.co/wp-content/uploads/2022/05/20220311_Guambia.pdf

CINEP/CERAC. (2021). *Segundo informe de verificación de la implementación del enfoque étnico en el Acuerdo Final de Paz en Colombia.* Bogota, Colombia: CINEP.

CNTI. (2021a). El Gobierno se comprometió a garantizar el derecho a la consulta previa, libre e informada para los pueblos indígenas en la implementación de la política del catastro multipropósito. https://cntindigena.org/documents/cntiopina/Comunicado-ruta-catastro-16072021.pdf

(2021b). Informe Panorama del proceso de restitución de derechos territoriales de los pueblos indigenas a 9 años de su implementación, nudos centrales y aportes para su impulso. https://cntindigena.org/documents/Informes/Informe-Proceso-de-Restitucio%CC%81n-de-derechos-terrritoriales-de-los-PI-ODTPI-7072021.pdf

(2021c). Tras 42 años de dilaciones, después de acciones administrativas y judiciales finalmente fue realizado el registro del resguardo indígenas Dochama Alto Ure en el Departamento de Cordoba. www.cntindigena.org/tras-42-anos-de-dilaciones-despues-de-acciones-administrativas-y-judi ciales-finalmente-fue-realizado-el-registro-del-resguardo-indigena-doc hama-alto-ure-en-el-departamento-de-cordoba/

Comisión Colombiana de Juristas. (2019). *Radiografía de la restitución de tierras en Colombia. Informe presentado ante la Comisión Interamericana de Derechos Humanos por incumplimiento de reparación a las víctimas despo- jadas de tierras en Colombia.* Bogotá: CCJ.

Comision Étnica. (2018). *Primer informe de cumplimiento del Capitulo Étnico en el marco de la implementación de acuerdo final de paz.* Bogotá.

Comisión Nacional de Territorios Indígenas [CNTI]. (2019). Informe, Estado de Cosas Inconstitucional de los Derechos Territoriales de Los Pueblos Indígenas. Bogota: SIT-CNTI. https://cntindigena.org/documents/Informes/COM_ESTADO-DE-COSAS-INCONSTITUCIONAL-DE-LOS-DERECHOS-TERRITORIALES-DE-LOS-PUEBLOS-INDIGENAS-14092020.pdf

Corte Constitutional. (2021). Political constitution of Colombia. www.corteconstitucional.gov.co/english/#Constitution

Defensoría del Pueblo. (2018). Derecho propio de los pueblos indígenas. *Imprenta Nacional de Colombia. Ombudsman's Office of Colombia (Defensoría del Pueblo de Colombia).* Bogota, Colombia.

(2019). *Comisiones de seguimiento a la Ley de Víctimas y Decretos Leyes Étnicos alertan sobre aumento de nuevos hechos de violencia.* Bogota, Colombia: Defensoría del Pueblo de Colombia.

Departamento Nacional de Planeación (DNP). (2019). *Asignación especial del sistema general de participaciones para resguardos indígenas, una propuesta de distribución.* www.dnp.gov.co/Paginas/Gobierno-nacional-le-sigue-cum pliendo-a-los-indigenas.aspx

Diaz Uribe, M. A. (2021). Performatividad política y cultural. El movimiento indígena colombiano y su participación en la Asamblea Nacional Constituyente de 1990. *Revista Jangwa Pana*, 20(3): 398–417.https://doi .org/10.21676/issn.1657-4923

El Tiempo. (1996). Continua la toma indígena en la coferencia episcopal. Archivo. www.eltiempo.com/archivo/documento/MAM-460641

Espinosa, F., Rodríguez, A.C., Galindo Gonzalez, C.M., & Rodriguez, N.O. (2020). The social use of rural land property (Surul) policy in Colombia: A review of its results in the municipality of Ovejas Sucre (2016–2019). *Annual World Bank Conference on Land and Poverty 2020.* www.oicrf.org/documents/ 40950/0/01-05-Espinosa-857_paper.pdf/bf894d3f-9481-4e33-8fea-b8fa9ae17988?t=1646044097607

Faguet, J. P., Sanches, F., & Villaveces, M. J. (2016). The paradox of land reform, inequality and local development in Colombia. *The London School of Economics and Political Science.* http://eprints.lse.ac.uk/67193/1/Faguet_ Paradox%20opf%20land%20reform_2016.pdf

Figueroa, I. (2016). Legislación marginal, desposesión indígena, civilización en proceso: Ecuador y Colombia. *NÓMADAS*, 45, 43–57. www.redalyc.org/ journal/1051/105149483005/html/

Guereña, A. (2017). A snapshot of inequality: What the latest agricultural census reveals about land distribution in Colombia. *Oxfam.* www.oxfam.org/en/ research/snapshot-inequality

Herreño Hernandez, A. L. (2004). Evolucion politica y legal del concepto de territorio ancestral indigena en Colombia. *El Otro Derecho*, 31–32. ILSA.

Martinez, P. (2013). *The victims and land restitution law in Colombia in context: An analysis of the contradictions between the agrarian model and compensation for the victims.* Berlin: FDCL, TNI.

Mayorga Garcia, F. H. (2004). Los derechos de los pueblos originarios sobre sus tierras de comunidad: Del Nuevo Reino de Granada a la Republica de Colombia. In M. G. Losano (ed.) *Un giudice e due leggi. Pluralismo normativo e conflitti agrari in Sud América (pp. 35-74).* Milán: Giuffré editore.

Mendes, I. (2020). Inclusion and political representation in peace negotiations: The case of the Colombian victim's delegations. *Journal of Politics in Latin America*, 11(3), 272–297. https://doi.org/10.1177/1866802X19889756

Mongabay. (2020). Minería y megaporyectos invaden "corazón del mundo" de Colombia. https://es.mongabay.com/2020/04/colombia-mineria-tierras-indi genas-sierra-nevada-santa-marta/

Morales Gomez, J. (1979). Vicisitudes de los resguardos en Colombia: Repaso historico. *Horizontes*, 10(10), 78–85.https://revistas.javeriana.edu.co/index.php/univhumanistica/article/view/10473

Muñoz Onofre, J. P. (2016). *La brecha de implementación de los derechos territoriales de los pueblos indigenas en Colombia*. Bogota: Universidad del Rosario.

Ortega-Roldan, J. L. (1993). *Reconocimiento legal de tierras a indígenas en Colombia. En Reconocimiento y demarcación de territorios indígenas en la Amazonia*. Bogota: CEREC and Gaia Foundation.

Paz Cardona, J. A. (2020, Oct. 21). Indigenas viajaron a Bogota y piden un debate politico con el president Ivan Duque. *Mongabay*. https://es.mongabay.com/2020/10/minga-indigena-colombia-protestas-bogota-por-masacres/

Rappaport, J. (2005). *Cumbe Renaciente: Una historia etnográfica andina*. Instituto Colombiano de Antropología e Historia, Bogota, Colombia.

Restrepo, J. C. & Bernal, A. (2014). La Cuestión Agraria. Tierra y Posconflicto en Colombia. Bogotá.

Rights and Resources Initiative [RRI]. (2014). What future for reform? Progress and slowdown in forest tenure reforms since 2002. https://rightsandresources.org/publication/what-future-for-reform/

Rodriguez, G. A. (2017). *De la consulta previa al consentimiento libre, previo e informado de los pueblos indigenas en Colombia*. Universidad del Rosario. Grupo editorial Ibañez, Bogota. Colombia.

Rodriguez, Garavito, Augusto, C., & Orduz Salinas, N. (2012). La consulta previa: Dilemas y soluciones. DeJusticia, Bogota. Colombia.

Romero Peñuela, N., & Granados C. (May 23, 2021,). Opinion. Paro Nacional 2021: Porque la Minga Indigena es fundamental en el dialogo para resolver la crisis? *El Espectador*. www.elespectador.com/colombia/paro-nacional-2021-por-que-la-minga-indigena-es-fundamental-en-el-dialogo-para-resolver-la-crisis/

RRI. (2015). Factsheet. Who owns the land in Latin America? The status of Indigenous and community land rights in Latin America. https://rightsandresources.org/wp-content/uploads/FactSheet_English_WhoOwnstheLandinLatinAmerica_web.pdf

(2018). At a crossroads: Consequential trends in recognition of community-based forest tenure from 2002–2017. https://doi.org/10.53892/UCYL3747

Sanchez Gutierrez, E., & Molina Echeverri, H. (2014). Documentos para la historia del movimiento indígena colombiano contemporáneo. Biblioteca Básica de los Pueblos Indígenas de Colombia. https://babel.banrepcultural.org/digital/collection/p17054coll8/id/0

Semper, F. (2018). *Los derechos de los pueblos indígenas en Colombia*. Bogotá: Editorial Temis.

Torres Solis, H. E. (2004). *Resurgiendo de la perdida: Desarrollo organizativo del pueblo Arhuaco. Periodo 2000–2003* [Thesis]. University of Andes,

Colombia.   https://repositorio.uniandes.edu.co/bitstream/handle/1992/21170/u245633.pdf?sequence=1

Tunubala Yalanda, D. (2016). Participación de la comunidad Misak en el movimiento de autoridades indígenas del Sur-Occidente (AISO) 1971–1991 [Thesis]. University of Valle, Cali Colombia. https://1library.co/document/y6ejjk5z-participacion-comunidad-movimiento-autoridades-indigenas-occidente-recurso-electronico.html

Ulloa, A. (2010). Colombia: Autonomías Indígenas en ejercicio. Retos de su consolidación. In M. Gonzales, A. B. Cal y Mayor, & P. Ortiz-T. (eds.), *La autonomía a debate: Autogobierno indígena y Estado plurinacional en América Latina. (pp. 149–176).* FLACSO, Quito, Ecuador.

Valencia-Hernández, J-G., Muñoz-Villarreal, E-M., & Hainsfurth, J. C. (2017). *Pueblos originarios y extractivismo minero.* Manizales, Colombia: Universidad de Caldas.

Vasco Uribe, L. G. (2008). Quintin Lame: Resistencia y liberación. *Tabula Rasa*, 9, 371–383. www.redalyc.org/pdf/396/39600918.pdf

Velasco Alvarez, A. (n.d.). La relacion pasado-presente en la creative resistencia del pueblos Misak. https://es.scribd.com/document/427470756/La-Creativa-Resistencia-Del-Pueblo-Misak#

Velásquez Ruiz, M. A. (2018). *Collective land tenure in Colombia: Background and current status.* Center for International Forestry Research. Bogor Indonesia. www.cifor.org/knowledge/publication/6902/

Villa, W., & Houghton, J. (2004). *Violencia política contra los pueblos Indígenas en Colombia 1974–2004.* Santafé de Bogotá: CECOIN, OIA, IWGIA.

Zambrano, L., & Gomez, F. (2013). Participation of civil society in the Colombian peace process. *NOREF: Norwegian Peace Building Resource Center.* https://reliefweb.int/sites/reliefweb.int/files/resources/colombia%20peacebuilding.pdf

5

Indigenous Land Rights in Chile

Dispossession, Misrecognition, and Litigation

ALEXANDRA TOMASELLI

Introduction

Almost 13 percent of Chile's population self-identified as "Indigenous" in the 2017 census, or 2,185,792 individuals (Instituto Nacional de Estadísticas Chile, 2018, p. 16). National legislation recognizes ten Indigenous Peoples (albeit by defining them as "ethnicities"): Aymara, Chango, Colla, Diaguita, Kawashkar o Alacalufe, Likan Antai (previously called Atacameños), Mapuche (the most populous), Quechua, Rapa Nui, and Yagán o Yámana (Article 1, paragraph 2 of the so-called Indigenous Law, *Ley Indígena*, Law 19.253 of 1993, as modified to include the Diaguita people in 2006 by Law 20,117 and the Chango people in 2020 by Law 21,273).

The majority of Indigenous individuals live in urban settings, and while poverty among Indigenous Peoples has slowly decreased in recent decades, the unemployment rates remain higher than the national average (Ministerio de Desarrollo Social, 2022). This is probably due to the widespread discrimination suffered by Indigenous Peoples throughout Chile (Briones & Lepe-Carrión, 2023; Molina, 2007).

Since the *Conquista*, Indigenous Peoples' lands, and their access to natural resources, have been dramatically reduced. Nowadays, the few preserved or restored Indigenous lands are constantly challenged by the neoliberal economic priorities pursued by the Chilean state. These include, among other things, the construction of hydroelectric plants (Anaya, 2009; Rosti, 2008), especially in the south (Aylwin & Silva, 2014); the aggressive extractivist agenda (Silva Neriz, 2013; Toledo Llancaqueo, 2006), principally in the north (Marimán Quemenado, 2011); the massive exploitation of forest resources (Silva Neriz, 2013; Stavenhagen, 2003); and the intense salmon farming in coastal areas (Aylwin & Silva, 2014; Soluri, 2011).

In recent years, some positive trends have emerged, including an official state apology that (then) President Bachelet offered to the Mapuche people in 2017 for the "errors and the horrors" committed or tolerated by Chile throughout its history. However, the election of (former) President Piñera (his second mandate, 2018–2022) had another dramatic effect on Indigenous policies (Didier et al., 2019). The nation-wide protests that took place in Chile starting in October 2019 relate to broad unequal access to public resources (education, justice, public transport, health services, etc.) that continue to heavily affect Indigenous Peoples too.

In July 2021, the first Constituent Assembly (the so-called Constitutional Convention, *Convención Constitucional*) started working on the new Chilean Magna Carta. The Assembly was formed by 155 delegates – all elected by the Chileans – out of which seventeen seats were reserved for Indigenous Peoples in accordance with the percentages of the 2017 census. This resulted in seven seats for the Mapuche elected representatives, two for Aymara, and one for each of the other eight Indigenous Peoples (Chango, Colla, Diaguita, Kawashkar/Alacalufe, Likan Antai, Quechua, Rapa Nui, and Yagán/Yámana) (El Ciudadano, 2020). Moreover, the first president of the Constituent Assembly, Elisa Loncón Antileo, was an Indigenous academic and Mapuche woman.[1]

A constitutional text was drafted between 2021 and 2022 and included a wide array of Indigenous rights (50 provisions of 380), with references to their pre-existence, their rights to self-determination, autonomy, independent institutions, justice systems, participation, consultation, culture, and free, prior, and informed consent; also included were references to their rights to natural resources, territories, and land (Convención Constitucional, 2022b). The proposal was rejected, likely due to an inappropriate communication strategy as well as conservative propaganda, which argued that the constitutional changes would undermine the legal foundations of the Chilean state (Velásquez Loaiza, 2022).

A second text was prepared from June 7 to November 7, 2023, by a constitutional council (*Consejo Constitucional*) that was elected in May with poor Indigenous representation (Proceso Constitucional, 2023a). This proposal included only three articles on Indigenous Peoples and rights: on their recognition, their international individual and collective

---

[1] Elisa Loncón Antileo was then replaced by María Elisa Quinteros as a new president, vice-president, and executive body (*mesa de la convención*) was appointed on January 5, 2022 (Convención Constitucional, 2022a).

rights, and interculturality; on mechanisms to promote their political participation; and on local rights at the regional and municipal levels (Proceso Constitucional, 2023b). Hence, land rights were not included. Nevertheless, this text was also rejected at the referendum held on December 17, 2023 (Sanhueza, 2023). Against this background, this chapter analyzes the process of dispossession faced by Indigenous Peoples in relation to their traditional lands, how they have contested the titles to ownership and possession of such territories, and the outcomes of their litigation strategy both in the north and in the south of Chile in recent decades. This chapter confirms the consensus in other chapters in this book: dispossession has been followed by processes for recognizing and reclaiming land rights, but implementation has been problematic. In addition, the chapter identifies how litigation in national courts has created an opportunity to safeguard land rights, at least at the jurisprudential level.

Processes for Dispossessing Indigenous Peoples of their Lands

The independence and the foundation of the Chilean state are officially dated as 1818 and 1810, respectively. However, the territory that forms the modern Chilean state was occupied and colonized by Spaniards during different periods. For instance, the areas covering the current towns of Arica, Iquique, Antofagasta, Calama, and Pozo Almonte in the north, and where the Aymara and Lika Antai/Atacameño Indigenous Peoples have been living for centuries, were annexed to Chile only after the so-called Pacific Wars of 1879–1884 (Gudermann, 2003). In the south, the fierce resistance of the Mapuche led to the signing of a number of bilateral treaties between their leaders and the colonizers.[2] Notwithstanding that these treaties *de facto* governed the territories south of the Bío-Bío river until the Civil War of 1859 (Bengoa, 2000), the occupation of Indigenous lands started well before. For

---

[2] The best known of such treaties is the so-called Parliament of Quilín or Quillín (*Parlamento de Quilín / Quillín*) of 1641 that, among other things, was supposed to seal the Bío-Bío River as the official border between the Mapuches and the colonizers. This was reiterated in the two following well-known Parliaments of Negrete (1726) and Tepihue (1738). However, the total number of these "Parliaments" was 18: 1641 (*Quilín or Quillín*), 1651, 1683, 1693–94, 1712, 1726 (Negrete), 1738 (Tepihue), 1746, 1756, 1760, 1764, 1771, 1774, 1784, 1787, 1793, 1803, and 1816 (Bengoa, 2000, pp. 38–40; Guevara, 1925, p. 373 as cited by Contreras Panemal, 2003, pp. 59–61; de Avila Martel, 1973 as cited by Aylwin, 2002, p. 3).

instance, the 1,600 Indigenous Peoples living in the Araucanía region were (immensely) outnumbered by the arrival of about 14,000 new settlers in the mid-nineteenth century (Aylwin, 1995). Such a high concentration of non-Indigenous Peoples justified the first state acts to regulate both the colonization and the occupancy of these territories (Aylwin, 1995).

In 1883, the so-called Peace of Araucanía (*Pacificación de la Araucanía*) ended two years of military occupancy in the region, and marked the beginning of the arbitrary confinement of the Mapuche peoples onto reserves (*Reducciones*) or other lodgings (Bengoa, 2000; Rosti, 2008). The concept of individual property rights was unknown to Mapuche at that time (Nesti, 2002). Overall, the original Mapuche territory was reduced by 95 percent (Rosti, 2008). In addition, other state initiatives, such as granting land concessions, attracting foreign settlers "in good health" to farm the land, creating new villages, and adopting ad hoc legislation legitimizing the new property titles, resulted in a further "colonization" of traditional Mapuche lands in the current Region of Araucanía (Aylwin, 1995). Mapuche organizations were set up in the early 1900s, but they did not make any significant gains in the return of their lands (Bengoa, 2000). A further 25 percent of Mapuche territory was "absorbed" before the agrarian reforms of the 1960s by non-Indigenous settlers that first unlawfully occupied the land, and then requested (and obtained) the titling for these territories (Bengoa, 2000).

Chile has a strong tradition of legal positivism, which constrains the expression of (Indigenous) customary law. Despite centuries of dispossession, Indigenous Peoples often retain their own laws, or, for instance, what the Mapuche call *Az Mapu*, "the law of the land." It is important to note that the term "law" is derived from Western values, understood by Mapuche as "state" or *wingkas* (non-Mapuche) law. *Az Mapu* refers to the group of norms and ways of relating that regulate Mapuche peoples and lands (Cloud, 2010). *Az Mapu* is intimately linked to the Mapuche cosmo-vision of a profound spiritual conception of equilibrium and harmony with the surrounding environment, and embedded in *Mapuzungun* (or Mapuche language), as *Az Mapu* is transmitted orally (Cloud, 2010).

On Easter Island, the dispossession of the lands of Rapa Nui Indigenous Peoples – and their dehumanization through slavery – started during the nineteenth century. The Rapa Nui decreased from 2,000 to 111 people between 1864 and 1877 (Rochna Ramirez, 1996). In 1868, the French merchant Jean Baptiste Onésime Dutroux-Bornier (better known as "Pitopito") "acquired" vast areas of land from the Rapa Nui by unlawful means, concluding contracts with children and taking advantage of the fact the Rapa Nui did not realize they were giving away their lands forever (Rochna Ramirez, 1996). In 1888, the Agreement of Wills – signed by the navy captain Policarpo Toro in representation of Chile and the Rapa Nui king Atamu Tekena – marked the annexation of the Easter Island to Chile (Chartier et al., 2011). In principle, the Rapa Nui should have remained the owners of their ancestral lands (Marimán Quemenado, 2011), but the Chilean state took control and gave concessions to the Rapa Nui's lands without any consideration of the Rapa Nui claims (Rochna Ramirez, 1996).

In 1933, the island was ultimately registered as *terra nullius* and formed part of the state lands of Chile in accordance with the then Article 590 of the Civil Code (Chartier et al., 2011; Marimán Quemenado, 2011). In 2012, a Rapa Nui family contested the validity of this registration before the Supreme Court. Nevertheless, the Supreme Court validated that title as well as other property titles enacted in the past that ignored the Rapa Nui's land titling (Silva Neriz, 2013). The Rapa Nui were kept in semi-slavery conditions until the adoption of the so-called Easter Law (*Ley Pascua*) 16.441 in 1967 (Chartier et al., 2011); thereafter, a national park over the island (called *Hanga Roa*) was established in the 1980s (Rochna Ramirez, 1996). The park is currently administered by the National Forestry Corporation (*Corporación Nacional Forestal* – CONAF) (Marimán Quemenado, 2012), but without the participation of any Rapa Nui (Cloud, 2013). Therefore, 13 percent of Easter Island is held by the Rapa Nui people, 17 percent is in the hands of private owners, and 70 percent is state land (Aylwin & Silva, 2014).

Only the agrarian reform of the 1960s brought some changes into Indigenous land titling. In particular, Law 17.729 of 1972 ruled a system of land restitutions (Article 17) and established an Institute for Indigenous Development (Articles 34 and ff.).[3] However, after the 1973 military *golpe* (coup), Law Decree 2,568 of 1979 modified the system of land restitution that became more arbitrary (Articles 9–26).[4]

---

[3] Law 17.729 of 1972, *Establece Normas sobre Indigenas y Tierras de Indigenas. Transforma la Direccion de Asuntos Indigenas en Instituto de Desarrollo Indigena. Establece Disposiciones Judiciales, Administrativas y de Desarrollo Educacional en la Materia y Modifica o Deroga los Textos Legales que Señala.*

[4] Law Decree 2.568 of 1979, *Modifica Ley N° 17.729, Sobre Proteccion de Indigenas, y Radica Funciones del Instituto de Desarrollo Indigena en el Instituto de Desarrollo Agropecuario, Decreto Ley 2568 Ministerio de Agricultura.* See also Nesti (2002).

Moreover, the dictatorship introduced a system of land "normalization," which was realized through revocations or expropriations and reallocation (via reselling) of land titles via unscrupulous transactions – for example, by concluding contracts with illiterate or poorly literate individuals, including Indigenous Peoples. This transformed all the lands that had been given back during the agrarian reform into private lands by the early 1980s (Toledo Llancaqueo, 2006, p. 56). Finally, the Water Code (Decree 1,122 of 1981)[5] legitimized the privatization and appropriation of watercourses, depriving Indigenous Peoples of water access (see more on this further below).

Once democracy was restored in 1989, the then presidential candidate and future first democratically elected president after the dictatorship, Patricio Aylwin, signed the so-called (first) Agreement of Nueva Imperial with some Indigenous representatives. Among other things, he promised to promote a constitutional reform that would include Indigenous Peoples and to recognize their socio-economic and cultural rights. Despite several attempts, the constitutional recognition never followed, and as mentioned, the recent attempts of the constitutional reforms failed too. Under Aylwin's mandate, the abovementioned "Indigenous Law" was eventually adopted in 1993.

The (Mis)Recognition of Indigenous Land Rights

Overview

The Chilean state has not protected Indigenous Peoples from dispossession. This failure has ultimately resulted in a number of socio-environmental conflicts. Since the late 1990s, Indigenous Peoples and their organizations have used different instruments to denounce this gap, such as peaceful marches or protests, as well as some frustration-led land occupations. However, the Chilean state has often (if not always) replied in an austere way, such as by ordering the police to repress the direct actions[6] or by using the military justice system under the anti-terrorism

---

[5] Decree 1,122 of 1981 of the Chilean Ministry of Justice (*Ministerio de Justicia*), *Código de Aguas. Decreto con Fuerza de Ley Nº 1.122.*

[6] For instance, the killing of the two Mapuche youngsters (Matías Valentín Catrileo Quezada and Jaime Facundo Mendoza Collio) who were shot by police during an uprising in the late 2000s (Cayuqueo 2008; Paillan 2009) or the most recent death of another youngster (Camilo Catrillanca) in late 2018 in Temucuicui (Ercilla) (Trincado Vera & Muñoz Sims, 2020); the forced displacement of those Indigenous Rapa Nui that were peacefully protesting against land

law – an inheritance of the dictatorship[7] – instead of the civil or criminal standard of justice. Furthermore, as mentioned, economic interests are prioritized over Indigenous land claims and rights.[8]

The Chilean economy is largely based on the export of raw materials (Equipo OCMAL, 2015), including some of the world's largest copper deposits, and is a leading exporter of lithium, iodine, molybdenum, silver (Prieto, 2015; Yáñez & Molina, 2008), and gold. All of these minerals are concentrated in the lands of the northern Indigenous Diaguita and Collas peoples (Molina, 2007, 2013). At the time of writing (December 2023), Chile had forty-nine ongoing mining conflicts, and was ranked fourth for the number of such conflicts in Latin America (Equipo OCMAL, 2023).

Chile has ratified the majority of the international human rights treaties, endorsed both the 2007 United Nations Declaration on the Rights of Indigenous Peoples (UNDRIP) and the 2016 American Declaration of the Rights of Indigenous Peoples (ADRIP), and, most importantly, it ratified the International Labour Organization (ILO) Indigenous and Tribal Peoples Convention of 1989 in 2008 (hereafter, C169).[9] The C169 entered into force on September 15, 2009.

The Indigenous Law

At the national level, Indigenous rights continue to be governed by the Indigenous Law (Law 19,253 of 1993), which might be changed by future constitutional reforms. The Indigenous Law has done the following:

---

dispossessions in August 2010 (Inter-American Commission on Human Rights, 2011: p. 78); or the violence against the Mapuche peoples of Temucuicui (Ercilla), which the Court of Appeal of Temuco defined as a place in a permanent state of militarization and repression (Corte de Apelaciones de Temuco, 2012).

[7] Law 18,314 of 1984, *Determina Conductas Terroristas y fija su Penalidad*. In accordance with this law, crimes such as setting fires (Article 2) have to be dealt with in front of military tribunals if there was an intention of menacing the population or a part of it, which makes this a crime of "terrorist" nature (Article 1). To provide evidence of such intentions, the plaintiff (usually the Chilean state) may call upon the so-called "faceless" witnesses (*testigos sin rostro*) (i.e., witnesses that cannot be identified and remain unknown to the defense) (Articles 15–18). Moreover, the penalties are longer than those foreseen under standard criminal law.

[8] The most glaring example is the controversial story of the construction of the Ralco's six hydroelectric plants on the Bío-Bío River by the National Electric Enterprise (ENDESA) (see Aylwin, 2002; Barrera-Hernández, 2005; Nesti, 2002; Tomaselli, 2012, 2016).

[9] Decree of the Ministry of Exterior No. 236 of 2008, *Promulga El Convenio N° 169 Sobre Pueblos Indigenas Y Tribales En Paises Independientes De La Organizacion Internacional Del Trabajo.*

- recognized the ten "ethnicities" (*etnias*) (i.e., Indigenous Peoples) of Chile (Article 1);
- established Indigenous "communities" and how they can be created (Articles 9–10);
- acknowledged Indigenous lands, also those registered in various statutes during the nineteenth and twentieth centuries (Articles 12–19);
- established a fund for the redistribution of land and water resources to Indigenous Peoples (Articles 20–22) and another fund to finance programs for Indigenous economic development (Articles 23–27);
- recognized Indigenous cultural rights (Articles 28–31);
- introduced intercultural and bilingual education (Articles 32–33);
- recognized some (albeit limited) political participation rights (Articles 34–35);
- created the National Corporation of Indigenous Development (*Corporación Nacional de Desarrollo Indígena*, CONADI), which is a public body charged with, among other things, promoting the national Indigenous policy and agenda, as well as implementing the Indigenous Law (Articles 38–40);
- established the CONADI steering body (National Council, *Consejo Nacional*) formed by seventeen members, of which eight must be elected by Indigenous communities (Articles 41–44); and,
- included a special protection for watercourses of the Indigenous Aymara and Likan Antai/Atacameño peoples, although without infringing on third-party "water rights"" of the same sources (Article 64; see further below).

However, the Indigenous Law contains many flaws, such as:

- referencing "ethnicities" and not Indigenous Peoples, thus ignoring their ancestral history and cultures;
- requiring the registration of Indigenous organizations at CONADI without respecting their own governance, and fueling divisions and conflicts (Instituto de Estudios Indígenas, 2003);
- establishing a very complicated system of land redistribution, resulting in many delays, causing unsuccessful investments, and creating overall discontent (Carruthers & Rodriguez, 2009);
- providing CONADI with an excessive concentration of power, which is easy to manipulate, as reflected in the notorious case of the Ralco-Endesa hydroelectric plant (Nesti, 2002);

- focusing on rural areas without considering its application in urban contexts, where most Indigenous Peoples live (Vergara et al., 2006); and,
- failing to prevent forced relocation and guarantee rights to natural resources (Instituto de Estudios Indígenas, 2003), with the abovementioned exclusion for the Aymara and Likan Antai/Atacameño peoples from water sources.

Importantly, the key problem, as expressed across most of the chapters in this book, is the overall lack of implementation of this law (Becerra Valdivia, 2023; Instituto Nacional de Derechos Humanos, 2013).

The land redistribution provided for in the Indigenous Law requires a procedure that has created a lot of confusion and even a speculative increase in prices for land acquisitions over the years (Stavenhagen, 2003). Most of the lands returned to Indigenous Peoples were marginal (Anaya, 2009), with more than 40 percent of lands returned between 2000 and 2005 barely fertile (Toledo Llancaqueo, 2007). From 2009 until 2018, CONADI acquired only 125,000 hectares through the land fund (Didier et al., 2019). In 2010, CONADI spent only one-third of the allocated $158 million (USD). Two-thirds of that year's budget had to be returned due to incomplete land purchase contracts (Marimán Quemenado, 2011). This caused a decrease in CONADI's budgets in the following years (Aylwin & Silva, 2014; Didier et al., 2019; Marimán Quemenado, 2012).

Other Laws and Norms

The "Law on Marine Coastal Spaces of Native Peoples," also known as "Ley Lafkenche," which refers to those Mapuche peoples of the coast,[10] regulates the establishment of coastal marine space(s) for those Indigenous Peoples who have customarily used them (Article 3). This law has been poorly implemented (Aylwin & Silva, 2014; Kaempfe & Ready, 2011). Currently, Indigenous Peoples, especially women, have been particularly active in claiming the creation of their marine spaces according to this law. However, of more than 100 requests only 13 percent have been completed due to long and bureaucratic procedures (Arce et al., 2023).

Indigenous land rights are also often infringed upon by laws that favor the Chilean resource extraction model. These laws were adopted under

---

[10] Law 20,490 of 2008, *Crea el Espacio Costero Marino de los Pueblos Originarios.*

the dictatorship but were never amended afterwards. They have been widely used, especially after the return of the democracy. These are the Law on Mining Concession (Law 18,097 of 1982, *Ley Orgánica Constitucional sobre Concesiones Mineras*); the Mining Code (*Código de Minería*; Law 18,248 of 1983 and following amendments); and Article 19.24, paragraph 6 of the constitution that recognizes the exclusive, inalienable, and imprescriptible property right of the state to mining resources, as well as state power to grant concessions to private entities for both exploration and exploitation purposes (Yáñez & Molina, 2008) through a presidential decree (Article 8 of the Mining Code), thus giving a high level of discretion to the executive.

In addition, legislation enacted during the dictatorship that is still in force favors foreign investors who have the right to compete on equal footing with national enterprises (Legislative Decree 600 of 1974); foresees a customs and fiscal system that promotes the mining sector in the north (Legislative Decree 889 of 1975); and regulates the fiscal system on economic activities in Chile (Law 18,293 of 1984), which suffers from a huge tax evasion. Furthermore, Chile used to have the lowest tax rate in the whole of Latin America until the adoption of Law 20,026 of 2005 on Mining Royalties, which, however, covers only the royalties of copper mining (Yáñez & Molina, 2008).

National water legislation inherited from Pinochet's dictatorship (Article 19, paragraph 24 of the Chilean constitution) created private "water rights" to water resources, which could be traded (*derecho de aprovechamiento de aguas*) once recorded in the national register, in accordance with Article 6 of the Water Code. This has caused a massive privatization of water resources that heavily impacts Indigenous Peoples, especially in the north. After long debates, Law 20,411 of 2010 excluded the possibility to register new water rights in northern and central Chile, although without infringing on those rights that were already recorded.

Finally, the recent legislation on the Right to Consultation of Indigenous Peoples (Decree 66 of 2013) and the Environmental Impact Assessment System (Decree 40 of 2013) have, ironically, further undermined Indigenous Peoples' voice on economic activities on their lands. There is no obligation to fully comply with a consultation process (Tomaselli, 2019).

Litigation for Land Rights

Indigenous Peoples have used litigation to advance and safeguard their land rights. Four specific cases are analyzed in this section, one in the north of Chile, and three in the south. Each of these demonstrate how national courts have become – in the last decades – *the* avenue to secure land rights, notwithstanding the unfavorable national legislative framework.

The El Morro Case: Northern Chile

In the north, the so-called El Morro case involved the Indigenous Diaguita community of Huasco Altinos (*Comunidad Agrícola Diaguita de los Huasco Altinos*). The community filed an *Amparo* proceeding for the protection of its constitutional rights[11] before the Court of Appeal of Antofagasta against the Atacama regional branch of the National Environmental Commission (*Comisión Nacional del Medio Ambiente*, CONAMA). CONAMA had approved the open-pit gold mining project "El Morro" in March 2011; covering 2,463 hectares, the project area spanned a significant part of Diaguita (registered) territory (Corte de Apelaciones de Antofagasta, 2011). The Court of Appeal found this project adversely impacted the Diaguita's land rights (recognized under Article 64 of the Indigenous Law), as well as their rights to culture and way of life as a consequence of forced relocation (per Article 16 of the C169) (Corte de Apelaciones de Antofagasta, 2011). Their right to consultation in accordance with C169, Articles 6, 7, 15, and 16.2, was also infringed (Corte de Apelaciones de Antofagasta, 2011). The Court declared CONAMA's authorization as null and void, thereby blocking the project and safeguarding Indigenous Diaguita land (Corte de Apelaciones de Antofagasta, 2011). The Chilean Supreme Court upheld this decision in April 2012 (Corte Suprema, 2012).

Despite these rulings, this case did not end here. CONAMA subsequently approved the mining project after these decisions. The Diaguita filed another lawsuit directly with the Supreme Court, which ultimately declared null and void the second of CONAMA's authorizations (Corte Suprema, 2014).[12]

---

[11] In Chile, this type of proceeding is called *Recurso de Protección*; see Article 20 of the Chilean constitution.

[12] The El Morro project was halted for a while. In 2015, it was merged with another mining site (*Relincho*) into a new, larger mining project – that is, the "NuevaUnión" (initially called "Corredor"). This project is owned and managed by Canada's Goldcorp, one of the Canadian companies involved in El Morro, and another Canadian company, Teck Resources. Both companies declared that this project had changed substantially from the previous ones, and that they had taken into consideration the environmental and social impacts. However, the Diaguita, together with other local associations, complained that this project did not respect environmental laws, would impact the Huasco river and the valley, and that the companies started the mining activities without obtaining the

Decisions from Southern Chile

In the south, three cases illustrate the impact of Indigenous strategic litigation. The first involved a traditional healer (*Machi*), Francisca Linconao Huircapan, against a logging company (*Sociedad Palermo Itda*) that had unlawfully extended its activities into Mapuche lands. The Court ruled that in accordance with Articles 13 and 14 of C169, Mapuche were to be protected against invasive logging activities that had seriously damaged sacred Mapuche sites (*menocos*), affecting herb collection and the gathering of traditional medicines (Corte de Apelaciones de Temuco, 2009). The Supreme Court confirmed the judgment of the Court of Appeal of Temuco in November 2009 (Corte Suprema, 2009).

In the second case, Mapuche Huilliche Pepiukelen had their lands adversely affected by the salmon farming activities of the *Los Fiordos SA* company, in the region of Puerto Montt. The Court of Appeal of Puerto Montt eventually condemned the salmon farming company for contaminating a natural lake in Mapuche Huilliche Pepiukelen territory, and ruled that access to water is one of the essential parts of Indigenous land rights in accordance with Article 13, paragraph 2 of C169 (Corte de Apelaciones de Puerto Montt, 2010). The Supreme Court upheld this decision in September 2010 (Corte Suprema, 2010).

The third case, heard by the Court of Appeal of Valdivia, and brought by the Mapuche Lanco-Panguipulli communities against the Region of Los Lagos' CONAMA office, involved the authorization of a dump in a ceremonial area. No consultation was carried out, and because of this, the Court declared the authorization null and void (per Articles 6 and 7 of C169). Importantly, the Court reasoned that Indigenous Peoples' enjoyment of their lands for ceremony was an important component of land rights (Corte de Apelaciones de Valdivia, 2010). The Court also cited Article 25 of the UNDRIP to stress the importance of supporting Indigenous Peoples' spiritual relationships with their territories.[13] The Supreme Court confirmed this lower court decision in January 2011 (Corte Suprema, 2011).

---

environmental impact assessment (Chile Minería, 2021; Equipo OCMAL, 2019; Tapia, 2018). It remains to be seen whether the Diaguita and the other local associations will take legal action again.

[13] Article 25 of the UNDRIP affirms that "Indigenous peoples have the right to maintain and strengthen their distinctive spiritual relationship with their traditionally owned or otherwise occupied and used lands, territories, waters and coastal seas and other resources and to uphold their responsibilities to future generations in this regard."

Conclusions

For Chile's ten recognized Indigenous Peoples, the nation's history has been characterized by dispossession, encroachment, and conflict. Indigenous Laws, like the *Az Mapu*, of the Mapuche, are ignored. There are significant pressures on Indigenous lands. Unique among Latin American countries, there is no constitutional recognition of Indigenous rights in Chile. The recent failed constitutional reforms would have strengthened Indigenous rights in a revitalized constitution. The future for Indigenous land rights, largely entrenched in the problematic Indigenous Law, remains uncertain.

The litigation strategy pursued by Chile's Indigenous Peoples has been quite successful for safeguarding their land rights. The chapter presented four cases brought before the Chilean national courts, where Indigenous land rights – despite an unfavorable legislative framework – have ultimately been protected due to the Indigenous parties' arguments and the courts' use of international standards of Indigenous rights (the C169 and UNDRIP). The courts have embraced a broad conceptualization of Indigenous land rights, recognizing these rights are intimately linked with the right to access water, the rights to culture and way of life, the right to traditional medicine, and the preservation of Indigenous ceremonial areas due to the spiritual relationship that Indigenous Peoples enjoy with their lands. The courts' rulings are becoming more aligned with the Indigenous customary conceptions of land, such as the Mapuche's *Az Mapu*, and the balance it sustains between people and nature.

Chile's national courts have matured on Indigenous rights issues, taking account of international standards and norms. However, the independence of the judiciary is fragile, being heavily influenced at times by the executive. Now, after two referendums that rejected a new and very progressive constitutional text in 2022 and a rather conservative proposal in 2023, it remains unclear how to move beyond Pinochet's unequal constitution from 1980. In the meantime, despite many other implementation challenges, Indigenous Peoples in Chile may at least enjoy some jurisprudential protection of their lands and rights.

References

Anaya, J. (2009). Informe del Relator Especial sobre la situación de los derechos humanos y las libertades fundamentales de los indígenas. Human Rights Council, UN Doc. A/HRC/12/34/Add.6.

Arce, L, Aylwin, J., Didier M., Crisóstomo S., & Vargas K. (2023). *The Indigenous World 2023: Chile*. IWGIA. www.iwgia.org/en/chile/5081-iw-2023-chile.html

Aylwin, J. (1995). *Estudio sobre Tierras Indígenas de la Araucanía: Antecedentes Históricos Legislativos (1850–1920)*. Temuco: Instituto de Estudios Indígenas, Universidad de la Frontera.

(2002). *Tierra y territorio mapuche: un análisis desde una mirada històrico jurídica*. Proyecto Mapu Territorialidad. Temuco: Instituto de Estudios Indígenas, Universidad de la Frontera.

Aylwin, J., & Silva, H. (2014). Chile. In International Work Group for Indigenous Affairs (IWGIA) (eds.), *The Indigenous World 2014* (pp. 203–213). Copenhagen: IWGIA.

Barrera-Hernández, L. (2005). Indigenous Peoples, human rights and natural resource development: Chile's Mapuche Peoples and the right to water. *Annual Survey of International and Comparative Law*, 11(1): 1–28.

Becerra Valdivia, K. (2023). Chile sin derechos colectivos indígenas. Factores institucionales y organizacionales de la cuestión. In R. Cammarata and M. Rosti (eds.), *I popoli indigeni e i loro diritti in America Latina. Dinamiche continentali, scenari nazionali* (pp. 497–516). Milan: University of Milano Press.

Bengoa, J. (2000). *Historia del Pueblo Mapuche Siglo (XIX y XX)*. Santiago de Chile: LOM Ediciones.

Briones, C., & Lepe-Carrión P. (2023). Racialization in Wallmapu: Contemporary perceptions of the 'Mapuche threat.' *Latin American and Caribbean Ethnic Studies*, 19 (1): 7–20.

Carruthers, D., & Rodriguez, P. (2009). Mapuche protest, environmental conflict and social movement linkage in Chile. *Third World Quarterly*, 30(4), 743–760.

Cayuqueo, P. (2008). Muerte de Matías Catrileo Quezada: Estado policial en zona Mapuche. *El Ciudadano*. www.elciudadano.com/pueblos/muerte-de-matias-catrileo-quezada-estado-policial-en-zona-mapuche/03/11/

Chartier, C., Chirif, A., & Tomas, N. (2011). *The human rights of the Rapa Nui people on Easter Island*. Santiago de Chile: Observatorio Ciudadano and International Work Group for Indigenous Affairs (IWGIA Report No.15).

Chile Minería. (2021, October 7). Aseguran que proyecto Minero NuevaUnión comenzó a realizar actividades sin evaluación ambiental. *Chile Mineria*. www.chilemineria.cl/2021/10/aseguran-que-proyecto-minero-nuevaunion-comenzo-a-realizar-actividades-sin-ingresar-a-evaluacion-ambiental

Cloud, L. (2010). *Az Mapu*. El derecho 'invisible' o el derecho de los Mapuche (Chile). *Thule – Rivista italiana di studi americanistici*, 26–29, 501–542.

(2013). La patrimonialización de Te Pito O Te Henua: Historia del Parque Nacional Rapa Nui – Chile. *Revista de Estudios Sociales Comparativos*, 7(1), 18–31.

Contreras Panemal, C. (2003). Los Parlamentos. In C. Contreras Panemal (ed.), *Actas del Primer Congreso Internacional de Historia Mapuche* (pp. 59–61). Siegen: Eigenverlag.

Convención Constitucional. (2022a). Mesa de la Convención. www .chileconvencion.cl/convencionales.

(2022b). Propuesta Constitución Política de Chile 2022. www.chileconvencion .cl/wp-content/uploads/2022/07/Texto-CPR-2022.pdf

Corte de Apelaciones de Antofagasta. (2011). Rol No. 618-2011, 17 February.

Corte de Apelaciones de Puerto Montt. (2010). Rol No.36-2010, 27 July.

Corte de Apelaciones de Temuco. (2009). Rol No. 1773-2008, 16 September.

(2012). Rol No. 838-2012, 20 December.

Corte de Apelaciones de Valdivia. (2010). Rol No. 243-2010, 4 August.

Corte Suprema. (2009). Rol No.7287-2009, 30 November.

(2010). Rol No.5757-2010, 15 September.

(2011). Rol No. 6062/2011, 4 January.

(2012). Rol No. 2211-2012, 27 April.

(2014). Rol No. 11, 299-2014, 7 October.

COTAM-Comisión de Trabajo Autónoma Mapuche. (2003). Informe de la Comisión Histórica y Nuevo Trato, Chile.

de Avila Martel, A. (1973). *Régimen jurídico de la guerra de Arauco*. III Congreso del Instituto Internacional de Historia del Derecho Indiano. Madrid: Instituto Internacional de Estudios Jurídicos, Madrid.

Didier, M., Aywin, J., Silva, H., & Guerra, F. (2019). Chile. In International Work Group for Indigenous Affairs (IWGIA) (eds.), *The Indigenous World 2019* (pp. 143–152). Copenhagen: IWGIA.

El Ciudadano. (2020). Guía El Ciudadano para Elección de Constituyentes – Escaños Reservados para Pueblos Originarios. https://drive.google.com/file/ d/1N3kPmPLeV-gUus4ave3kD4uQNSms5tr_/view

Equipo OCMAL-Observatorio de Conflictos Mineros de América Latina. (2015). *Conflictos Mineros en América Latina: Extracción, Saqueo y Agresión. Estado de situación en 2014.* www.ocmal.org/wp-content/uploads/2017/03/ Conflictos-Mineros-en-America-Latina-2014-OCMAL.pdf

(2019). *Conflicto Minero: Comunidades del Valle del Huasco se oponen a Minera Nueva Unión.* https://mapa.conflictosmineros.net/ocmal_db-v2/con flicto/view/988

(2023). Conflictos Mineros en América Latina. https://mapa.conflictosmineros .net/ocmal_db-v2

Gudermann, H. (2003). Las poblaciones indígenas andinas de Chile y la experi- encia de la ciudadanía. In H. Gudermann, R. Foester, & J. I. Vergara (eds.), *Mapuches y Aymaras: El debate entorno al Reconocimiento y los Derechos Colectivos* (pp. 19–104). Santiago de Chile: RIL Editores.

Guevara, T. (1925). *Chile prehispanico*. Santiago de Chile: Universidad de Chile.

Instituto de Estudios Indígenas. (2003). *Los derechos de los pueblos indígenas en Chile: Informe del Programa de Derechos Indígenas.* Santiago de Chile: LOM Ediciones.

Instituto Nacional de Derechos Humanos. (2013). *Situación de los Derechos Humanos en Chile. Informe 2013.* Santiago de Chile: Instituto Nacional de Derechos Humanos.

Instituto Nacional de Estadísticas Chile. (2018). Síntesis de resultados Censo 2017. www.censo2017.cl

Inter-American Commission on Human Rights. (2011). Annual Report of the Inter-American Commission on Human Rights 2011, Chapter III C. Petitions and cases before the Inter-American Commission on Human Rights. Precautionary measure (PM) No. 321/10, Rapa Nui Indigenous People, Chile.

Kaempfe, I., & Ready, G. (2011). Comentarios a la Ley N° 20.249, que crea los ECMPO y su Relación con el Convenio N° 169 de la OIT. *Ideas para-Chile*, 1(9), 1–33.

Marimán Quemenado, P. (2011). Chile. In International Work Group for Indigenous Affairs (IWGIA) (eds.), *The Indigenous World 2011* (pp. 211–219). Copenhagen: IWGIA.

 (2012). Chile. In International Work Group for Indigenous Affairs (IWGIA) (Eds.), *The Indigenous World 2012* (pp. 204–213). Copenhagen: IWGIA.

Ministerio de Desarrollo Social. (2022). Informe de Desarrollo Social 2022. www.desarrollosocialyfamilia.gob.cl/storage/docs/ids/Informe-desarrollo-social-2022.pdf

Molina, R. (2007). Identidad Diaguita, derechos indígenas y proyectos mineros en el Husaco Alto. In N. Yáñez & J. Aylwin (eds.), *El gobierno de Lagos, los pueblos indígenas y el "nuevo trato": Las paradojas de la democracia chilena.* Santiago de Chile: LOM Ediciones.

 (2013). Artículo 5. Los collas: Identidad y relaciones interculturales en Atacama. In J. Durston (ed.), *Pueblos originarios y sociedad nacional en Chile: La interculturalidad en las prácticas sociales* (pp. 99–113). Santiago de Chile: Programa de las Naciones Unidas para el Desarrollo.

Nesti, L. (2002). The Mapuche-Pehuenche and the Ralco Dam on the Bíobío River: The challenge of protecting Indigenous land rights. *International Journal on Minority and Group Rights*, 9(1), 1–40.

Newsroom Infobae. (2021). Chile decreta su primer Día Nacional de los Pueblos Indígenas. www.infobae.com/america/agencias/2021/06/17/chile-decreta-su-primer-dia-nacional-de-los-pueblos-indigenas

Paillan, E. (2009, Aug. 12). Jaime Facundo Mendoza Collio, de 24 años, es mapuche asesinado por carabineros. *El Ciudadano.* www.elciudadano.com/justicia/mapuche-asesinado-por-carabineros-seria-jaime-facundo-mendoza-collio-de-24-anos/08/12

Prieto, M. (2015). Privatizing water in the Chilean Andes: The case of Las Vegas de Chiu-Chiu, Mountain Research and Development. *Mountain Research and Development*, 35(3), 220–229.

Proceso Constitucional. (2023a). Consejo Constitucional. www.procesoconstitucional.cl/consejo-constitucional

(2023b). Propuesta Constitución Política de la República de Chile. www.procesoconstitucional.cl/wp-content/uploads/2023/11/Propuesta-Nueva-Constitucion.pdf

Rochna Ramirez, S. (1996). *La Propriedad de la Tierra en la Isla de Pascua.* Santiago de Chile: CONADI & AECID.

Rosti, M. (2008). Reparations for Indigenous Peoples in two selected Latin American countries. In F. Lenzerini (ed.), *Reparations for Indigenous Peoples: International and comparative perspectives* (pp. 345–362). Oxford: Oxford University Press.

Sanhueza, A. M. (2023, Dec. 18). Así es la Constitución que seguirá vigente en Chile y que se intent cambiar dos veces en cuatro años. *El País.* https://elpais.com/chile/2023-12-17/asi-es-la-constitucion-que-seguira-vigente-en-chile-y-que-se-intento-cambiar-dos-veces-en-cuatro-anos.html

Silva Neriz, H. (2013). Chile. In International Work Group for Indigenous Affairs (eds.), *The Indigenous World 2013* (pp. 188–196). Copenhagen: IWGIA.

Soluri, J. (2011). Chile's Blue Revolution, commodity diseases, and the problem of sustainability. *Latin America Research Review*, 46(1), 55–81.

Stavenhagen, R. (2003). Report of the Special Rapporteur on the situation of human rights and fundamental freedoms of indigenous people, submitted in accordance with Commission resolution 2003/56. Addendum, Mission to Chile. Commission of Human Rights, sixtieth session, UN Doc. E/CN.4/2004/80/Add.3, 17 November.

Tapia, D. (2018, Nov. 26). ¿En qué está el proyecto NuevaUnión? *Revista Nueva Minería y Energía.* www.nuevamineria.com/revista/en-que-esta-el-proyecto-nuevaunion

Toledo Llancaqueo, V. (2006). *Pueblo Mapuche. Derechos Colectivos y Territorios: Desafíos para la Sustentabilidad Democratica.* Programa Chile Sustentable. Santiago de Chile: LOM Ediciones.

(2007, October 28). Presupuesto del Sector Público y Políticas Indígenas. Chile 1994–2008. *Documentos de Politicas Públicas y Derechos Indígenas – Informe Nº 36.* Santiago de Chile.

Tomaselli, A. (2012). Natural resources claims, land conflicts and self-empowerment of indigenous movements in the Cono Sur: The case of the Mapuche People in Chile. *International Journal of Minority and Group Rights*, 19(2), 153–174.

(2016). *Indigenous Peoples and their right to political participation. International law standards and their application in Latin America.* Baden-Baden: Nomos.

(2019). Processes and failures of prior consultations with Indigenous Peoples in Chile. In C. Wright and A. Tomaselli (eds.), *The prior consultation of*

Indigenous Peoples in Latin America: Inside the implementation gap (pp.119–132). New York: Routledge.

Trincado Vera, P., & Muñoz Sims, A. (2020, January 23). Violencia policial contra el pueblo mapuche: Aún queda mucho por avanzar. Amnesty International, Santiago, Chile. https://amnistia.cl/noticia/violencia-policial-contra-el-pueblo-mapuche-aun-queda-mucho-por-avanzar

Velásquez Loaiza, M. (2022, September 5). Las razones detrás del rechazo a la nueva constitución de Chile y lo que sigue. *CNN Español*. https://cnnespanol .cnn.com/2022/09/05/razones-rechazo-no-plebiscito-nueva-constitucion-chile-lo-que-sigue-orix/#0

Vergara, J. I., Gundermann, H., & Foerster, R. (2006). Legalidad y legitimidad: Ley indígena, Estado chileno y pueblos originarios (1989–2004). *Estudios Sociológicos*, 71(24), 331–361.

Yañez, N., & Molina, R. (2008). *La gran minería y los derechos indígenas en el norte de Chile*. Santiago de Chile: LOM Ediciones.

PART II

Australia, Canada, and New Zealand

The common thread connecting Australia, Canada, and New Zealand is what Kirsty Gover (2015) described as the "Western settler-state view," where the focus of settler governments is "embedding ... indigenous identities and jurisdictions in [their] constitutional orders" (p. 346). Professor Gover also observed that across these countries there is a "persistent lack of indigenous consent to settler governance ... one that undermines the liberal premises of a state's legitimacy," hence these countries have sought to resolve this legitimacy deficit via the "restoration of indigenous property and governance authority ... to negotiate indigenous consent," such as through the "redistribution of public goods" like land (p. 346). However, the transfer of lands has been slow, and where this occurs, is typically only a fraction of the lands claimed.

6

Aboriginal Land Rights in Australia

Neither National nor Uniform

FRANCIS MARKHAM AND HEIDI NORMAN

Introduction

Aboriginal Land Rights: A National Story?

After a near complete dispossession, since 1966 a collective land titling process has been underway across Australia, with significant areas returned to Indigenous Peoples. Today, Indigenous Peoples have recognized land interests to over more than half the Australian continent – nearly four million square kilometers, with more under claim. Estimates suggest that Indigenous Peoples hold exclusive possession of native title and fee simple to around 26 percent of Australia's landmass. When non-exclusive native title is included, that number rises to 54 percent of the country and includes national parks, conservation areas, and vast expanses of the continent. However, Aboriginal land restitution,[1] when considered nationally, is uneven and fragmented, with little consistency in the rights that are afforded, or in the amount of land returned.

This spatial heterogeneity is sometimes elided in a rush to celebrate land restitution. For example, in the National Agreement on Closing the Gap, all Australian Governments and the Coalition of Peak Aboriginal and Torres Strait Islander Organisations agreed to a target increasing the area of "Australia's land mass subject to Aboriginal and Torres Strait Islander people's legal rights or interests" by 15 percent (Coalition of Aboriginal and Torres Strait Islander Peak Organisations and Australian Governments, 2020). The notion of "legal rights and interests" is not

---

[1] We use the term "land restitution" to cover both the *granting* of land to Indigenous Peoples by governments through various land rights schemes and the *recognition by the state* of native title, a form of title based on the laws and customs of Indigenous Peoples that predates colonization and has been continued despite colonization.

further specified in the agreement, and in practice will likely be met by the recognition of limited, non-exclusive rights of access and use to traditional owners over pastoral leases. Other accounts and spatial mapping of land restitution have tended to gloss over the differences among land rights regimes. For example, Altman and Markham (2015), in mapping Indigenous landholdings in 2013, categorized land into three groups: exclusive possession native title, non-exclusive possession native title, and a third catchall category termed "land rights lands and reserves." While they noted the heterogeneity among land rights regimes (and the content of native title determinations), this is bracketed in favor of an abstracting move that obscures jurisdictional differences.

This chapter details the fragmented nature of the last sixty years of Aboriginal land rights across Australia and offers an account as to how and why this came about. Standard accounts of the spatial distribution of land rights stress "remoteness" – or the closeness of non-Indigenous settlement, itself a function of colonization history and the value of the land to the settler economy – as the primary determinant of the presence or absence of land restitution (e.g., Jackson, 2017; Young, 1992). Other accounts focus on the agency of Indigenous activists and their networks of allies as determinative of land restitution outcomes in Australia (e.g., Foley & Anderson, 2006). In this chapter, we do not aim to dispute these inarguable propositions. Rather, we aim to draw attention to a further factor that has influenced the pattern of Indigenous rights and interests in land restitution across Australia: the federal dimension in Indigenous public policymaking.

Across the federation of states and territories that make up the Australian Commonwealth, the legislative responses to enduring Indigenous land demands have taken many different forms. What sits underneath the post-1966 land restitution are varied federal and state-based laws, and from 1992, recognition of native title rights and interests by the High Court, and their subsequent codification and restriction by the Commonwealth Government. Any account of Indigenous land rights therefore reflects these distinct and overlapping bases for land recognition. Multiple arrangements have developed over time in different jurisdictions that variously recognize Indigenous interests and rights in their land, and sometimes offer political recognition and cultural heritage protection. Accordingly, the "national story" of the post-1966 Indigenous land titling is inevitably a federal one, based not only on the idiosyncratic nature of Indigenous land rights campaigns in each state and the particularities of state government responses, but also on the disposition of various

Commonwealth Governments to centralism in public policy. Indeed, we argue that the story of land rights is at least in part a story of the shifting place of Indigenous public policy within the federal politics of Australia. The patchwork of land returns that we now see and will explore later in this chapter results from the intersection of not just Indigenous-settler politics, but also intergovernmental politics within the federation and the tendency of Labor governments and the High Court toward centralism in the federation of Australia (Galligan, 1987).

Land Rights as State and Territory Business, 1960s–1972

In the 1960s, Aboriginal activism thrust the issue of Aboriginal land rights onto the national political agenda, paralleling and engaging with global movements for decolonization and land reform, as well as the civil rights movement in the United States (Cooms, 2012; Piccini, 2019). At that time, government policy toward Indigenous Peoples in Australia was largely left to the states. It was only in the territories where the Commonwealth maintained a role in Indigenous policy and administration matters, especially in the Northern Territory, where the Australian Government acted as a regional government (Sanders, 2013).

Indigenous land rights in the 1960s was seen as a matter for the states. In some parts of the country, Indigenous Peoples lived on (and were often confined to) specifically designated land "reserved" by state and territory governments for Indigenous use. But reserves existed only so long as it pleased settler governments: they could be and were often revoked by state governments, a denial of land that often provided the spark that ignited Aboriginal land rights movements. It was perhaps unsurprising then that the first legislative reforms in response to calls for Aboriginal land rights came from the states, and dealt with reserves, specifically in South Australia and Victoria.

Accordingly, the first statutory Aboriginal land rights scheme in Australia was introduced in 1966 by the newly elected South Australian Labor Government. Speaking on the passage of the legislation, Don Dunstan – a former non-Indigenous advocate for Aboriginal rights and newly appointed Minister of Aboriginal Affairs – acknowledged the harm and alienation Aboriginal peoples experienced due to colonial dispossession (Rowse, 2012). The *Aboriginal Land Trust Act* 1966 was aimed at reparative objectives, creating an organization controlled by Aboriginal peoples, tasked with holding and managing former Aboriginal reserves for the benefit of Aboriginal peoples.

However, Victoria became the first state to grant freehold title to communities themselves, allowing them to own their land outright. In Victoria, the revocation of Aboriginal reserves had long been a cause for Aboriginal organizing and activism (Broome, 2005; Moore, 1981), with almost all of the 1,000 square kilometers of lands reserved for Aboriginal purposes revoked over the century prior to 1960. By 1960, only two Aboriginal reserves remained, at Lake Tyers and Framlingham, both home to small communities. The long-serving Bolte Liberal government had planned to revoke these final reserves over the course of the decade. However, the Black Power movement emerging in Victoria in 1960s under the auspices of the Aborigines' Advancement League was able to successfully fight off these proposals. In 1970, the Bolte government passed idiosyncratic legislation – the *Aboriginal Lands Act* 1970 – to grant these two small parcels of land in a freehold title to these communities, in two separate trusts.

These early moves toward distinctive state responses to land rights coincided with a major shift in federal arrangements for Indigenous public policy that commenced after the 1967 Referendum. At the start of the 1960s, the six states were responsible for Indigenous policy within their borders, with the Commonwealth having played an equivalent role in the Northern Territory since 1911. Dissatisfaction with this federal allocation of responsibility had been developing throughout the 1920s and 1930s, with Aboriginal activists campaigning for rights and white "humanitarians" pushing for a federal takeover of Indigenous affairs (Davis & Williams, 2021; Holland, 2019). It ultimately took two attempts to see the constitution changed to this end, first as part of a failed overhaul of Commonwealth-state relations in 1944 (Fox, 2008) and ultimately as part of a successful constitutional alteration referendum in 1967 (Davis & Williams, 2021).

By the early 1970s, no land reform had been attempted by the Commonwealth, despite the expectations raised by the 1967 Referendum, and it seemed that the Coalition government had no intention of using its new constitutional rights or acting on the mandate of the referendum to do so. Events in the Northern Territory forced the hands of the Coalition government in its dying days. In 1971, a legal challenge by the Yirrkala people regarding the excision of their reserved land for a government-approved bauxite mine, against the asserted interests of the Yolngu people, was unsuccessful (see Nikolakis, Chapter 1, this book). Pressure mounted on the government for a statutory response to the failure of the legal system to provide for land rights. But on Australia Day in 1972, Prime Minister McMahon's long-awaited announcement of the Coalition government's new land rights policy was a bitter disappointment for campaigners. Not only did the McMahon government oppose the Yirrkala petition to stop this excision, but it also announced that it would not legislate Aboriginal land rights in the Northern Territory. The government instead supported leasing a limited amount of land, subject to application and ministerial approval. The government also continued some of the key features of authoritarian welfare regime and left the Northern Territory's Aboriginal Affairs administration unchallenged (Dexter, 2015). This was despite significant momentum for change and some evident shift in the prevailing assimilation policy in southeastern Australia.

The Australian Labor Party (ALP), propelled by the "Yirrkala problem" in Arnhem Land and the Gurindji's walk-off from Wave Hill, had begun developing a position on Aboriginal land rights in 1963. Their Aboriginal Affairs Committee recommended what became a forerunner of the land rights response and the land purchase fund we write more about below. While these changes were developing, including ALP conversations with the Commonwealth's Council for Aboriginal Affairs (CAA), the three-member group appointed immediately after the 1967 Referendum to advise the Commonwealth's new policy role, the conservative Liberal and National Country party government maintained an official policy of assimilation. Aboriginal land rights were nowhere on Coalition government's agenda (Norman, 2015).

Following Prime Minister McMahon's 1972 Australia Day announcement of a much-promised new direction in Aboriginal Affairs, a group of young Aboriginal men, then living in and around Redfern, were compelled to drive overnight to Canberra. There in protest, they erected beach umbrellas and later tents and camped on the manicured lawns opposite the Australian Parliament, deploying a not unfamiliar form of Aboriginal housing: the "Tent Embassy" dramatically registered the effects of being made alien in one's own country and announced a seismic shift in Aboriginal and Australian politics. Optimism for change following a referendum in 1967 – cast in terms of equal rights but in fact about giving the Commonwealth the power to make laws for Indigenous Peoples – was already characterized as the stuff of "fools and dreamers" (Walker, 1969). Demands for Aboriginal rights from the far north to the southern island grew louder in response to the unfulfilled promise of

1967, and attracted a growing band of supporters in new networks of solidarity.

Although Prime Minister McMahon's unsatisfying announcement related specifically to the Northern Territory, it mobilized Kooris and Murris in Redfern, Sydney, and catalyzed a national protest movement. Many thousands more over the coming months joined a growing appreciation of Aboriginal land rights, with unique local claims shaped by a history of colonialism and dispossession that began to conceptualize land rights variously as property, rights, and lore, and as central to the ability to exercise self-determination. The Tent Embassy protest first propelled the emergence of a shared land rights claim across very different political geographies and sparked a growing awareness among Australians of the demand for land rights.

Aboriginal peoples across tropical northern Australia encountered the invasion of their lands more than one hundred years later than in the southeast, and in different circumstances that saw a fragile co-existence over territory granted as pastoral leases. In the south, from the 1960s onwards, Aboriginal reserve land was under threat of revocation as "inclusion" – a version of assimilation was pursued that included the promise of town housing for Indigenous Peoples. In New South Wales (NSW) and elsewhere, the security of reserve lands, alongside the protection of sacred sites, was a leading concern for political organizing by Indigenous Peoples (Goodall, 2008). Placards from the Tent Embassy revealed an evident shift in the scope of land demands over the course of the few months between January 1972 and mid-1972. Over the course of several months, the demands for land rights connected over a much larger space and were imbued with claims of spiritual attachment captured by the phrase "Ningla-Ana," we are "Hungry for our Land" (Cook & Goodall, 2013; Norman, 2015). The new national politics eschewed the assimilation discourse that inhered in the 1967 referendum citizenship campaign in favor of cultural identity connected to land.

McMahon's Liberal government met the new politics with violent disavowal. The police were repeatedly ordered to dismantle the Tent Embassy over the months that followed. Images of excessive numbers of police marching in formation across the front of the Parliament House, careering ambulances and police wagons, followed by a knockdown and drag-out mayhem, reached national audiences via the relatively new family ritual of viewing the evening news on television. Not a single lease promised by McMahon in his Australia Day address was delivered before the election.

Centralism Interrupted, 1972–1975

The Opposition Labor Party had long been more receptive to Aboriginal demands. Visiting the Tent Embassy, Gough Whitlam, the Leader of the Opposition, showed support for and comprehension of the new politics. At the November 1972 Labor Party policy launch, Whitlam announced his program to an already electrified Blacktown civic center audience. "A rightful place in this nation" was both Whitlam's challenge and promise to a nation coming to terms with its colonial past, projecting its independent future, and reckoning with ancient peoples who not only refused to disappear but were contesting the legitimacy of government and the interests of capital accumulation.

The Whitlam Labor Opposition's promises in Blacktown were radical and progressive – but they also represented a watering down of the national ambition of the Australian Labor Party platform. No doubt capitalizing on the national attention focused on the Northern Territory – not least by Aboriginal activists at the Tent Embassy – Whitlam promised that a system of land rights would be established in the Northern Territory should a Labor government be elected. Specifically, Whitlam promised legislation that would vest in Aboriginal communities in land "for aboriginal use and benefit a system of aboriginal tenure based on the traditional rights of clans and other tribal groups" (Whitlam, 1972, p. 30). In doing so, Whitlam narrowed the national ambition of the Labor Party platform of 1971 and its promise of inalienable title and full mineral rights for all "Aboriginal communities that demonstrate a strong tribal structure" (Young, 1971, p. 31). Beyond the Commonwealth's jurisdiction in the Northern Territory, Whitlam promised much less, the creation of an Aboriginal Land Fund, to acquire lands for "... significant continuing aboriginal communities" (Whitlam, 1972).

Eleven days after Whitlam was elected as prime minister in December 1972, a commission of inquiry, known as the Woodward Commission, was announced to recommend ways to achieve Aboriginal land rights. The Whitlam government announced that it would legislate land rights first in the Northern Territory, where the Commonwealth was responsible for legislation and public administration prior to self-government in 1978. The Commonwealth was leading the way, not by centralist coercion but by example.

This contrasted with the Whitlam government's approach to other questions of Indigenous public policy. There it was enacting a suite of reforms – including the establishment of the National Aboriginal Consultative Committee (NACC), the creation of a mechanism for Aboriginal organizations to form and pursue community social and eco-nomic aspirations, the creation of a separate department for Aboriginal Affairs, and the enactment of a legislative prohibition on racial discrimin-ation – that amounted to an unprecedented Commonwealth intervention into Indigenous policy, previously a state domain (Bennett, 1988; Sanders, 2013). In quick time, the government, with the CAA, made significant changes in Aboriginal Affairs policy that had proven impossible under the previous government, comprised as it was of hostile bureaucrats and ministers who stubbornly refused to depart from assimilationism. That policy was swiftly abandoned in favor of so-called "self-determination." The old Ministry for the Interior – that bastion of assimilation and authoritarian welfare, which held sway in the previous Cabinet – was abolished. Barrie Dexter from the CAA was installed as head of the new Department of Aboriginal Affairs, and Gordon Bryant appointed as the responsible minister. By 1975, the election promise of a legislative prohib-ition for discrimination on the grounds of race had been implemented through the enactment of the *Racial Discrimination Act* 1975. This Commonwealth leadership in Indigenous policy was part of Whitlam's centralist approach to the question of federalism, described in his 1972 elec-tion speech as "a national endeavour to expand and equalise opportunities for all our people" (Whitlam, 1972, p. 32).

In July 1974, the Whitlam Cabinet accepted most of the recommenda-tions of the two reports produced by the Woodward Commission on land rights and issued drafting instructions for legislation affecting Aboriginal land claims in the Northern Territory. The first report (April 1973) had recommended the federal government set up a Central Land Council and a Northern Land Council in the Northern Territory, each to represent the distinct central and northern parts of the jurisdiction. The second report drew on submissions provided by the new land councils and provided a "blueprint" for an Aboriginal land rights regime in the Northern Territory. Among other things, the report rec-ommended that:

• Reserve lands be returned to Aboriginal corporations (known as Land Trusts) in fee simple through an inalienable and/or perpetual form of land title.
• Regional Land Councils be established to support Land Trusts and to advance the interests of traditional owners.

- A process be established to allow Regional Land Councils to make claims based on traditional ties to "vacant" Crown lands.
- Land be acquired and returned to Aboriginal peoples by an Aboriginal Land Commission (with no cash compensation to be paid for Aboriginal peoples whose traditional lands cannot be returned).
- Development on Aboriginal land to take place only with the consent of the relevant Land Trust.
- Entry to Aboriginal land by settlers be regulated by a permit system.
- Minerals remain the property of the Crown, but traditional owners have the power to prevent mineral exploration on their lands.
- A royalty equivalent payment of 2.5 to 3.75 percent of the selling price of the mineral, less costs of treatment and transport, be paid to Aboriginal peoples through the Regional Land Councils.

Woodward's second report essentially provided a roadmap for the implementation of Whitlam's agenda promised in 1972 but recommended that full mineral rights remain with the Crown rather than Aboriginal landowners. While Woodward's second report was welcomed in some circles, the newly formed NACC was disappointed by the narrow geographical scope of the government's ambition. At its May 1974 meeting, the NACC resolved to reject Woodward's second report and called for the government to establish Commissions for Land Rights in the six states, as well as offer cash compensation for those whose traditional lands could not be redeemed (Hiatt et al., 1976).

The Whitlam government's land rights response was not entirely focused on the Northern Territory. By December 1974, Woodward's recommendation regarding the purchase of pastoral leases was already on the way to implementation, delivering on a promise in Whitlam's 1972 Blacktown speech. Enacting the *Aboriginal Land Fund Act* 1974, the Commonwealth created a statutory authority with a budget of $5 million for ten years to purchase property on the market in the states and territories, which could then be held on behalf of traditional owners or Aboriginal groups with long-standing ties to the land (Palmer, 1988). Significantly, the Aboriginal Land Fund Commission had a national focus and responsibility that went beyond the Northern Territory.

Whitlam had expressed an intention to extend his centralist approach to national Aboriginal land rights legislation, but when his government was dismissed in 1975, the Aboriginal Land Rights Bill was yet to be passed by the Senate. While the *Aboriginal Land Rights (Northern Territory) Act* 1976, which implemented most of Woodward's recommendations, was eventually passed in a somewhat watered-down form by the Fraser coalition government, the legislation was limited to the Northern Territory.

Fraser's "New Federalism" and Commonwealth Deference to the States, 1976–1983

Two different approaches to the federal question in land rights policy were to play out over the next two decades. While Fraser's coalition government came to power with a policy of passing the *Aboriginal Land Rights (Northern Territory) Act* 1976 more or less in line with Woodward's recommendations,[2] beyond that, the land rights agenda would be left to the states. A coercive strategy of compulsory acquisition by the Commonwealth was not contemplated. Instead, Fraser's approach to Commonwealth–state relations, known as "New Federalism," empha-sized negotiation as the preferred method for managing inter-governmental relations. He deliberately avoided antagonism or confron-tation with the states (Weller, 1989). The Coalition's position was that outside the Northern Territory, mining and development should con-tinue on existing Indigenous reserves "but under strict governmental control which would reflect the needs and views of the aboriginal people" with the "rights of the Aboriginal people where the land surface and use are concerned . . . fully protected" (Liberal Party of Australia & National Country Party of Australia, 1976, p. 53). The main active role foreseen by Fraser for the Commonwealth outside the Northern Territory was through funding the acquisitions of the Aboriginal Land Fund (Liberal Party of Australia & National Country Party of Australia, 1976), a role that was drastically curtailed when funding to the ALFC was dramatically frozen by Fraser in his austere first budget.[3]

In contrast, the Labor Party's approach to federalism was for uniform-ity and a centralized role for the Commonwealth in coercing potentially

---

[2] The primary distinction between the land rights legislation proposed by Labor in 1975 and the one enacted by the Fraser government in 1976, as stipulated in the *Aboriginal Land Rights Act* (NT) 1976, is that the latter did not mandate Aboriginal consent for mining activities on petroleum leases filed before November 1976 or within the Ranger uranium region.

[3] Expenditure by the Aboriginal Land Fund Commission was reportedly $2.02 million in 1975–76, and then cut to zero in 1976–77 by the incoming Fraser government, before being restored to sums of $0.75 million in 1977–78, and $0.54 million in 1978–79 (West, 1980, p. 61).

intransigent states. Whitlam, running as Labor Leader of the Opposition in 1977, maintained his promise to pursue land rights "in the states" even against the wishes of state Premiers, in order to discharge the responsibility given to the Commonwealth during the 1967 Referendum (Whitlam, 1977). The ALP's platform from 1977 professed that "the principles and recommendations of the Aboriginal Land Rights Commission (Woodward Report) should form a pattern for legislation. An Australian Labor Party government will … seek the co-operation of State Parliaments to adopt similar legislation and, only where the States fail to co-operate, would an Australian Labor Government introduce legislation to implement those principles and recommendations" (Combe, 1977, p. 113).

The limits of the Fraser government's New Federalist strategy of negotiation rather than coercion quickly became apparent over his eight years in power. Perhaps unsurprisingly, different states took radically different trajectories in their approaches to Aboriginal land rights, some-times shifting in their approaches over time. As we will see, intransigent state administrations had ample opportunity to obstruct the land rights agenda.

In South Australia, the pioneer for land rights nationally, successive Labor and Liberal governments proved willing and able to implement much of the Woodward vision. Most of the Aboriginal reserve land in the state had not been returned under the *Aboriginal Lands Trust Act* 1966 (Tedmanson, 2016). In particular, the North West Aboriginal Reserve lands traditionally belonging to Pitjantjatjara, Yankunytatjara, and Ngaanyatjara peoples remained under settler control. Inspired by devel-opments across the border in the Northern Territory, in 1976 Anangu formed the Pitjantjatjara Council to campaign for land rights. The Pitjantjatjara Council's demands were receptively heard by Don Dunstan, now the state Premier. The Pitjantjatjara Land Rights Bill, introduced in 1978, would provide for "a form of tenure consistent with that now being proposed in the Northern Territory as a result of Commonwealth initiatives" (Tedmanson, 2016). After the sudden resig-nation of Premier Dunstan, and a change of government, an amended Bill was passed that was largely unchanged, aside from the lessening of Anangu control of mineral exploration. The *Maralinga Tjarutja Land Rights Act* 1984 established a similar regime for lands in the southwest of the state, resulting from another Aboriginal campaign (Hiskey, 2021). However, no scheme was put in place for Aboriginal claims to Crown land outside of bounds of the areas outlined in the three South Australian acts.

NSW took a different path in its legislation of statutory land rights during this period, arguably demonstrating the potential of Fraser's hands-off approach to federalism to deliver statutory land rights tailored to the specific needs of different jurisdictions. Activism for land rights in NSW had been long in the making, but blossomed with the establishment of the Tent Embassy by Kooris and Murris in Canberra and as resistance grew to the revocation of Aboriginal reserves in NSW (Norman, 2015). Partly in response to pressure from the embryonic NSW Aboriginal Land Council, and partly in response to the party's national policy, the NSW Labor Party – in government since 1976 – adopted a land rights policy at its 1978 state conference. First proposed through an inquiry report in 1980, and subsequently watered down through green papers and cabinet processes, the once-radical proposal for land rights in NSW was met with significant resistance from Aboriginal activists in the state.

When finally enacted, the *Aboriginal Land Rights Act* 1983 (NSW) was an innovative departure from the Woodward model, adapted to the very different circumstances facing Aboriginal peoples in NSW. It established a tiered structure of statutory local, regional, and state-level land councils. As recommended by the Woodward Report, remaining reserves were transferred to the relevant land councils, and a claims process was established to allow certain "claimable" Crown lands to transfer to land councils, mostly in the form of freehold title.[4] A key point of difference with the Woodward model was the reparative approach adopted in NSW. The approach to land repossession was compensation for lost land and colonial dispossession, considering both pre-colonial and historically formed networks among Aboriginal peoples. Membership in Local Aboriginal Land Councils (LALCs) is open to all Aboriginal and Torres Strait Islander peoples, based on current residence or cultural connection. Further, the Act provided for a measure of financial redistribution, with a percentage of land tax revenue in NSW transferred to an Aboriginal-controlled capital fund for a period of fifteen years. The Act also provided a strong form of mineral rights, with the rights to most minerals vested in land councils and LALCs generally being able to withhold consent for mining on their land. However, the realization of

---

[4] Except in the Western Lands Division, where perpetual leases may be granted instead of freehold title. Since 1990, land granted or claimed under the Act can be alienated under certain conditions.

these rights has been frustrating in practice, with less than 1 percent of land in the state returned under the Act.

Whereas Labor Governments in South Australia and NSW took the Woodward model of land rights forward, similar ambitions were frustrated in Victoria. After John Cain led the Labor Party to its first election victory in 27 years without an upper house majority, it was sometimes remarked that Labor was "in government, but not in power" (Coghill, 1997). In March 1983, the Victorian government, led by John Cain's ALP administration, introduced the Aboriginal Land Claims Bill, which aimed to provide a process for the claiming of various types of public land by Aboriginal groups based on their historical association with the land, traditional rights and needs, or as compensation for dispossession (Victorian Government, 1983). Once a claim was approved, the land would be granted in freehold title, subject to certain conditions such as restrictions on the sale and transfer of the granted land and specific guidelines for mining activities. However, the Bill faced controversy regarding compensation for lost land and, under pressure from the Aboriginal community, its passage was delayed pending a report from an Aboriginal Task Force. Ultimately, the Cain government was unable to secure enough support in the upper house to pass the 1983 Aboriginal Land Claims Bill (Broome, 2005). Instead, five more highly specific acts were passed to transfer particular parcels of land to Aboriginal peoples. At one point, the Victorian Labor government circumvented the upper house entirely, enlisting the Commonwealth to pass the *Aboriginal Land (Lake Condah and Framlingham Forest) Act* 1987 (Commonwealth), which returned two further specific parcels of former reserve land to Aboriginal peoples. However, a systematic land claims process was not reconsidered in Victoria for several decades to come.

It was in Western Australia and Queensland, however, that the limitations of Fraser's decision to leave land rights to the states became most apparent. In Queensland, the state government had long exercised unfettered control over reserves and oppressive supervision of their Aboriginal residents. In the 1950s, the discovery of bauxite on the Weipa reserve saw the Queensland Government all but revoke the 5,870-square kilometer reserve in favor of a mining company. By 1962, the remainder of the reserve was revoked to grant a mining lease over the remainder of the reserve close to Mapoon, with protesting Aboriginal residents forcibly relocated by the Queensland police, who burnt their houses to prevent their return (Anderson, 1981). With land rights coming on to the agenda nationally, the Country Party government led by Joh Bjelke-Petersen had, in September 1972, decided to oppose "proposals to acquire large areas of additional freehold or leasehold land for development by Aborigines" (Palmer, 1988, p. 67). Accordingly, the Queensland government actively sabotaged the purchase of leasehold properties by the Commonwealth's Aboriginal Land Fund Commission. In particular, it attempted to block the transfer of the Archer River and Glenore pastoral leases to Aboriginal traditional owners, first by failing to approve their transfer, and then, in the case of Archer River, by resuming the land as a national park. The resulting public confrontation between the Bjelke-Petersen and Fraser governments was highly embarrassing for Ian Viner, the minister of Aboriginal Affairs, and had two important consequences. First, Viner, frustrated by the independence of the Aboriginal Land Fund Commission, which he saw as responsible for mismanaging the relationship with the Queensland Government, announced the commission's abolition in 1978 (Palmer, 1988). Second, this created the space for the High Court of Australia to set land rights policy, with a successful challenge to the resumption of Archer River in *Koowarta v Bjelke-Petersen* in 1982 ultimately upholding the constitutional validity of the *Racial Discrimination Act* 1975 (Commonwealth) and its ability to override discriminatory state laws. Where the Fraser government was engaged in negotiation to enact its land rights agenda, the High Court was acting in a centralizing manner to enhance Commonwealth powers.

Similarly, the Bjelke-Petersen government frustrated the Fraser government in its attempts to provide Aboriginal control over mining on Aurukun reserve (Brennan, 1991; Nettheim, 1981). When no negotiated agreement could be reached between the Queensland and Commonwealth governments, the Commonwealth attempted to override state legislation and hand control of reserves to their Aboriginal residents. This move was side-stepped by Bjelke-Petersen, who degazetted the Aurukun reserve and reclassified it as a shire, outside of the control of the new Commonwealth legislation. By 1978, the Queensland government had succeeded in maintaining control of the shire, with Fraser and Viner choosing to back down rather than risk further confrontation with Bjelke-Petersen. This did little to reassure Aboriginal activists, who by 1982 were planning to disrupt the Brisbane Commonwealth Games with protests for land rights. The Bjelke-Petersen government's response was to use an existing mechanism in the *Land Act* 1962 (Qld) to provide title to reserves to local Aboriginal councils in the form of a "deed of grant-in-trust" (or DOGIT). This form of tenure fell far short of those in the Northern Territory, particularly with regard to mining (no provisions for a veto over exploration or for royalties were provided) and security of tenure (the government could rescind DOGITs at any time, subject to eventual parliamentary oversight). This was far short of the Fraser government's commitment to land rights, but – in the spirit of the New Federalism – it did not elicit a legislative response but merely a threat by the Aboriginal Affairs Minister Senator Baume that the rescinding of a DOGIT by the Queensland government would be met with a legislative response from the Commonwealth government (Brennan, 1991).

In Western Australia, the government of Premier Charles Court adamantly opposed land rights, and particularly Aboriginal control over minerals, bringing it into conflict with the Fraser government. In 1972, the government of Western Australia had established the Aboriginal Affairs Planning Authority to oversee reserve lands held for Aboriginal peoples. However, it did not take steps to grant the Aboriginal residents' control or ownership of these lands. The developmentalist Court government was deeply opposed to any reforms which might slow or reduce the profitability of mineral extraction. After the Aboriginal Land Fund Commission bought Noonkanbah Station for the Yungngora community in 1975, Amax Petroleum's plans to explore for oil there led to a significant clash in 1979 and 1980 (Ritter, 2002). Sacred sites were at risk, and despite legal opposition and a physical confrontation by the Aboriginal community, the Western Australian government, led by Premier Court, facilitated Amax's exploration. Ultimately, no oil was found, but the event soured relations between the Court government – which had no intention of legislating land rights – and the Fraser government and particularly its new minister of Aboriginal Affairs, Fred Chaney. From 1980, the Court government obstructed the transfer of any new pastoral leases purchased by the Aboriginal Land Fund Commission into Aboriginal ownership (Palmer, 1988). While Chaney was perceived to have supported the Yungngora community in their resistance to drilling, in practice the Fraser government had proven unwilling to intervene substantively and legislate for land rights in Western Australia. Noonkanbah demonstrated once again Fraser's willingness to see the national land rights agenda stall in the face of reactionary state governments, with little political capital expended to advance the platform of the federal Liberal Party.

By the end of Fraser's third term in 1983, the limitations of his "New Federalism" were evident when it came to Aboriginal land rights. While the Commonwealth had advanced land rights in the Northern Territory where it held jurisdiction and had established an Aboriginal Land Fund

Commission with a national mandate, state responses varied. In South Australia and NSW, Labor governments had legislated regimes that were more or less consistent with the spirit of the principles of the Woodward Royal Commission. In Victoria, attempts at progress by the Cain Labor government were stalled by an uncooperative upper house. In Tasmania, little had been achieved. The Queensland and Western Australian governments continued their obstruction of the federal Liberal Party's land rights policy, resisting the work of the Aboriginal Land Fund Commission and showing little interest in legislating land rights. Any semblance of a national approach to Aboriginal land rights was in disarray.

National Uniform Land Rights Betrayed: Labor's "Practical Reconciliation with Federalism," 1983–1992

As the Labor government prepared to contest the 1980 and 1983 elections, they responded to criticism of the Fraser government's passivity by strengthening their policy platform on national land rights. The 1982 platform committed a future Labor government to "Grant land rights and compensation to Aboriginal and Islander communities, using the principles and recommendations of the Aboriginal Land Rights Commission (Woodward Report) as a basis for legislation" (McMullan, 1982, pp. 4–5). What was new was not just the promise of compensation, as advocated by the NACC some years earlier, but also the promised mechanism for achieving national land rights. While a Labor government would seek "complementary state or territory legislation" where this was not introduced, they would "use Commonwealth constitutional powers and legislation to achieve these objectives" (McMullan, 1982, p. 5), just as Whitlam had promised in 1977 (Combe, 1977; Whitlam, 1977). With respect to the political flashpoint of mineral extraction on Aboriginal land, the Northern Territory model of an Aboriginal veto right and royalties paid to Aboriginal peoples was promised. However, out of recognition that the *Aboriginal Land Rights Act* 1983 (NSW) had granted ownership of most minerals to Aboriginal land holders, the Woodward principles were intended to place a floor, not a ceiling, on Aboriginal rights.

After winning the 1983 election, the Hawke Labor government faced the challenging task of delivering on this promise. The new minister of Aboriginal Affairs, Clyde Holding, argued that support for land rights assisted the nation in coming to terms with itself. Land rights recognition by the states, as Goot and Rowse (2007) explained, was Holding's response to the expected opposition to national land rights, an expression of the racist strain in Australian society. In practical terms, he interpreted the commitments in the Labor platform in two ways. First, he derived five principles which the Labor government recognized (Libby, 1989):

1. Aboriginal land was to be held under inalienable freehold title.
2. Aboriginal sacred sites were to be protected.
3. Aboriginal peoples were to have control of mining on their land.
4. They were to have access to mining royalty equivalents.
5. Compensation for lost land was to be negotiated between the federal government and Aboriginal peoples.

Minister Holding's strategy involved drafting federal legislation in collaboration with Aboriginal groups, particularly the NACC, which would play a crucial role in its formulation (Libby, 1989). The minister committed to not presenting the draft to Parliament without NACC's approval. This draft was intended to pressure state governments into enacting similar Aboriginal land rights legislation. If states failed to legislate by a set deadline, the Commonwealth planned to override their authority in this matter using the powers granted by the Australian people in the 1967 referendum. This approach was not just politically risky but also faced legal hurdles, in particular the likelihood that the states would be constitutionally entitled to just terms compensation for any Crown land granted to Aboriginal peoples.

Holding's brinkmanship in land rights policy stood in contrast to Prime Minister Hawke's approach to federal–state relations. The Hawke government has been described as the culmination of what Galligan and Mardiste (1992) termed "Labor's practical reconciliation with federalism." Hawke preferred a co-operative consensual federal model rather than a centralist role for the Commonwealth, primarily as a pragmatic strategy.

Holding's confrontational plan, emphasizing federal dominance in land rights, was soon to clash with Hawke's pragmatic preference for cooperative intergovernmental relations (for a book-length account, see Libby, 1989). Delays in implementing the minister's plan had given time for critics to attack the policy. Aboriginal members of the steering committee advising the minister were concerned that the approach didn't go far enough, particularly on questions of which land might be available for claim and compensation. By late 1984, the plan was unravelling. The Burke Labor government of Western Australia – which had also come to power in 1983 with a strategy of cultivating friendly relations with business elites – was under pressure from the mining lobby to resist the Commonwealth's land rights agenda. Over the course of 1983, Burke came to a position that decisively and vigorously opposed Holding's five principles, especially regarding mineral extraction. The mining industry had been campaigning heavily in Western Australia on the issue, spooking politicians nationally (Goot & Rowse, 2007). Faced with advocacy by Burke, conflict among Labor factions, and polling in Western Australia suggesting that Aboriginal land rights were unpopular, Prime Minister Hawke unilaterally decided in October 1984 to remove the Aboriginal veto over mining from Labor policy. He did not discuss the matter with Aboriginal interests, or even Minister Holding. With the Labor Party heading toward an early election in December, neither Holding nor his Aboriginal advisors were able to advance the Woodward land rights agenda.

By the end of 1984, the Labor agenda of uniform, national land rights was in tatters but not yet abandoned. A period of negotiation between Aboriginal interests and the mining industry ended in stalemate in February 1986. The mining lobby was unsuccessful in its efforts to remove the *de facto* veto on mining in the existing Northern Territory legislation, and Aboriginal interests were unable to advance the national uniform land rights legislation. Hawke's consensual approach to the federal dimension in Aboriginal land rights had defused a potential political crisis – but at the cost of abandoning the Woodward principles for land rights. Recognition of this failure can be seen in the passage of special land rights legislation for the small Aboriginal community at Wreck Bay in Jervis Bay Territory, the final mainland territory in which the Commonwealth had legislative responsibilities for an Indigenous population. The *Aboriginal Land Grants (Jervis Bay Territory) Act* 1986 (Commonwealth) granted Woodward-style land rights to that community in response to protest, and in an admission that no national legislation was forthcoming. Labor's practical reconciliation with federalism meant the betrayal of the promise of national uniform land rights, with the states – and crucially the judiciary – once again becoming the focus of activism for land restitution.

Yet few states were responsive to this renewal of legislative responsibility. Only in Queensland was land rights legislation enacted during this period, and there it was weak and belated (Brennan, 1991). After its initial reforms in 1982, the Bjelke-Peterson government further modified the DOGIT regime to both strengthen Indigenous security of tenure (ultimately requiring an act of Parliament to revoke DOGITs) and to facilitate the granting of perpetual leases over dwellings to individual residents. When the Goss Labor government came to power in late 1989 after three decades of conservative rule, it did so with the promise of substantive reform to Indigenous policy in Queensland, including land rights. Its approach to land rights was to offer the mining and pastoral industries a choice: support the introduction of a weak package, or publicly resist land rights and have a Northern Territory style scheme legislated. Business elites chose the former path, and it was thus that the Goss Labor government legislated a weak form of land rights in 1991 without substantive Aboriginal input and in the face of significant Aboriginal resistance.

Judicial Centralism and Reaction, 1993–2007

The fierce opposition to land rights from Queensland's Bjelke-Petersen government and its plan in 1981 and 1982 to issue DOGITs over former Indigenous reserves, catalyzed the preparation of a new legal challenge to settler dispossession (Keon-Cohen, 2000). Known as the Mabo case, the litigants were successful in overturning the myth that Australia at the time of colonization was *terra nullius* or land belonging to no one. In their decision in 1992 in *Mabo v. Queensland (No. 2)*, the majority of High Court justices recognized the fact that Indigenous Peoples had lived in Australia for thousands of years and enjoyed rights to their land according to their own laws and customs. The High Court decision altered the foundation of land law in Australia, finding that while the Australian system of real property law could, and does, include native title, such native title rights could also be extinguished a number of ways, including by governments granting rights to land to others (like freehold or leasehold titles) that are inconsistent with the continued existence of native title. In certain limited situations, such extinguishment might create a right for native title holders to be compensated.

The Keating Labor government's response to the Mabo decision came after a period of intense negotiation between the states and an "A Team" representing Indigenous interests. Seeking consensus, Keating's Native Title Bill had several objectives. Among them, it created a framework for the recognition of native title and a claims system through which such recognition might be sought. Crucially for settler interests, it sought to legalize (or "validate") the extinguishment of native title, which, since the passage of the *Racial Discrimination Act* 1975, was illegal. The bill did not result in grants of inalienable freehold title to land, but instead the recognition of native title rights in certain parcels of land so long as customary connection to such land continued, with the right to exclude others from such lands granted in cases such as on reserves and Crown land where it had not already been extinguished. Crucially, no veto over mining or statutory royalty scheme was introduced, with the bill instead granting certain native title holders a "right to negotiate" for compensation with proponents of mining on their land. In 1992, the *Native Title Act* 1993 (Commonwealth) was passed through the Australian Parliament, opening the way for claims by Aboriginal and Torres Strait Islander peoples to their traditional rights to land and compensation. While our chapter is focused on legislated land rights, native title rights and interests emerge from 1993 as the leading mechanism for Indigenous recognition by the settler-state.

The High Court's decision in 1992 and the subsequent *Native Title Act* 1993 finally introduced a form of national uniform land restitution. The High Court's "judicial revolution" represented a significant intervention into Australian constitutionalism. While the Mabo decision was celebrated by Indigenous activists, critics argued it amounted to law-making by judiciary, with at least three of the justices directly confronting the question in their decisions and arguing that a change in Australian law was warranted (Chesterman & Galligan, 1997). Alternatively, the Mabo decision may be seen as a move by the judiciary to force the Parliament to legislate on the unresolved question of national land rights, which the Commonwealth had abandoned for almost a decade. As such, the High Court acted in its familiar role as centralizer in the Australian federal system (cf. Galligan, 1987). The Keating government was finally drawn into legislating a national response to the dispossession of Aboriginal land two decades after the election of Whitlam. But its response was reformist rather revolutionary, falling far short of the principles in the Woodward Report.

The Commonwealth's introduction of even this modest legislation was too much for some conservative state governments, however (Chesterman & Galligan, 1997). In Western Australia – led by a conservative government and with no land rights legislation introduced – competing legislation was introduced in an attempt to reduce Aboriginal rights by extinguishing native title and replacing it with weaker statutory rights of usage. This Western Australian legislation was found to be invalid by the High Court, however, which ruled not just that the legislation contravened the *Racial Discrimination Act* 1975, but also that Commonwealth's power to legislate for Aboriginal peoples granted in 1967 empowered it to pass the *Native Title Act* 1993. Having forced the Commonwealth to act in response to the Mabo decision, the judiciary had once confirmed the Commonwealth's role in legislating for national land restitution.

Yet, as the subsequent years revealed, centralizing Indigenous land restitution was no guarantee of positive reform for Indigenous Peoples. When native title was recognized in 1993, a significant portion of the Australia landmass was subject to pastoral leases ranging from 34 percent of land tenure in Western Australia to 54 percent in Queensland. As native title law evolved through the common law, the High Court ruled in 1996 that the Wik peoples' native title rights and interests in northern Queensland were not extinguished and could co-exist with the granting of a pastoral lease. That is, both the Wik people and the lessee could exercise their rights, so long as one didn't conflict with the other. This decision mobilized the new conservative government, led by Prime Minister John Howard (1996–2007) to develop a response known as the "10-point plan" and by 1998 the Native Title Act was amended under the heading, "Confirmation of past extinguishment of native title." The prime minister's stated ambition was to provide "certainty to pastoralists and miners" (Howard, 1997). The 1998 amendments undercut the intent of the native title legislation and foreclosed options for pursuing beneficial outcomes through the courts.

In 2007, with the long-serving Prime Minister John Howard approaching electoral defeat, a suite of measures were hastily crafted in relation to the Northern Territory, ostensibly in the interests of the "safety and well-being of children" and "designed to ensure the protection of Aboriginal children from harm" (Brough, 2007). To enact this package of legislation, several existing laws were affected or partially suspended, which included the *Racial Discrimination Act* 1975, the *Aboriginal Land Rights (Northern Territory) Act* 1976, and the *Native Title Act* 1993 (Commonwealth). The laws gave the Commonwealth powers to compulsorily acquire townships held under the *Native Title Act* 1993. Sixty-five Aboriginal communities were compulsorily acquired and subject to five-year leases that gave the government unconditional authority over and access to those lands, and, to an extent, resident Traditional Owners. While both Prime Ministers Keating and Howard had centralizing approaches to Indigenous land questions, they took very different ideological approaches.

Commonwealth Disinterest and the Negotiated Settlements

Since Howard, no Commonwealth government has pursued any substantive agenda on land rights or native title. Dreams of national uniform land rights along the lines of the Woodward principles are long forgotten. And governments have shown little appetite to change the statutory framework for native title enacted in the *Native Title Act* 1993, despite numerous reviews suggesting that reform is necessary (Law Reform Commission review, Juukan Gorge review). Instead, it has been left to state governments (and, with respect to native title, the courts) to provide solutions to Indigenous land issues, some innovative, some less so.

In 1995, Tasmania recognized Aboriginal land rights through the Tasmanian *Aboriginal Lands Act*, transferring significant lands to the Tasmanian Aboriginal Land Council (TALC). This legislation came after the High Court acknowledged the fallacy of *terra nullius* and recognized native title rights. It reflected a broader national movement toward reconciliation and acknowledging past injustices against Aboriginal peoples. The Act aimed to reconcile with the Aboriginal community by granting lands of historic and cultural importance. Clyde Mansell, Chair of the TALC, emphasized that the Act recognized their historical presence and resilience against colonial oppression. The Launceston TALC office displays photos capturing the community's journey, illustrating both the grief of past injustices and the joy of recognition.

The TALC consists of eight elected Aboriginal representatives. This council manages fifteen areas as of 2021, often under plan and including culturally important sites like *putalina*/Oyster Cove and Mount Cameron West. Despite initial progress, the transfer of additional lands has stalled, leading to frustration among community leaders.

In Victoria, a more substantial land rights response was developed that offered a viable alternative to the Commonwealth native title process while still operationalizing the Native Title Act. Unlike earlier laws that were site specific, the *Traditional Owner Settlement (TOS) Act* 2010 (Vic) emphasized a series of Recognition and Settlement Agreements drawn between Aboriginal peoples and the state relating to land transfer agreement, land use activity agreement, natural resources agreement, and funding agreements. By entering into an agreement with the Victorian Government under the TOS Act, Traditional Owners agree to withdraw any native title claims and suspend any future claims. Under the TOS Act, there is no requirement to recognize or extinguish native title but it allows the state's recognition of a group of people as the Traditional Owners for a particular area, together with other negotiated benefits. A Recognition and Settlement Agreement under the TOS Act is underpinned by the registration of an Indigenous Land Use Agreement (ILUA) on the Register of Indigenous Land Use Agreements. Preparations for treaties are also underway at the time of writing, which – if eventually negotiated and implemented – promise to deliver further negotiated land and other reparative settlements with the Aboriginal Traditional Owners of Victoria.

In Western Australia, a settlement process has been underway. In 2018 the largest native title settlement, known as the Noongar Settlement, was registered with the Native Title Registrar. The Noongar Agreement was the culmination of several years of negotiation to amalgamate six native title claims into a single claim encompassing Noongar country. The settlement has been characterized as the largest and most comprehensive agreement relating to Aboriginal interests in land in Australian history (Hobbs & Williams, 2018b). The Noongar Settlement was struck on behalf of 30,000 Noongar Traditional Owners, covering 200,000 square kilometers of land in southwestern Australia, and is valued at $1.3 billion. The wide-reaching agreement covers rights, obligations, and opportunities relating to land, resources, governance, finance, and cultural heritage. Critical to the agreement, and which runs counter to the recommendations of the Woodward Report, Noongar peoples had to concede any current or future claims. Yamatji people, from mid-west Western Australia, also reached a comprehensive settlement in February 2020. In the Yamatji case, native title rights and interests and alternative settlements were reached simultaneously. Yamatji groups were awarded possession of traditional lands, non-exclusive native title and a $450 million economic package to Yamatji people's social and economic independence. The Noongar and Yamatji comprehensive settlements show the evolution of the Native Title Act, led by state governments negotiating outcomes beyond native title rights and interests.

Uneven Outcomes

This chapter section illustrates the kinds of inconsistent outcomes of land rights created by variations in legislation and court decisions over time and space. The analysis above has described how land rights at the state level were contingent on political dynamics, demonstrating how the varying stances of Commonwealth and state governments on land rights and federal–state relations have led to a patchwork of land rights laws across Australia. The two maps below illustrate this patchwork of outcomes using the examples of tenure and veto rights over mineral extraction.

These maps have been produced by compiling spatial data separately on land restored to Indigenous Peoples under each land rights regime, as well as on native title determination outcomes. While every effort has been made to compile comprehensive information, there are some spatial data we were unable to access: lands held by land councils in NSW that entered the estate in ways other than the claims process; lands transferred as part of settlements in Western Australia, in particular through the Noongar Settlement Agreement, the Yamatji Settlement Agreement, and the Yawuru Global Agreement; some Community Living Areas in the Northern Territory that are held under various forms of tenure other than freehold; lands purchased using government funds by organizations such as ATSIC or the Aboriginal Development Commission; lands divested from the Aboriginal Lands Trust estate in Western Australia; and, various other one-off or ad hoc arrangements.

Nevertheless, we believe we have compiled spatial data on the vast majority of land held by Indigenous Peoples. Methodologically, we have followed the approach outlined by Altman and Markham (2015), but accessed a more comprehensive set of data. Almost all data are current as of July 1, 2023, or more recently. For each parcel of land, we have attempted to classify the rights enjoyed by land holders in terms of land tenure and alienability, and whether landholders have a veto right over mining (*de facto* or *de jure*). In doing so, we have relied on the summary by Nettheim et al. (2002), as well as our own interpretation of the relevant legislation, a process of abstraction which – even as it illustrates heterogeneity – hides much of the real legal complexity and diversity in rights.

Figure 6.1 maps the varying land tenure underlying the multitudes of different land rights and native title lands returned. It shows a patchwork of land tenures, with freehold titles predominantly outside Western Australia. Only in the Northern Territory, the western parts of South Australia, Cape York in Queensland, and in small pockets of land in Victoria is land returned under inalienable freehold as Woodward recommended.

The map also shows how native title has acted as a baseline form of uniform land restitution. In Western Australia in particular native title is the primary means by which Aboriginal peoples have gained legally enforceable rights in land. It does this in two ways, extensively and substantively. First, it extends Aboriginal rights in land to vast areas of Crown land far beyond those available for Aboriginal peoples through the Aboriginal Land Trust, pastoral lease transfers and other arrangements. Second, it substantively strengthens the rights of traditional owners in areas like reserves that are already set aside for Aboriginal peoples. This second function also acts to strengthen legal protections against alienation under arrangements like the Aboriginal Land Trust in

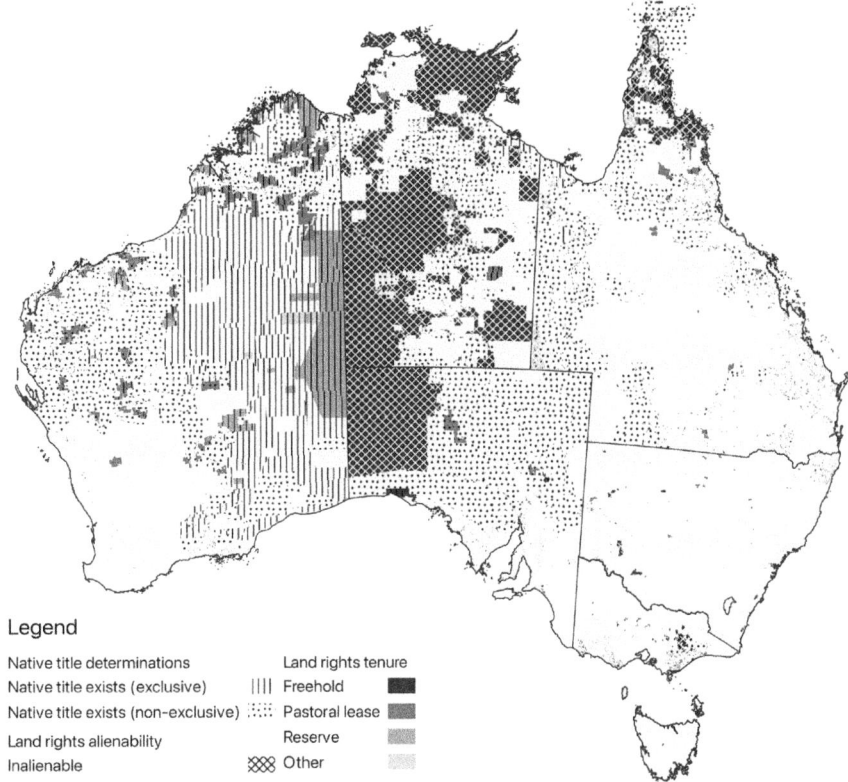

Legend

Native title determinations		Land rights tenure	
Native title exists (exclusive)	‖‖	Freehold	■
Native title exists (non-exclusive)	⁞⁞⁞	Pastoral lease	▨
Land rights alienability		Reserve	▨
Inalienable	▧	Other	▨

Figure 6.1 Indigenous land restitution in Australia, 2023, showing land tenure, alienability and native title recognition (Source: Produced by the authors from data provided by state and territory, and Commonwealth government agencies)

South Australia, while complicating Indigenous rights by intersecting the traditional ownership basis of native title with the residency basis of the *Aboriginal Lands Trust Act* 2013 (South Australia).

Figure 6.2 shows the extent of a further crucial element of land rights as envisaged by Woodward, the *de facto* or *de jure* right to veto mineral extraction. It shows a tiered system of three levels of rights. Land holders in the Northern Territory can control mining on their land, holding *de facto* veto rights over mining in areas of land held subject to the *Aboriginal Land Rights (Northern Territory) Act* 1976 (Commonwealth), with mining prohibited on the smaller community living areas in the territory. In NSW, most minerals are owned by land

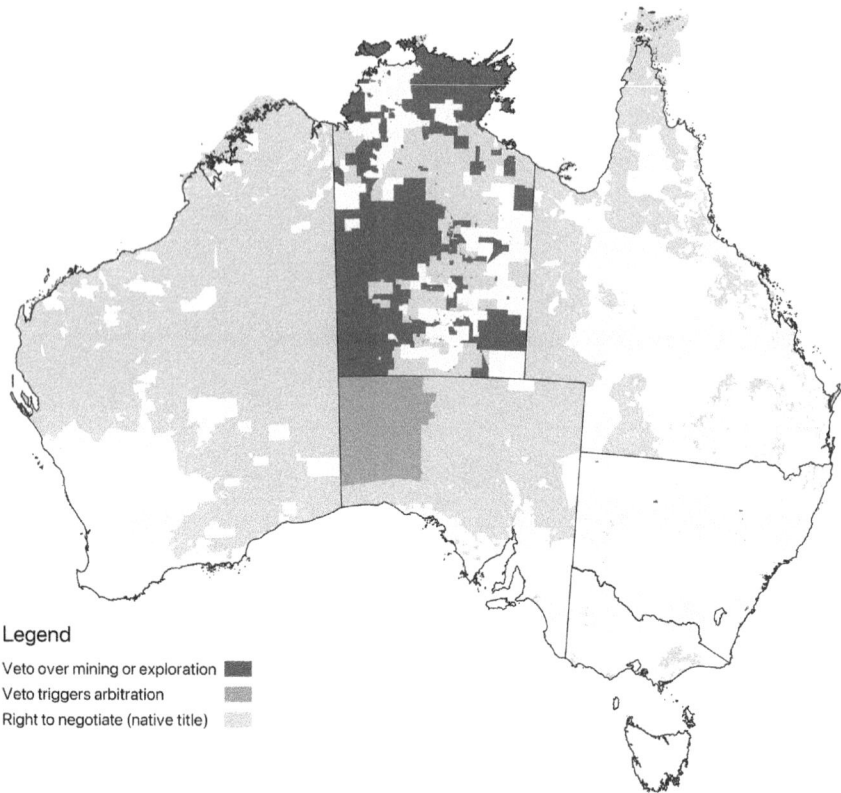

Figure 6.2   Indigenous land restitution in Australia, 2023, by type of mineral extraction veto rights enjoyed by landholders (Source: Produced by the authors from data provided by state and territory, and Commonwealth government agencies)

holders under the *Aboriginal Land Rights Act* 1983 (NSW), although the amount of land restored to Aboriginal peoples under that scheme is relatively small. In South Australia, traditional owners of the Anangu Pitjantjatjara Yankunytjatjara lands and the Maralinga Tjarutja lands have similar rights to veto mineral extraction, although doing so may trigger an arbitration process. For much of the rest of the country, most notably Queensland and Western Australia, Indigenous land holders lack powers to veto mineral development, instead having only a time-limited "right to negotiate" compensation with proponents of extractive developments. As such, the rights enjoyed by Aboriginal landholders with regard to mineral extraction vary radically across the continent, a consequence of the uneven and contested political process that has unfolded across the Australian federation since the 1960s.

Conclusion

Legislative responses to recognize Aboriginal land rights were initially led by the states, and the Commonwealth in the Northern Territory. The Woodward Report was intended to guide state-based responses; however, both the Fraser coalition government in the late 1970s and the Hawke Labor government in the 1980s failed to advance a national land rights agenda that left advancing Aboriginal interests in land to the states and litigation through the courts. The land rights model outlined in the Woodward Report was limited in influence on NSW and South Australia. Litigation that successfully challenged the legality of occupation necessitated a Commonwealth Government response confirming land dealings and creating a mechanism for the recognition of native title. State-based responses after recognition of native title rights and interests have continued to evolve. Accepting the difficulty of proving native title, the Tasmania state government responded with limited land rights recognition. In Victoria and Western Australia, settlement processes have been underway that utilize the structures of the Native Title Act, and that also engage the states in the negotiation of a range of social justice aspirations that go beyond land repossession.

In this chapter we argue the land rights recognition in Australia is an outcome of shifting state–Commonwealth relations within the Australian federation. This has led to a hugely varied and spatially uneven set of legislative land rights regimes across Australia, placing onus on Indigenous Peoples to work to advancing their rights and interests in the absence of agreed-upon national standards or leadership from the Commonwealth government.

References

Altman, J. C., & Markham, F. (2015). Burgeoning Indigenous land ownership: Diverse values and strategic potentialities. In S. Brennan, M. Davis, B. Edgeworth, & L. Terrill (eds.), *Native Title from Mabo to Akiba: A vehicle for change and empowerment* (pp. 126–142). Melbourne: Federation Press.

Anderson, C. (1981). Queensland. In N. Peterson (ed.), *Aboriginal land rights: A handbook* (pp.53–114). Canberra: Australian Institute of Aboriginal Studies.

Bennett, S. (1988). Federalism and aboriginal affairs. *Australian Aboriginal Studies (Canberra)*, 1, 18–27. https://doi.org/10.3316/informit.177910165588169

Brennan, F. (1991). *Land rights Queensland style: The struggle for Aboriginal self-management—Australian National University*. University of Queensland Press, Brisbane Australia.

Broome, R. (2005). *Aboriginal Victorians: A history since 1800*. Allen & Unwin, Crows Nest, Australia.

Brough, M. (2007). 'National emergency response to protect Aboriginal children', Media Release 21 June 2007, Minister for Families, Community Services and Indigenous Affairs. Available at: https://formerministers.dss.gov.au/3581/emergency_21june07/

Chesterman, J., & Galligan, B. (1997). *Citizens without rights: Aborigines and Australian citizenship*. Cambridge University Press, Cambridge, UK.

Coalition of Aboriginal and Torres Strait Islander Peak Organisations & Australian Governments. (2020). *National agreement on closing the gap*. National Indigenous Australians Agency, Canberra, Australia. http://web.archive.org/web/20200926040101/www.closingthegap.gov.au/sites/default/files/files/national-agreement-ctg.pdf

Coghill, K. (1997). In government but not in power: Victorian Labor 1982–92. *Legislative Studies*, 11(2) 76–77.

Combe, D. (1977). *Australian Labor Party Platform, constitution and rules as approved by the 32nd National Conference, Perth 1977*. Australian Labor Party, National Secretariat, Barton, Australia.

Cook K., & Goodall, H. (2013). *Making change happen: Black and white activists talk to Kevin Cook about Aboriginal, Union and Liberation Politics*. Canberra: ANU Express.

Cooms, V. (2012). *Free the blacks and smash the Act! Aboriginal policy and resistance in Queensland between 1965 and 1975* [PhD dissertation, Australian National University]. https://doi.org/10.25911/5c6e71395b26c

Davis, M., & Williams, G. (2021). *Everything you need to know about the Uluru Statement from the Heart*. Sydney, Australia: NewSouth Publishing.

Dexter, B. and edited by G. Foley & E. Howell (2015). *Pandora's box: The Council for Aboriginal Affairs 1967–1976*. Southport, Queensland: Keeaira Press. See https://scholarly.info/book/pandoras-box-the-council-for-aboriginal-affairs-1967-1976/.

Foley, G., & Anderson, T. (2006). Land rights and Aboriginal voices. *Australian Journal of Human Rights*, 12(1), 83–108. https://doi.org/10.1080/1323238X.2006.11910814

Fox, C. (2008). The fourteen powers referendum of 1944 and the federalisation of Aboriginal affairs. *Aboriginal History*, 32, 27–48.

Galligan, B. (1987). *Politics of the High Court: A study of the judicial branch of government in Australia*. Brisbane: University of Queensland Press.

Galligan, B., & Mardiste, D. (1992). Labor's reconciliation with federalism. *Australian Journal of Political Science*, 27(1), 71–86. https://doi.org/10.1080/00323269208402182

Goodall, H. (2008). *Invasion to embassy: Land in Aboriginal politics in New South Wales, 1770–1972*. Sydney: Sydney University Press.

Goot, M., & Rowse, T. (2007). *Divided nation? Indigenous affairs and the imagined public*. Melbourne: Melbourne University Press.

Hiatt, L., Luther, M., O'Donoghue, L., & Stanley, J. (1976, November). *National Aboriginal Consultative Committee: Report of Committee of Inquiry*.

Hiskey, G. (2021). *Maralinga: The struggle for return of the lands*. Cambridge, MA: Wakefield Press.

Hobbs, H., & Williams, G. (2018b). Australia's First Treaty. www.auspublaw.org/blog/2018/04/australias-first-treaty

Holland, A. (2019). *Breaking the silence: Aboriginal defenders and the settler state, 1905–1939*. Melbourne: Melbourne University Press.

Howard, J. (1997). "WIK 10 POINT PLAN", The Department of Prime Minister and Cabinet, Australian Government, Canberra, Australia. Media Release, accessed 20 February 2024 at https://pmtranscripts.pmc.gov.au/release/transcript-10323

Jackson, S. (2017). Land rights: A postcolonial revolution in land title. In S. Jackson, L. Porter & L. Johnson, (eds.), *Planning in Indigenous Australia: From imperial foundations to postcolonial futures* (pp. 155–174). Routledge, London, UK. https://doi.org/10.4324/9781315693668

Keon-Cohen, B. (2000). The Mabo litigation: A personal and procedural account. *Melbourne University Law Review*, 24, 893–951.

Libby, R. T. (1989). *Hawke's law: The politics of mining and Aboriginal land rights in Australia*. Perth: University of Western Australia Press.

Liberal Party of Australia & National Country Party of Australia. (1976). *The New government policies: A complete guide to the official announced policies of the Fraser Liberal/National Country Party Government which took office in Australia in December, 1975*. Canberra.

McMullan, R. F. (1982). *Australian Labor Party Platform, Constitutional and Rules as approved by the 35th National Conference, Perth 1982*. Australian Labor Party, National Secretariat. https://parlinfo.aph.gov.au/parlInfo/download/library/partypol/1032121/upload_binary/1032121.pdf;fileType=application/pdf

Moore, B. (1981). Victoria. In N. Peterson (ed.), *Aboriginal land rights: A handbook* (pp. 148–167). Australian Institute of Aboriginal Studies, Canberra, Australia.

Nettheim, G. (1981). *Victims of the law: Black Queenslanders today*. Allen & Unwin, Crows Nest, Australia.

Nettheim, G., Meyers, G. D., & Craig, D. (2002). Australian land rights legislation. In G. Nettheim (ed.) *indigenous Peoples and governance structures:*

A comparative analysis of land and resource management rights (pp. 237–317). Canberra: Aboriginal Studies Press.

Norman, H. (2015). *What do we want? A political history of Aboriginal Land Rights in NSW*. Canberra: Aboriginal Studies Press.

Palmer, I. (1988). *Buying back the land: Organisational struggle and the Aboriginal Land Fund Commission*. Canberra: Aboriginal Studies Press.

Piccini, J. (2019). *Human rights in twentieth-century Australia*. Cambridge: Cambridge University Press.

Ritter, D. (2002). The fulcrum of Noonkanbah. *Journal of Australian Studies*, 26(75), 51–58. https://doi.org/10.1080/14443050209387803

Rowse, T. (2012). *Rethinking social justice: From 'peoples' to 'populations.'* Canberra: Aboriginal Studies Press.

Sanders, W. (2013). Changing agendas in Australian Indigenous policy: Federalism, competing principles and generational dynamics. *Australian Journal of Public Administration*, 72(2), 156–170. https://doi.org/10.1111/1467-8500.12014

Tedmanson, D. (2016). Shifting state constructions of Anangu Pitjantjatjara Yankunytjatjara: Changes to the South Australian Pitjantjatjara Land Rights Act 1981–2006 [PhD dissertation, Australian National University]. https://doi.org/10.25911/5d763524705f3

Victorian Government. (1983). Explanatory Memorandum: Aboriginal Land Claims Bill 1983. Available from: https://classic.austlii.edu.au/au/legis/vic/bill_em/alcb1983187/alcb1983187.html

Walker, K. (1969). The black commandments. *Koorier*, 1(10), 25.

Weller, P. (1989). *Malcolm Fraser, PM: A study in prime ministerial power*. Penguin Books, Melbourne Australia.

West, S. (1980). *Aboriginal affairs: A guideline to labor policies*. Australian Labor Party, Canberra, Australia. https://parlinfo.aph.gov.au/parlInfo/download/library/partypol/1011080/upload_binary/1011080.pdf;fileType=application%2Fpdf

Whitlam, G. (1972, November 13). It's time for leadership. https://parlinfo.aph.gov.au/parlInfo/download/library/partypol/1022125/upload_binary/1022125.pdf;fileType=application%2Fpdf#search=%22library/partypol/1022125%22

(1977). Address at the National Press Club on 5 December 1977 [sound recording]. Available from http://nla.gov.au/nla.obj-215135396

Young, E. A. (1992). Aboriginal land rights in Australia: Expectations, achievements and implications. *Applied Geography*, 12(2), 146–161. https://doi.org/10.1016/0143-6228(92)90004-7

Young, M. (1971). *Australian Labor Party Platform, Constitutional and Rules as approved by the 29th Commonwealth Conference, Launceston 1971*. Australian Labor Party, Federal Secretariat. https://parlinfo.aph.gov.au/parlInfo/download/library/partypol/1042679/upload_binary/1042679.pdf;fileType=application/pdf#search=%22labor%20party%20constitution%20rules%22

7

Dispossession by Treaty, Dispossession by Statute

Indigenous Title in Eastern and Western Canada

DANIEL DIAMOND AND DOUGLAS SANDERSON
(AMO BINASHII)

Introduction

To bring insight to the development of land rights in Canada, this chapter compares how various manifestations of the British Crown took very different approaches to Indigenous-held lands during the early and middle encounter periods (1500–1800) in eastern North America, as compared to the nineteenth-century encounters in Australia and British Columbia. We trace just a few contextual differences to demonstrate motivations for British Columbia's denial of Indigenous claims to land in opposition to earlier British policy. We then demonstrate how the introduction of the Torrens system of land-title registration, first proposed and adopted in Australia in 1858, proved the perfect vehicle to ensure that Indigenous claims did not survive the assertion of a title interest by settler and colonial officials. The vastly different circumstances of government officials in the pre-Confederation era, compared with those in post-Confederation British Columbia, go a long way to explaining the profoundly different regimes of land management and, eventually, registration by colonial officials on the East and West Coasts of what we now call North America.

While critical analyses of the Indigenous-settler encounters across Canada have produced a significant literature on the *theoretical* justifications for land appropriation, very few scholars have addressed the *legal mechanisms* that converted Indigenous lands into the privately held property of European settlers. We show how the transition to settlement required that Indigenous claims to land be sidelined to make room for increased European settlement, and how the Torrens system facilitated the *en masse* appropriation of Indigenous lands in western Canada. This contrasts to eastern Canada, characterized by a steady acquisition of Indigenous lands by the Crown and private entities, in a long series of what are termed the Peace and Friendship treaties. The legal mechanisms for appropriation have implications for how lands are reclaimed today.

British Land Law before the Nineteenth Century

In the common law, land plays a unique role distinct from property in chattels. The first mention of land as property is found in St. German's *Doctor and Student* published in 1530 (Jones, 2018) where, for the first time, land was "equated with property, rather than treated as a special case." Even so, it takes a while for this practice to become standard. Coke's *Reports*, published from 1600 to 1615, treat property in goods separately to ownership of land. Coke's *Institutes*, from 1628, uses the terms more interchangeably, and generalize land and goods as property (Jones, 2018).

Land and property were distinct because their treatment under the law was fundamentally different. Specifically, "[i]n theory, land was held for a feudal lord, and could not be devised by will. In practice, land can sustain many overlapping claims by many individuals, and be used casually or regularly by many others" (Jones, 2018, p. 194). Jones found the 1600s was marked by a shift from qualitative to quantitative measurements of land (p. 197). By the early 1600s, Gunter's chain, twenty-two yards made of one hundred links, was used to plan the entirety of the British Empire (Jones, 2018, p. 194). Despite this shift towards quantitative measurement, the fungibility of land as a commodity was severely constrained well into the nineteenth century because the process of buying and selling land was expensive, rudimentary, and slow.

Land conveyancing was largely governed by contract (Pottage, 1994). Validity of title turned on the soundness of contracts, through which ownership was conveyed from one party to another (Pottage, 1994). In practical terms, this meant lawyers would evaluate "the plausibility of a paper title against a practical sense of property which had arisen from land use, and which lay in local memory" (Pottage, 1994 p. 363). Put simply, a prudent purchaser of land needed to ensure that the purported owner had a valid title to sell. Since there was no registry that the owner could reference to demonstrate that they had legal title to the land, the seller had to provide documentation illustrating a valid chain of title going as far back as possible. Yet, this documentation could not be relied on in isolation. Lawyers would evaluate the likelihood that the paper documentation was legitimate, and weigh that against knowledge of land use embedded in local and community memory (Pottage, 1994).

For example, as one senior ordnance survey officer explained to the Registration and Conveyancing Commission, even in cases where it is easy to show title, through deeds and paper documentation, showing the exact boundaries of the property down to the very border "depend[ed] on the evidence of tenants, and old laborers, and persons of great age, and to the practice that may have prevailed with different occupiers" (Pottage, 1994, p. 364).[1] Indeed, lawyers relied heavily on community knowledge. Accordingly, until the early nineteenth century, land surveyors would be accompanied by local residents as their knowledge was essential to creating an accurate estate map. Land was not a particularly fungible form of property.

Feudal property relationships, lawyers, and the aristocracy slowed the transition towards a commoditized and fungible real-property regime based on registration in the United Kingdom. Primarily, this is because the aristocracy, still land-rich from feudal property arrangements were not inclined to make the alienation of their vast estates any easier. "As Stone and Stein note, in 1833, '24 peers in the realm of England' each held estates in excess of 100,000 acres" (Bhandar, 2015, p. 272). Lawyers, in turn, resisted a system of land registration because the time-consuming nature of title research was profitable (Bhandar, 2015). This was the deed registration system imported to the American colonies.

British–Indigenous Relationships to Land from the Sixteenth to Eighteenth Centuries

The assertion of Crown sovereignty over distant lands was just that – an assertion – which, without more, such as an actual occupation or sale, provided no rights to land. This was widely accepted in European, and certainly British, encounters with Indigenous Peoples (Banner, 2005). Royal Charters were certainly granted, but upon arrival, colonists, or Hudson's Bay Company (HBC)[2] traders, did their best to secure their

---

[1] Cited from the evidence that Capt. Yolland reported in the First Report of the Registration and Conveyancing Commission, PP(1850) XXXII (p. 591). Pottage notes that this may overstate the difficulties of conveyancing, because members of the Commission were enthusiastic in their advocacy of large-scale land surveys.

[2] In 1670, the Hudson's Bay Company was granted a Royal Charter over a tract known as Rupert's Land, which would in time be revealed to be a territory larger than the Holy

interests through treaty or purchase. Certainly almost no one in the eastern colonies imagined that the lands before them were barren or unused. Applying a doctrine of possession, based on an imagined empty landscape, would have struck anyone as ludicrous (Banner, 2005). Before 1763, purchases of Indian lands were ordinary contracts entered into by individual colonists, corporations and towns, as well as governors and other Crown representatives. Whatever else the colonists might have called the Indigenous population, it was clear that they understood Indigenous Peoples as proprietors and owners of their lands (Banner, 2005).

The tension of *imperium* and *dominium* (the assertion of sovereignty and the actual possession of property) was resolved in North America through Crown assertion of British sovereignty in the form of patents for land purchases – patents guaranteeing the right to land only if the patent was coupled with a purchase of sale from the relevant Indigenous party. In this way, the British could say that their sovereignty extended in some jurisdictional sense, even if no Indigenous party on the ground was even remotely aware of visitors from another continent, or of their assertion of sovereignty. After 1763, the *Royal Proclamation*'s[3] prohibition on the sale of Indian land to anyone other than the Crown created a distinction between Indigenous and settler held lands. Until then, the two property interests were treated identically – but after 1763, Indigenous title came to be seen as something different than the sort of title that settler people held in the lands they called fee simple.

Roman Empire at its height. The grant provided an exclusive monopoly over the trade of furs and minerals within a watershed that stretched from the Rocky Mountains in the West to James Bay in the east, encompassing a land mass of some 3.9 million square kilometers. Though technically a mere corporation acting pursuant to the grant of the Royal Charter, the HBC established trading posts along the coast and eventually in the interior, which were empowered to empanel courts though never did, and at one point would also be placed in charge of the Empire's outpost on Vancouver Island, and over the interior of what would become British Columbia.

[3] George R., Proclamation, October 7, 1763, reprinted in RSC 1985, App II, No. 1. The Royal Proclamation of 1763 drew a line that was to separate Indian and settler-held lands. To the east were the colonies, and to the west was Indian country. The Proclamation declared that henceforth only the Crown could buy or obtain Indigenous lands – settler-to-Indian contracts were discouraged and not enforced. The boundary line was continually moved further west until the American Revolution, after which any pretense to the protection of Indian lands was set aside in favor of a murderous campaign of dispossession and relocation in the United States, and further treaty engagement between Indigenous Peoples and the Crown to the north in Canada.

One consequence of this pattern of land acquisition was that, even after 1763, a very large number of titles to land traced their purchase to an original Indigenous seller. After 1763, and as a consequence of the *Royal Proclamation*'s requirement that land be ceded first to the Crown, and all subsequent land grants traced to grants from the Crown. After the *Proclamation* was issued, contracts for sale of Indian lands were void unless the sale was via a treaty negotiated with the Crown.

Once purchased, the Crown would then issue patents to would-be landowners. But the British found themselves still bound by treaty relationships with their military allies. Since the early seventeenth century, the British had been engaged in a complex and deepening alliance with an Indigenous confederacy known as the Five Nations. The formal name for the British–Five Nation relationship was the Covenant Chain, described as a symbolic silver chain that bound the parties in a military and trade alliance (Morito, 2012). After 1763, the British attempted to further their influence in the west through an extension of the Covenant Chain relationship.

Under William Johnson's term as Superintendent of Indian Affairs, this influence was possible because Johnson was himself deeply enmeshed in an Indigenous worldview. Johnson had an Indigenous wife, spoke Indigenous languages, and had taken the time to read through volumes of reports on and histories of treaty making between his predecessors and Indigenous nations. Johnson employed Indigenous diplomatic protocols and processes to affirm peace with Indigenous nations. After his death, Johnson's relations carried on, but over time the various governors general and superintendents of Indian Affairs grew slowly less familiar with the details of a once-close and sustained relationship between the Crown and its Indigenous allies.

The annual treaty meetings and distribution of presents came to be seen as an unnecessary expense, and by 1836 it was possible for Sir Francis Bond Head to remark that "on our part, little or nothing documentary exists – the promises which were made, whatever they might have been, were almost invariably verbal; those who expressed them are now moldering in their graves" (Head, 1836, as cited in Corbiere, 2019). The once vital Covenant Chain relationship was now no longer even a distant memory – the commitments of the *Royal Proclamation* became rote and boilerplate, when they were remembered at all.

After 1850, the Crown began a series of treaty negotiations for lands that became Canada. The treaty regime after 1850 used boilerplate language in treaties with distinct Indigenous nations – giving an almost spooky uniformity to these treaties. Except in the west, where, throughout most of

British Columbia, land was both unpurchased and not subject to treaty. Future property interests in British Columbia would turn not on the need to formally recognize original Indian title, as was the case in the east, but rather on the need to eliminate all prior Indigenous claims. Without treaty or purchase, it was hard to imagine how this could be accomplished.

Relations to Land in Australia: The Torrens System

Unlike in the United Kingdom and eastern North America, land in Australia was conceptualized as a fungible commodity "without any owners, to be claimed, partitioned, securitized and cultivated" (Bhandar, 2015, p. 256). In practice, this meant that a more efficient system of land conveyancing was needed to accommodate the increasing number of land transactions. Indeed, the colony "required something less costly, less artificial, something which [...] may [be] handle[d] with more freedom and rapidity" (Torrens, 1859, p. 4). By this time, the commoditization of Australian land was already well underway. To illustrate, the "Colonization Commissioners for South Australia noted that by 1839 (three years after the first settlers had landed on the coast St. Vincent's Gulf) 250,320 acres of public land had been sold for the sum of £229,756" (Bhandar, 2015, p. 267). Yet, without a centralized registry, the system was almost as cumbersome to manage as that in the United Kingdom. Flaws in title could still be passed down from owner to owner without their knowledge, the risk of fraud and forgery was high, and ownership still needed to be traced as far back as possible to confirm the buyer was receiving valid title to land. Consequently, the expense, difficulty, and legal uncertainties of land conveyancing under the British law were perceived as a barrier to the settlement of the Australian colony.

With this problem in mind, Robert Torrens, a member of the House of Assembly for the City of Adelaide, devised a centralized land-registry system based on the "shipping system, where funded property was bought and sold within a system of registration" (Bhandar, 2015, p. 258). Bhandar (2015) noted that Torrens emphasized that there was no difference in principle between land and other forms of property for the purposes of conveyancing (pp. 258–259). The Torrens system was made into law under the *Real Property Act* 1858.[4] This supported the

---

[4] *An Act to simplify the Laws relating to the transfer and encumbrance of freehold and other interests in Land, House of Assembly*, South Australia, 1858. See www.foundingdocs.gov .au/item-sdid-43.html.

process of British settlement in the Australian colony, as land transactions were now relatively easy and inexpensive. The Torrens system was popular with already landed Australian settlers because it made ownership of land more attainable for the majority of citizens (Taylor, 2008). Moreover, "the settler colony of South Australia was the ideal space for the imposition or trialling of this technique, treated, as it was, as a *terra nullius*" (Bhandar, 2015, p. 256). The treatment of Indigenous lands as legally empty, without owners or sovereigns in Australia, stands in stark contrast to the well-established colonial practice in eastern Canada. Indeed, rather than acquire rights to Indigenous lands through treaty and purchase, in Australia the very existence of Indigenous ownership was, and arguably still is, simply denied.

Relations to Land in British Columbia

Prior to the mid-nineteenth century, European presence in Canada's westernmost province, British Columbia, was minimal and primarily dedicated to fur trading. Europeans were limited to geographically small settlements, with equally small populations; and there was neither the motivation nor the ability to claim ownership of vast swaths of Indigenous lands. In addition, Indigenous Peoples were not passive victims; they actively asserted claims to land and land ownership. Thus, European settlement cannot be characterized as the acquisition of "empty" lands. Indigenous Peoples did not simply occupy the land, extracting resources as they made seasonal rounds of their traditional territories. Indigenous Peoples adapted to the changing economic and political landscape by engaging in European-style agrarian farming and capitalism. Nevertheless, as we discuss in the following section, racist discourses of the "savage" Indian painted Indigenous Peoples as incapable and uninterested in agrarian capitalism – such that their lands were considered "wastelands" and thus legally empty and open for appropriation by European settlers.

In the west, the years between 1800 and 1858 are characterized by Robin Fisher as the "fur trade era." During this period, Indigenous Peoples and settlers enjoyed a reciprocal and mutually beneficial relationship with minimal conflict. Fisher (1977) suggested that Indigenous Peoples "to a large extent controlled both the trade and their culture, and European traders did not attempt any major interference with their way of life. The mutually beneficial nature of the land-based fur trade was indicated by the continued absence of interracial conflict" (p. 24). Several factors underpinned this dynamic.

Indigenous Peoples were skilled hunters and trappers, and they provided the HBC with their desired otter, marten and beaver pelts (Fisher,
1977). The power dynamic between the two groups was relatively stable
because Indigenous Peoples were skilled and competitive bargainers.
Both American and Russian traders provided alternative trading options
and thus economic competition was intense (Fisher, 1977).
In recognition of this fact, the Northwest Company introduced a debtor
system which was continued by the HBC after it took control of the area.
Under this system, Indigenous communities were supplied with goods
and equipment in the fall, with the understanding that they would pay
for the goods with pelts in the coming spring (Fisher, 1977).[5]
    The mutually beneficial nature of the relationship encouraged many
Indigenous communities to engage in the fur trade for the benefits to be
gained, and the settler population in the region was still dwarfed by the
surrounding Indigenous communities. As a result, some Indigenous
groups were able to resist participation in the fur trade. For example, in
1829, the HBC built a fort in Tsilhqot'in territory, in central British
Columbia, with an eye to engaging them in the fur trade. Yet, the
Tsilhqot'in,

> according to their representative, could see no advantage in the presence
> of whites and expected them to leave the fort so that they would have
> the opportunity to burn it down. In reply, the head trader had to
> concede that the Indians were at liberty to act as they pleased, to hunt
> or not to hunt, because there was no compulsion in the trade.
> Essentially, the Chilcotin [sic] opted out of the fur trade, and there was
> little that the company could do but recognize the fact by abandoning the
> post in 1844. (Fisher, 1977, p. 35)

This passage is significant, demonstrating the power of local Indigenous
communities to actively and confidently assert control over their territories. Moreover, the small population of HBC trading posts rendered the
traders highly vulnerable. Fisher (1977) believes it is likely that
Indigenous Peoples could have destroyed them, but refrained from doing
so because the settler presence was valued.
    Indigenous Nations such as the Haida engaged with settlers and other
Indigenous communities through alternative economic means. Indeed,
Indigenous Peoples in British Columbia participated in both agrarian-

---

[5] It is possible that what was viewed as a "debtor" system by HBC fur traders was viewed by
Indigenous communities as a necessary act of generous gift-giving that creates and
sustains positive relations between two communities.

style capitalism and sophisticated trading relationships with European settlers. For example, the Haida grew potatoes and manufactured carvings and cedar canoes for sale (Fisher, 1977). HBC reports indicate that by 1836, the Haida engaged in large-scale potato farming, and by 1860, potato farming had spread to the majority of Indigenous communities in the interior of what would become British Columbia (Thomson, 1994).

Importantly, during this era there was no incentive for settlers to alter Indigenous Peoples' traditional ways of life. Indeed, exactly the opposite, settlers had "a considerable investment and interest in keeping much of the Indian way of life intact. Obviously it did not want to see the kind of radical change that would prevent the Indians from being efficient fur hunters. For this reason there was little intrusion on Indian land during the fur-trading period" (Fisher, 1977).

The very existence and maintenance of the fur trade turned, in some sense, on Indigenous Peoples remaining in control of hunting grounds that supplied the HBC with pelts. Thus, the economic pull of a steady supply of furs was substantial enough to render ineffectual calls for increased efforts at "civilizing" Indigenous Peoples (Fisher, 1977).

There was even a grudging respect for the property laws of Indigenous nations along the coast. A mass "culture area" of interconnected peoples, speaking a wide variety of unconnected language groups, bound coastal nations through familial bonds expressed and given shape in the form of totemic and house identities (Graeber & Wengrow, 2021). Land in these communities was the property of a House Chief – a title that provided exclusive rights to direct labor and to allocate resources within a defined property boundary or within the House Chief's territories. Ascension to the status of House Chief required a long history of study of, and immersion into, the cultural histories of the House to which one belonged, and further required not only the affirmation of House members, but even more importantly, the approval of neighboring House Chiefs whose interests were intertwined through marriage (Mills, 1994).

Although interests in particular fishing spots or berry-gathering areas descended matrilineally, broader control over border maintenance and the allocation of hunting resources fell to the House Chiefs whether they be male or female. Upon first seeing Gitxsan and Wet'suwet'en communities, HBC Chief Trader William Brown remarked that these were "men of property," just as traders along the East Coast referred to Indigenous Peoples as "proprietors" (Banner, 2005, p. 22).

Property law disputes within a House clan were resolved at the level of the House Chief. Disputes involving other House Chiefs required the gathering of regional chiefs to assemble in a regional *potlatch* (Mills, 1994). There, House business was discussed and settled, and the wealth and acumen of the Chiefs were demonstrated through a massive redistribution of wealth in the form of almost competitive gift giving called *potlatch*. With each gift, a House chief affirmed his or her ability to master the reciprocal relationship to the lands – one of "perpetual gift exchange" – such that the wealth of the people fed the land, and the land fed the people in abundance (Daly, 2007, p. 271).

Indigenous Peoples were not merely inhabiting the land: they were owners, stewards, sovereigns, and lawmakers over their traditional territories. As such, they actively asserted rights over their traditional territories, embraced aspects of agrarian cultivation, and engaged in trade relationships with both settlers and other Indigenous communities. At that time, European encroachments on Indigenous lands were minimal and allowed to occur because the trading relationship was mutually beneficial.

Indigenous–Settler Relationships in the Transition to Settlement

With a looming threat of American expansionism, the colony of Vancouver Island was established in 1849 through Royal Charter to HBC for the purpose of settling a colony of the United Kingdom (Martin, 1849). Despite the Oregon Treaty, signed by the United Kingdom and the United States in 1846, and settling boundaries on the west coast, the Colonial Office feared their interests, protected by assertions of sovereignty, were of little force or effect in comparison to physical occupation and settlement (Wrinch, 1932). HBC had the capital and administrative reach to oversee and regulate the process of European settlement in the area (Wrinch, 1932).[6]

The colony was barely more than a fur trading post, with little appeal for settlers, and "by 1852, as few as 435 emigrants had been sent to the colony, [and] only 11 had purchased land, and another 19 had applied for land" (Fisher, 1977, p. 58). Nearly all of the settlers were servants of the HBC (Blanshard, 1851, as cited in Fisher, 1992). Despite the HBC and Colonial Office's efforts, immigration and settlement of the colony remained stagnant until the Fraser River gold rush in 1858. While most

---

[6] Citing C. Grey (1849, June 29) in the House of Lords.

of the new immigrants were miners seeking gold, many developed ties to the region and sought to settle there. As settlement of the Colony expanded, competition between settlers and Indigenous Peoples for land, and particularly the highest quality farmlands, increased. Besides mining, new settlers primarily engaged in agriculture as a means of subsistence. This created tensions, because "[a]gricultural settlement was destructive to the Indian's methods of food gathering. In the Fort Victoria area, for example, Indian camas grounds were broken up by the plough" (Fisher, 1977, p. 66). Indigenous Peoples were also utilizing agrarian techniques for producing food, and serious competition emerged for the most arable sections of land.

Just weeks after the HBC received the Royal Grant, and in keeping with the general tenor of British land policy in the East, James Douglas, Chief Factor for HBC, and soon-to-be Governor of the Vancouver Island Colony, wrote to the HBC secretary in London making it clear that arrangements would have to be made for the purchase of Indigenous lands, as had been the well-established practice in Eastern Canada for over a century (Douglas, 1849).

The HBC replied by citing a report compiled by the Committee of the House of Commons examining claims of the New Zealand Company. Within, it was argued that Indigenous Peoples "had only 'qualified Dominion' over their country, consisting of a right of occupancy but not title to land" (Fisher, 1977, p. 66). Accordingly, Douglas was permitted to engage in treaty-making with Indigenous Peoples with respect to lands that had been cultivated or had houses built by the year 1846 when they came under the sovereignty of Great Britain.[7] All other land was to be regarded as waste and therefore available for colonization (Fisher, 1977). Douglas set about negotiating treaties with local Indigenous communities. In total, Douglas made fourteen treaty agreements between 1849 and 1854.

By 1854, Douglas had acquired more land than could be effectively settled and defended (Harris, 2002). Engaging in treaty-making was a time-consuming endeavor, and a process that required the Crown's commitment to substantial annual gift giving to Indigenous treaty partners. Thus, further treaty-making was likely not a priority unless there was actual need and use for the lands to be acquired. Interestingly, Douglas maintained a policy until 1859 for compensating Indians for

---

[7] 1846 is the date of the signing of the Oregon Treaty with the United States.

the surrender of their lands. Yet, this policy would end in both intent and practice because in 1858 the severing of the colony's ties with the HBC reduced the amount of goods available[8] for purchasing Indigenous lands.

In illustration of this rapid swing in policy toward Indian lands, John Trutch, Chief Commissioner of Lands and Works for British Columbia in 1864, wrote that "the Indians had to [be] relieved of as much land as possible so that it could be 'properly' and 'efficiently' used by European farmers" (Fisher, 1977, p. 162). Later, Trutch argued that the lands reserved for Indigenous Peoples were "entirely disproportionate to the numbers or requirements of the Indian tribes," and that it was "very desirable ... that it should be placed in possession of white settlers as soon as practicable" (Fisher, 1977, p. 163).[9]

By 1866, the reserves of the Shuswap peoples were adjusted so that a forty-mile stretch of land was reduced to three reserves each of no more than four square miles, a unilateral process that would have been unimaginable during the earlier era in the east. Further reductions soon after totaled 40,000 acres (Fisher, 1977, p. 163). Yet, rendering lands as legally empty or wasted was insufficient to get land into the hands of settlers.

The Torrens title system of land registration was implemented under the *Land Registry Act* 1860.[10] Under the Act, any person who possessed title that had been registered for a period of five years was deemed

---

[8] Cole Harris provided the best explanation for why Douglas stopped. By 1854, Douglas had acquired more land than he could effectively settle and defend.

[9] See Good to Trutch, (1865, Sept. 26). British Columbia, Colonial Secretary, Outward Correspondence, September 1860–May 1872, Letters to Lands and Works Department, PABC.

Reserves were not coextensive with Indigenous communities understanding of the boundaries of their traditional territories. These were allotted with some measure of consultation with Indigenous communities, but ultimately decisions were made by colonial administrators. We emphasize the reduction of reserve lands because this represents erasure of Indigenous land rights that were clearly recognized and affirmed by colonial administrators. For a more fulsome discussion of the reserve creation process, see Diamond (2022) and Harris (2002).

[10] *Land Registry Act* 1860. Despite the title, the Act did not receive Royal Assent until January 18, 1861. Later that year, the *British Columbia Land Registry Act*, which was similar but did not create indefeasible titles, was implemented on the mainland colony of British Columbia. Registered titles, however, were still privileged over non-registered interests. The Torrens system was implemented on the mainland in 1870 after the colonies united. Colony of British Columbia, *British Columbia Land Registry Act*, August 26, 1861 (25 Vict.), Appendix to the Revised Statutes of British Columbia, 1871, no. 20.

"absolutely and indefeasibly entitled to the interest in respect of [that land]" (*Land Registry Act 1860*, s. 20). In simple terms, five years after registering a newly created title to lands the owner had an exclusive right to land that was unaffected by any other unregistered interests (i.e., Indian land interests).

Bhandar (2018) observed that "the most radical aspect of a system of title by registration is that it renders all prior ownership claims irrelevant" (p. 95). Taylor (2008) argued that what separated the Torrens systems from other systems of deed registration is that it made deeds easier to find – it did not cure any defects in the title.

Validation versus Elimination of Indigenous Claims

By 1875, Télesphore Fournier, the Minister of Justice in Ottawa, now aware that Indigenous lands in British Columbia were, with the minor exception of the fourteen Douglas treaties, not acquired in accordance with the established protocol of purchase through treaty, reprimanded Lieutenant-Governor Trutch. He recommended that *An Act to Amend and Consolidate the Laws Affecting Crown Lands* in British Columbia be disallowed and postponed until the last possible date because it ignored Indigenous land rights (Hodgins, 1896). Ultimately, the federal government and British Columbia agreed to the creation of a joint commission to address the allotment of Indian reserves. Yet Harris (2002) maintained that the Joint Indian Reserve Commission had little interest in casting doubt upon vast swaths of settler land titles and were determined to leave sufficient land open for further settlement.

We may never fully know why colonial policy was set aside, but we can point to four points of context. First, the relationship between Indigenous Peoples and settlers was, on the West Coast, recent and shallow compared to the hundreds of years old relationships in the east. In British Columbia, Indigenous and settler families were not intermarried, contacts were comparatively few, and there was no motivation for anything more complex than a commercial trading relationship. As the rhetoric of race began to influence relations between colonial officials and Indigenous Peoples, there was no long history to buffer growing racism. The language of efficiency and waste came to dominate the characterizations of Indigenous lands and what to do with them. In the east, settler colonial deeds of possession could be traced to original Indigenous possession, and so to question the validity of Indigenous title was to cast doubt upon every subsequent purchaser. But in the west, as in Australia, there were no prior settler titles, and each new title was to be based on occupation of land noted in a centralized registry. Settler claims to land were in direct competition with Indigenous histories and patterns of occupation. Valid titles thus depended not on a valid chain of prior titles, but rather a complete wiping clean of any prior owners, and a fresh start with settler names on the deeds. In this, Australia and British Columbia found themselves in identical positions – and so it is no surprise they are the first and second jurisdictions to adopt the most efficient methodology for eliminating Indigenous title to the land: the issuance of indefeasible title under the Torrens system.

Contemporary Indigenous Land Rights Claims and Their Relationship to Torrens Title

Of course, the issue of Indigenous land claims has never gone away. Indigenous communities in British Columbia have actively asserted their rights to land throughout the nineteenth, twentieth, twenty-first centuries. Most notably, in *Tsilhqot'in Nation v. British Columbia* (2014), the Tsilhqot'in successfully brought a claim for Aboriginal title over a large portion of their traditional territories.

Aboriginal title is grounded in Indigenous legal systems, derived from Indigenous use, occupancy, and control of their lands prior to the Crown's assertion of sovereignty (*Tsilhqot'in Nation*, 2014). Nevertheless, the Supreme Court of Canada described the content of Aboriginal title as analogous to ownership rights, rather than a jurisdictional or sovereign authority over the land. As a result, Aboriginal title claims have overlapped – and may continue to overlap, as well as come into conflict with fee simple ownership rights of property owners in contemporary British Columbia.

Importantly, in *Tsilhqot'in Nation*, the plaintiffs carefully drew the borders of their claimed territory to exclude any overlap with privately owned lands held in fee simple. Hence, the Supreme Court was not required to consider this issue of conflict and primacy.

Nevertheless, in some cases avoidance of overlap between Indigenous land rights and privately owned and registered property is simply not possible. This was the case of the Grace Islet dispute in British Columbia, where the Cowichan Nation sought a declaration of title for ancient burial grounds on fee simple lands (which were threatened by development) (Borrows, 2015). This dispute was settled out of court by the Cowichan and the provincial government, "to avoid potentially precedent-setting litigation that favourably pitted Aboriginal title against 'private' ownership" (Borrows, 2015, p. 99). As such, the relationship between overlapping Aboriginal title rights and privately owned and registered fee simple under the Torrens title system remains an open question.[11]

Registrability of Aboriginal Title

Thus far, attempts by Indigenous communities to register their Aboriginal title rights under the Torrens title system have been rejected by the courts. In *Skeetchestn Indian Band and Secwepemc Aboriginal Nation v. Registrar of Land Titles* (*Skeetchestn Indian Band*, 2000),[12] the plaintiffs appealed a decision by the Registrar of Titles to refuse to register "a certificate of pending litigation against certain lands in the Kamloops Land Title District, which many years ago, the Crown had granted in fee simple." In addition, the plaintiffs also sought a declaration that they held Aboriginal title rights over the land in question. Relying on a proceeding associated with the *Delgamuukw* case, indexed as *Uukw* (1988), the Court noted that the claim for Aboriginal title is "upstream of the certificate of indefeasible title" (in *Skeetchestn Indian Band*, 2000, para. 50), exists outside the four corners of the legislative framework of the *Land Titles Act* and is therefore not an interest capable of registration.

The Court added that "Aboriginal title is not marketable and is therefore not registerable" (*Skeetchestn Indian Band*, 2000, para. 20). In simple terms, the idea is that Aboriginal title is an interest that arises outside the legislative framework of the *Land Titles Act*, and therefore cannot be registered. In addition, because Aboriginal title lands are only alienable to the Crown, they are not marketable and incapable of registration.

The important point for our purposes is that the Torrens title system continues to secure settler land rights from competing Aboriginal title claims. This has two major implications. First, as Aboriginal title interests cannot be registered, landowners and prospective landowners alike may not receive notice that certain lands held in fee simple are currently or likely to be the subject of an Aboriginal title claim. The presence of a current or impending Aboriginal title claim is likely to alter the market value of the land. Second, allowing for registration of Aboriginal title

---

[11] For fruitful discussions of how overlapping Aboriginal title and private property rights claims might be resolved, see Borrows (2015) and Sanderson and Singh (2021).

[12] *Skeetchestn Indian Band v. Registrar of Land Titles (Kamloops), (2000) 143 B.C.A.C.*

interests on lands regulated under the *Land Titles Act* would notify and motivate Aboriginal title claims to be proactively addressed by the provinces and the federal government. A potentially fruitful and simple solution, then, would be to amend the *Land Titles Act* to make possible the registration of Aboriginal title interests. Landowners and Indigenous claimants alike would benefit from the notice, and the ability to register a claim.

Conclusion

The legal nature of Indigenous tenure in what we now call British Columbia is unique. But the use of property law and land title regulation, as efficient tools of dispossession, is a common theme in spaces wherever settlement encountered prior occupiers – as, for example, shown in the Aotearoa New Zealand chapter elsewhere in this book. There a Native Land Court was designed to identify customary title holders, and to convert customary titles into fee simple titles. These fee simple titles could then be bought and sold on the open market, thereby making it possible for settlers to acquire said titles. Likewise, as shown by Koné, in the Democratic Republic of Congo Indigenous land rights were totally denied by a legal regime that viewed all lands not held by settlers as "vacant" and therefore the property of the state. In each of these spaces, Indigenous communities were dispossessed of their lands through law, policy, and bureaucracy, rather than brute force or conquest.

Righting historical wrongs is a complex but achievable goal. Our intervention should be viewed as an initial step in this process – namely, to accurately and coherently identify the wrong in order to illuminate avenues for redress. In the context of Indigenous dispossession in British Columbia, this requires an empirical analysis of the laws and policies that facilitated dispossession.

While British policy toward Indigenous land in North America remained constant after 1763, the actual practice varied by region and era. Along the eastern seaboard and around the Great Lakes, Indigenous claims to land were affirmed, which enabled Indigenous sellers to engage with British and colonial buyers. In British Columbia, virtually no Indigenous rights to land were recognized by treaty, and direct purchases of Indigenous land were essentially non-existent.[13] The one hundred or so

---

[13] A few direct purchases were made but these purchases were quickly outlawed and deemed to be invalid. See Douglas to Lytton, March 14, 1859, in Victoria, Government

years between the colonial experience in the eastern Americas and the west coast of British Columbia provide context for the differing treatments.

During these intervening years, social and political theories began casting Indigenous Peoples as backwards and inferior, which promoted discourse around Indigenous lands as being waste due to inefficient use. In British Columbia, there was no long history of Indigenous–settler alliances or even any need for such alliances – the relationships were almost purely commercial, in sharp contrast to close relationships in the east that the British enjoyed with their Indigenous military and commercial allies during the seventeenth and eighteenth centuries. The lack of close bonds made it easy for late nineteenth-century colonists to make (racist) assumptions about Indigenous Peoples and their relationships to land. Perhaps more importantly, once Indigenous title to land had been recognized as it was in the east and around the Great Lakes, future deeds for the same land could be traced to an original Indigenous seller. To deny Indigenous rights to land would thus jeopardize the long chains of settler title made after purchase from an Indigenous seller. Precisely the opposite situation obtained in the West: there, valid setter title turned on the complete erasure of Indigenous interests in the land – *terra nullius* – because without purchase, no settler interests in fee could be recognized.

The history we present here in this chapter is important for understanding the current distribution of land rights in British Columbia and has implications for how we might think about contemporary Aboriginal title claims, because it is clear that Indigenous lands were taken without consent or sale. The vast disparity in the treatment of Indigenous lands by colonial officials between the seventeenth and mid-nineteenth centuries strongly suggests that official policy had changed, and so that perhaps even if immoral, the settlement of British Columbia was at least legal. But this is not the case, and the settlement that occurred was wrong in both law and policy.

References

Banner, S. (2005). *How the Indians lost their land: Law and power on the frontier.* Cambridge, US: Harvard University Press.

Bhandar, B. (2015). Title by registration: Instituting modern property law and creating racial value in the settler colony. *Journal of Law and Society*, 42(2), 253–282.

Printing Office James' Bay, *Papers Connected with the Indian Land Question 1850–1875* (Victoria: Richard Wolfenden, Government Printer), p. 15.

(2018). *Colonial lives of property: Law, land and racial regimes of ownership.* Durham, US: Duke University Press.

Borrows, J. (2015). Aboriginal title and private property. *The Supreme Court Law Review: Osgoode's Annual Constitutional Cases Conference,* 71(1), 5.

Corbiere, A. (2019). *Anishinaabe treaty-making in the 18th- and 19th-Century northern Great Lakes: From shared meanings to epistemological chasms* [Doctoral dissertation, Osgoode Hall Law School, York University). https://yorkspace.library.yorku.ca/items/8f5cec7f-9b7b-4750-944e-66fd4a2e9b21.)

Daly, R. (2007). *Our box was full: An ethnography for the Delgamuukw plaintiffs.* Vancouver, Canada: University of British Columbia Press.

Diamond, D. (2022). *Dispossession and resistance: A history of Indigenous and settler relations to land in British Columbia, 1800–1890* [LLM thesis, University of Toronto].

Douglas, J. (1849). *Fort Victoria letters, 1846–1851.* https://royalbcmuseum.bc.ca/sites/default/files/sites/default/files/images/Douglas_Treaties_Correspondence1.pdf

Fisher, R. (1977). *The land-based fur trade, contact and conflict: Indian-European relations in British Columbia, 1774–1890.* Vancouver: University of British Columbia Press.

(1992). *Contact and conflict: Indian-European Relations in British Columbia, 1774–1890.* Vancouver: University of British Columbia Press.

Graeber, D., & Wengrow, D. (2021). *The dawn of everything: A new history of humanity.* London, UK: Penguin.

Harris, C. (2002). *Making native space: Colonialism, resistance, and reserves in British Columbia.* Vancouver, Canada: UBC Press.

Hodgins, W. E. (1896). Correspondence, Reports of the ministers of Justice and Orders in Council Upon the Subject of Dominion and Provincial Legislation 1867–1895, "Compiled Under the Direction of the Honourable The Minister of Justice" Ottawa: Government Printing Bureau, at 1024–1028

Jones, H. (2018). *Property, territory, and colonialism: An international legal history of enclosure.* Cambridge UK: Cambridge University Press.

Martin, R. M. (1849). *Hudson's Bay territories and Vancouver's Island: With an exposition of the chartered rights, conduct, and policy of the Hon'ible Hudson's Bay Corporation.* London, UK: T. and W. Boone. https://open.library.ubc.ca/viewer/bcbooks/1.0221805#p183z-1r0F:168

Mills, A. (1994) *Eagle down is our law: Witsuwit'en law, feasts, and land claims.* Vancouver: UBC Press.

Morito, B. (2012). *An ethic of mutual respect: The covenant chain and Aboriginal-Crown relations.* Vancouver: UBC Press.

Pottage, A. (1994). The measure of land. *Modern Law Review,* 57(3), 361–384. https://doi.org/10.1111/j.1468-2230.1994.tb01946.x

Sanderson, D., & Singh, A. C. (2021). Why is Aboriginal title property if it looks like sovereignty? *Canadian Journal of Law & Jurisprudence*, 34(2), 417–460

Taylor, G. (2008). *The law of the land: The advent of the Torrens system in Canada*. Toronto, Canada: University of Toronto Press.

Thomson, D. (1994). The response of Okanagan Indians to European settlement. *BC Studies*, 101, 96–117.

Torrens, R. R. (1859). The South Australian System of conveyancing by registration of title, with instructions for the guidance of parties dealing, illustrated by copies of the books and forms in use in the Lands Titles Office, Adelaide, South Australia.

Wrinch, L. A. (1932). *Land policy of the colony of Vancouver Island 1849–1866* [Unpublished master's thesis]. University of British Columbia.

8

Māori Land Law in Aotearoa New Zealand

Recognizing Land as tāonga tuku iho

CARWYN JONES AND SANDRA CORTÉS ACOSTA

Introduction

During the nineteenth century, the New Zealand Government used a series of legislative mechanisms to facilitate the alienation of land from Māori (Boast, 2008). The Māori customary regime was seriously altered, and land titles were individualized to facilitate land transactions and settlement. The conversion from a customary regime into a fee simple (or freehold title system) revealed difficulties in reconciling the "new" system with the customary regime. Under the customary regime, land is held in accordance with *tikanga* Māori (Māori law, values, and practices)[1] and represents a source of identity (Durie, 1998), while under the "new" Crown land tenure system, land was and is today seen in terms of market potential and commercial interests.

The freehold title system resulted in the alienation of the land, undermined tribal authority, and imposed complex ownership arrangements (Belgrave et al., 2004). Indeed, the *Land Transfer Act* 1870 introduced the Torrens system for land titles, where those with indefeasible title were guaranteed full ownership to the land, thus extinguishing customary title. As Diamond and Sanderson argue in this book, the Torrens system created the administrative tool for dispossession with ongoing ramifications for land rights. The freehold system also created two categories of private land: general land and Māori freehold land. General land, under

This chapter is based, in part, on Sandra Cortés Acosta's PhD dissertation at Te Herenga Waka Victoria University of Wellington.

[1] *Tikanga* is not equivalent to customary law. *Tikanga* operates in all aspects of Māori life and comprises cultural, spiritual, and practical aspects that are beyond a set of rules, which apply to distinct areas of social life or a strictly legal domain (Jones, 2014).

private ownership, is not subject to the distinct statutory regime of Māori freehold land and can be owned by Māori or any other New Zealander. Māori freehold land is usually collectively held and today is regulated by the *Te Ture Whenua Māori/Māori Land Act* 1993 (TTWM). The status of Māori freehold land indicates that the land title is ultimately derived from a determination by the Native/Māori Land Court based on customary regime and ancestral connections, and has been converted by the Court to a freehold title.

The TTWM has roots in the relationship of Māori with the land, the transition of customary land to an individual title, and various attempts to address challenges associated with fragmented titles and multiple owners. It is estimated that Māori freehold land is about 5 percent of Aotearoa New Zealand's 26.8 million hectares of total land area (Harmsworth, 2018).[2]

For Māori, attitudes toward land are multidimensional and continue to be deeply influenced by *mātauranga* Māori (Māori knowledge systems) (Harmsworth & Awatere, 2013; Mead, 2016; Marsden, 2003). The political and legal processes preceding the enactment of TTWM illustrated that Māori saw a recognition of land as a basis of identity (Durie, 1999; Mead, 2016). Additionally, the pressure to develop the land with commercial interests motivated a "new role" for the land as a sustainable economic base for Māori. Therefore, the TTWM focuses on retention alongside utilization, and recognizes land as *tāonga tuku iho* – a treasure that connects current generations with their ancestors and future generations. Safeguarding this land is critical moving forward.

Te whenua Te iwi, the Land and the People

While many aspects of Māori culture are integrated into mainstream culture in Aotearoa New Zealand, it remains distinct in several ways. For example, Māori rights and obligations to land are primarily founded upon ancestral connection to the land over successive generations. Maintaining that connection through use of the land and participation in the community is also important. The resolution of disputes about land and the assertion of rights in relation to land are framed by a

---

[2] The total area of Māori freehold land differs by source. Te Puni Kōkiri (2014) estimates that Māori freehold land varies between 1.43 million and 1.77 million hectares, while Kingi (2008) suggests that Māori freehold land is about 5.6 percent of New Zealand's total land area of 26.8 million hectares.

distinctive worldview. According to this worldview, both rights and duties are held in accordance with *tikanga* Māori, which Jones (2014) articulates is a Māori values-based system that "[d]escribes the right or correct way of doing things within Māori society. It is a system comprising practices, principles, processes and procedures, and traditional knowledge. It encompasses Māori law but also includes ritual, customs, spiritual and socio-political dimensions that go well beyond the legal domain" (p. 189).

Before European arrival in Aotearoa New Zealand and the signing of *Te Tiriti o Waitangi* (the Treaty of Waitangi), Māori association with the land was shaped by the belief that people belong to the land rather than owning it (Mead, 2016). For Māori, the relationship between people and land comes from an ancestral connection based on customary practices, protocols, and values. Land is a source of identity for Māori, as they see themselves as *tangata whenua* or the people of the land. *Whenua* is the word for land in *Te Reo Māori* (Māori language). As Mead (2016) states, "whenua carries a wide range of meanings. Whenua, as placenta, sustains life and the connection between the foetus and the placenta is through the umbilical cord. This fact of life is a metaphor for whenua, as land, and is the basis for the high value placed on land" (p. 285).

Under a Māori customary regime, rights of occupation and use were determined collectively by Māori tribal authorities, subdivided into *whānau, hapū* and *iwi* (family, sub-tribe and tribe). As observed by Durie (1987), "in the beginning land was not something that could be owned or traded. Maoris did not seek to own or possess anything, but to belong. One belonged to a family that belonged to a hapū that belonged to a tribe. One did not own land. One belonged to the land" (p. 78).

The Māori customary regime and association to land involved collectively held rights of occupation, access, and use over land without claiming ownership (Durie, 1998; Kingi, 2008; Bennion, 2009). The rights to land were evidenced through occupation by establishing *kāinga* (settlement) and cultivation, but also through the use of resources for the sustainability and survival of the settlement. Association with the land was predominantly recognized by an ancestral connection based on historical occupation (*ahikāroa*) or spiritual connection with the land – for example, birth or death of their ancestors. Given this ancestral connection with a specific land or area, the association with the land could be retained even when rights over the land were lost (Waitangi Tribunal, 2003).

Although the Crown has altered the customary regime, attitudes toward land are still profoundly influenced by *mātauranga* Māori

(Māori knowledge systems) (Harmsworth & Awatere, 2013; Mead, 2016; Marsden, 2003). *Mātauranga* Māori provides the basis for *Te Ao Māori* (Māori world view) and Māori values through which Māori experience and interpret their environment and determine their attitudes toward land (Harmsworth & Awatere, 2013; Marsden, 2003; Mead, 2016; Phillips & Hulme, 1987). Guiding land use decisions were principles of interdependency and intergenerational equity. Interdependency is a reciprocal relationship between people and the land, and comprises *manaaki whenua* (caring for the land) and *manaaki tangata* (caring for people) (Harmsworth & Awatere, 2013). Intergenerational equity can be seen as a concern for resource sustainability and protection of the land across generations. With these decision drivers in place, land is passed from one generation to the next in as good a condition as it was received.

Te Tiriti o Waitangi

Land tenure and the mechanisms for recognizing *tikanga*-based or Māori customary forms of title were specific matters addressed in *Te Tiriti o Waitangi*/the Treaty of Waitangi, signed in 1840 by Māori leaders and the British Crown. Te Tiriti is recognized as a foundational constitutional document, which established the formal relationship between Māori and British spheres of authority. It was signed in the context of a system of *tikanga* that provided for a range of intersecting rights and duties in relation to land and the natural environment. Te Tiriti is central to any discussion of Māori land.

The essential bargain set out in Te Tiriti was that the British Crown could exercise governmental authority, at least over British subjects in Aotearoa, in exchange for the protection of Māori authority. Te Tiriti contains specific guarantees for Māori to retain the undisturbed possession of their lands, unless and until Māori wished to sell any such land. The Māori text of Te Tiriti frames this as a broad guarantee of authority over all things that are highly valued to Māori, whereas the English text uses the specific language of property rights in relation to resources such as land, forests, and fisheries.

Partly on the basis of Te Tiriti and partly on the basis of "discovery," the British Crown asserted sovereignty over Aotearoa New Zealand, notwithstanding the fact that exclusive Crown sovereignty would have been entirely inconsistent with the guarantees of Māori authority contained in Te Tiriti.

Te Tiriti is now recognized as a foundational component of Aotearoa New Zealand's unwritten constitution. In 1975, the Waitangi Tribunal was established to hear claims based on "the principles of the Treaty" and has subsequently published a large body of reports addressing both historical and contemporary breaches of Treaty principles and making recommendations to the government of the day to redress well-founded claims and to prevent future breaches of Treaty principles. Many of these claims relate specifically to land alienation that has occurred in breach of Te Tiriti.

However, without formal constitutional protection, legally enforceable rights under Te Tiriti are limited. Aotearoa New Zealand's unitary and unicameral system of government centralizes power in the Parliament, which, in turn, has historically been dominated by the Executive branch, at least until the introduction of proportional representation in 1996. Settlements of historical Treaty claims are negotiated political agreements, rather than a recognition of rights. Both the Māori Land Court and the ordinary courts have a limited statutory jurisdiction in relation to Māori rights to land. As a consequence, Māori have been able to use Te Tiriti more effectively as a political instrument, rather than the source of legally enforceable rights to land.

An Era of Land Dispossession, Alienation and Title Individualization

From the 1860s onwards, the Crown drastically altered the Māori customary regime to facilitate the trading of the land for European settlement purposes. The Torrens system, an ownership arrangement with individual and indefeasible title-recording owners and shareholders, replaced the customary regime. Though some land blocks remained under Māori ownership (today known as Māori freehold land), this individualization undermined tribal authority and affected the social cohesion between *whānau*, *hapū*, and *iwi*.

The Crown enforced a range of legal mechanisms to dispossess and alienate land from Māori and individualize the property rights of the land without reference to the wider community. The main mechanisms used were land confiscation, Crown land purchases and alienation facilitated by the Native Land Court (Boast, 2008; Bennion, 2009).[3] The Native Land Court was established to stipulate who held the rights on customary

---

[3] Land confiscation was a coercive expropriation of customary land by statutory fiat and was a way to individualize the land that was under Māori customary tenure and make it recognizable under English Common Law (Boast, 2008).

land and had the authority to convert customary lands into fee simple.[4] Land was surveyed and divided up into blocks of varying sizes, and lists of "owners" were drawn up and allocated with shares (Mead, 2016). As a result, two parallel ownership arrangements took place: European land (today known as general land) and Māori freehold land. Since then, Māori freehold land has evolved into a complex multiple ownership structure with fragmented titles and multiple interests (Kingi, 2008; Waitangi Tribunal, 2008).[5]

The Current Māori Land Law Framework

During the twentieth century, the Crown was deeply involved in the administration and management of Māori freehold land with commercial purposes in mind. Before the Second World War, policies regarding Māori land development relied on a process of amalgamation and incorporation as an attempt to consolidate land blocks into economic units and simplify ownership (Belgrave et al., 2004).[6] After the mid-twentieth century, the *Māori Affairs Act* 1953 and its amendments led to an era of title reforms and schemes for administering Māori freehold land. Furthermore, policies were mainly implemented through the Māori Land Court (formerly the Native Land Court), the Department of the Māori Affairs,[7] and the Māori

---

[4] To claim rights over customary land, the Native Land Court used three *take* (foundations), *take tuku* (gift), *take ōhāki* (deathbed deposition), and *take raupatu* (conquest) (Sinclair, 1977).

[5] The legislation in the 1860s made it mandatory that all descendants from the former "owners" had an equal right to the land. For that reason, land titles allocated to some Māori owners were handed down through successive generations. With an additional situation, descendants now have an absolute right of ownership to the land interest of both parents. Register owners in the last few generations have then exponentially increased (Kingi, 2008).

[6] The Incorporations system was established under the *Native Land Court Act* 1894. Given that this system facilitated the amalgamation of land titles into groups, Sir Āpirana Ngata recognized incorporations as an attempt to revert the individualization of the land titles and emulate the former regime of collective ownership, with one important difference: the administration of the land was centralized in a group of committee members (Durie, 1999; Kingi, 2008).

[7] Although the roots for the Department of Māori Affairs can be traced back to former agencies created in the 1800s, it was formally established in 1947 (Fleras & Spoonley, 1999). This government body was in charge of implementing and conducting initiatives regarding Māori policy and land development, vocational training, welfare, and housing (Durie, 1999). Initially, it was constituted under the philosophy of supporting tribal leaders and encouraging collective strategies with tribal aspirations for developing their land (Fleras & Spoonley, 1999).

Trustee[8] (Belgrave et al., 2004; Fleras & Spoonley, 1999; Waitangi Tribunal, 2016).

The *Māori Affairs Act* 1953 introduced a leasing regime, set out reforms for the operation of Māori incorporations, and created a system of trusts, known as 438 trusts.[9] This Act also conferred the Māori Land Court with special powers to (1) appoint the Māori trustee as an agent to dispose of unproductive land; (2) allow others apart from landowners to develop a specific Māori land block, when it was proved that it was fertile and was not being put to "good use"; and (3) establish an incorporation over any block of Māori freehold land with three or more owners under the intent to occupy and use the land for any agricultural, pastoral, or timber activities. However, the implementation of the reforms introduced in the *Māori Affairs Act* 1953 and its amendments were not an easy task for the Crown. By the end of the twentieth century, Māori opposition was vocal and well organized, demanding the return of unjustly alienated land and the retention of land in Māori ownership according to *tikanga* Māori. This led to the current Māori land law framework, regulated by the TTWM.

The TTWM explicitly references *Te Tiriti o Waitangi* and recognizes that *whenua* (land) is a *taonga tuku iho* or a treasure for Māori people that connects current generations with their ancestors and those to come. The TTWM recognizes that Māori cultural values influence Māori behavior and relationships with land, driving decisions relating to collaboration, investment, diversification, and management of Māori freehold land. The TTWM promotes the retention of land in the hands of its owners, their *whānau* (extended family) and their *hapū* (sub-tribe). It also facilitates the use, development and control of Māori freehold

---

[8] The position of the Māori Trustee was formerly established at the beginning of the twentieth century under the *Native Trustee Act* 1920. It was originally created to provide support in concerns such as the management and productivity of Māori land. The Māori Trustee was established under the *Māori Trustee Act* 1953 and later replaced by the *Māori Trustee Amendment Act* 2009. According to the more recent Act, the Māori Trustee has the capacity and power to carry on or undertake any business or activity or to enter into any transaction.

[9] Incorporations were provided with special provisions for the sale and purchase of Māori freehold land within the incorporation. Conversely, the 438 trusts allowed land to be vested in trustees, often the Māori Trustee, who had the power to administer the trust property for the benefit of Māori or their descendants (Waitangi Tribunal, 2016). The introduction of 438 trusts of the *Māori Affairs Act* 1953 were the basis for the creation of the other statutory trusts in the *Te Ture Whenua Māori Act* 1993. Today, 438 trusts are known as Ahu Whenua trusts.

land, recognizing several different land uses, not only commercial use. To meet these objectives, the TTWM sets strong rules that restrict the alienation of Māori freehold land, including sales or lease (Durie, 1998).

Moreover, to administer and facilitate decisions, the TTWM provides a scheme for the Māori land governance structures. These structures have become an important body to overcome absentee ownership and title fragmentation. They have been used as a vehicle to try to revert to collective ownership, but they cannot be easily compared with any "institutions" observed under the customary regime (Kingi, 2008).

Foreshore and Seabed

Aotearoa New Zealand has not experienced the same kind of landmark Aboriginal title cases that jurisdictions such as Australia and Canada saw in the latter part of the twentieth century (see the chapters on Australia and Canada in this book).[10] The primary reason for this is that the Native Land Court was extremely effective in its task of converting customary title into freehold title. As discussed above, Māori lands and title have been regulated by a comprehensive statutory regime since the 1860s. Although the current legislation, *Te Ture Whenua Māori Act* 1993, maintains the Māori Land Court's jurisdiction to identify customary title, it is estimated that very few, if any, areas of land remain that are held according to customary title. Most Māori land is now held as Māori freehold land. However, in recent years, the nature of potential customary title in the foreshore and seabed has been the subject of litigation, legislation, and significant political debate.[11]

The nature of Māori rights in the foreshore and seabed became an issue of significant public controversy following the Court of Appeal's 2003 decision in *Ngāti Apa v Attorney-General*. In that case, the Court of Appeal (at the time, the highest appellate court based in Aotearoa, with only the United Kingdom's Privy Council superior in hierarchy) recognized that areas of the foreshore and seabed may still be held under Māori customary title. The *Ngāti Apa* decision did not address any specific claims of customary title, so the Court did not make any findings of customary title existing in any particular area of the foreshore. Rather,

---

[10] See, for example, *Mabo v Queensland (No 2)* (1992) 175 CLR 1; *Delgamuukw v British Columbia*, [1997] 3 SCR 1010.

[11] See *Ngāti Apa*; *Foreshore and Seabed Act* 2004; *Marine and Coastal Area (Takutai Moana) Act* 2011; and *Edwards*.

the Court determined that such title could theoretically exist. That is, a Native Land Court determination of customary title in coastal land, and conversion of that title to freehold title, did not imply any determination about title to the adjacent foreshore. What is more, the Court held that there was no general legislative bar to the existence of Māori customary title to the foreshore. The Court noted that it would not necessarily be easy to prove continuing customary title, and it may be that very few areas of customary title in the foreshore still exist, but, nevertheless, such rights and title could potentially be proven. *Ngāti Apa* overruled a previous Court of Appeal decision, *In Re the Ninety-Mile Beach*,[12] and, in doing so, upended existing assumptions of title in the foreshore.

The Court of Appeal's decision sparked an intense political debate. Within days, the then Labour-led government announced that it intended to introduce legislation removing the court's ability to recognize either common law Aboriginal title or customary title under TTWM for the foreshore and seabed. The government's proposals were highly controversial, with many Māori viewing them as a confiscation of property rights.[13] The government's intention was to provide a more limited legislative scheme for the recognition of Māori customary rights in the foreshore and seabed than would have been provided by the recognition of common law Aboriginal title or by a Māori Land Court finding of customary title. The central plank of the legislation provided that title to the foreshore and seabed would be held by the Crown. Māori would be able to apply for the recognition of customary rights in these areas, but not exclusive title.

Prior to legislation being introduced, the Waitangi Tribunal agreed to urgently hear claims alleging that the Crown's proposals were inconsistent with the principles of the Treaty of Waitangi. The Tribunal found the Crown's proposed policy was in breach of Treaty principles in several ways. First, the Tribunal determined that, even if no specific customary title to the foreshore had at that point been recognized, the removal of the ability to test such claims of title in the courts would be tantamount to the removal of a property right. Second, the Tribunal noted that the Crown already had the ability to compulsorily purchase land under public works legislation, but the proposed policy would remove property

---

[12] In Re the Ninety-Mile Beach [1963] NZLR 461.
[13] A Māori Cabinet Minister, Tariana Turia, resigned over this issue and went on to establish the Māori Party, whose MPs held ministerial portfolios in subsequent administrations and were influential in repealing the *Foreshore and Seabed Act*.

rights to the foreshore and seabed without compensation. Third, because the proposals would exempt any areas of the foreshore already explicitly covered by a certificate of title, only Māori property rights would be abrogated. The Tribunal had many other concerns with both the substance of the proposals and the process by which they were developed and recommended that the Crown engage in a longer conversation with Māori before progressing the proposed policy. However, the government was not bound to follow those recommendations, and the *Foreshore and Seabed Act* was enacted in 2004.

Foreshore and Seabed Act

The *Foreshore and Seabed Act* 2004 provided for two different types of recognition of customary rights. "Territorial customary rights" could be recognized where a group could prove they had exclusive use and occupation of an area of the public foreshore and seabed without substantial interruption since 1840, and that the group also had continuous title to contiguous land. Any Māori kin group – a *whānau*, *hapū*, or *iwi* – was able to make a claim for territorial customary rights under the Act. A successful application for the recognition of territorial customary rights could lead to one of two outcomes. The successful applicant group could apply to the High Court for an order referring the matter to the attorney-general and minister of Māori Affairs to negotiate appropriate redress. Alternatively, the applicant may apply for an order establishing a foreshore and seabed reserve.

The other customary rights recognition mechanism established by the *Foreshore and Seabed Act* is a "customary rights order." Both the High Court and the Māori Land Court had jurisdiction to determine applications for customary rights orders under the 2004 Act. Customary rights orders provide recognition of specific customary practices. Māori groups could apply for a customary rights order in relation to an activity or practice that meets the following criteria:[14]

- the activity or practice is, and has been since 1840, integral to *tikanga* Māori; and
- has been carried on, exercised, or followed in accordance with *tikanga* Māori in a substantially uninterrupted manner since 1840, in the area of the public foreshore and seabed specified in the application; and

---

[14] s 50, *Foreshore and Seabed Act* 2004.

- continues to be carried on, exercised or followed in the same area of the public foreshore and seabed in accordance with *tikanga* Māori; and
- is not prohibited by any enactment or rule of law; and
- the right to carry on, exercise or follow the activity, use, or practice has not been extinguished as a matter of law.

As noted above, the *Foreshore and Seabed Act* was highly contentious. Legal scholars noted that the statutory tests in the Act drew on the most restrictive aspects of tests for Aboriginal rights and native title in Canada and Australia (Dorsett, 2007; McNeil, 2007). The general election in 2008 ushered in a new government, with the National Party as the majority party in government. In a confidence and supply agreement with the Māori Party, the National Party agreed to review the *Foreshore and Seabed Act*. This review eventually led to the repeal of the *Foreshore and Seabed Act* and the enactment of its replacement, the *Marine and Coastal Area (Takutai Moana) Act* 2011.

The *Marine and Coastal Area Act* maintains the same basic structure as the *Foreshore and Seabed Act*. "Territorial customary rights" is replaced by "customary marine title" and "customary rights orders" and replaced by "protected customary rights." The tests for recognition were also adjusted slightly. Customary marine title still requires exclusive use and occupation since 1840 without substantial interruption, but now recognizes that the specified area is to be held in accordance with *tikanga* and no longer requires continuous title to contiguous land. A protected customary right is defined as a right that:

(a) has been exercised since 1840; and
(b) continues to be exercised in a particular part of the common marine and coastal area in accordance with *tikanga* by the applicant group, whether it continues to be exercised in exactly the same or a similar way, or evolves over time; and
(c) is not extinguished as a matter of law.

These minor changes mean that the tests for rights recognition under the *Marine and Coastal Area Act* should be able to be met more easily by applicant groups. Another significant change from the *Foreshore and Seabed Act* is that rather than title over the foreshore being held by the Crown, under the *Marine and Coastal Area Act*, this space, now described as the common marine and coastal area, cannot be owned by anyone. While this change has little practical impact, as the Crown continues to exercise many of the functions of a landowner, it is, nonetheless, a symbolically important change. Although the *Marine and Coastal Area Act* is generally viewed as being a vast improvement on the *Foreshore and Seabed Act*, the new legislation maintains some of the most problematic aspects of the previous legislation. The fundamental basis of the Act is that it prevents Māori from being awarded exclusive title to areas of the foreshore and replaces that possibility with a statutory scheme of lesser rights without compensation. Furthermore, the 2011 Act is still discriminatory, continuing the exemption of existing, privately held title from the new regime. At the time of writing, only three High Court decisions have addressed the substantive recognition of customary rights in the marine and coastal area. These decisions have recognized customary marine titles and protected customary rights in areas on the Titi Islands,[15] in the eastern Bay of Plenty,[16] and northern Hawke's Bay.[17]

Any applications under the *Marine and Coastal Area Act* were required to have been submitted by April 2017. The first substantive decision in relation to a contested application for customary marine title was *Re Edwards (Te Whakatohea (No.2))*.[18] This case involved multiple parties and a lengthy hearing covering complex evidence and legal arguments, and the judgment is, accordingly, substantial and covers a range of issues in careful detail. For current purposes it is sufficient to note that the Court placed significant weight on the requirement that the specified area of the common marine and coastal area be "held in accordance with tikanga" as part of the test for customary marine title. In particular, the Court took the view that there was no reason why "held" should import common law concepts of how property is held. Rather, "according to tikanga" suggests that Māori law ought to inform the content of this part of the test. The Court wrote, "[h]olding an area of the takutai moana [foreshore] in accordance with tikanga is something different to being the proprietor of that area."[19] Consequently, other parts of the test for customary marine title, such as what would constitute "exclusive use and occupation" and "substantial interruption," will be determined by Māori law and may be different to how such elements might be considered according to English property law. While the

---

[15] *Re Tipene* [2016] NZHC 3199.
[16] *Re Edwards (Te Whakatohea (No.2))* [2021] NZHC 1025.
[17] *Re Ngāti Pāhauwera* [2021] NZHC 3599.
[18] *Re Edwards (Te Whakatohea (No.2))* [2021] NZHC 1025.
[19] *Edwards*, at [130].

recognition of customary rights in *Edwards* is significant, the potential benefit to the applicants of the recognition of customary marine title and protected customary rights is limited. The statutory rights that will accrue to applicants are rights to participate in conservation processes and enhanced rights in planning and consenting processes under the *Resource Management Act* 1991. Customary rights holders will enjoy greater ability to influence these processes under the statute but this is far short of a recognition of common law Aboriginal title, which the Court of Appeal determined in *Ngāti Apa* could have been available to Māori prior to the enactment of the *Foreshore and Seabed Act* 2004.

Treaty Settlements

One further area that has a bearing on the nature of Māori land rights is the settlement of historical claims based on Crown breaches of *Te Tiriti o Waitangi*. Since the early 1990s, the Crown has been engaged in a systematic programme of direct negotiation with Māori groups to settle historical claims. These settlements often involve redress related to land, including the return of land acquired by the Crown in breach of its Tiriti obligations. Where title to land is returned, this is usually returned as general land and, while forming an important part of treaty settlements, does not raise any novel or distinctive legal issues.[20]

However, there are many forms of redress relating to land that are used in treaty settlements, including various models of co-governance or co-management of specific sites. These models may include partnership arrangements between settling groups and the Crown and collective management by multiple Māori groupings. For example, the Tāmaki Makaurau Collective Settlement vested a number of volcanic cones in the Auckland area in a joint governance body made up of six representatives appointed by thirteen Māori groups included in the settlement and six representatives from Auckland Council (the relevant municipal body). These sites retain the status of public reserves, with the joint governance body now overseeing the management and administration of these sites.

In relation to the lands which formerly comprised Te Urewera National Park in the central North Island (now simply "Te Urewera"),

---

[20] Te Arawhiti – The Office of Māori Crown Relations provides a quarterly update of progress in Treaty settlements. See www.govt.nz/browse/history-culture-and-heritage/treaty-settlements/quarterly-reports/.

the joint governance arrangements are underpinned by a recognition of the legal personality of the land itself. *Te Urewera Act* 2014 provides that Te Urewera is, itself, a legal entity with "all the rights, powers, duties, and liabilities of a legal person."[21] Te Urewera is now managed by a joint governance board. Six members of the board are appointed by Tūhoe (the settling group), and three members are appointed by the Crown. The legislation requires that the board must consider and give expression to customary values and law in the management of Te Urewera. The recognition of legal personality of a landscape feature has also been used in the settlement of claims in relation to Te Awa Tupua (formerly, the Whanganui River)[22] and Ngā Maunga o Taranaki, Pouākai me Kaitake (Mount Taranaki, Pouākai, and the Kaitake Ranges).[23]

Pathways toward Land Rights

With no formal constitutional protection, recognition of Māori land rights remains limited and precarious. The enactment of the *Foreshore and Seabed Act* 2004 illustrates that the New Zealand Government continues, even into the twenty-first century, to be willing to expropriate Māori property rights and limit the jurisdiction of the courts to recognize Māori rights to land.

Any land that falls within the statutory category of "Māori land" is regulated by the Māori Land Court and its empowering statute, *Te Ture Whenua Māori Act* 1993. That statute has been effective at slowing the alienation of Māori land but has done so by placing significant restrictions on the rights of Māori landowners. The statute is primarily an attempt to ameliorate the problems created by earlier legislation which was designed to facilitate the sale of Māori land.

Negotiated agreements aimed at settling historical breaches of the Treaty of Waitangi have resulted in some land being returned to Māori ownership. However, the amount of land made available in these settlements is tiny compared to the scale of historical land loss. The Waitangi Tribunal is prohibited from recommending the return of private land to Māori and private land is excluded from Treaty settlement agreements. Only surplus Crown land is available to be used in Treaty settlements,

---

[21] Te Urewera Act 2014, s 11 (1).
[22] Te Awa Tupua (Whanganui River Claims Settlement) Act 2017.
[23] Te Anga Pūtakerongo (20 Dec 2017).

which means that in practice very little land is returned by way of Treaty settlements.

Treaty settlements have, however, provided innovative mechanisms for co-governance and opportunities for Māori to participate in conservation or resource management processes. Aside from the small percentage of Aotearoa New Zealand's land area that is retained as Māori land under TTWM, this is perhaps the area in which Māori have had most success in securing an ability to influence land management. Similar participation rights are likely to result in the coming years from applications made under the *Marine and Coastal Area (Takutai Moana) Act* 2011.

Conclusion

Prior to the assertion of British sovereignty in Aotearoa New Zealand, Māori land rights were recognized and governed by *tikanga* Māori (Māori law, values, and practices). Today, however, Māori land is primarily regulated by TTWM. The state legal system has recognized Māori land rights via a legislative scheme ever since the enactment of the Native Land Acts in the 1860s. Those statutes were intended to recognize the customary owners of land and to convert the customary title into freehold title. TTWM now aims to support the retention of Māori freehold land in the hands of Māori and to promote their utilization of that land. Although filtered through the framework of the legislation, *tikanga* Māori remains relevant to decisions about land use, the implementation of the legislation, and the operation of the Māori Land Court. Recent developments in relation to the foreshore and seabed and the settlement of historical treaty claims further illustrate the New Zealand Government's preference to give effect to Māori land rights via legislation. This legislative approach has generally tended to narrow the scope of Māori land rights and has ensured that the recognition of Māori land rights is subject to the political whims of the government of the day. Although *tikanga* Māori has always been a key thread of state law recognition of Māori land rights, to a greater or lesser degree recent developments show a state legal system that is still struggling to give appropriate effect to land rights sourced in *tikanga*. Without constitutional protection and a land rights framework aimed at strengthening Māori land title in ways that meet Māori needs, the promise of land as *tāonga tuku iho* remains elusive.

References

Belgrave, M., Deason, A., & Young, G. (2004). *Crown policy with respect to Māori Land, 1953–1999* (Report No. A66). Crown Forestry Rental Trust's Central North Island Stage One Research Programme.

Bennion, T. (2009). Māori land. In D. Brown, R. Thomas, E. Toomey, R. Muir, & K. Palmer (eds.), *New Zealand land law* (2nd ed., pp. 293–343). Wellington, New Zealand: Brookers.

Boast, R. (2004). Māori customary law and land tenure. In R. Boast (ed.), *Māori land law* (2nd ed., pp. 21–40). Wellington, New Zealand: LexisNexis.

(2008). *Buying the land, selling the land: Governments and Māori land in the North Island 1865–1921*. Wellington, New Zealand: Victoria University Press.

Dorsett, S. (2007). An Australian comparison on Native Title to the Foreshore and Seabed. In C. Charters & A. Erueti (eds.), *Māori property rights and the foreshore and seabed: The last frontier* (pp. 59–82). Wellington, New Zealand: Victoria University Press.

Durie, E. (1987). The law and the land. In J. Phillips (ed.), *Te Whenua, te iwi. The land and the people* (pp. 78–81). Wellington, New Zealand: Allen & Unwin/ Port Nicholson Press in association with the Stout Research Centre for the Study of New Zealand Society, History and Culture.

Durie, M. (1998). *Te mana, te kāwanatanga: The politics of Māori self-determination*. Auckland, New Zealand: Oxford University Press.

(1999). Māori development: Reflections and strategic directions. *He Pukenga Kōrero. A Journal of Māori Studies*, 5(1), 4–11.

Fleras, A., & Spoonley, P. (1999). *Recalling Aotearoa: Indigenous politics and ethnic relations in New Zealand*. Auckland, New Zealand: Oxford University Press.

Harmsworth, G. (2018). *Landcover class (LCDBv4) intersected with Māori land blocks for New Zealand*. Lincoln, New Zealand: Manaaki Whenua Landcare Research.

Harmsworth, G., & Awatere, S. (2013). Indigenous Māori knowledge and perspectives of ecosystems. In J. Dymond (ed.), *Ecosystem services in New Zealand: Conditions and trends* (1st ed., pp. 274–286). Manaaki Whenua Press, Auckland, New Zealand1. www.landcareresearch.co.nz/__data/assets/pdf_file/0007/77047/2_1_Harmsworth.pdf

Jones, C. (2014). A Māori constitutional tradition. *New Zealand Journal of Public and International Law.* 135(12), 187–203. https://papers.ssrn.com/sol3/papers.cfm?abstract_id=2538900

Kingi, T. (2008). Māori landownership and land management in New Zealand. In Australian Agency for International Development (ed.), *Making land work, Volume 2: Case studies on customary land and development in the Pacific* (pp. 129–151). Department of Foreign Affairs and Trade, Canberra, Australia. www.dfat.gov.au/sites/default/files/MLW_VolumeTwo_CaseStudy_7.pdf

Marsden, M. (2003). *The woven universe: Selected writings of Rev. Māori Marsden* Te A. C. Royal (ed.). Ōtaki, New Zealand: The Estate of Rev. Māori Marsden.

McNeil, C. K. (2007). Legal rights and legislative wrongs: Maori claims to the foreshore and seabed. In C. Charters & A. Erueti (eds.), *Māori property rights and the foreshore and seabed: The last frontier* (pp. 83–118). Wellington, New Zealand: VUP.

Mead, S. M. (2016). *Tikanga Māori: Living by Māori values* (Revised ed.). Wellington, New Zealand: Huia.

Phillips, J., & Hulme, K. (1987). *Te Whenua, Te iwi: The land and the people.* Wellington, New Zealand: Allen & Unwin/Port Nicholson Press in association with the Stout Research Centre for the Study of New Zealand Society, History and Culture.

Sinclair, D. (1977). Land: Māori view and European response. In M. King (ed.), *Te Ao hurihuri: The world moves on: Aspects of Māoritanga* (Rev. version). (pp.115–140). Wellington, New Zealand: Hicks Smith & Sons/Methuen NZ Ltd.

Te Puni Kōkiri. (2014). *The potential utilisation of Māori land.* Wellington, New Zealand: Te Puni Kōkiri.

Waitangi Tribunal. (2003). *Te Whanganui a Tara: Me Ona Takiwa* (Waitangi Tribunal Report 2003 No. WAI 145). https://forms.justice.govt.nz/search/ Documents/WT/wt_DOC_68452530/Wai145.pdf

(2008). *Papatuanuku (Papaahurewa/Papauenoko) and land ownership: Maori land alienation, and Maori land and title administration in the Central North Island* (Waitangi Tribunal Report 2008 No. Wai 1200 Volume 3). https://forms.justice.govt.nz/search/WT/reports.html

(2016). *He Kurawhenua Karokohanga: Report on claims about the reform of Te Ture Whenua Māori Act 1993* (Waitangi Tribunal Report 2016 No. Wai 2478). https://forms.justice.govt.nz/search/Documents/WT/wt_DOC_ 101113166/Te%20Ture%20Whenua%20Pre-pub%20W.pdf

PART III

Africa and Asia

Countries from Africa and Asia are grouped together in this book because of the complexities around, and resistance to, the concept of "Indigenous Peoples" and for the recognition of customary land rights (Barume, 2010; Morton & Baird, 2019; Xanthaki, 2003). While many of the countries covered in this section from Africa and Asia have constitutions that recognize customary land rights, seldom do they recognize Indigenous Peoples. Also, land rights are largely unprotected; thus, dispossession and tenure insecurity remain ongoing problems across these continents (Aiken & Leigh, 2011; Barume, 2010; He, 2011).

Despite the challenges, Indigenous Peoples are mobilizing to secure and safeguard their land rights across Africa and Asia, but this often pits Indigenous Peoples against parochial national interests and an ever expanding agricultural, mining, and energy sector.

9

Land Rights of Indigenous Peoples in the Democratic Republic of Congo

"First Come, Last Served"

LASSANA KONÉ

Introduction

The Law on the Protection and Promotion of the Rights of Indigenous Pygmy Peoples[1] was adopted by the Democratic Republic of Congo's (DRC's) Parliament in April 2021, and then became law in November 2022. Until this point, the collective ownership of land was largely unrecognized: with Indigenous Peoples' occupying lands they did not "legally" own and over which they had no enforceable rights (Ubink, 2009). The precariousness of customary land tenure in the DRC has contributed to the persistent poverty experienced by Indigenous Peoples. Without secure rights to land, the survival of Indigenous Peoples has been, and continues to be threatened.

In addition, Indigenous Peoples were largely unrecognized as distinct legal peoples with unique rights in the DRC. Indeed, the country has for many years contested the adoption of specific laws for protecting Indigenous Peoples and securing their land rights.[2] The mobilization and advocacy of non-government organizations (NGOs) and Indigenous Peoples led to the adoption of the Law on Indigenous Peoples in 2022, but there remain many deep-seated barriers to the implementation of this law.

The opinions expressed in this chapter are exclusively those of the author and do not necessarily reflect the opinion of the Forest Peoples Programme.

[1] DRC. (2020). Draft Law on the Protection and Promotion of the Rights of Indigenous Pygmy Peoples. National Assembly, third legislature of the third Republic, ordinary session of September 2020.

[2] The 2006 Constitution does not provide a definition of Indigenous Peoples, and the 2002 Forest Code does not use the term Indigenous Peoples either.

The DRC asserts ownership to all lands in the country. The state does allow, on a discretionary basis, Indigenous communities to exercise some access and use rights to their lands through various institutional mechanisms, including individual titling and registration. However, legal gaps and loopholes mean customary tenure is seldom recognized and titled, and the result is that Indigenous Peoples have pursued an alternative pathway to have their land tenure strengthened (Ubink, 2009).

This pathway consists of statutory opportunities to secure customary rights over forests and forest lands through the *local communities' forest concessions* (CFCLs).[3] The CFCLs have been the main option for Indigenous communities to secure some form of collective property rights over lands and resources. The CFCLs are one of the most ground-breaking legal developments in the Congo Basin rainforests in recent years.

While there is much to celebrate with the CFCLs, there are major shortcomings in the current legal framework, including bureaucratic constraints and "red tape," institutional gaps, a lack of legal representation and gender mainstreaming, and the ongoing problem of elite capture (Rainforest Foundation UK, 2014).

This chapter first explains the concept of Indigenous Peoples in the DRC, and explores the nation's historical background to land tenure. The chapter then examines how various legal and institutional mechanisms support the recognition and reclamation of Indigenous Peoples' land rights. The chapter further explains how CFCLs emerged as an alternative pathway to secure some form of rights to customary lands in the DRC, drawing on a successful example from Kasai-Central province in reclaiming lands. Despite this success, the CFCLs do not offer a strong form of land tenure, and the chapter reflects on ways to strengthen the recognition and reclamation of Indigenous Peoples' land rights.

Indigenous Peoples and the DRC

The Baka, Bambuti, and Batwa peoples are recognized as the first inhabitants of the DRC – they are the nation's Indigenous Peoples.[4] In many

---

[3] DRC. (2002). Forest Code, Article 22.

[4] In this chapter, the term "Indigenous Peoples" is used, rather than the generic term "pygmies," which while commonly applied in the DRC, including in the recently adopted Law on Indigenous Peoples, is considered as having a negative connotation and denigrates Indigenous Peoples. Indigenous Peoples themselves consider this generic appellation as

instances, they continue to live in close connection to their lands. From 2000 BC onwards, other groups such as the Bantu, Nilotes, and Sudanese also migrated to this territory, where they set up the Kongo, Luba, and Lunda kingdoms. Indigenous Peoples often sought refuge in the equatorial forests (Musafiri, 2009).

The Baka, Bambuti, and Batwa peoples have, for political and other reasons, been referred to as "Pygmy" peoples and nomadic hunter-gatherers by those who came after them – the Bantu, Nilotes, Sudanese, and then the Europeans with the goal of dispossessing them of their lands, such as under the concept of *terra nullius* (Barber, 2022).

Unlike the typically agricultural and pastoral-based Bantu, Nilotes, and Sudanese societies, the Baka, Bambuti, and Batwa do not have structured chieftainships; rather, they have kinship-style systems and relationships to land connected to the spirits of their ancestors. Land ownership and access are based on family lineage and social groupings. Areas for hunting and gathering tend to be extensive and overlap with other uses and users. Traditional Indigenous society has been characterized as essentially egalitarian. Men are born heads of family, while women manage household resources and decide on important family matters. At the group level, decisions are made on a consensus basis and elders are acknowledged and respected for their wisdom (IWGIA, 2012).

Until the 1950s, the Baka, Bambuti, and Batwa lived as nomadic hunter-gatherers, dependent on the forest or savannah and its produce. Many Indigenous Peoples today reside in permanent settlements away from their lands, a result of the expansion of agriculture, logging and mining concessions, and the creation of protected areas and other nature conservation initiatives. Evicted from their ancestral lands, many of the Baka, Batwa, and Bambuti have ended up as landless squatters on the outskirts of Bantu villages, increasingly dependent on a cash economy to which they have very limited access (IWGIA, 2012). Sedentarization also means acculturation and the loss of social and cultural identities.

Today, the DRC is a multi-ethnic country with some 250 ethnic groups. The exact number of Indigenous Peoples in the DRC is unknown, but official estimates suggest they number around 600,000 people, or one percent of the total population. NGOs estimate that this number is likely around one million Indigenous Peoples. Between 30,000 and 40,000 Indigenous Peoples live in the forest as nomadic hunter-

negative. Furthermore, the African Commission, in its concluding observations in 2010, recalled that this term had a negative connotation.

gatherers or in semi-nomadic or sedentary communities. A sizable number of Indigenous Peoples live as internally displaced persons in the still conflict-ridden eastern part of the country (IWGIA, 2012). Indigenous Peoples more often experience poverty in the country, and they are more likely to suffer from weak livelihood conditions, are regularly exposed to human rights violations, and continue to be neglected in forest governance issues. Indigenous Peoples are more likely to lack access to health care and education. They are the victims of pervasive discrimination, have no political representation at the local or the national level, and their traditional cultures are at serious risk (IWGIA, 2012).

Dispossession

> The treaties must be as brief as possible ... and in a couple of articles must grant us everything.
>
> King Leopold II (in reference to the Congo Free
> State, in Hochschild, 1998).

The arrival of Europeans saw them signing treaties and other agreements with the Kings or Chiefs of the Bantu, Nilotes, and Sudanese – marginalizing the Baka, Bambuti, and Batwa and dispossessing them of their lands and resources (Musafiri, 2009). While large parts of the DRC remain under customary governance and ownership (Land Portal, 2020), these systems are often ignored and conflict with the DRC's asserted sovereignty. There have been three defining periods of land tenure: first, the period of the Congo Free State (CFS) marked by the exploitation of the colony's resources for the exclusive benefit of King Leopold II (1885–1908); second, the colonial period characterized by the transfer of the CFS to Belgium, as an official Belgian colony (1908–1960); and third, the post-colonial period, marked by the independence of the DRC (1960 to present). All three periods show an uneasy co-existence between statutory law and customary law where customary rights are constantly denied or ignored.

The Congo Free State

In 1885, King Leopold II of Belgium annexed the territory that became the CFS, the precursor to the modern DRC. From 1885 and throughout the colonial period, a new land tenure system was established that denied

Indigenous Peoples formal legal title to their traditional lands – these lands were *terra nullius* (or nobody's land). However, the state legally recognized all land acquired by missionaries and European traders. Remaining land, including forests under customary ownership and use, and land occupied semi-nomadically by Indigenous Peoples, was considered "vacant and without masters" and transferred to the state's private domain (Kipalu et al., 2016). King Leopold II exploited the country's natural resources to cover the colony's running costs and for his own personal economic gain. Rubber extraction was developed to meet growing demand in Europe. An objective of the tenure system was to expand the amount of land classified as "vacant" to allow the CFS to take control. Many forest peoples were dispossessed during this period (Sakata, 2009).

The doctrine of *terra nullius*, rooted in the Doctrine of Discovery, meant that colonial powers did not recognize the territorial sovereignty of Indigenous communities, viewing them as societies without proper territorial sovereignty (Gilbert, 2016). Indeed, in 1885, when the existence of the CFS was formally proclaimed, a number of royal decrees from Brussels declared that all "vacant land" there became the property of the state. There was no definition of what made land "vacant" (Hochschild, 1998).

The Belgian Congo

The CFS became the Belgian Congo in 1908, and then in 1912 adopted a decree stating that "all ownerless things belong to the Colony, except for respect for customary indigenous rights and what may be said on the subject of the right of occupation" (Hochschild, 1998). The Great War's demand for resources intensified the exploitation of the Congo's forests. Much of the state domain, including large portions of customarily held territories, were granted to companies. The subordination of Indigenous Peoples' customary land rights was legally established by a 1920 law providing that private land ownership required a certificate of registration from the registrar of land titles (akin to the situation in Australia, western Canada, and New Zealand, see Diamond and Sanderson, this book). Indigenous Peoples' customary rights could not be registered in this way, which established the administrative basis for dispossession (Ona, 2008). However, the 1908 colonial charter[5] admitted the legal character of customary law, and Indigenous courts (*tribunaux*

---

[5] Law of October 18, 1908, on the Government of the Belgian Congo, Article 4(2).

indigènes) could apply customs if they were not contrary to the general law and public order.[6]

The Independent Congo

When the Congo achieved independence under the Fundamental Law of 1960 (the nation's first constitution), all existing regulations were to remain in force unless repealed. This included the inherited colonial land tenure system, which went unchanged until 1973, when the DRC reformed land ownership by adopting the law on property, land tenure, real estate, and securities,[7] the basis of the DRC's current land tenure system. This 1973 law vested ownership of soil and subsoil interests to the state, which also retained ownership of all Indigenous and local community lands expropriated during the colonial era. The 1973 Land Law appears similar to the treaties signed by King Leopold II with local Congo Chiefs in 1884, who gave up their "sovereignty and governing rights to all their territories." Today, six decades years after independence, lands occupied by Indigenous Peoples are still said to be state-owned land.

Indigenous Peoples in the DRC Legal Framework

The DRC's 2006 Constitution affirmed the principle of non-discrimination: that is, all people are equal to other peoples; they have the right to be different, and to be respected in their difference.[8] The DRC endorsed the United Nations Declaration on the Rights of Indigenous Peoples (UNDRIP) in 2007, and is state party to various regional and international human rights instruments, including the African Charter on Human and Peoples' Rights,[9] the Convention on the Elimination of All Forms of Racial Discrimination,[10] and the Convention on the Elimination of All Forms of Discrimination Against Women,[11] among others. Despite these commitments, Indigenous Peoples continue to face discrimination, and are subject to extreme

---

[6] Decree of March 17, 1938, establishing the Indigenous courts, Article 18.
[7] DRC. (1973). Law 73-021 on the General Regime of Property, Land Tenure, Real Estate and Securities as amended and supplemented by Law 80-008 of July 18, 1980.
[8] Law of February 18, 2006.
[9] Ratified on July 20, 1987.
[10] Ratified on April 21, 1976.
[11] Ratified on October 17, 1986.

economic, social, cultural, and political inequality. Indeed, while there
has been intense activity at the international level to ratify these human
rights instruments, the Congolese government has done little to implement them in practice, and until the most recent Indigenous Peoples'
protection laws, were referred to as "local communities."[12]

The 1973 Land Law, and the national land use planning framework,
did not recognize Indigenous Peoples and their customary rights. The
2002 Forest Code[13] provided a definition of "local communities" referred
to as "a population traditionally organized on the basis of custom and
united by bonds of clan or parental solidarity that form the basis of its
internal cohesion. It is also characterized by its attachment to a specific
terroir."[14] The Congolese legislature has expressed a certain suspicion
towards the rights of minorities or vulnerable groups, similar to some of
the debate and misconceptions around the concept of "Indigenous" in
the African context more generally (ACHPR and IWGIA, 2006). The
most common reasons to justify this mistrust are, among others, the
principle of the indivisibility of the state and the promotion of
national unity.

The term "Indigenous Peoples" is used to draw attention to and
alleviate the particular form of discrimination these peoples suffer in
the DRC. The chief concern of Indigenous Peoples in the DRC is not just
to simply claim first inhabitant status – but for the recognition of their
basic human rights, and rights of access to land and natural resources
(ACHPR and IWGIA, 2006), and in turn, to seek protection in international human rights law and moral standards.

The UN Human Rights Committee's concluding observations on the
DRC expressed concerns about the generally precarious situation and
vulnerability of Indigenous populations:

> The Committee is concerned about: (a) the overall situation of insecurity
> and vulnerability of Pygmy communities; (b) reports that these commu-
> nities are discriminated against, particularly in the areas of health care and
> education; and (c) the State party's position that indigenous peoples are
> subsumed under the category of "local communities" in legislation, particu-
> larly in the Forestry Code. It is also concerned at the delay in adopting the
> law on the rights of indigenous peoples (United Nations Human Rights
> Committee, CCPR/C/COD/CO/4, 2017).

---

[12] See Articles 11, 12, 13, and 51 of the 2006 DRC Constitution.
[13] Law 11/2002 of August 29, 2002.
[14] Article 1, section 17.

The Committee expressly recommended that "legislation recognising the rights of the Indigenous Peoples be put in place as soon as possible." In recent years, the DRC has reviewed its position on "Indigenous Peoples," which is now accepted and endorsed by the government, and adopted in law as well as in climate change-related programs.[15]

Land Rights: A Legal Vacuum

The 1973 Land Law provided access to land for all individuals and legal entities, whether Congolese or foreign nationals. However, it left open the question of securing the customary land rights of local communities, providing that this would be resolved at a later date by presidential decree (Koné, 2017). According to Article 389 of the Land Law, "the rights of use of these lands, duly acquired, shall be regulated by decree of the President of the Republic." Although the Land Law considered this issue of customary rights in 1980, the presidential ordinance was never drafted, leaving customary land rights holders in a legal position akin to rights of occupation only (Mpoyi, 2013), an oversight that has never been addressed by various governments since then (Battory & Vircoulon, 2020). This situation creates tenure insecurity for customary rights holders who depend on the forest for their livelihoods (Koné, 2017).

This "tenure" vacuum has maintained dispossession, leaving the door open to forcible land grabs, illegal occupations and coerced sales, and fueling various types of land disputes, including between the Indigenous Peoples and local Bantu communities. This is evidenced by the case of the *Batwa* people evicted from their ancestral lands in the Kahuzi-Biega National Park in 1975 without their consent. They were dispossessed by a conservation approach that assumed that communities and the preservation of biodiversity are incompatible. Following the eviction, the DRC state failed to protect the Batwa from entrenched discrimination, and to provide alternative lands or access to basic public services. There has never been formal acknowledgement of the injustice of this dispossession, of their forced expulsion, or any compensation and reparations.

---

[15] In 2007, the Committee on the Elimination of Racial Discrimination (CERD) noted with regret the DRC's reluctance to acknowledge the existence of Indigenous Peoples in its territory. Referring to General Recommendation VIII on self-identification, CERD "remind[ed] the State party that the principle of non-discrimination requires it to take account of the cultural characteristics of ethnic groups and the way in which such groups perceive and define themselves." See, for example, DRC, 17/08/2007, CERD/C/COD/CO/15, paragraph 14.

They continue to live landless and in poverty and are frequently criminalized for their subsistence activities. As part of a review of the status of Indigenous Peoples in Africa, the African Commission on Human and Peoples Rights (ACHPR), which reviewed the situation of the Batwa in and around Kahuzi-Biega in 2003, highlighted the consequences of the evictions of the Batwa:

> Land should have been given to the Batwa, but this did not happen. Now the Batwa are forbidden to hunt in the park and forbidden to collect park products. They have no food resources or medicinal plants, and the forest is no longer their place of worship. The Batwa have been culturally and psychologically shattered by the loss of their forests. (ACHPR, 2003)

The Batwa of the Kahuzi-Biega National Park, with legal support provided by Minority Rights Group and Environment Natural Resources and Development, lodged a case for land restitution before the ACHPR in November 2015. The admissibility decision was received as a beacon of hope by Indigenous Peoples and their support organizations (MRG, 2019). By declaring the communication admissible within the meaning of Article 56 of the African Charter on Human and Peoples' Rights, the Commission found that the domestic remedies provided by the DRC authorities were not sufficiently available, effective or efficient to ensure adequate redress for the violations suffered by the complainants (MRG, 2019). The decision is a big step towards the recognition and protection of the Batwa's rights, who were evicted from their lands without compensation or restitution (MRG, 2019).

Collective Rights, Individual Titles and State Sovereignty

The constitution recognizes customary land tenure and guarantees rights to individual and collective title acquired in accordance with law or custom. Some estimates suggest that as much as 97 percent of land across the DRC is governed under customary law (USAID, 2010). At the same time, the constitution asserts state sovereignty over land and forests – which is problematic for Indigenous Peoples.[16] In addition, according to the Land Law, the state is the sole owner of the lands occupied by local and Indigenous communities.[17] The Land

---

[16] DRC. (2006). Constitution, Article 34.
[17] DRC. (1973). Land Law No. 73-021, Article 387, "The lands occupied by local communities become, from the entrance of this Act, domanial lands."

Law stipulates that "the right of utilization of a land is legally established only through a registration certificate of the deed assigned by the
State,"[18] meaning that customary land rights are not clearly affirmed
and recognized as a property right in practice. Only those customary
rights converted into land titles are recognized, with the certificate of
registration acting as an enforceable legal document to which probative
value is asserted.[19]

The process for obtaining a registration certificate is relatively long and
costly, meaning very few Indigenous communities have taken advantage
of it. There are administrative barriers for communities exercising legal
capacity in the country because the legal system presumes such rights can
only be exercised by individuals; what this means is that many
Indigenous communities are prevented from collectively managing property (Smith & Stein, 2020). If communities can enjoy legal personality,
they are denied legal capacity under the current legal framework. The
distinction between legal personality and legal capacity is merely an
administrative device that enables the state to regulate who may
exercise their rights, and to what extent, and through what modality they
may do so. In practice, the distinction recognizes and at times facilitates
the exercise of rights by some groups, while at times calcifying and
legitimizing paternalistic attitudes about other groups (Powell & Stein,
2016).

In the case of *Kakese Shumbusho Marcel v. Migambi Munyandatwa
et al.,*[20] the *Tribunal de Grande Instance* (High Court) of Goma was
asked to settle a land dispute between Mr. Kakese, the applicant, and five
members of the Bambuti Indigenous community in Masisi territory, in
North Kivu. The applicant was asking the High Court to confirm his
ownership rights to a concession of approximately 100 hectares, legally
acquired under a certificate of registration.[21] On the other side, the
defendants claimed customary ownership of their ancestral lands, based
on customary occupation.[22]

---

[18] Article 219
[19] DRC. (1973). Land Law No. 73-021, Article 227.
[20] RC 19.962. (2019). TGI Goma, *Kakese Shumbusho Marcel vs. Migambi Munyandatwa
   et al.*
[21] DRC. (1973). Land Law No. 73-021, Article 219.
[22] DRC. (1973). Land Law No. 73-021, Article 388, "The land occupied by local communities are the land that these communities inhabit, cultivate or exploit in any way –
   individually or collectively – in accordance with local customs and practices."

The High Court of Goma was emphatic in its judgement, writing that:

> [...] the defendants do not disclose the existence of any title or judgment against this registration certificate. The mere allegation of the enjoyment of customary rights is not sufficient against the existence of a registration certificate. In a sense, Congolese case law holds that "the evidence provided by the registration certificate has an *erga omnes*[23] effect, and third parties cannot claim that the rights established therein are '*res inter alios acta*'[24] against them."[25] This is why the registration certificate is enforceable against a person claiming to have customary land rights, even if the title was established by virtue of a contract between the sole holder and the Republic, the person claiming customary rights not being a party to it. (unofficial translation by the author)

As we can see, the court's intervention in land disputes does not consider the existing legal and institutional dualism provided for in the constitution; rather the court's perspective affirms that customarily held land rights are not equal in weight and validity to administratively granted land rights. The provisions of the constitution, the Land Law, and the recent Law on Indigenous Peoples (which took effect in 2022) must be used for implementing and enforcing customary land rights, otherwise Indigenous Peoples in the DRC will continue to face issues with tenure insecurity.

International Agreements and Article 215 of the Constitution

As a civil law country, the DRC's legal framework for recognizing Indigenous land rights relies on various formal sources, including international treaties (Zongwe et al., 2020). The DRC is a monist state, and as such international treaties are expected to become an integral part of national law upon ratification. According to Article 215 of the Constitution,[26] ratified treaties and international agreements prevail over Congolese legislation. However, the rigid distinction between monist and

---

[23] *Erga omnes* means "With respect to all." It means that a legal decision has the force of *res judicata erga omnes*, enforceable against all, not only against the parties involved. The term is therefore opposed, for example, to a contractual obligation, which is binding only on the signatories of the contract.

[24] *Res inter alios acta* ("a thing done by others") means that a contract cannot adversely affect the rights of a third party. It is a principle of the law of obligations and public international law.

[25] RJC, 1967, p. 40, cited by JP Kifwabala Tekilazaya, Kinshasa, August 23, 1966, Droit Civil, Les Biens, Tome 1, *Les droits réels fonciers*, Presses Universitaires de Lubumbashi, 2003, p. 428.

[26] DRC. (2006). Constitution, Article 215.

dualist[27] states is not played out in practice. There are some instances where the application of Article 215 is limited in practice, for example, when the Constitutional Court declares that an international treaty or agreement contains a clause contrary to the constitution, and as a result, subjects its application to the review of the constitution.[28] In addition, Article 214 binds the operation of Article 215 by requiring the domestication of specific types of international treaties. The DRC ratified the African Charter on Human and Peoples' Rights guaranteeing individuals their property rights, which applies as well to Indigenous Peoples.[29] In theory, then, the provisions of the African Charter form an integral part of Congolese law, and should therefore be "directly enforceable" in Congolese courts. If there is a conflict, international law prevails over ordinary law.

Also, the rights of Indigenous Peoples have been specifically addressed in the UNDRIP endorsed by the DRC in 2007. The UNDRIP protects Indigenous Peoples against discrimination,[30] and recognizes their rights to self-determination,[31] culture,[32] land,[33] spirituality or religion,[34] and health.[35] The UNDRIP also acknowledges the collective nature of Indigenous rights. Although the UNDRIP is not legally binding, some of its provisions may reflect customary international law. In any case, it is an important step towards setting standards for recognizing and protecting the rights of Indigenous Peoples in the DRC. However, the application of international law in domestic cases is rare and the courts continue to give precedence to registration certificates over communities' customary rights in land-related conflicts.[36]

The Law on the Rights of Indigenous Peoples

The Law on the Rights of Indigenous Peoples[37] was adopted by Parliament in April 2021, and became law in 2022. This new law – the

---

[27] According to international law theory, dualist states should in theory domesticate international norms before they become part of national law.

[28] DRC. (2006). Constitution, Article 216.

[29] Article 14 of the African Charter.

[30] Article 2.

[31] Articles 3, 4, 46.

[32] Articles 5, 8, 11, 12, 13, 15, 16, 31.

[33] Articles 8, 10, 20, 26, 27, 28, 29, 30, 32.

[34] Articles 12, 25.

[35] Article 24.

[36] *Kakese v. Migambi et al.*

[37] Law 22/030 of July 15, 2022, on the Protection and Promotion of the Rights of Indigenous Pygmy peoples.

outcome of a huge effort by Indigenous Peoples and civil society organizations – aimed to recognize and safeguard the customary and communal land rights of the Baka, Bambuti, and Batwa peoples, and "fill the
legislative void in terms of the protection of the rights of Indigenous
Peoples." The law makes direct reference to obligations under a series of
international and regional human rights instruments in its *Exposé des
motifs* (Thornberry, 2023).

Under this law, notwithstanding the state's property rights over the
soil and subsoil, Indigenous Peoples have the right to the lands and
natural resources that they own, occupy or use, in accordance with the
applicable law; and no relocation or resettlement can take place without
free, prior, and informed consent (FPIC).[38] Indigenous Peoples also have
the right to the full enjoyment of all natural resources, both timber and
non-timber, and the benefits of environmental services on the lands they
traditionally own, occupy or use.[39] In addition, Indigenous Peoples may
give or withhold consent to any project that may affect lands and natural
resources they traditionally own, occupy or use.[40]

While the law has provisions on FPIC relating specifically to displacement, more general FPIC provisions were watered down in the final text.
Whereas a previous draft of the text foresaw *prior consultation with a
view to obtaining consent* "for *any project* affecting the life of indigenous
Pygmy peoples directly or indirectly," as well as "appropriate mechanisms for consultation which take account of their customs, *before any
elaboration or implementation of administrative or legislative measures*,"
these provisions have been removed and replaced (Thornberry, 2023).

An Alternative Pathway to Strengthen Customary Land Tenure

Given that the Law on the Rights of Indigenous Peoples has not taken
effect at the time of writing, and the fact that few Indigenous Peoples have
formal title to their lands in the DRC, most legal efforts to advance land
rights have focused on individual land ownership through land titling and
registration. Disappointment with such approaches led to a search for an
alternative pathway in land tenure regulation that reconciles customary
land rights with those asserted by the state (Ubink, 2009). This pathway is
the through the Community Forest Concessions (*Concessions Forestières*

---

[38] Articles 42–48.
[39] Article 44.
[40] Article 42.

des Communautés Locales or CFCLs).[41] The 2002 Forest Code sets the legal framework for Indigenous Peoples to manage forests they traditionally occupy, even though they are not the "legal" owners according to state laws.

According to the Decree on CFCLs,[42] Indigenous Peoples (and local communities) can transform part of or all their customarily occupied forests into a community-controlled and managed concession – the CFCLs. It is, to date, the only legal option for many Indigenous communities to secure some form of recognized collective property rights to their forests – and to protect their lands against encroachment.

A local community's forest concession is granted to a community by the state, based on customary ownership, to manage it according to their customary laws and traditions, provided the uses are not contrary to existing laws and regulations, and subject to the obligation of applying the rules and practices of sustainable forest management.[43] Communities with CFCLs can engage in conservation or forestry or any other form of activity. These concessions are allocated upon request by the community, free of charge and in perpetuity.[44] The first threshold for establishing customary rights is customary occupation. Participatory mapping and land demarcation exercises can provide physical evidence of customary occupation. To date, more than 150 community forests covering three million hectares have already been established, with potentially tens of millions more available to local communities (RFUK, 2023).

The Batwa communities of Tshiefu, in Central Kasaï, hold a land title to their lands dating from the colonial era. They have been supported by the Dynamique des Groupes des Peuples Autochtones (DGPA) and Forest Peoples Programme (FPP) in formalizing this title, and they have also obtained recognized property rights through community forests. Four Batwa communities from Micha, Bondo, Kombe, and Tongonuena have secured 111,760 hectares of community forests in total.[45] The request was made separately because an Indigenous community can only request up to 50,000 hectares in a CFCL.[46] Now, with

---

[41] DRC. (2002). Forest Code, Article 22.
[42] DRC. (2014). Decree 14/018 establishing the Modalities for the allocation of local communities' forest concessions, Article 1. Hereafter referred to as the CFCL Decree.
[43] DRC. (2014). CFCL Decree, Article 2.
[44] Ibid.
[45] These are 29,347 ha for Bondo, 25,496 ha for Kombe, 31,069 ha for Misthia and 25,848 ha for Tongonuena.
[46] DRC. (2014). CFCL Decree, Article 18.

CFCLs, the Batwa of Tshiefu are supposed to be less vulnerable to land grabbing with greater legal standing, and can play a stronger role in forest management. However, community forest "titles" are effectively concessions and not titles of land ownership. While the CFCL can provide some protection against logging and mining exploitation, the level of protection is not as strong as it would be if the communities owned the land (Koné, 2023).

In support of their CFCLs, the Batwa have produced maps documenting their customary territory, which are being used for drafting subsequent forest management plans, with the goal of protecting their values and livelihoods. It is important to note that, to date, most of the CFCLs obtained in the DRC belong to Bantu peoples, sometimes to mixed communities (Bantu and Indigenous communities), and only occasionally to Indigenous Peoples – strengthening Indigenous engagement in CFCLs is critical moving forward. Because of the persistence of traditional discrimination and the perception of the subordinate status of Indigenous Peoples, there is a risk that the Bantu will give them a smaller share of the distributed collective resources, especially money (Moise, 2019).

Community forestry faces major challenges, including weak community ownership and capacity, and there is ongoing debate over communities' choices of socio-economic model. For example, should this model be conservation- or market-focused? CFCLs do focus on poverty reduction rather than tenure security, which can lead to forest degradation, and thus undermine the subsistence economy (Moise, 2019). CFCLs are governed by the local management committee (*Comité de Gestion – CdG*), a highly formalized structure with a president, vice-president, treasurer, etc. (Moise, 2019). To operate an enterprise, the community must form a cooperative society or a local development committee.[47] Traditional governance is typically ignored. Most communities have partnerships with outside corporations, which can open the door to corruption and elite capture (Kipalu et al., 2016). Some Congolese NGOs have reported a proliferation of CFCL applications facilitated by foreign NGOs, where the local communities have not been properly informed or consulted and are not fully engaged in the process.

A National Roundtable on Community Forestry was initiated in 2015 to address the risks outlined above, bringing together different stakeholders to develop a common national strategy for CFCLs through consensus. The

[47] DRC. (2014). CFCL Decree, Article 20.

National Roundtable also serves as a forum for sharing lessons from pilot projects across the DRC, in terms of best practices and in order to identify obstacles to the national CFCLs process (RFUK, 2018).

Conclusion

Apart from CFCLs, there are few examples where Indigenous Peoples in the DRC are successfully reclaiming their land back or registering title. However, the latest Law on the Rights of Indigenous Peoples may remedy this. While the state retains exclusive ownership of land and subsoil resources, these rights are mitigated to some extent by the specific new provisions of this law that aims to give legal recognition and protection to lands and resources traditionally occupied by Indigenous Peoples.

The country's legal dualism, which affirms customary and state ownership, does not reconcile these, and puts barriers in place to the recognition of customary ownership – for example by requiring cumbersome land title certificates to prove ownership. This means that most Indigenous communities endure tenure insecurity and vulnerability. The CFCLs have been the primary strategy for Indigenous Peoples to secure some form of access and use right to their lands, but are not an end in itself.

For the CFCLs strategy to be effective, Indigenous communities need to be aware, empowered, and possess the capabilities (legal and administrative) to make a request for the CFCLs, which frequently they are not. The CFCLs may offer some form of standing against encroachment of traditional lands; however, they are not focused entirely on commercial forest resources (and thus cannot generate the revenues for communities to pursue land reclamation strategies), and they do not offer security from elite capture or dispossession by more powerful actors. Therefore, CFCLs should not be considered as the end or a miracle solution, but one step on the road to genuine Indigenous land justice in the DRC.

CFCLs should build on existing and traditional forms of organization and governance in Indigenous communities, rather than imposing bureaucratic structures. This approach may create space for genuine participation in CFCL management and decision-making, and could support an equitable sharing of benefits arising from the exploitation of CFCL resources.

Looking forward, how the new Law on the Rights of Indigenous Peoples plays out in practice remains unknown. However, what we understand from previous experience is that a genuine *dualism* in the country, one that both recognizes and safeguards Indigenous land rights, has proven elusive. Strengthening the land rights of Indigenous Peoples through a meaningful recognition and protection of these rights requires, as a first step, a more supportive and simplified land titling process. This means building an institutional and regulatory framework that can implement and safeguard customary title and ownership, with a space for Indigenous voices in this framework.

References

ACHPR & International Work Group for Indigenous Affairs (IWGIA). (2006). *Indigenous Peoples in Africa: The forgotten peoples? The African Commission's work on Indigenous Peoples in Africa.* The Gambia: African Commission on Human and Peoples' Rights.

African Commission on Human and People's Rights (ACHPR). (2003). *Report of the African Commission's Working Group on Indigenous Populations/ Communities.* The Gambia: ACHPR and International Work Group for Indigenous Affairs (IWGIA).

Barber, N. (2022). *Baka representation: Rights, videomaking, and Indigenous identity in Southeast Cameroon* [Thesis, McGill University]. See https:// escholarship.mcgill.ca/concern/theses/sf268b447.

Battory, J., & Vircoulon, T. (2020). *Les pouvoirs coutumiers en RDC: Institutionnalisation, politisation et résilience.* Notes de l'Ifri. Centre Afrique subsaharienne, Paris, France.

Gilbert, J. (2016). *Indigenous Peoples' land rights under international law.* Leiden, Netherlands: Brill Nijhoff.

Hochschild, A. (1998). *King Leopold's ghost: A story of greed, terror and heroism in colonial Africa.* Boston: Mariner Books.

IWGIA. (2012). Country technical notes on Indigenous peoples' issues, Democratic Republic of the Congo. www.iwgia.org/es/documents-and-publi cations/documents/publications-pdfs/english-publications/341-ifad-iwgia-country-technical-note-on-indigenous-peopels-issues-democratic-republic-of-congo-2012-eng/file.html.

Kipalu, P., Koné, L., Bouchra, S., Vig, S., & Loyombo, W. (2016). *Securing forest peoples' rights and tackling deforestation in the Democratic Republic of Congo.* Moreton-in-Marsh, UK: Forest Peoples Programme.

Koné, L. (2017). *Garantir les droits fonciers coutumiers en République démocratique du Congo: Guide Pratique à l'intention des acteurs impliqués dans le processus de la réforme foncière.* Moreton-in-Marsh, UK: Forest Peoples Programme.

(2023). *Democratic Republic of the Congo: A rights-based analysis of mining legislation*. Moreton-in-Marsh, UK: Forest Peoples Programme. www .forestpeoples.org/sites/default/files/documents/DRC%20A%20rights-based %20analysis%20of%20mining%20legislation%20ENG.pdf.

Land Portal. (2020). *Customary rights key to land reform in Democratic Republic of Congo*. https://landportal.org/node/100435.

Minority Rights Group (MRG). (2019). *DRC: The admissibility decision of the African Commission on Human and Peoples' Rights on a case involving the eviction of indigenous people from their ancestral lands represents a beacon of hope*. https://minorityrights.org/2019/07/02/drc-admissibility-decision-afri can-commission-on-human-and-peoples-rights-on-eviction-of-indigenous-people-from-ancestral-lands-represents-beacon-of-h/

Moise, R. E. (2019). Making community forestry successful in DRC: Anthropological perspectives on community-based forest management. Rainforest Foundation, London, UK. www.rainforestfoundationuk.org/wp-content/uploads/2021/10/drc-moise-study-english.pdf.

Mpoyi, A. (2013). *Amélioration de la gouvernance du secteur foncier en République Démocratique du Congo*. Washington, DC: World Bank.

Musafiri P. N. (2009). *The dispossession of indigenous land rights in the DRC: A history and prospects*. Moreton-in-Marsh, UK: Forest Peoples Programme.

Ona, U. (2008). La gestion domaniale des terres rurales et des aires protégées au Sud-Kivu: Aspects juridiques et pratiques d'acteurs. In S. Marysse, F. Reyntjens, & S. Vandeginste (eds.), *L'Afrique des Grands Lacs. Annuaire 2008–2009* (pp. 415–442). Paris: L'Harmattan.

Powell, R., M., & Stein, M. A. (2016). Persons with disabilities and their sexual, reproductive, and parenting rights: An international and comparative analysis. *Frontiers of law in China*, 11(1), pp. 53–85. https://doi.org/10.3868/s050-005-016-0005-6

Rainforest Foundation UK (RFUK). (2014). *New community forest decree in the Democratic Republic of Congo: Opportunities, risks and implications for forest governance*. www.rainforestfoundationuk.org/media.ashx/37742-RFUK-CF-Briefing-Statement.pdf.

RFUK. (2016). *Note on community forests in the DRC: Towards equitable and sustainable forest management*. www.rainforestfoundationuk.org/media .ashx/3171759-eng-final-web.pdf.

(2018). *A national strategy for community forestry in Democratic Republic of Congo*. www.rainforestfoundationuk.org/media.ashx/a-national-strategy-for-community-forestry-2018.pdf.

(2023). *Community forests*. www.rainforestfoundationuk.org/our-projects/com munity-forests/.

Sakata, G. (2009). La réforme du secteur des ressources naturelles: Historique, enjeux et bilans. In S. Marysse, F. Reyntjens, & S. Vandeginste (eds.),

L'Afrique des grands lacs. Annuaire 2008–2009 (pp. 269–288). Paris: L'Harmattan.

Smith, M. S. & Stein, M. A. (2020). Connecting the right of collective legal capacity by Indigenous Peoples with the right of individual legal capacity by persons with disabilities. *International Human Rights Law Review*, 9, 147–183. https://brill.com/view/journals/hrlr/9/2/article-p147_147.xml.

Thornberry, F. (January 11, 2023). The new law on Indigenous Peoples' rights in the Democratic Republic of Congo: Moving towards implementation. LinkedIn. www.linkedin.com/pulse/new-law-indigenous-peoples-rights-democratic-republic-thornberry.

Ubink, J. M. (2009). Legalising land rights in Africa, Asia and Latin America: An introduction. In J. M. Ubink, J. A. Hoekema, & W. J. Assies (eds.), *Legalising land rights: Local practices, state responses and tenure security in Africa, Asia and Latin America* (pp. 7–32). Leiden: Leiden University Press.

United Nations Human Rights Committee (UNHRC), Centre for Civil and Political Rights (CCPR), CCPR/C/COD/CO/4. (2017). *Concluding observations on the fourth periodic report of the Democratic Republic of the Congo.* Geneva: UNHRC.

United States Agency for International Development (USAID). (2010). *Country profile: Democratic Republic of Congo, Land.* Washington, DC: USAID. www.land-links.org/country-profile/democratic-republic-congo/.

Zongwe, D. P., Butedi, F., & Mavungu, C. (2020). *Overview of the legal system of the Democratic Republic of the Congo.* New York: Hauser Global Law School Program. www.nyulawglobal.org/globalex/Democratic_Republic_Congo1.html#_ednref3.

10

San Land Rights in Botswana

A Critical Analysis

ROBERT K. HITCHCOCK, MARIA SAPIGNOLI, AND
SMITH MOETI

Introduction

As Africa's oldest multiparty democracy, the Republic of Botswana in
southern Africa has long been viewed as a country with a superb human
rights record (Samatar, 1999). However, in the past four decades, the
actions of the Botswana Government involving the country's Indigenous
minorities has called into question this reputation (Barume, 2014;
Ndahinda, 2011; Nyati-Ramahobo, 2009; Saugestad, 2001). Botswana
has a complex history when it comes to the recognition of Indigenous
Peoples, San and Bakgalagadi, and their rights to their ancestral
territories.

At the time of Botswana's independence on September 30, 1966, there
was only one place in the country where San (Bushmen) and Bakgalagadi
had constitutionally recognized land rights: the Central Kalahari Game
Reserve (CKGR). In 1997 and 2002, however, the residents of the Central
Kalahari were involuntarily relocated to areas outside of the CKGR by
the Botswana Government. Some of the former residents were only able
to return to the Central Kalahari after a two-and-a-half-year-long legal
battle in the country's High Court, the longest and most expensive
litigation case in the nation's history (Ng'ong'ola, 2007; Sapignoli, 2017;
Zips-Mairitsch, 2013). Some analysts have seen the situation in Botswana
as an example of the "judicialization of African politics" (Brett, 2018;
Sapignoli, 2018).

As a landlocked country, Botswana is 581,730 square kilometers in
size, roughly the size of Kenya. It is culturally diverse, supporting some
thirty-six different ethnic groups. Botswana endorsed the United Nations
Declaration on the Rights of Indigenous Peoples (UNDRIP) in

September 2007. However, the country raised objections to an earlier draft of the Declaration at a meeting in late 2006 of the Third Committee of the United Nations General Assembly in New York, and at a meeting of the Assembly of Heads of State and Government of the African Union in January 2007 (see African Group of States, 2006; African Commission on Human and Peoples' Rights, 2007). The concerns raised by Botswana, Namibia, and the other African states included the following: (1) the definition of Indigenous Peoples, (2) the issue of self-determination, (3) the issue of land ownership and the exploitation of resources, (4) the establishment of distinct political and economic institutions, and (5) the issue of national and territorial integrity (African Group of States, 2006; Barume, 2009). These concerns became a major topic of discussion in Botswana, and after endorsing the UNDRIP, efforts were made by various non-government organizations (NGOs) and the United Nations to distribute copies of the UNDRIP to people in both urban and rural communities. While Botswana endorsed the UNDRIP in September 2007, it has not been ratified in the Botswana Parliament. However, the UNDRIP has been used by San advocacy groups at the community level to familiarize them with human rights principles, including land rights.

While Botswana does not recognize its 60,000-plus San peoples as "Indigenous," holding instead that all citizens of the country are Indigenous, it does have a Remote Area Development Program with the target population being all those people living in remote parts of the country, which includes San peoples (Republic of Botswana, 2009). It also has an "Affirmative Action Framework" aimed at assisting people in what are known as "remote area communities," of which there are seventy-three at present (Ludick, 2018; Republic of Botswana, 2014) (see Figure 10.1). The problem for San in these settlements, however, is that people there do not have officially recognized land tenure rights. The remote area settlements are open to anyone who wants to come and live there.

Historically, San have faced dispossession as a result of several processes: (1) pre-colonial incursions of other groups, most of them agropastoralists over the past 2,000 years, who incorporated San into their social and economic systems, and denied them land rights; (2) the granting of land by the colonial administration to people of European backgrounds in the form of freehold ranches and farms; (3) the introduction of land reform programs in the post-colonial period (1966–present); and (4) the taking of land for mines, roads, trek routes, and protected areas.

This chapter considers two questions: (1) What are the mechanisms for recognizing Indigenous Peoples' land rights in Botswana? (2) How

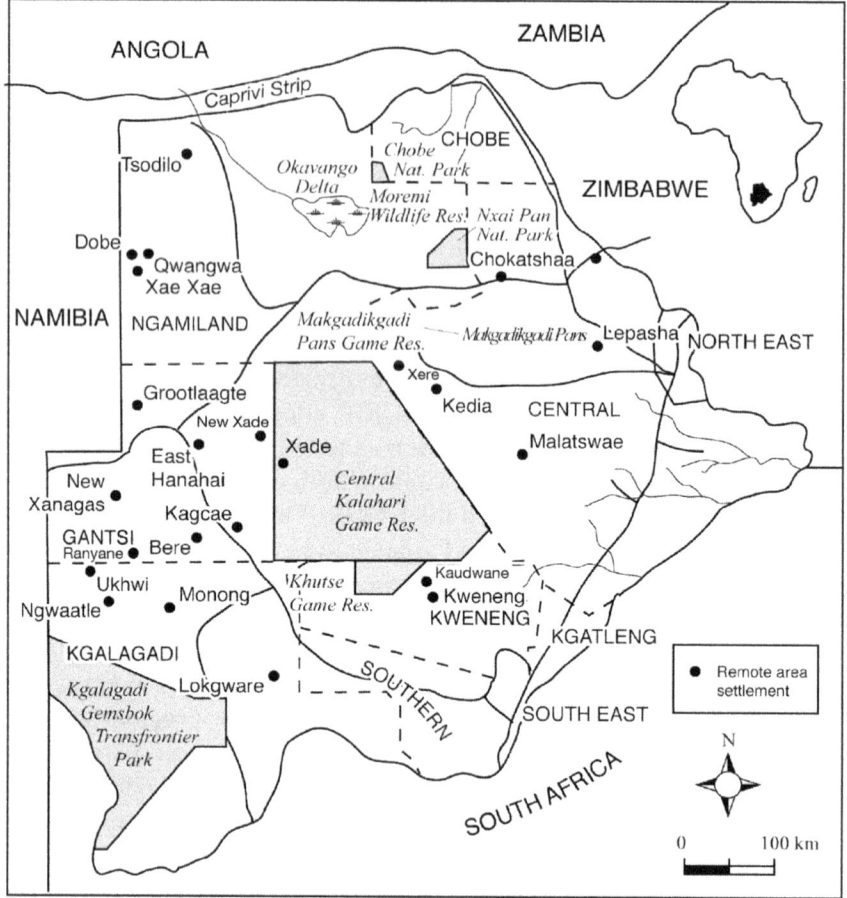

Figure 10.1   Remote area communities in Botswana

have these mechanisms and rights performed in practice? The balance of this chapter examines the ways in which the Government of Botswana has dealt with the land rights of San peoples, and then assesses the strategies employed by San and their supporters to get their land rights recognized.

A Brief History of San Dispossession

San and their ancestors resided in the Kalahari Desert region of Botswana for thousands of years. San moved about the landscape from one resource patch to another, depending on resource type and density, numbers of people in each group, and season (Barnard, 1992; Silberbauer, 1981; Tanaka, 1980). Virtually all San groups claimed rights to their territories, or areas they recognized as belonging to them, and had *de facto* rights of long-term occupancy and use (Barnard, 1992; Silberbauer, 1981; Tanaka, 2014). San territorial units are known as a *nong* (Naro), *gu* (G/ui), *g!u* (G//ana), *n//olli* (!Xõó), and a *n!ore* (‡X'ao-||'aen).

San were pressed into service as herders and field hands when agro-pastoralists moved into the Kalahari some 2,000 years ago. They had to seek permission from traditional authorities of other groups if they wanted land for residential, agricultural, or other purposes (Hitchcock, 1980; Schapera, 1938, 1943). As Schapera (1953, p. 37) pointed out:

> In the Western tribes, there was formerly also a class of "serfs" (*malata*) consisting mainly of Sarwa and Kgalagadi but also (in the north) of Pedi and Koba. These people, found in the country occupied by the Tswana, were parceled out in local groups among the chiefs and other leading tribesmen. They and their families were permanently attached to the families of their masters, to whom they paid special tribute and whom they served in various menial capacities; such property as they acquired was at their master's disposal.

Over time, the servile status of San and Bakgalagadi was transformed, with stipulations by Tswana chiefs and by the Bechuanaland Protectorate authorities who declared slavery illegal in the 1930s (Datta & Murray, 1989; Schapera, 1970).

The Colonial Period

The British sought to influence the positions of the Tswana *vis-à-vis* San in five ways. First, the British Protectorate and British government officials made proclamations in public meetings in 1926 and 1936 that slavery was illegal (Miers & Crowder, 1988). Second, in the early 1930s, the British Government called for an investigation into Tswana slavery (Tagart, 1933). Third, individuals who mistreated San were investigated and tried in local courts. Fourth, reports were sent to the British High Commissioner in Cape Town regarding persistent beatings, torture and murder, and enslavement of San in Bechuanaland. Fifth, individual Bechuanaland Protectorate officials sought to assist San communities, setting aside land for San in such places as Letlhakane in the Ngwato District, and Olifonts Kloof in Ghanzi District. It should be noted, however, that these resettlement sites did not last very long (Silberbauer, 1981).

The London Missionary Society and individual clergymen and clergy-women also sought to improve the lives of San under the Tswana during the British Protectorate (see the London Missionary Society, 1935). There were also individual anthropologists who sought to get better treatment for San through their reports, two examples being Schapera (1939) and Silberbauer (1965). Chiefs themselves also sought to get better treatment of San through proclamations, visits to officials in England, and efforts to resolve disputes between individual San and those who had employed them (Schapera, 1970). Despite all these efforts, San felt that they were worse off at the end of the British colonial period than they were at the beginning (Gulbrandsen, 2012).

The Constitutional Republic

At Independence on September 30, 1966, Botswana's new constitution addressed the land and resource rights of the country's citizens (Republic of Botswana, 1966). The introduction of a *Tribal Land Act* (1968), which took effect in 1970, removed power for land away from the chiefs and gave it to district land boards (Republic of Botswana, 1968). The intro-duction of a land reform program, the Tribal Grazing Land Policy (TGLP) in 1975, guaranteed that every Motswana (citizen) had the right to enough land to meet their needs (Republic of Botswana, 1975).

Today, Botswana is made up of three kinds of land: freehold (private), state land, and communal (tribal land). The rough breakdown is 5.7 percent freehold, 17.4 percent state land (including parks and reserves and national monuments), and 29.8 percent (or 173,432 km^2) communal (see Table 10.1). The tenure in tribal (communal) areas became alienable over time after the introduction of the Tribal Land Act, which went into effect in 1970. This alienability makes the Botswana case distinct from many other jurisdictions around the world (see the chapters from Australia and Canada for example).

The majority of San peoples reside in communal areas. The land use planning process introduced by the TGLP resulted in District Councils and Land Boards dividing tribal land up into subcategories, including commercial leasehold ranching zones, reserve areas (set aside for the future), and communal lands (Table 10.1). As it worked out, the com-mercial leasehold ranching zones became the primary focus of the District Councils and Land Boards, and what was then the Ministry of Local Government and Lands (Peters, 1994; Hitchcock & Sapignoli, 2019; Wily, 1979, 1981). Subsequent land use zoning efforts resulted in the

Table 10.1 Land zoning categories in Botswana

Type of Land	Land Zoning Category	Amount of Land	Percentage of Country
Freehold land	Freehold farms	32,970 km^2	5.7
State land	Parks and reserves	101,535 km^2	17.4
	Other	32,455 km^2	5.6
Tribal land	Communal	173,432 km^2	29.8
	Commercial	51,094 km^2	8.8
	Wildlife Management areas	129,450 km^2	22.2
	Leasehold ranches	3,351 km^2	0.6
	Remote area Dweller settlements	3,523 km^2	0.6
	Other land	53,910 km^2	9.3
Total	All land	581,720 km^2	100.0

Data obtained from the Ministry of Lands and Housing, the Ministry of Local Government and Rural Development and the Ministry of Environment, Wildlife and Tourism, Government of Botswana. The category "other" includes land in towns and land set aside for government purposes, such as trek routes and quarantine camps for livestock.

setting aside of Wildlife Management Areas (WMAs), multiple-use zones in which wildlife-related land uses were supposed to receive priority (Republic of Botswana, 1986). Over time, the land boards allocated water points for domestic animals not only in the communal and leasehold areas, but also in the WMAs, which shifted land use toward livestock production (Adams et al., 2003; Cullis & Watson, 2005; Keeping et al., 2019). In addition, community members in the settlements in WMAs engaged in small-scale livestock production and initiated gardening and tourism projects, which transformed local landscapes (Cadger & Keep, 2013; Hitchcock, 2021).

A Community-Based Natural Resource Program was introduced in 1990 (Republic of Botswana, 1990), which gave communities rights over wildlife if they formed community trusts – management bodies that had a constitution, land use plan, and formal structure (Rihoy & Maguranyanga, 2010). The communities had the option of leasing out rights to wildlife to private companies or keeping the wildlife quota for themselves and engaging in subsistence and tourism. By 2014, there were over 180 community trusts in the ten districts of the country. It is important to note that the community trusts had rights over wildlife but no rights to wild plant resources, grazing, or water in these areas. They also did not have *de jure* land rights or sub-surface rights.

Community trusts had management councils that were similar to traditional San community leadership systems. The difference is that officers in community trusts were elected by community members, while San leaders usually arose from within local bands based on their personal qualities, knowledge of San customs, even-handedness in dealing with others, and awareness of the natural resources and important places in their areas.

A countrywide hunting ban declared by the Botswana Government (Republic of Botswana, 2014) led to a shift from community management to private company management in the community trust areas. Many of the communities that had community trusts in 2014 found that wildlife rights and benefits from tourism were done away with. In community trusts in the North West District, for example, tourism benefits flowed to private safari tourism companies (Joseph Mbaiwa, personal communication, 2019; Mbaiwa, 2017, 2018). The rights to tourism and to hunting became a key focal point of debate in the lead-up to the 2019 elections. With the election of Mokgweetsi Masisi, moves were made toward opening up hunting, particularly to foreign safari hunters. No guarantees were provided by the new government for subsistence hunting rights for citizens dependent on wild fauna and flora.

The introduction of a new national land policy in Botswana in 2015 (Republic of Botswana, 2015) led to a trend toward privatization of tribal lands and a land rush into communal and wildlife management areas (Isaacs & Manatsha, 2016). The only places that did not experience this land rush were protected areas such as the Kgalagadi Transfrontier Park and Chobe National Park, and lands that were already in the hands of people with leasehold rights. The Central Kalahari Game Reserve was the only area set aside purposely for San in 1961, in this case to protect the *modus vivendi* of the people residing there, and at the same time conserve flora and fauna (Silberbauer, 2012).

Efforts to Secure Land Rights for San

Many of the efforts to secure land rights for San consisted of setting up settlements in which San could reside and pursue their livelihoods, particularly in the 1930s, such as the case of Olifants Kloof, in what is now the Ghanzi District, and one in the Letlhakane area of the Ngwato (Central) District (Silberbauer, 1981). Faith-based institutions established mission stations aimed at assisting San, as seen, for example, at D'Kar in Ghanzi District in 1973 and Ka/Gae in Ghanzi District in 1975–76. There are only two places where San own their own land in Botswana (i.e., they have *de jure* [legal] tenure rights). These are D'Kar, a 3,000-hectare community in central Ghanzi District, north of Ghanzi Township, which belongs to a church (originally, the Gereformeerde Church, the Dutch Reformed Church in Namibia); and the Dqae Qare Game Farm in Ghanzi District, a 7,500-hectare freehold farm that is now owned by a Naro San community trust, the D'Kar Trust (Bollig et al., 2000).

An important effort to promote San land rights was led by Elizabeth Alden Wily, who persuaded the government to establish a Bushmen Development Program (BDP) in the Ministry of Local Government and Lands in Gaborone in 1973 (see Wily, 1979). This program initially supported San, but subsequently expanded to cover all people in remote areas living outside of government-recognized settlements (Gulbrandsen et al., 1986). In the 1970s and 1980s, communal service centers were established in commercial ranching areas, and people from the ranches were moved into them. In those service centers, the residents were provided with water, social infrastructure (schools, health posts), community centers, and meeting places (*dikgotla*) where community members could meet with government officials and village headmen and headwomen (Hitchcock, 1988).

San Land Rights in Ghanzi District

One of the strategies employed by the BDP was to establish a set of resettlement sites for San living in the Ghanzi Farms, or in the town of Ghanzi, and who for all intents and purposes were landless (Wily, 1982). The original plan was to establish four resettlement localities in Ghanzi District: East Hanahai, West Hanahai, Rooibrak, and Groot Laagte (see Figure 10.2 for a map of Ghanzi District). East and West Hanahai were made up primarily of Naro San and some G/ui and G//ana. Groot Laagte in the northern part of the district contained primarily Ju/'hoan-speaking ‡X'ao-||'aen. Rooibrak, which did not become a resettlement site because it lacked sufficient water to sustain the population, and would have supported Naro, as well as some G/ui and G//ana.

The implementation of the Ghanzi settlement schemes did not go as smoothly as hoped. As soon as the resettlement sites were designated,

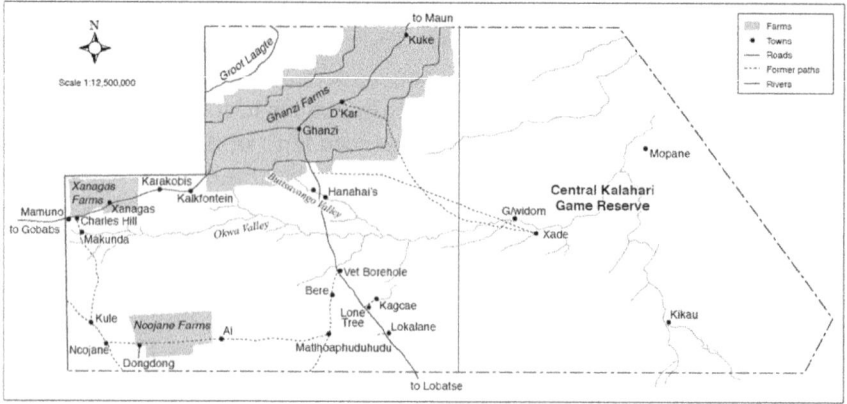

Figure 10.2   Map of Ghanzi District and CKGR

people from other groups began to move into them with their livestock. A second problem related to the size of the area to be allocated. While San and their supporters believed that the settlement areas should be large enough to accommodate foraging, residence, arable agriculture, and livestock raising, along with sufficient room for growth of human and livestock populations, the Ghanzi District Council decided to allocate blocks of land 20 by 20 kilometers in size (400 square kilometers) for the settlements (Hitchcock, 1988; Wily, 1979, 1982). These areas turned out to be too small to sustain people through hunting and gathering. In many of the settlements, much of the wildlife and wild plant resources were exploited heavily both by residents of the settlements and outsiders. Agriculture and livestock keeping expanded as wild resources declined, which affected livelihoods in the settlements.

Ghanzi District, it turns out, is an important district to examine for a variety of reasons. First, it is a large district, 117,910 square kilometers, and it lies in the western Kalahari Desert region of Botswana, an area with a high-water table that attracted livestock keepers and settlers (Russell & Russell, 1979). Second, it is the district with the highest percentage of San. Third, Ghanzi contains the most diverse types of land, from freehold farms to leasehold ranches, and from communal land to WMAs (see Table 10.2, see Ghanzi District Development Plan 2009). There are also some subcategories of land, including areas set aside as leasehold (long-term leases for commercial land) and land designated for specialized purposes (e.g., land for trek routes and veterinary camps).

Table 10.2 Land zoning categories in Ghanzi District, Botswana

Land category	Area (in square kilometers) (km²)	Percentage of district
Communal Area		
Mixed farming, grazing, and arable area	17,619	14.94
Remote Area Dwellers Settlements	2,415	2.05
Ghanzi Township	133	0.11
Miscellaneous land (e.g., trek routes, villages)	973	0.83
Freehold and Leasehold Land		
Ghanzi Freehold Block	10,480	8.88
Xanagas Freehold Block	1,374	1.14
Ncojane Leasehold Farms	1,664	1.41
State Land Extension Farms	3,784	3.2
Kuke State Land Leasehold Farms	430	0.36
Artificial Insemination (AI) Camp, Veterinary Services	15	0.001
Commercial Areas on Tribal Land		
Makunda FDA Ranches	444	0.37
SE Ghanzi SDA Ranches	924	0.78
Wildlife Management Areas		
Groot Laagte WMA	3,908	3.31
Matlo-a-Phuduhudu WMA	8,816	7.47
Okwa WMA	13,618	11.55
Conservation Area		
(State Land)		
Central Kalahari Game Reserve	52,313	44.36
Total	117,910	100.0

Note: Data obtained from the Ghanzi District Council. The abbreviations used here are as follows: WMA stands for Wildlife Management Area, FDA for First Development Area, SDA for Second Development Area (both TGLP commercial ranch areas), and RAD for Remote Area Dweller.

A sizable proportion of the Ghanzi district consists of a single pro-tected area, the Central Kalahari Game Reserve. The Central Kalahari is considered state land, and it is overseen by both the Ghanzi District Council and the central government which determines policy in the area. When the game reserve was first declared, European farmers in the Ghanzi Farms opposed the idea, because they feared the reserve would serve as a locale for people to escape farm work and potentially serve as a base for people engaged in livestock theft (personal communication, 1978; Silberbauer, 1981). At the time of its declaration, there were 3,000 to 5,000 people who had some form of rights in the CKGR. In the 1980s, however, the Government of Botswana established a commission of inquiry into the status of the CKGR, in part as a response to concerns expressed by ecologists and others that the wildlife and habitats in the reserve were being affected by the presence of large numbers of people who had moved to one of the communities in the reserve, !Xade (Government of Botswana, 1985). The government rejected many of the conclusions of the Central Kalahari Commission, recommending instead that reserve residents be relocated to other places. Several reasons were given for this decision: first, the government wanted to promote wildlife conservation in the reserve; second, the government felt that wildlife-related tourism was an important way to have the state benefit from the resources in the reserve; and third, it was argued that people inside the reserve were no longer living as hunter-gatherers, but instead were keeping livestock and engaging in other "non-traditional" activities inconsistent with wildlife conservation (Ministry of Commerce and Industry, 1986).

The Botswana Government began encouraging people to resettle outside of the reserve by utilizing a number of techniques, some of them coercive. Arrest rates for illegal hunting increased substantially, and people suspected of poaching were sometimes beaten and tortured (Mogwe, 1992). Food and water deliveries under the government's Remote Area Development Program slowed, and for some communities in the reserve stopped altogether. In some cases, individuals' livestock were confiscated. Eventually, two major relocations of reserve residents occurred, one in May–June 1997, where some 1,760 residents were moved from !Xade in the reserve to New Xade outside the western boundaries of the CKGR.

A second set of relocations took place in January–February 2002, when some 2,000 people were loaded on trucks and moved out of the reserve to three resettlement sites: New Xade, Kaudwane in Kweneng District, and Xere in Central District (Sapignoli, 2017, 2018; Zips-Mairitsch, 2013). At first San and Bakgalagadi in the reserve attempted to negotiate, but these negotiations did not change the government's mind about the relocations. Then people from the reserve engaged in demonstrations against the government's decisions. San formed their own non-government organizations aimed at promoting their rights. People from the central Kalahari and support organizations, notably the First People of the Kalahari which had been founded in 1993, engaged in lobbying efforts at the international level to highlight this injustice, traveling to New York, Geneva, and London, among other places. When these efforts failed, the people of the CKGR opted to go to court, filing a legal claim against the government (High Court of Botswana, Affidavit, 2002). While at first the High Court rejected the legal case on the basis of technicalities, eventually the Central Kalahari case was heard in the High Court over the period from July 2004 to December 2006 (see Sapignoli, 2018 for a detailed description of this legal case). A third small-scale removal of people from the Central Kalahari Game Reserve occurred in 2005 (Sapignoli, 2018).

In December 2006, three High Court judges ruled largely for the applicants, arguing that they (1) had the right to return to the Central Kalahari, and (2) had the right to hunt for subsistence in the reserve (High Court of Botswana, Affidavit, 2006). The day after the judgment was issued, however, the Attorney General of Botswana stated the government was under no obligation to offer services in the reserve, including food and water provision (Molokomme, 2006). The people of the Central Kalahari went back to court in 2009, seeking a right to water in the Court of Appeal, the country's highest court. The people of the Central Kalahari won this case, setting an international precedent for Indigenous and other peoples' right to water (Court of Appeal, Botswana, 2011; Morinville & Rodina, 2013; Sapignoli, 2018).

From our field work in January 2022, we documented some 350 people in five communities inside the CKGR, earning their livelihoods through gathering wild plant foods, delivering government food, growing crops in small gardens, and maintaining small-livestock (goats and sheep) and poultry production. People in the reserve are still not allowed to hunt, which is unlikely to change despite a promise by the Botswana Government in May 2019. It is important to note here that Botswana is the only country in Africa to have had a nation-wide subsistence hunting law, which lasted from 1979 to 2004. The regulations were specified in the Unified Hunting Regulations of 1979 (Hitchcock et al., 2012; Republic of Botswana, 1979). It should be pointed out, however, that dozens of people were arrested by wildlife officers and police despite their possession of subsistence hunting licenses in the period from 1970 to 2004, calling into question the effectiveness of the licensing system. One of the complaints about this hunting system in late 2021 related to communities' dissatisfaction with how private safari companies were getting allocations of animals to hunt, but communities were not allowed to benefit from the hunting license allocation.

The Ghanzi District Council and the Residents of Ranyane

The Ghanzi District Council also used heavy-handed tactics against San residents of villages in the communal areas of the district. This can be seen, for example, in the case of Ranyane, a small village consisting of several hundred Naro San, and a few Ngologa Bakgalagadi in the southern part of Ghanzi District. The Ghanzi Council argued in 2010 that the people of Ranyane had to move to another village, Bere, because Ranyane was located in a "wildlife corridor." Over the next two years the Ghanzi Council engaged in intimidation and harassment of Ranyane residents in an effort to get them to relocate (Gaotlhobogwe, 2012). Eventually, the Council shut down the borehole in Ranyane, leaving residents without water for themselves or their animals. The Council did this despite Botswana government policies, including the *National Settlement Policy* of 1998 (Republic of Botswana, 1998) which guarantees villages of over 500 people the right to water, and the National Water Policy of 2012 that guarantees all Botswana the right to water (Republic of Botswana, 2012).

In response, the people of Ranyane took the Council to court in 2013 (High Court of Botswana, 2013). The Ranyane people failed in their effort to get the High Court to support them remaining at Ranyane; about half of the population was moved in 2013 to Bere, another Ghanzi remote area settlement. The rest of the people remained at Ranyane and earned a living through foraging and working for livestock owners in the vicinity of the village. In 2018, the remaining residents of Ranyane sought government recognition of their community as an official gazetted settlement (see Baaitse, 2018; Mokwape, 2018), but as yet neither the Ghanzi District Council nor the Botswana Government has responded to this request.

The effort to establish three Remote Area Dweller (RAD) ranches in Ghanzi District was also largely unsuccessful. The three farms, designated NK 173 (near West Hanahai), NK 164 (near Chobokwane), and NK 145 (near Groot Laagte) were allocated officially to the Ghanzi District Council on behalf of San in February 1990. The Ghanzi District Council had approached a consortium of NGOs, including the Kuru Family of Organizations and Permaculture, to assist in the development of the farms. The Norwegian development agency (NORAD) pledged P360,000 (then about US$180,000) for water and fencing on the farms (NORAD office, personal communication, 1991). As it turned out, however, the government took over these ranches, a process that also occurred in Ghanzi District in the new millennium.

Barriers and Opportunities for San Land Rights

The government is the biggest obstacle for San land rights in Botswana. The government has steadfastly refused to negotiate San land rights. It has not honored requests by San organizations, the Commissioner for Indigenous and Human Rights, the Human Rights Council, and various international Indigenous rights NGOs to change its land rights policies.

In the 1990s, and the first decade and a half of the twenty-first century, a number of communities in Ghanzi District formed community trusts under the government's Community-Based Natural Resource Management Program (Republic of Botswana, 1990). San communities were able to get rights to resources through these trusts. This strategy worked until 2014, when the Government of Botswana imposed a hunting ban. Since that ban, the trusts have largely lost control of their areas to private safari companies. Table 10.3 presents data on these community trusts, which engaged in a variety of projects ranging from tourism to wild animal sales and to craft production. It is currently unclear what the status and rights of the community trusts are.

Another way that San who were dispossessed of their lands sought to get at least some land and resource rights was to form alliances with mining companies, some of whom, such as DeBeers Botswana and Gem Diamonds, argued on behalf of San with the government. It is estimated that at least 300 San were dispossessed by the establishment of the DeBeers Orapa diamond mine in 1967. In the case of the diamond mines around Letlhakane in Central District, another 500–1,000 San were dispossessed (Keikabile Mogodu, personal communication, August 2022). Compensation in the form of alternative land or cash was not provided to those people who were required to leave their residential, arable, and grazing lands (Botswana Khwedom Council, personal communication, 2022).

More recently, mining corporations have exercised a certain degree of social responsibility. San communities and individuals required to leave their areas because of mining operations in Ghanzi and North-West Districts have received some cash in exchange for the loss of their land rights. In the case of the new copper-silver mines in northern Ghanzi and southern Ngamiland (North-West District), San were consulted ahead of time and had the opportunity to argue for fair and just compensation for their losses. The problem, however, is that many of the promises of cash and alternative land have yet to be honored by the new mines and their owners.

Table 10.3 Community trusts in Ghanzi District, Botswana, that are or were involved in community-based natural resource management activities

Name of Trust and Date of Founding	Controlled Hunting Area (CHA), Support Organization	Number of Villages Involved, Population Size	Project Activities
Aushuxalu Conservation Trust (Bere), 2006	Okwa WMA (13,618 km²)	One village (Bere), 800 people	Community tourism, crafts, tracking activities, bush (veld) products
Huiku Community Based Conservation Trust, 1999	Groot Laagte WMA (GH 1), (3,908 km²) Kuru Family of Organizations	Two villages (Groot Laagte and Qabo), 1,013 people	Community tourism, lodge, crafts, bush (veld) products
D'Kar Kuru Trust, 1999	Dqae Qare freehold farm (7,500 ha), D'Kar Kuru Trust	One village, (D'Kar), 943 people	Community tourism, crafts, lodge at Dqae Qare in Ghanzi Farms
Kgoesakani (New Xade) Management Trust, 2000	GH 10 (1,248 km²), Government of Botswana	One village (New Xade) (Kgoesakani) 1,800 people	Community tourism, crafts related to the Central Kalahari Game Reserve
Xwiskurusa Community Trust, 1996	GH 10 (1,248 km²), Permaculture Trust	Three villages (East and West Hanahai, Ka/Gae), 1,247 people	Community tourism, crafts, bush (veld) products
Chobokwane Community Trust, 1999	GH 11, Matho-a-Phuduhudu WMA (8,816 km²)	One village (Chobokwane), 489 people	Community campsites, crafts, bush (veld) products
Komku Development Trust, 1999	GH 11 (8,816 km²), First People of the Kalahari	One village, Buitsavango, 200 people	Community campsites, crafts, dances

Note: Data obtained from the Ghanzi District Council, the Kuru Family of Organizations, and the IUCN (World Conservation Union) CBNRM Support Program (www.cbnrm.bw and www.iucnbot.bw).

Conclusion

In 2023, it was uncertain whether the community trusts in the communal areas and Wildlife Management Areas in Botswana still had the right to make their own decisions, and whether people there had resource and land tenure rights. The lack of clarity on the land issue in communal areas is the most crucial problem facing Indigenous and minority communities in Botswana. As Wily (2018) pointed out, Botswana's protections for the tenure rights of people in communal areas are weak, and as a result "the law is to blame" (Wily, 2011). San and other minority communities in Botswana's communal areas continue to be vulnerable to expropriation, a process seen, for example, among San communities not only in Ghanzi District, but also in Central, Chobe, Kgalagadi, Kgatleng, Kweneng, and North-West Districts. The land tenure status of gazetted remote area settlements is unclear as well. Majority San communities have thus far been unable to obtain *de jure* land and water rights in the tribal land areas of Botswana.

Another strategy that San employed in an effort to get their land rights recognized was to take part in the political process (for comparison, see the chapter by Baird on Cambodia and Thailand in this book). In 1989, several San from Ghanzi District ran for Parliament (Hitchcock & Holm, 1993). In 1994, only one San was elected to Parliament, Kgosi (Chief) Rebecca Banika, a Shua (//Gorokhwe) San from Chobe District. At the council level, however, a sizable number of San in Ghanzi have run successfully for positions in the Ghanzi District Council. In 2019, there were six San on the Ghanzi Council, one of whom, Hunter Sixpence, was the Ghanzi Council chairperson. Another San, Jumanda Gakelebone, a G//ana from Mothomelo in the Central Kalahari Game Reserve, was the district councillor for New Xade. Mr. Gakelebone was re-elected to the Ghanzi District Council during the recent October 23, 2019, elections in Botswana. He now plans to run for the chairmanship of the Ghanzi District Council. One of the issues he will be pushing for is clarification of the rights of the people of the Central Kalahari Game Reserve.

One of his strategies (and that of other San activists) has been to form alliances with international organizations such as the Forest Peoples Programme, Minority Rights Group International, the International Work Group for Indigenous Affairs, Land is Life, and in the past, Survival International. Some of these organizations have provided funding for the activities of San organizations, and others have provided resources to allow international travel. This strategy has been partially successful, but the drop-off in funds to cover the costs of legal cases continues to be a major challenge.

As it stands now, water and social services such as education and health are provided in most of the seventy-three recognized remote area settlements in Botswana. However, water provisions were stopped in those places where the government wanted people to relocate, such as Ranyane in western Ghanzi District and in the Central Kalahari Game Reserve. As discussed, these decisions were successfully challenged in the High Court. But as yet the government and district councils have failed to implement these High Court judgments.

A critical analysis of the land rights of San and Bakgalagadi in Botswana reveals that they generally lack clearly defined land tenure rights. While the government pays lip service to "land rights for all" in its constitution and land policy papers, it is apparent that the district land boards and the government ministries responsible for land, such as the Ministry of Lands and Housing, and the Ministry of Local Government and Rural Development, have deliberately chosen not to allocate land to Indigenous communities, nor have they ruled on behalf of those communities that have filed appeals with the government. The new Botswana land policy (Republic of Botswana, 2015) has mainly served to allow individuals with means (i.e., those who are wealthy) to take over land occupied by poorer people, including those who define themselves and who are recognized internationally as "Indigenous Peoples."

San, for their part, continue to seek recognition of their land rights through organizing themselves, seeking funding to support negotiations, lobbying government and, in some cases, taking the government to court, with a certain degree of success. One way that San can ensure that they have their rights to land defined more clearly is to have them spelled out in a future "white paper" on Botswana land policy. It would also be useful to have the rights of Indigenous Peoples included in a new version of the Botswana Constitution.

In many ways, Botswana provides an all-too-common example of the problems of land rights for Indigenous Peoples in Africa and elsewhere across the world, as reflected across this book. Part of the reason for this situation is the weak protections of communal land rights. San in Botswana have faced challenges when it comes to political recognition and acceptance by the government of the concept of Indigeneity as a basis for rights. Interestingly, Botswana government officials regularly attend the United Nations Permanent Forum on Indigenous Issues (UNPFII) where they meet with representatives of San organizations.

However, Botswana government officials have been reluctant to meet face-to-face with representatives of San communities in Botswana itself. Thus, it remains to be seen what progress local and international efforts will bring when it comes to ensuring greater security of land tenure for the country's Indigenous Peoples.

Acknowledgments

We thank the Government of Botswana for permission to carry out this research. Support for the research upon which this paper is based was provided by the U. S. National Science Foundation grants (NSF-Soc. 75-02253, BNS 76-19633), the International Work Group for Indigenous Affairs (IWGIA), Hivos (the Netherlands), the Norwegian Agency for International Development (NORAD), the U. S. Agency for International Development (USAID), the United Nations Development Program (UNDP), and the Remote Area Development Program, Government of Botswana. William Nikolakis, Jumanda Gakelebone, Melinda Kelly, Sidsel Saugestad, and Elizabeth Alden Wily provided useful information and editorial suggestions. We wish to express our sincere appreciation to my informants for the valuable information that they provided to us.

References

Adams, M., Kalabamu, F., & White, R. (2003). Land tenure policy and practice in Botswana: Governance lessons for Southern Africa. *Austrian Journal of Development Studies*, 1, 55–74.

African Commission on Human and Peoples' Rights. (2007). *Advisory opinion of the African Commission on Human and Peoples' Rights on the United Nations Declaration on the Rights of Indigenous Peoples*. Banjul, The Gambia: African Commission on Human and Peoples' Rights, African Union.

African Group of States. (2006). *Draft aide memoire: United Nations declaration on the rights of indigenous people*. New York: African Group of States.

Baaitse, F. (2018, Aug. 21). Fight for survival: Lawyers argue that Ranyane village deserves recognition. *The Voice*.

Barnard, A. (1992). *Hunters and herders of Southern Africa*. Cambridge: Cambridge University Press.

Barume, A. (2009). Responding to the concerns of the African states. In C. Charters & R. Stavenhagen (eds.), *Making the declaration work: The United Nations Declaration on the Rights of Indigenous Peoples* (pp. 170–182). Copenhagen: International Work Group for Indigenous Affairs.

(2014). *The land rights of Indigenous Peoples in Africa* (2nd ed.). Copenhagen: International Work Group for Indigenous Affairs.

Bollig, M., Hitchcock, R. K., Nduku, C., & Reynders, J. (2000). *At the crossroads: The future of a development initiative. Evaluation of KDT (Kuru Development Trust), Ghanzi and Ngamiland Districts of Botswana.* Amsterdam: Hivos Foundation.

Brett, P. (2018). *Human rights and the judicialisation of African politics.* New York: Routledge.

Cadger, K., & Keep, T. (2013). Contextualizing development projects among the San of Botswana: Challenges of community gardening. *Development in Practice*, 23(7): 811–825.

Court of Appeal, Botswana. (2011) *In the Court of Appeal of Botswana held at Lobatse. Court of Appeal No. CACLB-074-10. High Court Civil Case No. MAHLB 000 393-09 In the matter between Matsipane Mosetlhanyene, First Appellant, and Gakenyatsiwe Matsipane, Second Appellant, and the Attorney General Respondent. Heard 17 January 2011 and delivered 27 January 2011.* Lobatse, Botswana: Court of Appeal.

Cullis, A., & Watson, C. (2005). *Winners and losers: Privatizing the Commons in Botswana.* London: International Institute of Environment and Development.

Datta, K., & Murray, A. (1989). The rights of minorities and subject peoples in Botswana: A historical evaluation. In J. Holm & P. Molutsi (eds.), *Democracy in Botswana* (pp. 58–74). Gaborone: Botswana Society.

Gaotlhobogwe, M. (2012, March 15). Basarwa, Bakgalagadi in another forced relocation. *Mmegi On-Line*.

Government of Botswana. (1985). *Report of the Central Kgalagadi Reserve Fact Finding Mission.* Gaborone, Botswana: Government Printer.

Gulbrandsen, O. (2012). *The state and the social: State formation in Botswana and its precolonial and colonial genealogies.* New York: Berghahn Books.

Gulbrandsen, O., Karlsen, M., & Lexow, J. (1986). *Remote Area Development Programme.* Gaborone, Botswana: Government Printer.Republic of Botswan

High Court of Botswana. (2013). *MAHGB-000295-139 In the matter between Ditlhame Mmakgomo, First Applicant, and 11 others vs Ghanzi Land Board, First Respondent, Ghanzi District Council, Second Respondent, and Ghanzi District Commissioner, Third Respondent, 24 May 2013.* Lobatse: High Court of Botswana.

High Court of Botswana, Affidavit. (2002). *Central Kalahari Legal Case No. MISCA 52/2002 in the Matter between Roy Sesana, First Applicant, Keiwa Setlhobogwa and 241 others, Second and Further Applicants, and the Attorney General (in his capacity as the recognized agent of the Government of the Republic of Botswana).* Lobatse: High Court of Botswana.

(2006). *Judgment – Central Kalahari Legal Case No. MISCA 52/2002 in the Matter between Roy Sesana, First Applicant, Keiwa Setlhobogwa and 241 others, Second and Further Applicants, and the Attorney General (in his capacity as the recognized agent of the Government of the Republic of Botswana).* Lobatse: High Court of Botswana.

Hitchcock, R. K. (1980). Tradition, social justice, and land reform in Central Botswana. *Journal of African Law*, 24(1), 1–34.

(1988). *Monitoring, research, and development in the remote areas of Botswana.* Gaborone: Ministry of Local Government.

(2021). *Kgalagadi Drylands Ecosystem Project Indigenous Peoples Planning Framework (IPPF).* Gaborone, Botswana: Government of Botswana and United Nations Development Programme.

Hitchcock, R. K., & Holm, J. D. (1993). Bureaucratic domination of African Hunter-Gatherer societies: A study of the San in Botswana. *Development and Change*, 24(1), 1–35.

Hitchcock, R. K., & Sapignoli, M. (2019). The economic well-being of the San of the Western, Central, and Eastern Kalahari desert regions of Botswana. In C. Fleming & M. Manning (eds.), *The Routledge handbook of Indigenous well-being* (pp. 170–183). New York: Routledge.

Hitchcock, R. K., Sapignoli, M., & the San Caucus. (2012). Subsistence hunting and social justice in Botswana. www.justconservation.org

Isaacs, S. M., & Manatsha, B. T. (2016). Will the dreaded 'yellow monster' stop roaring again? An appraisal of Botswana's 2015 land policy. *Botswana Notes and Records*, 48, 383–395.

Keeping, D. R. Kashe, N., Langwane, H.K., Sebati, P., Molese, N., Gielen, M-C., Keitsile-Barungwi, A., Xhukwe, Q., & !Nate, B. (2019). Botswana's wildlife losing ground as Kalahari Wildlife Management Areas (WMAs) are dezoned for livestock expansion [Unpublished manuscript]. https://doi.org/10.1101/576496

London Missionary Society. (1935). *The Masarwa (Bushmen): Report of an Inquiry by the South African District Committee of the London Missionary Society.* Alice, South Africa: Lovedale Press.

Ludick, S. (2018, Dec. 3–5). *Botswana report.* Sub-Regional Workshop on Inclusive Development for San People in the Framework of the United Nations Declaration on the Rights of Indigenous Peoples, Windhoek, Namibia.

Mbaiwa, J. E. (2017). Poverty or riches: Who benefits from the booming tourism industry in Botswana? *Journal of Contemporary African Studies*, 35(1), 93–112.

(2018). Effects of the safari hunting tourism ban on rural livelihoods and wildlife conservation in Northern Botswana. *South African Geographical Journal*, 100(1), 41–61.

Miers, S., & Crowder, M. (1988). The politics of slavery in Bechuanaland: Power struggles and the plight of the Basarwa in the Bamangwato Reserve, 1926-1940. In S. Miers & R. Roberts (eds.), *The end of slavery in Africa* (pp. 172–200). Madison: University of Wisconsin Press.

Ministry of Commerce and Industry. (1986). *Report of the Central Kalahari Game Reserve Fact Finding Mission*. Gaborone, Botswana: Ministry of Commerce and Industry.

Mogwe, A. (1992). *Who was (t)here first? An assessment of the human rights situation of Basarwa in selected communities in the Gantsi District, Botswana*. Gaborone, Botswana: Botswana Christian Council.

Mokwape, M. (2018, Sept. 14). Ranyane residents want recognition. *Mmegi Online*.

Molokomme, A. (2006). *Attorney General's statement on the outcome of the case of Roy Seasana and others vs. the Attorney General*. Gaborone: Attorney General's Chambers, Government of Botswana.

Morinville, C., & Rodina, L. (2013). Rethinking the human right to water: Water access and dispossession in Botswana's Central Kalahari Game Reserve. *Geoforum*, 49, 150–159.

Ndahinda, F. M. (2011). *Indigenousness in Africa: A contested legal framework for empowerment of 'marginalized' communities*. New York: Springer.

Ng'ong'ola, C. (2007). Sneaking Aboriginal title into Botswana's legal system through a side door: Review of *Sesana and Others v. the Attorney General*. *Botswana Law Journal*, 6, 103–123.

Nyati-Ramahobo, L. (2009). *Minority tribes in Botswana: The politics of recognition*. London: Minority Rights Group International.

Peters, P. (1994). *Dividing the Commons: Politics, policy, and culture in Botswana*. Charlottesville, Virginia: University Press of Virginia.

Republic of Botswana. (1966). *Constitution of Botswana*. Gaborone, Botswana: Government Printer.

(1968). *Tribal Land Act (1968)*. Gaborone, Botswana: Government Printer.

(1975). *National policy on tribal grazing land*. Gaborone, Botswana: Government Printer.

(1986). *Wildlife Conservation Policy*. Gaborone, Botswana: Government Printer.

(1990). *Community-Based Natural Resources Management Policy*. Gaborone, Botswana: Government of Botswana.

(1998). *National Settlement Policy*. Gaborone, Botswana: Government Printer.

(2009). *Remote Area Development Program (RADP)*. Gaborone, Botswana.

(2012). *Botswana National Water Policy, October 2012*. Gaborone: Ministry of Minerals, Energy and Water Resources.

(2014). *Supplement C. Wildlife Conservation and National Parks (Prohibition of Hunting, Capturing, or Removal of Animals Order, 2014)*. Gaborone: Government of Botswana.

(2015). *Land Policy*. Gaborone, Botswana: Ministry of Lands and Housing.

Rihoy, L., & Maguranyanga, B. (2010). The politics of community-based natural resource management in Botswana. In F. Nelson (ed.), *Community rights, conservation, and contested land: The politics of natural resource governance in Africa* (pp. 55–78). London: Earthscan.

Russel, M. & Russell, M. (1979). *Afrikaners of the Kalahari*. Cambridge: Cambridge University Press.

Samatar, A. I. (1999). *An African miracle: State and class leadership and colonial legacy in Botswana development*. Portsmouth, New Hampshire: Heinemann.

Sapignoli, M. (2017). "Bushmen in the law": Evidence and identity in Botswana's High Court. *Political and Legal Anthropology Review (PoLAR)*, 40(2), 210–225.

(2018). *Hunting justice: Displacement, law, and activism in the Kalahari.* Cambridge: Cambridge University Press.

Saugestad, S. (2001). *The inconvenient Indigenous: Remote area development in Botswana, donor assistance, and the First People of the Kalahari*. Uppsala, Sweden: Nordic Africa Institute.

Schapera, I. (1938). *A handbook of Tswana law and custom*. London: Frank Cass.

(1939). A survey of the Bushman question. *Race Relations*, 6(2), 68–83.

(1943). *Native land tenure in the Bechuanaland Protectorate*. Alice, South Africa: Lovedale Press.

(1953). *The Tswana*. London: International African Institute.

(1970). *Tribal innovators: Tswana Chiefs and social change, 1795–1940*. London: Athlone Press.

Silberbauer, G.B. (1965). Report to the Government of Bechuanaland on the Bush Man Survey. Government of Bechuanaland.

(1981). *Hunter and habitat in the Central Kalahari Desert.* New York: Cambridge University Press.

(2012). Why the Central Kalahari Game Reserve? *Botswana Notes and Records*, 44, 201–203.

Tagart, E. S. B. (1933). *Report on the conditions existing among the Masarwa in the Bamangwato Reserve of the Bechuanaland Protectorate and certain other matters appertaining to the Natives living therein.* Pretoria, South Africa: Government Printer.

Tanaka, J. (1980). *The San, hunter-gatherers of the Kalahari: A study in ecological anthropology* (D. W. Hughes, Trans.). Tokyo: Tokyo University Press.

(2014). *The Bushmen: A half-century chronicle of transformation in hunter-gatherer life and ecology* (M. Sato, Trans.). Kyoto: Kyoto University Press.

Wily, E. A. (1979). *Official policy towards San (Bushmen) hunter-gatherers in modern Botswana: 1966–1978*. Gaborone, Botswana: National Institute of Development and Cultural Research.

(1981). *The TGLP and hunter-gatherers: A case study in land politics*. Gaborone, Botswana: National Institute of Development and Cultural Research.

(1982). A strategy of self-determination for the Kalahari San (The Botswana government's programme of action in the Ghanzi farms). *Development and Change*, 13(2), 291–308.

(2011). 'The Law is to Blame': The vulnerable status of common property rights in sub-Saharan Africa. *Development and Change*, 42(3), 733–757.

(2018). Collective land ownership in the 21st century: Overview of global trends. *Land*, 7(2), 68.

Zips-Mairitsch, M. (2013). *Lost land? (Land) rights of the San in Botswana and the legal concept of Indigeneity in Africa*. Copenhagen: International Work Group for Indigenous Affairs.

11

Rights to Land among *Amazigh* Peoples in Morocco

The Case of the High Atlas

AHMED BENDELLA, UGO D'AMBROSIO, EMILY CARUSO,
GARY MARTIN, SOUFIANE M'SOU, MARI CARMEN
ROMERA, AND PABLO DOMINGUEZ

Introduction

Morocco sustains a rich diversity of cultures, languages, and livelihoods. Like in other countries, the social organization of the rural populations is closely linked to their historical relationship to land and to their immediate biophysical environment, as well as to centuries-old and ever-evolving demographic, legal, cultural, economic, and political transformations. In this chapter, we focus on *Amazigh* peoples living in the Moroccan High Atlas (see map, Figure 11.1), who have demonstrated resilience in the face of significant scarcity and uncertainty, through customary systems of natural resource governance – the *agdal* systems. Despite the many social, cultural, and legal shifts and its degradation or disappearance in many places, the *agdal* system still remains a robust institutional framework, which is not only a bulwark against the dispossession of communal lands but also sustains the cultural and economic relationships for stewarding resources among High Atlas populations.

Socio-cultural Context of Morocco

Morocco is home to a conglomerate of culturally diverse populations whose geographical or historical connections extend well beyond the country's borders into the wider Maghreb region, the whole of northwest Africa and the Iberian and Arabic peninsulas. This expansiveness gives life to a multiplicity of traditions, identities, languages, and dialects belonging to an immense array of cultural influences. However, in the

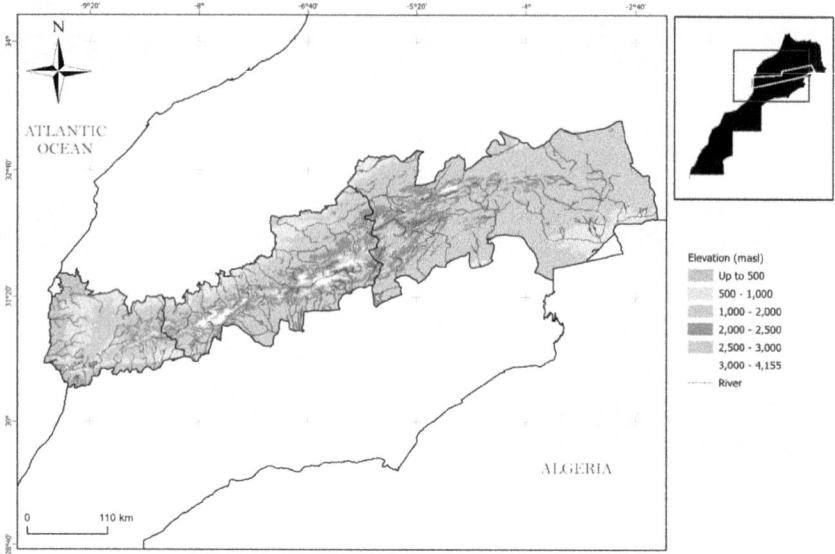

Figure 11.1 High Atlas within present-day Morocco: Giandanielle Castangia, High Atlas Cultural Landscapes project run by the Global Diversity Foundation and financed by the MAVA foundation and the Darwin Initiative (DEFRA)

High Atlas, a common macro-linguistic family can be identified, which connects with the wider *Berber/Amazigh* ethnicity. For a long time denominated as Berbers, especially by Europeans but not exclusively (Basset, 1908), in the last decades the term *Amazigh* has been used, especially by the *Berberist/Amazighist* movements. *Amazigh*, for many, means free or noble men (Chaker, 2004). The *Berber/Amazigh* peoples are often spoken of as the *aborigine* populations of northern and north-western Africa, in reference to the idea that many of their cultural traits were already present in the region before the Arab conquest of the seventh and eighth centuries AD.

However, the arrival of proto-*Berber/Amazigh* cultures to the Maghreb from the regions of the Red Sea can be dated to around the local Neolithic period (approximately 3,000–5,000 BC), and they were of course preceded by other cultures that disappeared or fused with their onset (Camps, 1995). Several millennia after their installation in the Maghreb, the first commercial colonies of other Mediterranean peoples appeared, first along the seacoast, which then moved into the hinterland. This was particularly the case with Greeks and Phoenicians, the latter notably turning later into Carthaginians through their intermingling with local *Amazighs*. These were then followed by wider conquests by Romans, Vandals, Byzantines, Arabs, Ottomans, Portuguese, Spaniards, and French.

The first Arab arrivals came with the Islamic conquest of the seventh century AD, and continued through to the eighth century (Valérian, 2011). This was followed by new invasions of Arab Bedouin tribes coming from the Middle East, like the Beni Hilal and the Beni Sulaim toward the eleventh century (Camps, 1995). A few centuries later, populations of Arab or Arabized Muslims and Jewish peoples immigrated to the Maghreb from the Iberian Peninsula, escaping the Christian *Reconquista* of the fifteenth century (Zayas, 2017). So did populations from Nigerian West Sudan (*blad sudan*) immigrate, especially during and after the Moroccan invasion of the Songhai Empire in the late sixteenth century (Mouline, 2009). Moreover, there has also been a constant arrival of *chorfas* (descendants of the prophet) from the Arabian Peninsula at different moments during Morocco's history (Ferhat, 1999).

This movement of people created a significant ethno-linguistic diversity across Morocco. A significant portion of the Moroccans of the country's population speaks one of various *Amazigh* languages,[1] yet until the creation of the new Moroccan Constitution in 2011, and particularly Article 5 which recognizes the linguistic and cultural rights of the *Amazigh/Berber*-speaking populations, Arabic was the only state-recognized language and was the promoted identity (Aït Mous, 2011). As a result, since 2011, *Amazigh* languages (increasingly referred to as Tamazight in an effort to unify the diverse idioms and dialects that compose the *Amazigh* linguistic family), have been recognized as official, even if the relevant laws were only promulgated in September 2019,[2] and even if Arabic remains the language of the state administration, schools, business, and work (Benzakour, 2007).

Morocco can be roughly divided into two large ethnolinguistic segments, one Arabophone (to refer to those populations speaking Darija, the Moroccan Dialectal Arabic with many *Amazigh* imprints) and one Amazighophone (to refer to those populations speaking one of the three

---

[1] Unfortunately, official statistics for ethnic or language groups in Morocco are not available, despite the inclusion of questions about language usage in the 2014 official census.

[2] This organic law specifies the procedures and stages for recognizing the Amazigh language as official, detailing how it will be integrated into the educational system and various other public-life sectors.

main *Amazigh* linguistic variants as their mother tongue: Tarifit in the north, Tamazight around the Middle Atlas and Central High Atlas, and Tachelhit around the southern High Atlas and southern parts of Morocco). Arabophone populations constitute the majority of the population, and are concentrated mainly in the plains, generally in the most fertile areas, while Amazighophones are mainly concentrated in the mountains, in arid areas or in the south before the western Sahara, generally distant from the cities and the coast.

The 2011 Constitution recognizes in its preamble the Arab-Islamic, *Amazigh*, Saharo-Hassani, African, Andalusian, Hebrew, and Mediterranean components of Moroccan identity, demonstrating a progressive development toward the recognition of Morocco's great cultural diversity. Since Morocco's independence from France and Spain in 1956, the country's territorial organization has blurred traditional tribal and ethno-lineage distributions (Chanbergeat, 1961), although the reference to its tribal organization remains sociologically significant. However, in order to promote fraternity among the different groups in Morocco, and to avoid what could be unproductive *Indigenist* competitions, a broad agreement in Morocco emerged decades ago to speak of rural and local communities instead of "Indigenous Peoples." To respect this social contract, which is still held by the majority of Moroccans, we will treat terms such as common lands or local community lands as synonymous with Indigenous Peoples' lands. In addition, in order to be context-based, we will use the terms *Berber* and *Amazigh* according to the period of history discussed.

The Socio-cultural History of High Atlas Communities: The Resilience of Customary Systems

Until the time of independence, rural Morocco, and most particularly the High Atlas, was organized into tribal groups. High Atlas tribes implied a common real but also symbolic kinship ascendance, which, according to each situation and need, could conglomerate into greater social structures (tribal confederations) or smaller units connected by a system of alliances called *leff-s* or *çoff-s* (Lakhsassi & Tozy, 2000). These multifractal groups maintained relations with the *Makhzen* (the state or central power, the head being the King or Sultan of Morocco), but this varied according to the region and shifting political interests and hierarchies. (While these socio-political systems are largely deactivated today, they still have a certain functionality at the lower scales of the tribal system such as with tribal subfractions, and the tribe is still very often a source of social and cultural identities.) At the same time, the populations of the cities were diverse, even if social groupings along ethnic and tribal lines could be found, especially through the crafts organized by certain social guilds (Massignon, 1925).

These frameworks of belonging and cooperation among tribal society cohered, case by case, permanently, punctually or ad-hoc, depending on the stakes of the moment, according to a model described by many anthropologists as segmental (Gellner, 1969). They mainly oscillated between basic structures like the *douar* (hamlet) and large tribal confederations passing through tribal fractions or cantons and tribes, nested as if a set of Russian matryoshka dolls.

While recognizing one way or another the primacy of the Sultan of Morocco, at least on the spiritual level, as well as Islamic law, and at the same time accepting the physical presence of political, administrative, or judicial personnel among them (e.g., *caid*[3], *adoul*[4]), the tribes retained a variable but generally quite important degree of autonomy, or even a *de facto* independence (Montagne, 1930). All tribes had community institutions in charge of local government, natural resource distribution and use, deliberation, and justice. In this sense, local customary law applied most prominently, without questioning the status of Islamic law, which remained in effect for certain areas like personal and moral conduct.

Although there were some common basic principles for these customary legal systems among all tribal groups and subgroups (e.g., cantons or tribal fractions) (Berque, 1978; Dresch, 1939), their provisions could vary greatly, especially across geographical distances. However, the institutions responsible for enforcing these laws did not have jurisdiction beyond the territory of each tribal grouping. Thus, parties settled inter-tribal issues either through force or more likely through negotiated pacts in order to avoid violence (Berque, 2001). In this context, while central power changed hands regularly over time, local High Atlas communities maintained a great customary diversity without really ever seeing a unified system imposed. Even the units of measurement linked to taxation under the prerogative of the *Makhzen* were never unified before the French and Spanish twentieth-century Protectorates (Hibou & Tozy, 2020).

---

[3] Representative of the Sultan and *Makhzen* (the state) at the local level, mainly linked to the Ministry of the Interior today.
[4] Traditional public notary.

In this context of highly diversified territorial autonomies, the *faqihs* (Muslim clerics) were also forced to adapt. Rural Berberophone populations displayed great ingeniousness in the interpretation of Islamic law or what is locally called the use of *hyal-s fiqhya*, meaning creative or crafty "*fiqhing*" (doing the *faquih*). These practices allowed for continuous syncretism between pre-Muslim and Muslim religious traditions in a way that always managed, nevertheless, to avoid a direct confrontation between the two, and somehow astoundingly maintained a generalized sense of the whole as being strictly Muslim. This great flexibility permitted the inclusion of very important rural contingents into the broader Moroccan Muslim community, building a solid base for future Moroccan political expansions or consolidations.

The Berber Policy: The Colonial Interpretation of the Moroccan Ethnicity

During the colonial period and most particularly in the French Protectorate that was the most prominent (1912–1956), the foreign powers reinforced different status and laws between Arabs, Berbers (Basset, 1908), old Jewish communities (Zafrani, 1999), and *Haratines*, the descendants of enslaved peoples from Sub-Saharan Africa (Ilahiane, 2001). The French Protectorate conveyed an image that there was only one government, the *sharifian* government, led by the Sultan of Morocco who was also its spiritual leader, and that the French "simply" assured its protection while supporting Morocco's progress. However, the French also provided *de facto* internal and external control and guardianship over a reinvented and reconverted *Makhzanian* apparatus, the Arabic part of the state, still functioning under the Protectorate. The Protectorate monopolized the production of some of the most important norms, such as those concerning key economic affairs, international relations, and the rights and duties of the French citizens and of other nationals holding privileges in Morocco under treaties and international agreements prior to 1912 (notably the Treaty of Algeciras of 1906).

At the same time, the foreign powers took charge of the internal "pacification" process according to the colonial terminology (Ladreit de Lacharrière, 1936), which involved intense warfare to submit the different tribes that opposed the *Makhzen* and/or the Protectorate, and which took place mainly in *Berber* areas. This "pacification" was especially harsh in the High Atlas, and most particularly with the Ait Atta tribal confederation who were the last to be defeated in 1933.

The *Berber* tribes have been always the most important and permanent threat to Morocco's central powers. Therefore, the French Protectorate chose to institutionalize the *Berber* tribes to better control them, and it did so through the politics of the great *caids*, also called the *Berber policy* (Ageron, 1971). This policy reinforced the powerful men of the *Amazigh* areas, traditionally called *amghars*, often initially chosen by the tribes to represent them, in order to then turn them into state *caids*. The *caid* is a Moroccan traditional figure that, unlike the *amghars*, is designated by the *Makhzen* or Moroccan state to represent it. These *caids*, once reinforced with the help of the French powers (e.g., often they facilitated the rule of several tribes), intertwined with French interests, and were then mobilized to exercise an indirect French control over those same tribes.

There was also a shift in the 1930s, with the transition in these areas from a traditional Muslim policy – which prior to the Protectorate applied to all Morocco, at least in theory – to a *Berber* policy that provided an official and public state recognition of a second legal system within the country. This was formalized on May 16, 1930 with the *dahir* Berbère, and marked the beginning of a legal dualism in Morocco (Hart, 1997). This was formalized on May 16, 1930, with the *dahir* Berbère, and marked the beginning of a legal dualism in Morocco (Hart, 1997).

This new *dahir* officially granted customary law a regulatory function for local justice among the *Berber* tribes, thus paving a path, among other things, to avoiding the *mahkamas* (Islamic Courts) for the application of the *Chrâa* (Islamic Law). This shift toward legal dualism was a turning point, and built on previous reforms by the Protectorate, including the *dahir* of September 11, 1914, relating to the administration of the *Berber* tribes of the Empire; the Vizieral Decree of September 12, 1914, on the designation of tribes of *Berber* custom; and the *dahir* of November 21, 1916, recognizing the value of the traditional *j'maa* (tribal assemblies where each household had one vote and one voice for important decisions of the tribal group).

This legal dualism (two officially recognized legal systems within one country) triggered a great wave of opposition among the dominant Arabophone urban populations of the country, led by the nationalist elites of the country, who saw it as a divide-and-rule policy (Halstead, 1967). After independence, this dualism was pushed back. There was also a rejection of traditional local institutions and the discourse of pluralism. The Pan-Arab stance was motivated to develop a unified ideology for the nation. In the struggle for the liberation from colonial powers, the subtleties and nuances of Morocco's diversity were sacrificed (Rachik, 2003).

After independence in 1956, the new Moroccan state inherited this increased perception of mistrust and rejection toward *Berber* tribes, and turned it into policy (El Qadéry, 1998). This attitude lasted many decades, to the detriment of tribes' autonomy, and even if greatly diminished, it still continues today toward certain tribes and regions. The new state equated the existence of tribes with archaic tendencies and primitivism, and reinforced the consolidation of the exclusive power of the central state against any competition from local authorities. It also encouraged the prevalence of a unitary ideology favoring a sole national identity along with the unity of law, the centrality of law's production and its general application.

No Country for Tribesmen

In the post-independence context, *Berber* and High Atlas tribal institutions and customary systems were mainly framed by this new nationalist class as traitors and collaborators of the colons (El Qadery, 1995). This was most greatly symbolized by the role of the *Berber* tribal chief El Glaoui (one of the aforementioned great *caids* of the High Atlas) in the deposition of Mohammed V's status as Sultan during the crisis of August 1953, which subsequently led to his exile first in France and then in Madagascar (Julien, 1978). This resulted in post-independence policies that marginalized Berbers in rural areas, with particularly violent repressions in Tafilalet in the eastern High Atlas regions and even more in the Rif mountains between 1957 and 1959 during and after the two respective revolts (Gellner, 1981). However, tribal communities of the High Atlas and other rural Moroccan populations maintained some of their traditional institutions of local governance through the principle of "nonintervention" implemented by the new independent state (often called the *laissez faire* policy), as long as peace was kept in these regions and there were no conflating interests.

Even for all this spiny history, within a twentieth-century state, there is still space for a certain autonomy of the tribal group according to its traditional regulatory practices for land management and natural resource governance. Nevertheless, this autonomy does not avoid the constant erosion and threat of arbitrary treatment by the state concerning land tenure and land use of *Amazigh* communities of the High Atlas and other regions of Morocco, depending on its interests at stake in each moment (Bendella, 2016). And of course, in such context, the Moroccan state has not yet endorsed the 1989 International Labour Organization

Convention on Indigenous and Tribal Peoples (ILO 169) or the 2007 United Nations Declaration on the Rights of Indigenous Peoples (UNDRIP).

The Survival of *Amazigh* Land Rights in the High Atlas

The main Moroccan laws governing access to rural lands and other natural resources, such as those held by the tribes of the High Atlas, date from a few years after the Protectorate in 1912. These have not changed much since then — and will not change much even if certain *nouveautés* are announced in the leadup to publication.[5] Examples include the laws regulating the public domain, *habous* (mortmain, or lands and property held inalienably), registration of land, forest estates, collective lands, and the arganeraie (argan tree forests), among others. The *dahir* (Moroccan legal decree) of April 27, 1919, on collective lands, sought to meet the needs of colonialists and Berbers. Today, more than 100 years after this *dahir*, it poses a series of challenges, to which a recent amendment to this law has tried to respond, without questioning the basis of the original text.

This decree on collective lands largely ignores the notion of common property and provides only cursory mention of customary law (Bouderbala, 2013). Nevertheless, this regulatory system has been reappropriated and reinterpreted by different actors to recognize common property or land use rights for *Amazigh* communities. The state has also used this system to recognize its rights to use land and natural resources considered public property, like water, forests, arganeraie or extensive pastoral lands. The state has been able to use this decree to seize communal land for projects considered "of general interest" (the definition and content changing with political trends). *Amazigh* have only

---

[5] The Moroccan government has recently released a draft legislation concerning the preservation and sustainable development of forests. If enacted, this legislation would replace and repeal the existing legislative framework governing forest areas in Morocco, including the 1917 *dahir* on forest exploitation and the 1925 *dahir* on Argan forests. The initial version of the legislation, open for public consultation, incorporates provisions for the usage rights of local populations, but especially for tribal members with traditional usage rights over Argan forests, comprising only a small part of Morocco's local community lands (Article 26). Moreover, the participatory mechanisms in the legislation do not explicitly recognize traditional groups, tribes, or local communities as such, but rather focus on associations and user cooperatives.

been able to preserve the traditional management of lands and natural resources where no clashes with the "general interest" are found.

The tensions weighing on this delicate balance are accentuated by new forms of land grabbing (Mahdi, 2014), and new attitudes and political hierarchies in local communities that alter preferences from traditional communal lands to new systems (Kadiri & Er-rayhany, 2019). These new systems range from simple open access to the individualization and privatization of common lands.

In any case, the "title of occupation" (i.e., use right) varies, referring to a mere presumption of collective status, an administrative delimitation, or a collective land registration. The Ministry of the Interior oversees the identification and registration of the landowning communities and their lands, and ensures their preservation. The problem in practice is that the title, whatever its form (presumed collective, delimited administratively, or even registered as a collective), ultimately does not protect these lands. For example, see the case of the Gharb in western Morocco (Karsenty, 1988). The Ministry of the Interior has, in the last instance, the right of interpretation of these titles, and can ignore these as part of its "supervisory authority."

Since 1919, the government has removed communal lands from the jurisdiction of the legislature and the judiciary. A law passed by the Moroccan Parliament in 2019[6] governs the question of collective land, but like the 1919 decree that it replaced, it guarantees the exclusive control of the executive over communal lands. A joint circular from the Minister of Justice and the Minister of the Interior even prohibited the courts from hearing cases on collective land for some time.[7] An article in the 1919 decree made it impossible to appeal to the courts against decisions of the Tutorship Council (an administrative arbitration commission chaired by the Minister of Interior), making it one of the only

---

[6] The collective lands were governed by a royal decree adopted during the colonial period, in 1919. This text entrusted their exclusive guardianship to the Ministry of the Interior, with virtually no oversight by legislative or judicial powers. However, in 2019, a new code was adopted through a law voted on by the Parliament, which, while retaining the same previous mechanism, introduced two new provisions that will probably induce profound and lasting transformations: the admission of women as rights holders, and the possibility of transferring lands to private investors.

[7] Joint circular from the Minister of the Interior and the Minister of Justice, addressed to magistrates and authority agents: "Circulaire interministérielle n° 8/62 sur les conflits de compétence en matière de propriété collective,"", in Ministère de l'Intérieur, *Guide des terres collectives*, Rabat, 1995.

administrative authorities not subject to judicial review. While the 2019 reforms opened the door to judicial review on communal land decisions, these new provisions restrict the court from interpreting the rules of management of this particular type of property, which remains the exclusive responsibility of the executive power.

The type of property right decreed by the *dahir* of April 27, 1919, on collective lands is restrictive. It is a right exercised under the tutelage of the state, and it is inalienable (Guillaume, 1960). The state, in contrast, has the ability to appropriate a portion of these lands for projects of "general interest," which can include everything from a dam for hydroelectric power and water provision to golf and tourist resort construction, military training grounds, and hunting grounds for Saudi clients. Ultimately these appropriations can mean the sale of traditionally common land to private investors. These transfers trigger resistance, but they generally succeed when they are fully backed up by the state. The recent land law reforms in 2019 have opened more possibilities for collective land sales to investors, and enabled further land-grabbing (Mahdi, 2014).

Land Governance by *Amazigh* Communities: The *Agdal* System

The contemporary legislative framework provides a precarious but nuanced layer of protection for High Atlas populations and their land rights. While the state can appropriate communal lands, there is a certain recognition of inalienable collective ownership, thus institutionalizing the communal dimension linked to the tribes, inherent in land and resource stewardship.

There is an intricate legal mosaic in the High Atlas, which includes individual private ownership (e.g., rights to fruit-bearing trees or livestock), public or state dominion (e.g., over forests, pastures and hydrological resources), communal or collective usufruct rights (e.g., water management systems, pastoralism and certain forms of wood collection), along with recognized communal property rights over certain grazing lands. Central to the well-functioning of this interplay is the capacity of traditional communities to effectively enforce a customary regulatory framework and make it be respected by all the members of the community of users (e.g., the tribes or smaller parts of the tribes), by their neighbors and by the state, for which the existence of a well and strongly present community is always necessary.

This Indigenous governance mechanism is instrumental not only in the preservation of the different tribal identities, cultural norms, and traditional land governance customs, but harmonizes relationships and often competing interests. The *agdal* system, historically and culturally integral to *Amazigh* High Atlas communal governance (Dominguez et al., 2010, embodies the complex intertwining between different human groups and actors, land and natural resources within a traditional legal context), embodies the complex intertwining between different human groups and actors, land, and natural resources within a traditional legal context.

Rooted in the cultural heritage of *Amazigh* peoples, these self-regulated *agdal-like* units can be counted by hundreds of thousands across the Maghreb region, but they are legally unrecognized in Morocco, yet they are still indispensable to sustainability and community-driven governance. They exemplify the resilience and adaptability capacities of High Atlas communities, crucial for maintaining socio-political and environmental equilibriums (Auclair and Alifriqui, 2012; Borrini-Feyerabend, 2010; Da Silva et al., 2020).

The Agdal Polyvalent Institution: The Example of Pastoralism

Agdals are island-like units at the local level, which are composed of an assembly of people who have a stake in the *agdal*, granting them a great deal of legitimacy in the eyes of the local population. *Agdals* are not built on a written legal or state-structured institutional framework (Gellner, 1969), which means they are based on a fragile consensus that can easily change depending on shifting alliances.

Of collective lands, 85 percent are rangeland in the High Atlas. Pastoral *agdals* typically involve assemblies of herders, who control or limit access to pasturelands during periods of the year, particularly in spring and early summer, to protect the most sensitive period for the growth and reproduction of plants (Dominguez et al., 2012). While herd ownership is usually private, grazing occurs on collective or public lands mainly considered state-owned forestland (*domaine forestier*), even if most of the time forest cover is nearly nonexistent. Communities manage and regulate pastoral activity in such areas according to different modalities, depending on the configuration of the pastoral social system and geographical scale. They engage in nomadism, moving livestock to locations of rainfall during the year, and transhumance, consisting of an annual movement of the herds between two complementary fixed areas of a group's territory. These collective property rights can be de facto divided among the lineages. Groups may, however, have grazing rights to rangelands in other communities, and communities may share some in common.

Water Turns

Water is public property in Morocco, but the law recognizes traditional rights of use acquired before the adoption, in 1914, of the present water law. Communities typically manage the equipment for collecting, storing and distributing water, as well as the social institutions that govern all the processes for their creation, maintenance, supervision and repair of irrigation systems. Communities typically manage the equipment for collecting, storing, and distributing water, as well as the social institutions that govern all the processes for their creation, maintenance, supervision, and repair of irrigation systems. These are directly linked to the communal cosmo-vision in which *agdals* and all High Atlas societies are rooted.

Communities also manage the distribution of water according to private collective property rights known as "water turns," rights to successively withdraw water in a pre-established and negotiated order of priority. In this arrangement, water ownership is public and "water turns" are private, while the community plays a key role in the governance of this water and associated infrastructure.

Community management mobilizes the memory of rights and their transmission, adapted to the irregularity of the cycles and whims of nature. The transposition of rights, as water-withdrawal turns, are calculated with extraordinary precision to generate a robust scheme that takes into account the different contingencies. The scheme might involve rotations of the "turns" to avoid the same users always receiving their turn at inconvenient hours, splitting water turns of larger shareholders to avoid long waits for those who have small plots or simply smaller shares of water, or adaptation of the distribution to the physical morphology and imposed constraints. The management and monitoring of the network guarantees respect for the recognition of rights-holders, as well as the prevention and management of conflicts. Furthermore, the body responsible for water management can sanction offenders, ranging from assessment of payment in crops, animal products or money to the contribution of work to the community, the exclusion from the resource during a given period, or even exclusion from the community if the offense is taken too far. Furthermore, the body responsible for water management can sanction offenders, ranging from assessment of payment in crops, animal products, or money to the contribution of work to the community, the exclusion from the resource during a given period, or even exclusion from the community if the offense is taken too far. The governance body can mobilize the whole community when it comes to exceptional, vital and urgent work. The governance body can mobilize the whole community when it comes to exceptional, vital, and urgent work.

Arboriculture

Arboriculture in orchards incorporates a significant share of collective farming and community management. For orchards, property regimes overlap among public (land and water), private (trees), and collective (water management and sometimes even grazing under the fruit trees or even "on" fruit trees as it happens in the argan forests of Southern Morocco), managed also through the *agdal* institution (Romera, 2021). Local oral legal agreements assure collective use and community regulation of fruit trees. Along with their integration into other agricultural activities and water management, such use and regulation ensure control and rationalization of resources and preserve the often-fragile ecological balance. This system of community regulation may also be applied to medicinal or other gathered plants, High Atlas forest or forest management for wood production (firewood or timber), or fodder, or other resources of the sort produced in local community lands.

Challenges to the Agdal System

Many *agdals* have disappeared, though stories and memories of them sometimes persist. Others are eroding fast (Dominguez & Benessaiah, 2017), but still many persist, and a few are even reborn or created. As a mechanism for managing natural resources and regulating their use, *agdals* integrate prohibitions and quotas, monitor resource use, and wield the possibility of sanctioning and enforcing them to make the system effective. Removing *agdals* can weaken systems where there is social conflict. However, the *agdal* is increasingly supplanted by the state, and the *agdals* are constrained in how they can deal with any conflict, for the state remains uncompromising in monopolizing ultimate control.

Oral Traditions and the Agdals

Amazigh laws are most commonly orally transmitted, negotiated, agreed, and renegotiated, generation after generation. These systems are socially constructed and adaptive, where a precedent is not always authoritative, and an analysis of each case is always necessary. The content of the rules varies from one community to another, and no community institution has the power to enforce judgments beyond its borders. However, within each system, there is coherence as well as shared principles among the different groups participating in the individual ethnic-tribal-legal system (Mahdi & Tozy, 1990).

For some issues, such as water rights (Lazarev, 2005) or customary rights in argan forests, which are exceptionally valued today (Chamich, 2008), the provisions are extremely specific and detailed. The prescriptive rules regulating water use, for example, are generally formulated when a case is submitted for the deliberation to the competent authority, the *j'maa*, or deliberative assembly, where all household heads or rights holders participate with vote and voice. In these deliberations, general debates and close negotiations are bound by norms of consensus-based decision-making (Mahdi & Tozy, 1990), which can strengthen cooperation, trust, and accountability.

Recent socio-political transformations have weakened the collective, increasingly empowering certain members and diminishing enforceability of common decisions. Micro-local power struggles come into play, allowing decision-makers to bend the rules more than in positive or statutory law. However, cheaters, free riders, or ambitious members of local tribal assemblies who try to excessively bend the rules are brought into conformance through collective norms (Bendella, 2009). The *de facto* collective ownership to land is one of the strongest contributory elements to the maintenance of local communities' land and natural resource regulatory systems in Morocco. It is through this relative stability that intra-tribal cooperation occurs for the collective governance of resources that can today be observed almost daily in many regions of the High Atlas.

Discussion: From Dispossession to Preserving Cultural and Ecological Resilience

Since 1919, collective lands like those held and stewarded by the *Amazigh* in the High Atlas have been under the control of the executive powers, and the 2019 law affirms this. The state can, and has, appropriated these lands for reasons of "general interest" or public utility.[8] The state today

---

[8] Article 20 of 2019 Law 62.17 amendment details the conditions and procedures for the transfer and exchange of collective lands. It allows for the transfer of these lands through various forms of agreements, including sale and exchange, primarily to state institutions, public entities, and collective communities. Additionally, the law permits transfer to private operators under certain conditions, ensuring these transactions align with the public interest and are approved by the relevant supervisory councils.

considers the mobilization of a significant part of these communal lands as a national development priority by members of the communities (on an individual and private basis), or more often for the benefit of outside investors.

The existing legal framework threatens the survival of *Amazigh's* collective modes of social organization, and their lands and resource governance – for example, the *agdal* system. The challenge in the High Atlas today is not so much access to or recovery of land by *Amazigh*, but rather the preservation of what exists from appropriation. There are many forces at play that encroach on customary institutions, such as nationalism, the state bureaucracy, and other assimilative forces that focus on private interests and development. It is important to frame the cultural institutions, language, and rights of *Amazigh* as an essential part of the country's national heritage, central to the preservation of a cultural and linguistic wealth, and foundational to the resilient management of fragile natural resources in an environment characterized by harshness.

In considering future prospects for the peoples of the High Atlas, there are several opportunities that can be leveraged to move forward. A key opportunity lies in the increasing global recognition of the protection of Indigenous Peoples and local communities, and their customary practices, alongside Morocco's growing national and international commitments in this area. These international frameworks provide a robust foundation for advocating enhanced legal protections and greater autonomy in managing Indigenous Peoples' lands and resources. The alignment of Morocco's policies with these instruments presents an opportunity for the High Atlas communities to reinforce their traditional practices within a legal structure that recognizes and values their cultural and environmental contributions, and which is already being put into practice in collaboration with local, national, and international NGOs and other public and private development agents.

Additionally, there are opportunities in exploring community-led initiatives in sectors such as agroecology, which blends traditional agricultural practices with sustainable approaches to food production, or community-managed tourism or eco-friendly projects that capitalize on the unique natural and cultural assets of the High Atlas region. Such initiatives can not only contribute to local economic development but also promote social cohesion and environmental stewardship, while reinforcing *Amazigh* identity and cultural rights.

Conclusion

The recognition of *Amazigh* languages and identities in the 2011 Moroccan Constitution, and the importance of the High Atlas population in all of this, seems to be a significant step toward a more plural society. However, this recognition does not necessarily translate into practical and operational guarantees for *Amazigh* and their lands, and this connection must still be sought from both the macro (national and international) and the micro (local) perspectives. Indeed, communities such as those in the High Atlas have managed to preserve much of their identity, culture, and legal systems, particularly in respect to the land, and this despite facing numerous challenges throughout history, still exist today. Nonetheless, *Amazigh* culture, lands, and institutions remain largely unprotected by the state.

The protection and promotion of traditional ways of life and governance, as well as the preservation of languages and cultural practices, require tangible actions that go beyond symbolic declarations. Therefore, it is essential to develop integrated strategies involving *Amazigh* populations that reflect their values and priorities. There is also much to learn from the *agdal* system, which offers resilience in an increasingly uncertain world. These systems have been effective in sustainably managing resources in a harsh environment, and have supported very adaptive and dynamic societies able to transform themselves and maintain a strong local sense of identity and micropolitical control of their lands, natural resources, and social affairs.

The role of the *j'maa* (the local assembly), the consensus-based nature of decisions, and the customary sanctions, are all based on oral law, which form the bedrock of rural *Amazigh* community governance. The oral laws of the High Atlas *Amazigh* peoples are deeply intertwined with their cultural and social fabric. Passed down and constantly evolving through generations, this oral tradition ensures that the laws are living, dynamic entities, adaptable to changing circumstances while retaining their core principles. Its effectiveness lies in its inclusive and participatory oral nature, embodying a form of direct democracy that takes into account the many voices of community members, and knows the keystones of the local societies, while allowing for effective and dynamic negotiation. However, it must be remembered that women and younger generations are still excluded from the *j'maa*, since generally it is the male head of the household that speaks, negotiates, and votes in the name of all the household.

Future prospects for the High Atlas communities are relatively promising after decades and even centuries of conflict with the state and discrimination. Opportunities are now slowly appearing alongside Morocco's growing international commitments that can support the advocacy of national and transnational *Amazighs* movements.

References

Ageron, C. R. (1971). La politique berbère du protectorat marocain de 1913 à 1934. *Revue d'Histoire Moderne & Contemporaine*, 18(1), 50–90.

Aït Mous, F. (2011). Les enjeux de l'amazighité au Maroc. *Confluences Méditerranée*, 78(3), 121–131.

Auclair, L., & Alifriqui, M. (eds.) (2012). *Agdal, patrimoine socio-écologique de l'Atlas Marocain*. Rabat, Morocco: IRCAM-IRD. https://horizon .documentation.ird.fr/exl-doc/pleins_textes/divers13-07/010059469.pdf.

Basset, R. (1908). Notice « Amazigh ». In M. Th. Houtsma, R. Basset & T. W. Arnold (eds.), *Encyclopédie de l'Islam* (p. 329). Leyde & Paris: Ed. Brill & A. Picard et fils.

Bendella, A. (2009). Les modes de régulation des conflits. Entre régulation communautaire et régulation judiciaire. In P. Bonte, M. Elloumi, H. Guillaume, & M. Mahdi (eds.), *Développement rural, environnement et enjeux territoriaux. Regards croisés sur l'Oriental marocain et le Sud-Est tunisien*. Tunis: Cérès Editions (pp. 291–304).

(2016). Une catégorie juridique pour gouverner la question du social. In B. Hibou, & I. Bono (eds.), *Le gouvernement du social au Maroc*. Paris: Karthala (pp. 275–320).

Benzakour, F. (2007). Langue française et langues locales en terre marocaine: Rapports de force et reconstructions identitaires. *Hérodote*, 3(126), 45–56.

Berque, J. (1978). *Structures sociales du Haut Atlas*. Paris: PUF.

(2001). *Opera minora*. Saint-Denis: Bouchène.

Borrini-Feyerabend, G. (ed.) (2010). *Bio-cultural diversity conserved by indigenous peoples and local communities — examples and analysis*. ICCA Consortium and Cenesta for GEF SGP, GTZ, IIED and IUCN/CEESP. https://www.iied .org/sites/default/files/pdfs/migrate/G02786.pdf.

Bouderbala, N. (2013). *La Loi entre ciel et terre*. Rabat: Faculté des lettres et des sciences humaines.

Camps, G. (1995). *Les Berbères: Mémoire et identité*. Paris: Errance.Chaker, S. (2004). Berber, a "long-forgotten" language of France. In Language and (Im)migration in France, Latin America, and the United States: Sociolinguistic Perspectives, transl. L Chaker, A Chaker, pp. 1–14. Austin: Univ. Tex. https://minio.la.utexas.edu/webeditor-files/france-ut/pdf/chaker_ english.pdf.

Chamich, M. (2008). *Gestion des conflits liés aux ressources naturelles dans l'arganeraie de Souss (Maroc)* [doctoral dissertation, Université Toulouse].

Chanbergeat, P. (1961). Les Elections Communales Marocaines du 29 Mai 1960. *Revue française de science politique*, 11(1), 89–117.

Da Silva, P., D'Ambrosio, U., Dominguez, P., & M'Sou, S. (2020). What is an *agdal*? *Alliance for Mediterranean Nature and Culture*. https://www .mednatureculture.org/what-is-an-agdal/.

Dominguez, P., & Benessaiah N. (2017). Multi-agentive transformations of rural livelihoods in Mountain ICCAs. *Quaternary International*, 437, 165–175. https://doi.org/10.1016/j.quaint.2015.10.031.

Dominguez, P., Bourbouze, A., Demay, S., Genin, D., & Kosoy. (2012). Diverse ecological, economic and socio-cultural values of a traditional common natural resource management system in the Moroccan High Atlas: The Aït Ikiss tagdalts. *Environmental Values*, 21, 277–296. https://doi.org/10.3197/ 096327112X13400390125939.

Dominguez, P., Zorondo, F., & Garcia-Reyes, V. (2010). Relationships between saints' beliefs and mountain pasture uses. *Human Ecology*, 38, 351–362.

Dresch, J. (1939). Caractères généraux de la vie pastorale dans le massif du grand Atlas. 4ème congrès de la Fédération des soc, Savantes de l'Afrique du Nord, Algiers.

El Qadéry, M. (1995). *L'état-national et les berbères : Le cas du Maroc. Mythe colonial et négation nationale* [Doctoral dissertation, Université Montpellier]. https://www.iamm.ciheam.org/ress_doc/opac_css/index.php? lvl=notice_display&id=28080.

(1998). Les Berbères entre le mythe colonial et la négation nationale: Le cas du Maroc. *Revue d'histoire moderne et contemporaine*, 45(2), 425–450.

Ferhat, H. (1999). « Chérifisme et enjeux du pouvoir au Maroc ». Oriente moderno, 79, 473–481.

Gellner, E. (1969). *Saints of the atlas*. London: Weidenfeld & Nicolson.

(1981). Patterns of rural rebellion in Morocco during the early years on independence. In E. Gellner (ed.), *Muslim Society* (pp. 194–206). Cambridge: Cambridge University Press.

Guillaume, A. (1960). *La propriété collective au Maroc*. Rabat: Editions La Porte.

Halstead, J. P. (1967). *Rebirth of a nation: The origins and rise of Moroccan nationalism, 1912–1944*. Harvard University Press.

Hart, D. M. (1997). The Berber Dahir of 1930 in colonial Morocco: Then and now (1930–1996). *The Journal of North African Studies*, 2(2), pp. 11–33.

Hibou, B., & Tozy, M. (2020). *Tisser le temps politique au Maroc. Imaginaire de l'Etat à l'âge néolibéral*. Paris: Karthala.

Ilahiane, H. (2001). The social mobility of the Haratine and the re-working of Bourdieu's *Habitus* on the Saharan Frontier, Morocco. *American Anthropologist*, 103(2), 380–394.

Julien, C. A. (1978). *Le Maroc face aux impérialismes, 1415–1956*. Paris: Éd. Jeune Afrique.

Kadiri, Z., & Er-rayhany, H. (2019). La politique foncière de privatisation des terres collectives à l'épreuve des réalités d'appropriations et des conflits. *Alternatives Rurales*, 7, 1–20. https://doi.org/10.60569/7-a8.

Karsenty, A. (1988). « Les « terres collectives » du Gharb et le protectorat », *Annuaire de l'Afrique du Nord*, Vol. XXVII, pp. 430–446.

Ladreit de Lacharrière, J. (1936). *La Pacification du Maroc, 1907–1934*. Paris: Publications du Comité de l'Afrique française.

Lakhsassi, A. & Tozy, M. (2000). « Segmentarité et théorie des leff-s : Tahuggawat-Taguzult dans le sud-ouest marocain », *Hésperis-Tamuda*, vol. XXXVIII, pp. 183–214.

Lazarev, G. (2005). La gestion participative des terroirs de montagne au Maroc, condition d'une maîtrise de la "production d'eau." *Critique économique*, 15, 141–154.

Mahdi, M. (2014). Devenir du foncier agricole au Maroc. Un cas d'accaparement des terres. *New Medit*, 4, 2–10.

Mahdi, M., & Tozy, M. (1990). Aspects du droit communautaire dans l'Atlas marocain. *Droit et Société*, 15, 203–210.

Massignon, L. (1925). *Enquête sur les corporations musulmanes d'artisans et de commerçants au Maroc* (p. 251). Paris: Ernest Leroux.

Montagne, R. (1930). *Les Berbères et le Makhzen dans le sud du Maroc, essai sur la transformation politique des Berbères sédentaires (groupe chleuh)*. Paris: Alcan.

Mouline, N. (2009). *Le califat imaginaire d'Ahmed al-Mansûr. Pouvoir et diplomatie au Maroc au XVIe siècle* (p. 371). Paris: Presses Universitaires de France.

Rachik, H. (2003). *Symboliser la nation: Essai sur l'usage des identités collectives au Maroc*. Casablanca: Éd. Le Fennec.

Romera, M. C. (2021). *Towards an inclusive environmental governance model: Analyzing the interface between the Arganeraie Biosphere Reserve and two local communities in Morocco* [Doctoral dissertation], Institute of Environmental Science and Technology, Universitat Autònoma de Barcelona.

Valérian, D. (2011). *Islamisation et arabisation de l'Occident musulman médiéval (VIIe-XIIe siècle)* (p. 407). Paris: Publications de la Sorbonne.

Zafrani, H. (1999). *Deux mille ans de vie juive au Maroc* (p. 325). Paris: Maisonneuve et Larose.

Zayas (de), R. (2017). *Les Morisques et le racisme d'Etat* (p. 668). Paris: La Différence.

12

Adivasis and Land Rights in India

Dispossession and the "Implementation Gap"

JAGANNATH AMBAGUDIA

Adivasis, or India's Indigenous Peoples, constitute 8.6 percent of India's total population (Government of India, 2013). Land and forests are the "twin pillars of the Adivasi economy" (Ambagudia, 2010, p. 61). The term "*Adivasi*" is believed to have originated in the state of Bihar during the 1930s (Ambagudia, 2019; Hardiman, 1987) and was popularized by social worker A. V. Thakkar in the 1940s to advance the unique cultural, property, and political rights of *Adivasis*. Today, many tribal communities employ it as a political term of self-reference in contemporary India. Despite being a signatory to the International Labour Organization ILO Convention 107 (1957), the first international instrument to protect Indigenous Peoples from labor market discrimination, and endorsing the United Nations Declarations on the Rights of Indigenous Peoples (UNDRIP) (2007), India recognizes neither the term "Indigenous Peoples"[1] nor *Adivasi* for that matter. The contention revolves around the additional rights and privileges that recognition may grant Indigenous Peoples or *Adivasis*, particularly around rights to lands and natural resources (particularly as these relate to consent) (Nikolakis & Hotte, 2020).

The Indian state uses the statutory and constitutional term "Scheduled Tribes" (STs) to differentiate *Adivasis* from other social groups.[2]

---

[1] Although the working definition of the United Nations Working Group on Indigenous Populations may not apply to all *Adivasi* communities living across India *in toto*, they can be considered Indigenous Peoples by employing the region-specific criteria within India (Ambagudia, 2019). The tribal communities in central India and northeast India would perhaps prefer to call themselves *Adivasis* and Indigenous Peoples, respectively. *Adivasis*, tribes, tribal communities, and STs are used interchangeably in this chapter for analysis. In Assam, tea tribes are known as *Adivasis* and are not recognized as STs.

[2] The STs are different from Scheduled Castes (SCs), another social group for whom similar constitutional and statutory provisions are enacted for protecting and promoting their rights and interests.

To paraphrase Article 342(1) of India's Constitution, STs are "the tribes or the tribal communities or parts of or groups within tribe or tribal communities" whom the president may specify as STs. There are no criteria set out in the constitution for declaring STs. The Indian state has adopted five criteria for determining STs – primitive traits, a distinctive culture, geographical isolation, shyness of contact with the community at large, and backwardness – prescribed by the Lokur Committee in 1965 for recognizing an ST. Most of these criteria are outdated in contemporary India but continue to be used and have important implications for *Adivasi* recognition and land rights – being granted ST status provides additional rights and privileges. *Adivasis*, however, would prefer to define themselves based on their relationship with land, water, and forests.

In 2006, the Indian state enacted one of the key *Adivasi* land rights mechanisms, the *Scheduled Tribes and Other Traditional Forest Dwellers (Recognition of Forest Rights) Act* (commonly known as *Forest Rights Act*, FRA). The FRA grants *Adivasis* the heritable, inalienable and non-transferrable legal rights to four hectares of forest land per person. There are also other statutory provisions, such as the *Scheduled Castes and Scheduled Tribes (Prevention of Atrocities) Act* 1989, the *Panchayat (Extension to the Scheduled Areas) Act* 1996 (PESA), the *Right to Fair Compensation and Transparency in Land Acquisition, Rehabilitation and Resettlement Act* 2013 (LAA), Compensatory Afforestation Fund Rules 2018, and many others at the federal and state levels to recognize and safeguard the land interests of *Adivasi*.

Against this backdrop, the chapter analyzes the various nuances of *Adivasi* land rights. First, the chapter discusses the land tenure systems in *Adivasi* areas. Second, it briefly describes the legislative measures enacted by various federal and state governments to protect *Adivasi* land rights and their ramifications over *Adivasis*. Third, it deals with federal legal measures to allot land to *Adivasis*. Fourth, it delves into the land situation in the *Adivasi* area. Fifth, it discusses the nature and scale of *Adivasi* land alienation. Sixth, it explores the various strategies that *Adivasis* have adopted to advance and safeguard their land rights. This is followed by the conclusion. Recommendations are offered for strengthening *Adivasi* land rights in practice, which includes the need for safeguards, consistent governance, and independent monitoring of land rights.

Land Tenure Systems in *Adivasi* Areas

While there is heterogeneity, traditionally, *Adivasi* communities had individual and communal ownership, and these have continued into the contemporary period, albeit with some changes. Individual land ownership broadly includes kitchen garden/homestead land; swidden land, terrace land; paddy land; wetland acquired through inheritance, purchase, gift, and mortgage; and dry lands or up lands. Individual lands are transferred through the patrilineal system of inheritance. In contrast, collective areas include sacred sites, such as ritual places, funerals and cremation sites, and sacred groves; swidden land (*dangar*) owned collectively by clan members or belonging to the village; socio-culturally significant lands; village grasslands and grazing land; and commons for thatching grass and firewood (among others) (Kumar & Choudhary, 2005).

In central and eastern India, *Adivasis* use a clan-based land tenure system that provides customary rights to land, trees, and forests, with collective decision-making around use (Kumar & Choudhary, 2005). Among the tribes of northeast India, the Nagas of Manipur, for example, have village community land, clan, or lineage land, and individual private land defines the land ownership system (Devi, 2006). In contrast, a feudal system of land ownership exists among the Kuki and Kuki-Chin-Mizo tribes' villages, where the village chief owns village lands, and the villagers are considered tenants. The tribal communities of the Sixth Scheduled area of Assam, Meghalaya, Mizoram, and Tripura of northeast India largely have community ownership of almost all lands, except the land under reserve forests, with customary legal and institutional mechanisms for their management and governance, and some individual ownership of lands (Land Portal, n.d.). Nevertheless, the state now controls most of the lands under communal ownership.

Federal Constitutional Framework and Land Legislation

Adivasi lands include lands located in the Fifth and Sixth Schedule Areas, and those that the *Adivasis* possess outside the Scheduled Areas. At the institutional and federal levels, the Indian state has established the National Commission for Scheduled Tribes and the Ministry of Tribal Affairs. These examine issues concerning *Adivasi* land, and both conduct or commission studies to understand the *Adivasi* land rights, and the extent of land alienation and restoration. State governments have *Adivasi* welfare departments to advance and safeguard *Adivasi* land rights. The states also have dedicated research institutes to conduct studies on *Adivasi* socio-economic needs and land rights.

On the legislative front, both the federal and state governments have enacted laws to protect and promote *Adivasi* land rights (see Table 12.1). Central laws such as the PESA, the FRA, and the LAA protect and

Table 12.1 Legislation for protection and promotion of land rights of adivasis

Federal /state	Legislative measures	Descriptions
Federal	The *Scheduled Castes and Scheduled Tribes (Prevention of Atrocities) Act* 1989	Makes it a punishable offence to wrongfully occupy or cultivate any land owned by or allotted to a member of a ST, or allotted or transferred lands.
Federal	The *Panchayat (Extension to the Scheduled Areas) Act* 1996	Empowers the Gram Sabha to prevent *Adivasi* land alienation and restore lands that were unlawfully dispossessed in Scheduled Areas.
Federal	The *Scheduled Tribes and Other Traditional Forest Dwellers (Recognition of Forest Rights) Act* 2006	Grants land rights to *Adivasis*. Endows the Gram Sabha with a critical role in customary forest and resource governance, including decision-making for *Adivasi* land alienation and forest conversion.
Andaman and Nicobar Islands	The Andaman and Nicobar Islands (Protection of Aboriginal Tribes) Regulation 1956	Mandated to protect the STs in the four tribal reserves. This regulation empowers the government to prohibit and regulate the entry of outsiders, and restricts the transfer of lands to non-tribals in the reserves.
Andhra Pradesh	The Andhra Pradesh (Scheduled Areas) Land Transfer Regulation 1959, amended by the Andhra Pradesh (Scheduled Areas) Land Transfer (Amendment) Regulations of 1970, 1971, and 1978	Prohibits transfer of land to non-tribals in Scheduled Areas. Authorizes government to acquire land in case a tribal purchaser is not available. There is, however, no legal protection to ST land outside the scheduled areas.
Assam	The Assam Land and Revenue Regulations 1886, amended in 1981	Chapter X of the Regulation prohibits land alienation in tribal belts and blocks.
Arunachal Pradesh	Bengal Eastern Frontier Regulation 1873, as amended	Prohibits transfer of tribal land.

Chhattisgarh	(a) Sections 165 and 170 of Madhya Pradesh Land Revenue Code 1959	Sections 165 and 170B of the Code protects STs against land alienation.
	(b) *Madhya Pradesh Land Distribution Regulation Act 1964*	The 1964 Act is in force in the scheduled areas.
Dadra and Nagar Haveli	Dadra and Nagar Haveli Land Reform Regulation 1971	Protects tribal interests in lands.
Gujarat	The *Bombay Land Revenue Code as amended by Bombay Land Revenue (Gujarat Second Amendment) Act 1980*	Sections 73A, 73AA, 73AB, 73AC, and 73AD prohibit transfer of tribal lands and provide for restoration of alienated land in Gujarat.
Himachal Pradesh	The *Himachal Pradesh Transfer of Land (Regulation) Act 1968*	Prohibits transfer of land from tribals to non-tribals.
Jharkhand	(a) *Chhota Nagpur Tenancy Act 1908* (applies to old Ranchi district, mostly comprising Mundas and Uraons)	Prohibit alienation of tribal land and provide for restoration of alienated land.
	(b) *Santhal Parganas Tenancy (Supplementary Provision) Act 1940*	
	(c) Bihar Scheduled Areas Regulation 1969	
	(d) Wilkinson's Rule 1837 (applies to Hos of Singhbhum)	
Karnataka	The *Karnataka Scheduled Caste (SC) and Scheduled Tribes (Prohibition of Transfer of Certain Lands) Act 1975*	Prohibits transfer of land assigned to SCs and STs by government. No provision to safeguard SC/ST interest in other lands.
Kerala	The *Kerala Scheduled Tribes (Regulation of Transfer of Land and Restoration of Alienated Land) Act 1975*	Act of 1975 made applicable in effect from June 1, 1982, by notification of January 1986. Prohibits transfer of land of tribals and provides for restoration.
Lakshadweep	The Laccadive Islands and Minicoy Regulation I of 1912.	Alienation of tribal lands prohibited in entire union territory of Lakshadweep.
	Lakshadweep (Protection of Scheduled Tribes) Regulation 1964	

Table 12.1 (*cont.*)

Federal /state	Legislative measures	Descriptions
Madhya Pradesh	(a) Sections 165 and 170 of Madhya Pradesh Land Revenue Code 1959 (b) *Madhya Pradesh Land Distribution Regulation Act 1964*	Sections 165 and 170B of the Code protect STs against land alienation. The 1964 Act is in force in Scheduled Areas of Madhya Pradesh.
Maharashtra	(a) The Maharashtra Land Revenue Code 1966, as amended in 1974 (b) *The Maharashtra (Restoration of Lands to Scheduled Tribes) Act 1974*	Prohibits alienation of tribal land and provides for restoration of both illegally and legally transferred lands of a tribe.
Manipur	The *Manipur Land Revenue and Land Reforms Act 1960*	Section 153 forbids transfer of tribal land to non-tribals without permission of the District Collector. The statute has not been extended to hill areas; therefore, hill area tribals are not covered.
Meghalaya	*Meghalaya Transfer of Land (Regulation) Act 1971*	Prohibits alienation of tribal land.
Nagaland	Bengal Eastern Frontier Regulation 1873 and Assam Land and Revenue Regulation 1866, as amended vide *Nagaland Land and Revenue Regulation (Amendment) Act 1978*	Prohibition of transfer of tribal lands.
Odisha	The Orissa Scheduled Areas Transfer of Immovable Property (by Scheduled Tribes) Regulation 1956. The *Orissa Land Reforms Act 1960*	Prohibits transfer of tribal land and provides for its restoration, both in Scheduled Areas (1956 Regulation) and non-Scheduled Areas (1960 Act).
Punjab	The *Punjab Land Alienation Act 1916*	Prevents alienation of tribal lands to non-tribals.
Rajasthan	The *Rajasthan Tenancy Act 1955* The *Rajasthan Land Revenue Act 1956*	Sections 175 and 183B specifically protect tribal interest in land and provide for restoration of alienated land to them.

State	Law	Remarks
Sikkim	Revenue Order No. 1 of 1917 The *Sikkim Agricultural Land Ceiling and Reform Act 1977*	Order of 1917 still in force. Chapter 7 of the 1977 Act restricts alienation of lands by STs but is not in force.
Tamilnadu	Standing Orders of the Revenue Board BSO 15–40. Law against land alienation not enacted	BSO 15–40 apply only to Malayali and Soliga tribes. Prohibit transfer of assigned land without approval of District Collector.
Tripura	*Tripura Land Revenue and Land Reform Act 1960*, as amended in 1974	Act prohibits transfer of tribal land to others without permission of the Collector. Only lands transferred after January 1, 1969 are covered under restoration provision.
Uttar Pradesh (UP)/Uttarakhand	*Uttar Pradesh Zamindari Abolition and Land Reforms Act 1950*, as amended by *U. P. Land Laws (Amendment) Act 1981*	Provides protection of tribal land. However, amending Act stayed by Allahabad High Court in *Swaran Singh v. State Govt* (1981).
West Bengal	*West Bengal Land Reforms Act 1955*	Chapter II-A prohibits the alienation of tribal land and provides for restoration.

Source: Government of India, not dated, pp. 87–92.

advance *Adivasi* land rights. The PESA prohibits *Adivasi* land alienation and restores lands unlawfully dispossessed in Scheduled Areas. The FRA grants *Adivasis* communal and individual rights to forest land and empowers them to make decisions on *Adivasi* land alienation and forest conversion. The LAA prohibits land alienation in Scheduled Areas. In the case of unavoidable circumstances where land acquisition is essential, the prior consent of the *Gram Sabha* (village council) is mandatory. In addition, the *Scheduled Castes and Scheduled Tribes (Prevention of Atrocities) Act* 1989 punishes those guilty of wrongfully occupying or cultivating *Adivasi* land.

As Table 12.1 shows, the legal framework for *Adivasi* land rights is a complex mix of federal and state legislations. These legal measures grant land rights to *Adivasis* and promote and safeguard them from alienation by empowering the grassroots-level collective institutions (Gram Sabha). However, there are examples where the Gram Sabha has been misused and manipulated, and has enabled the alienation of *Adivasi* land.

Land Allotment to *Adivasis*

The most prominent legislative measures for providing land to *Adivasi* are the *Central Land Ceiling Act*[3] and state land ceiling laws, and the FRA.

Land Ceiling Act

The federal and state ceiling laws were enacted to impose a ceiling on agricultural holdings and prioritize *Adivasi* land tenure when distributing any surplus agricultural land. Implementing these laws across India resulted in the redistribution of 795,886 acres of surplus lands in 2007;

---

[3] By 1961–1962, all states had enacted ceiling laws as part of land reform measures to address skewed agricultural land ownership. However, ceiling levels vary from state to state and, in some cases, even within the same state. The need for some consistency in land holding ceilings across states prompted the Parliament to pass the *Urban Land (Ceiling and Regulation) Act* 1976, which applied to eleven states, such as Andhra Pradesh, Gujarat, Haryana, Himachal Pradesh, Karnataka, Maharashtra, Odisha (Orissa), Punjab, Tripura, Uttar Pradesh, West Bengal, and union territories. Other states, such as Madhya Pradesh, Rajasthan, Bihar, Assam, Manipur, and Meghalaya, later adopted the central law. However, due to the failure to achieve the objectives, the law was repealed in 1999, followed by the repeal in Madhya Pradesh (2000), Odisha (2002), and Assam (2003). This law was repealed in 2011 by Bihar, Maharashtra, Andhra Pradesh, and Jharkhand. However, various state ceiling laws continue to exist, albeit with numerous amendments in recent times. It has been observed that eleven states have amended the land ceiling laws that favor the industry (Lopes & Chari, 2021).

779,858 acres in 2008; and 789,288 acres in 2009.[4] In December 2007, the surplus land distributed to the *Adivasis* under land ceiling laws constituted 16 percent of the total area of land distributed, and 15 percent of the total number of beneficiaries (Government of India, 2009). The government informed the Lok Sabha[5] on September 6, 2012 that 7.96 lakh (0.796 million) acres had been distributed under the land ceiling laws to the *Adivasi* communities in India by March 31, 2012.[6] The *Committee on State Agrarian Relations and the Unfinished Task in Land Reforms* expressed its disenchantment with a lack of statewide data on landless *Adivasi* communities (Government of India, 2009); and that most *Adivasi* received less than the required 1.26 hectares of land.

Forest Rights Act

The Indian Parliament enacted the FRA to undo the historical injustices meted against *Adivasi* forest dwellers. The FRA recognizes and grants legal land rights to a maximum of four hectares of forest land. Section 6 of the FRA outlines the procedure for evaluating and recognizing *Adivasi* forest land tenure claims (Government of India, 2007; Nikolakis & Hotte, 2020). To commence a claim, the Gram Sabha (village assembly) forms a Forest Rights Committee (FRC) consisting of 10–15 members, two-thirds of whom should be *Adivasis*. The FRC evaluates claims by employing criteria of (i) whether the claimant is an *Adivasi* and (ii) in case of a non-*Adivasi* claimant, whether the member has resided and depended on the forest for their livelihood for at least three generations prior to December 13, 2005. The FRC makes recommendations to the Gram Sabha, which evaluates these and makes recommendations to a Sub-Division Level Committee (SDLC), which, in turn, can accept or reject them and recommend them to the District Level Committee (DLC). An individual or community can appeal any SDLC or Gram Sabha decision within sixty days to the SDLC and the DLC. The decision of the DLC is final and binding.

As Table 12.2 highlights, by March 31, 2022, a total of 4,429,065 claims have been made under the FRA, consisting of 4,260,247 individual claims

---

[4] Lok Sabha Unstarred Question No. 1383, dated November 27, 2009, available at http://164 .100.47.193/Annexture_New/lsq15/3/au1383.htm.

[5] The Lok Sabha is the Lower House of the Indian Parliament, with members elected directly by the people. *Adivasis* can elect their own Lok Sabha members under Article 332 of the Indian Constitution to protect and promote their community's rights and interests.

[6] Lok Sabha Unstarred Question No. 4225, dated September 6, 2012.

Table 12.2 Forest land allotted to tribal people

States	No. of claims received up to March 31, 2022 (individual = I; community = C)			No. of titles distributed up to March 31, 2022 (individual = I; community = C)			Extent of forest land for which titles distributed (in acres) (individual = I; community = C)		
	I	C	Total	I	C	Total	I	C	Total
Andhra Pradesh	274,078	3,294	277,372	210,828	1,822	212,650	436,606	526,454	963,060
Assam	148,965	6,046	155,011	57,325	1,477	58,802	NA/NR	NA/NR	NA/NR
Bihar	8,022	NA/NR	8,022	121	0	121	NA/NR	NA/NR	NA/NR
Chhattisgarh	866,955	50,806	917,761	445,573	45,303	490,876	898,010	478,3047	568,1057
Goa	9,758	378	10,136	138	11	149	299	17	316
Gujarat	182,869	7,187	190,056	91,686	4,597	96,283	156,926	1,236490,	1,393,416
Himachal Pradesh	2,746	275	3,021	129	35	164	5.96	4,742	4,748
Jharkhand	107,032	3,724	110,756	59,866	2,104	61,970	153,396	103,759	257,155
Karnataka	288,357	5,938	294,295	14,680	1,343	16,023	19,989	36,340	56,329
Kerala	43,466	1,109	44,575	26,745	183	26,928	35,449	0	35,449
Madhya Pradesh	585,326	42,187	627,513	266,609	27,976	294,585	902,750	1,463,614	2,366,365
Maharashtra	362,679	12,037	374,716	165,032	7,084	172,116	392,929	2,736,661	3,129,589

Odisha	627,998	15,282	643,280	452,164	7,624	459,788	666,089	337,043	1,003,132
Rajasthan	85,243	2,016	87,259	45,135	361	45,496	63,788	12,290	76,078
Tamil Nadu	33,755	1,082	34,837	8,144	450	8,594	9,626	NA/NR	9,626
Telangana	204,176	2,808	206,984	97,434	102	97,536	310,916	3,631	314,547
Tripura	200,696	277	200973	127,931	55	127,986	460,182	91	460,274
Uttar Pradesh	92,577	1,162	93,739	180,49	861	18,910	19,190	120,776	139,966
Uttarakhand	3,587	3,091	6,678	184	1	185	0	0	0
West Bengal	131,962	10,119	142,081	44,444	686	45,130	210,14	572	21,586
Andaman and Nicobar Island	0	0	0	0	0	0	0	0	0
Ladakh	0	0	0	0	0	0	0	0	0
Total	4,260,247	168,818	4,429,065	2,132,217	102,075	2,234,292	4,547,166	11,365,529	15,912,694

Source: Lok Sabha Unstarred Question No. 3510, dated August 8, 2022, available at http://164.100.24.220/loksabhaquestions/annex/179/AU3510.pdf (NA/NR: Related figure is either not available or not reported.

(96.18 percent) and 168,818 community claims (3.81 percent). Table 12.2 also shows a total of 2,234,292 titles distributed to *Adivasi* communities and other traditional forest dwellers, and just over 95 percent of these were for individuals (or 2,132,217 titles), and the remainder were communal titles (or 102,075 titles). In total, just over 15.9 million acres of forestland were distributed to *Adivasi*, of which just over 11.36 million acres were communal lands (71.42 percent), and the remainder were for individuals. It is argued that the state has given undue importance to and expanded individual rather than collective rights (Nikolakis & Hotte, 2020), and thus dilutes the constitutional and collective rights of *Adivasi* communities (Bose et al., 2012). Also, it is important to note that for nomadic and pastoral communities, their rights are not recognized through the FRA. However, they access forest resources, collecting non-timber forest products and other traditional resources, and their stock can access grazing lands and water (Government of India, 2007).[7]

Overall, the lands granted under the ceiling laws and the FRA have expanded *Adivasis'* marginal and small-scale land holdings across India.[8]

Landholding Patterns in *Adivasi* Areas

The data on *Adivasi* communities and land tenure, especially the number of operational holdings and area of operational holdings,[9] are largely drawn from different Agricultural Census reports. Though the Agricultural Census commenced in 1970–1971 with an interval of five years, and the most recent in 2015–2016,[10] the data on *Adivasi* land

---

[7] The nomadic or pastoralist communities do not fulfil the criteria of occupying the forest land for three generations or 75 years prior to December 13, 2005 and depending on forests for livelihood under the FRA due to the nature of occupation they practice for their living.

[8] The state follows a standard definition of land holdings across the country and categorizes them into five groups based on size, such as marginal (below 1 hectare), small (1–2 hectares), semi-medium (2–4 hectares), medium (4–10 hectares), and large (above 10 hectares).

[9] Operational holding refers to entire tracts of land under the same management used entirely or partially for agricultural production using the same means of production. Area of operational holdings includes land owned and cultivated by self, leased land and encroached land, forcibly occupied land, and unauthorized or disputed land (which cannot be owned or leased). The operational holder may be an individual, joint, or institutional, who gets the right to cultivate or lease the land to others for fixed money, fixed produce, share of production, etc. (Government of India, 2015).

[10] The fieldwork for the Eleventh Agricultural Census (2021–22) is planned to start in August 2022.

holdings were collected separately in the Third Agricultural Census (1981–1982) and continued since then. Tables 12.3 and 12.4 illustrate the statewide distribution and area of *Adivasi* operational holdings in last two Agricultural Census, and the percent changes over time (2005–6 to 2010–11, 2010–1, and 2015–6).

Table 12.3 shows that in 2005–2006 and 2010–2011, there was a decline in the number of *Adivasi* operational holdings in Andhra Pradesh, Jammu and Kashmir, and Maharashtra. Similarly, in 2010–2011 and 2015–2016, there was a decline in seven states: Andhra Pradesh, Bihar, Gujarat, Maharashtra, Mizoram, Sikkim, Uttar Pradesh, and one union territory, Daman and Diu. The number of operational holdings is significantly less in smaller states and union territories such as Sikkim and Daman and Diu.

Table 12.4 demonstrates a decline in operational holdings in twelve states and one union territory in 2005–2006 and 2010–2011. Similarly, there was a decline in eighteen states in 2010–2011 and 2015–2016.

The statistics show a general negative trend in *Adivasi* land holdings that accelerated during 2015–2016. The average area of holdings has declined from 1.76 hectares in 2000–2001 to 1.64 hectares in 2005–2006 (Government of India, 2012, p. 44) and 1.40 hectares in 2015–2016 (Government of India, 2020, p. 49). The socio-economic and caste census in 2011 shows that 5.47 percent of rural *Adivasi* households were landless in India.[11] In 2003, 35.5 percent of *Adivasi* households, against 41.6 percent of all households, did not own any land other than their homestead (Bakshi, 2008, p. 101).[12] The unit-level data from various rounds of the National Sample Survey Office (NSSO) shows that the *Adivasi* household that did not own any land, not even the homestead land, has increased from 16 percent in 1987–1988 to 24 percent in 2011–2012 (Karat & Rawal, 2014). The same data set indicates that *Adivasi* households that did not possess any land increased from 13 percent in 1987–1988 to 25 percent in 2011–2012. Similarly, landlessness among *Adivasis* has increased from 28 percent in 1987–1988 to 39 percent in 2011–2012 (Karat & Rawal, 2014). In short, landlessness among rural *Adivasi* households has increased over time, with alarming rates of tenure insecurity.

---

[11] See https://secc.gov.in/homepage.htm.
[12] Homestead is land used for house construction and surrounding land used for kitchen garden.

Table 12.3 Statewide distribution of number of operational holdings for STs during agriculture census 2005–2006 to 2015–2016 (in'00)

States/Union Territories (UTs)	2005–06	2010–11	2015–16	Percent of Variation in 2010–11 over 2005–06	Percent of Variation in 2015–16 over 2010–11
Andhra Pradesh	9,267	3,871	4,056	−58.22	−61.72
Arunachal Pradesh	1,064	1,065	1,103	0.09	3.57
Assam	4,379	4,382	4,431	0.07	1.12
Bihar	1,906	2,121	2,030	11.28	−4.29
Chhattisgarh	11,054	11,768	12,565	6.46	6.77
Goa	118	211	215	78.81	1.90
Gujarat	4,875	5,043	4,981	3.45	−1.23
Haryana	0	0	0	0.00	0.00
Himachal Pradesh	447	560	572	25.28	2.14
Jammu and Kashmir	1,844	1,813	2,087	−1.68	15.11
Jharkhand	NA	9,670	9,791	–	1.25
Karnataka	4,391	4,726	5,213	7.63	10.30
Kerala	873	952	1,079	9.05	13.34
Madhya Pradesh	16,274	17,823	20,005	9.52	12.24
Maharashtra	8,798	8,635	8,560	−1.85	−0.87
Manipur	642	643	645	0.16	0.31
Meghalaya	2,026	2,088	2,287	3.06	9.53
Mizoram	897	917	896	2.23	−2.29

Nagaland	1,687	1,778	1,959	5.39	10.18
Odisha	14,074	14,255	14,605	1.29	2.46
Punjab	0	0	0	0.00	0.00
Rajasthan	9,673	11,198	12,281	15.77	9.67
Sikkim	302	365	312	20.86	-14.52
Tamil Nadu	686	744	946	8.45	27.15
Telangana		6,724	7,125		5.96
Tripura	1,558	1,635	1,641	4.94	0.37
Uttarakhand	297	297	793	0.00	167.00
Uttar Pradesh	556	709	281	27.52	-60.37
West Bengal	5,516	5,823	5,996	5.57	2.97
Andaman and Nicobar Islands	0	0	0	0.00	0.00
Chandigarh	0	0	0	0.00	0.00
Dadra and Nagar Haveli	127	129	132	1.57	2.33
Daman and Diu	6	7	6	16.67	-14.29
Delhi	0	0	0	0.00	0.00
Lakshadweep	93	94	95	1.08	1.06
Puducherry	0	0	0	0.00	0.00
Total	103,431	113,322	126,687	9.57	5.53

Source: Government of India (2015, pp. 108–109; 2020, pp. 85–86).

Note: #excluding Jharkhand; Neg, negligible; NA, not applicable.

Table 12.4 Statewide distribution of area operated by operational holdings for STs during agricultural census 2005–2006 to 2015–2016 (area in'00 ha.)

States/Union Territories (UTs)	2005–06 (hectares, 00s)	2010–11 (hectares, 00s)	2015–16 (hectares, 00s)	Percentage of variation in 2010–11 over 2005–06	Percentage of variation in 2015–16 over 2010–11
Andhra Pradesh	12,120	4,774	4,321	-60.61	-9.49
Arunachal Pradesh	3,516	3,803	3,763	8.16	-1.05
Assam	4,901	5,166	5,098	5.41	-1.32
Bihar	995	1,055	1,032	6.03	-2.18
Chhattisgarh	22,103	21,587	21,241	-2.33	-1.60
Goa	79	241	224	205.06	-7.05
Gujarat	9,690	9,685	9,584	-0.05	-1.04
Haryana	0	0	0	0.00	0.00
Himachal Pradesh	427	502	490	17.56	-2.39
Jammu and Kashmir	1,435	1,298	1,347	-9.55	3.78
Jharkhand	NA	14,306	13,879	-	-2.98
Karnataka	7,249	7,052	7,297	-2.72	3.47
Kerala	302	344	383	13.91	11.34
Madhya Pradesh	32,333	31706	31,379	-1.94	-1.03
Maharashtra	15,288	15,580	15,099	1.91	-3.09
Manipur	789	790	792	0.13	0.25
Meghalaya	23,77	2,862	2,974	20.40	3.91
Mizoram	1,068	1,045	1,114	-2.15	6.60
Nagaland	11,696	10,715	9,535	-8.39	-11.01

Odisha	17,483	16,147	15,380	-7.64	-4.75
Punjab	0	0	0	0.00	0.00
Rajasthan	17,658	17,850	17,511	1.09	-1.90
Sikkim	569	568	473	-0.18	-16.73
Tamil Nadu	752	747	754	-0.66	0.94
Telangana	7,707	7,707	7,406		-3.91
Tripura	1,126	1,239	1,246	10.04	0.56
Uttarakhand	482	799	895	65.77	12.02
Uttar Pradesh	703	479	464	-31.86	-3.13
West Bengal	3,958	3,966	3,964	0.20	-0.05
Andaman and Nicobar Islands	0	0	0	0.00	
Chandigarh	0	0	0	0.00	0.00
Dadra and Nagar Haveli	172	169	172	-1.74	1.78
Daman and Diu	2 (Neg)	3 (Neg)	2 (Neg)	0.00	
Delhi	0	0	0	0.00	
Lakshadweep	14	23	23	64.29	0.00
Puducherry	0	0	0	0.00	
Total	163,949	182,207	177,841	11.14	-2.40

Source: Government of India (2015, pp. 109–110; 2020, pp. 87–88).

Note: #excluding Jharkhand; Neg, negligible; NA, Not applicable

Dispossession and tenure insecurity were heightened during the COVID-19-imposed lockdown. In a report to the United Nation's Special Rapporteur on the Rights of Indigenous Peoples, the Housing and Land Rights Network, New Delhi, claimed that between March and June 2020, both the Indian federal and state governments engaged in at least twenty-two cases of forced eviction of *Adivasis* without due process. Incidents in Odisha, Manipur, Gujarat, and Madhya Pradesh involved activities ranging from setting fire to *Adivasi* houses, to forcible eviction, destroying *Adivasi* standing crops, and using police force to quell *Adivasi* protests (Housing and Land Rights Network, 2020). Several other dispossession activities occurred during COVID-19 that Ambagudia (2022b) argues undermines *Adivasi* land rights further, including the extension of mining leases and the approvals of major projects, many of which are on *Adivasi* lands.

The number of marginal land holdings among *Adivasi* communities has increased from 2.728 million in 1981–1982 to 7.127 million in 2015–2016 (Figure 12.1). A similar increasing trend is also visible in small and semi-medium land holdings; however, there is a gradual decline in the number of medium and large-scale land holdings held by *Adivasis* across India.

Figure 12.2 examines the operational holdings of *Adivasis* in 1981–1982 and 2015–2016. It shows a sharp decline in medium and large-scale holdings, decreasing in size from 5.596 million hectares and 3.729 million hectares in 1980–1981 to 3.984 million hectares and 1.434 million hectares in 2015–2016, respectively. However, marginal, small, and semi-medium land holdings gradually increased, except for 2000–2001, 2005–2006, and 2015–2016 for semi-medium.

The comparative land picture paints *Adivasis* as at the margin of society and lagging behind other social groups, such as SCs and others (non-*Adivasis* and non-SCs) regarding the number of operational holdings (Figure 12.3). However, they are above the SCs concerning the area of operational holdings in 1985–1986 and 2015–2016 (Figure 12.4).

Five Dispossession Pathways

Figure 12.5 shows the nature and scale of *Adivasi* land dispossession and alienation in post-independence India, which occurs broadly in five different ways.

First, land is alienated in private transactions, such as *Adivasis* mortgaging their lands to non-*Adivasis* to meet their basic needs, perform rituals and religious ceremonies, celebrate festivals, or meet the

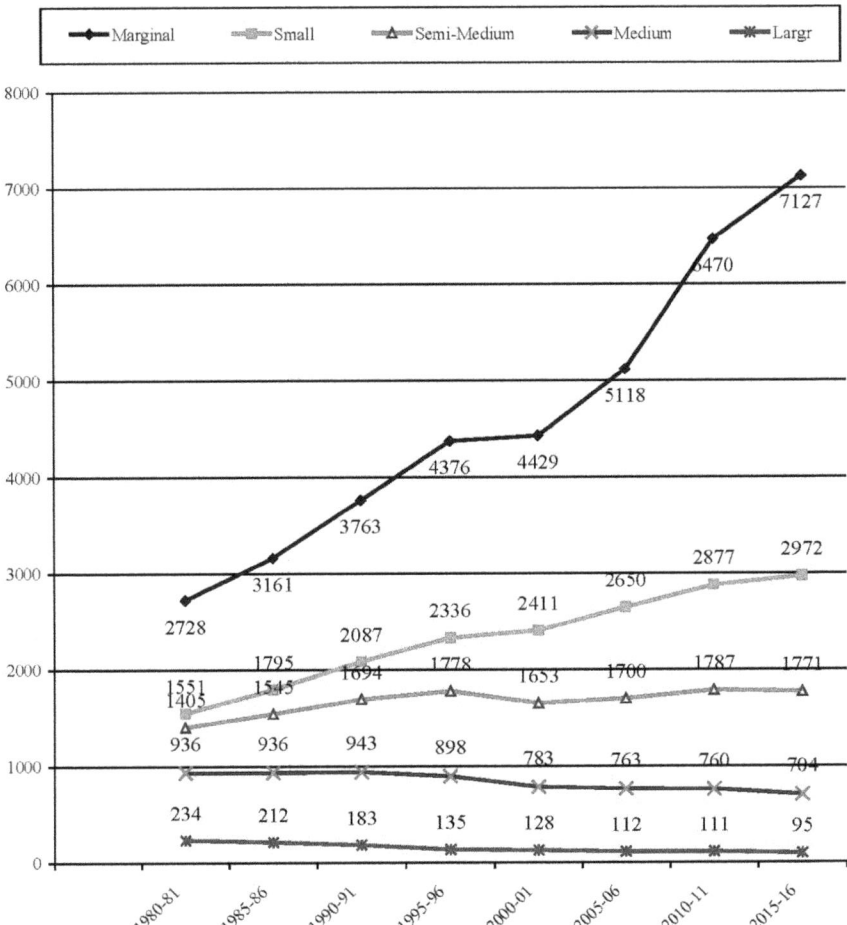

Figure 12.1 Number of operational holdings in India by size groups for STs, 1980–1981 to 2015–2016 (in '000 ha)
Source: Government of India (2020, p. 50)

expenditure of a daughter's marriage (among other reasons), which sometimes leads to the illegal transfer of land. Until the 1950s and 1960s, non-*Adivasis* could purchase *Adivasi* lands with permission from relevant authorities. In some cases, records and permissions were manipulated to acquire *Adivasi* lands (Government of India, 2014). In some states, *Adivasi* communities also seek permission to sell land to non-*Adivasi* communities. For instance, in Tripura, seventy-four cases

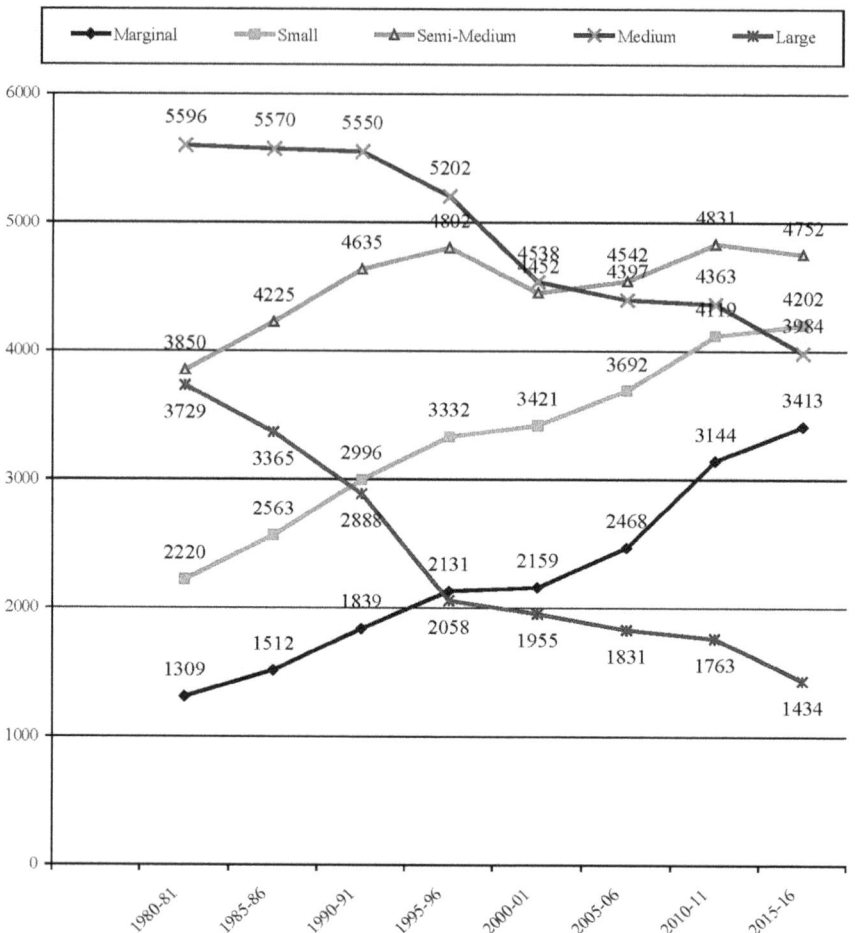

Figure 12.2   Area operated by holdings in India by size groups for STs, 1980–1981 to 2015–2016 (in '000 ha)
Source: Government of India (2020: p. 51)

were submitted to and approved by the Tribes Advisory Council (TAC) in 2006–2007 and 2015–2016, transferring 52.2956 acres of *Adivasi* lands (Centre for Equity Studies, 2016). *Adivasi* communities also suffer land loss due to encroachment of their land by non-*Adivasis* (Ambagudia, 2019; Buckles et al., 2013; Viegas, 1991).

Second, the state acquires land for public purposes (such as development projects, highways, railways, and even conservation) through the

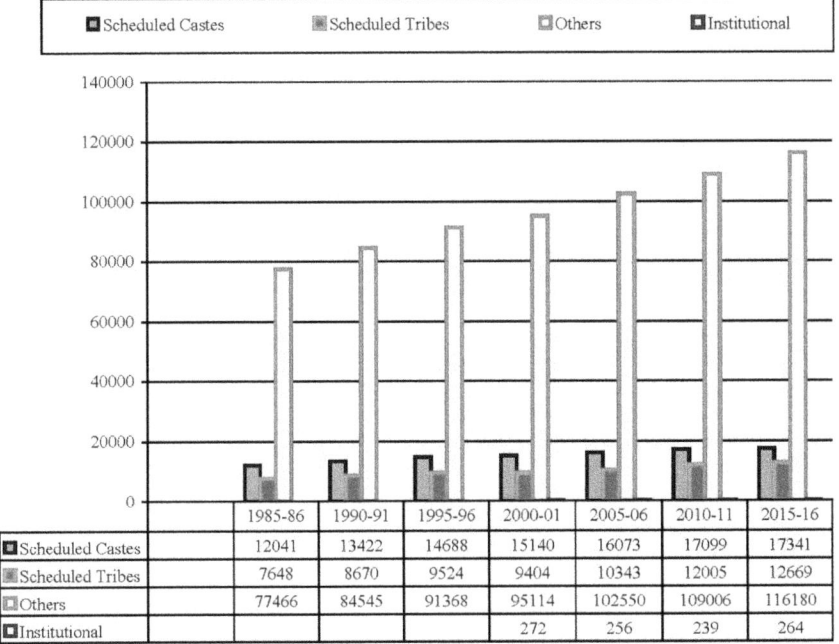

	1985-86	1990-91	1995-96	2000-01	2005-06	2010-11	2015-16
Scheduled Castes	12041	13422	14688	15140	16073	17099	17341
Scheduled Tribes	7648	8670	9524	9404	10343	12005	12669
Others	77466	84545	91368	95114	102550	109006	116180
Institutional				272	256	239	264

Figure 12.3   Number of operational holdings in India by social groups 1980–1981 to 2015–2016 (in %)
Source: Government of India (1998, p. 68; 1995–1996, pp. 59–61; 2012, p. 38; 2015: p. 47; 2020: p. 40) * Excluding Jharkhand

"eminent domain principle" under the *Land Acquisition Act* 1895 (Levien, 2015). On March 19, 2015, the government informed the Lok Sabha that 15,363 hectares of *Adivasi* lands were acquired for power plants, affecting 2,133 *Adivasi* families.[13] Similarly, Coal India Limited acquired 691 hectares of *Adivasi* lands in 2014–5; 990 hectares in 2015–6; 1,332 acres in 2016–7; and 884 acres in 2017–8 (till February 2018).[14] The state also acquires *Adivasi* lands to rehabilitate migrants in various parts of *Adivasi* territories in India (Ambagudia, 2019; Government of India, 2014; Singh, 2010).

[13] Lok Sabha Unstarred Question No. 3837, dated March 19, 2015, available at http://164 .100.47.193/Annexture_New/lsq16/4/au3837.htm.
[14] Lok Sabha Unstarred Question No. 5440, dated March 28, 2018, available at http://164 .100.24.220/loksabhaquestions/annex/14/AU5440.pdf.

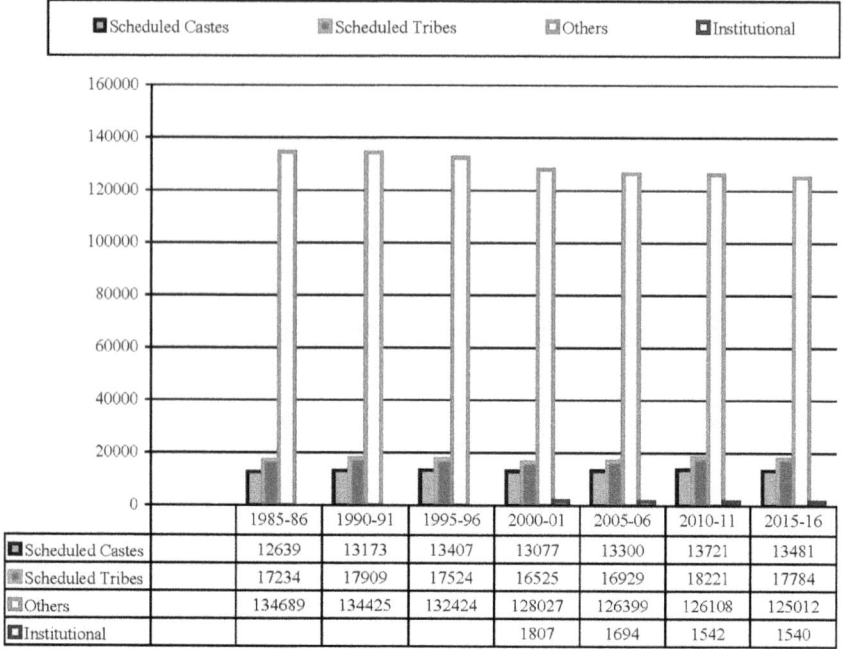

	Scheduled Castes		Scheduled Tribes		Others		Institutional

	1985-86	1990-91	1995-96	2000-01	2005-06	2010-11	2015-16
Scheduled Castes	12639	13173	13407	13077	13300	13721	13481
Scheduled Tribes	17234	17909	17524	16525	16929	18221	17784
Others	134689	134425	132424	128027	126399	126108	125012
Institutional				1807	1694	1542	1540

Figure 12.4   Area operated by social groups 1980–1981 to 2015–2016 (in '000 ha)
Source: Government of India (1998, p. 68; 1995–1996, pp. 59–61; 2012, p. 38; 2015, p. 47; 2020, p. 40) * Excluding Jharkhand

Third, surveys and settlements of *Adivasi* areas in eastern India were delayed until the 1960s, allowing lands to be transferred to non-*Adivasis*. Sometimes, due to flawed surveys, most of the land in *Adivasi* areas was registered as government land, and correspondingly, the privately owned land was significantly less (Ambagudia, 2019; Government of India, 2014).

Fourth, the continuation of landlessness among the *Adivasi* communities is due to the poor distribution of government wastelands, land acquired through land ceilings, and the FRA (among others).

Fifth, the *Adivasi* communities' access to land also gets reduced due to areas being designated forests or protected areas, which limits access for traditional uses.

As Figure 12.5 outlines, the state not only dispossesses *Adivasis* in the name of "national development" but also facilitates the transfer of land and forest resources to non-*Adivasis* and multinational corporations (MNCs). While the government does not assess the socio-economic

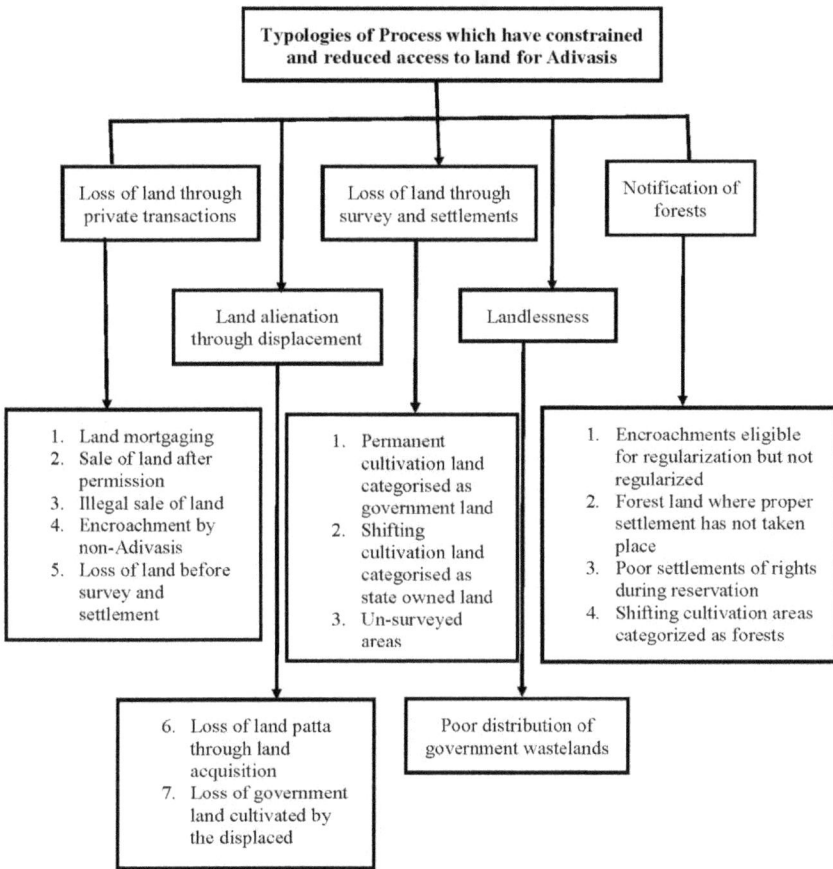

Figure 12.5 Process of Adivasi land alienation
Source: Kumar and Choudhary (2005, p. 38)

outcomes of *Adivasis* following land acquisition,[15] it is clear that dispossession is a major driver of poverty and inequality among *Adivasis*. This issue, in turn, has mobilized *Adivasi* resistance and social movements.

Strategies for Protecting *Adivasi* Land Rights

Adivasis have employed various strategies to advance and protect their land rights across India. These strategies range from working with non-

---

[15] Lok Sabha Starred Question No. 265, dated August 19, 2011, available at http://loksabhaph.nic.in/Questions/.

governmental organizations (NGOs) to launching social movements and pursuing land justice through the courts. The *Adivasi* educated class has been meeting and putting pressure on their political representatives to raise questions on *Adivasi* land rights in decision-making bodies such as the Parliament and state assemblies. However, the two most prominent strategies are *Adivasi* social movements and litigation.

Adivasi Social Movements

Land alienation in *Adivasi* areas, Mohanty (2001) argues, was driven by the colonial state's land revenue policy and exploitative policies. A new land tenure system and the British introduction of non-*Adivasi* intermediaries and administrators accelerated *Adivasi* land dispossession (Xaxa, 2021). The colonial state also diluted the *Adivasis'* relationship with forest resources by introducing various forest policies, thereby restricting their access. Subsequently, it commercialized and extracted the forest resources in *Adivasi* areas. *Adivasis* were compelled to work as laborers in the land they once possessed. Nevertheless, the *Adivasis* launched a series of rebellions against resource alienation, albeit with little or no success.

Dispossession accelerated in the post-colonial period (Murdia, 1975). *Adivasi* territories have abundant natural resources, which have been an easy target for the state and its treasury. The Twelfth Five Year Plan (2012–2017) document acknowledged that the proportion of displaced *Adivasis* was at least 55 percent of the total displaced people in India, and it was around 76 percent in Gujarat (cited in Government of India, n.d., p. 60). In the post-colonial period, the *Adivasi* movements mounted against land alienation demanded restoration of alienated land and advocated for recognizing *Adivasi* land rights within the country's constitutional framework. *Adivasi* movements have focused their attention on the state and MNCs extracting mining and forest resources from *Adivasi* lands, especially since the 1990s (Ambagudia, 2017).[16] *Adivasi* movements, involving direct action, lobbying, and advocacy, were critical for

---

[16] The state signs memorandum of understandings (MoUs) with MNCs reflecting mutually acceptable terms and conditions, where the former is perceived to provide liberal terms and conditions to the latter to attract capital. As part of the MoU, the state acquires *Adivasi* lands and makes them available to MNCs for establishing industries and project plants. The state also creates infrastructural facilities for MNCs to extract natural resources from the *Adivasi* region.

developing two of India's most progressive land rights statutes: the PESA and the FRA (Nikolakis & Hotte, 2020). Both of these laws seek to secure and safeguard *Adivasi* lands, a response to the unprecedented dispossession experienced across the country.

Litigation

The *Adivasis* of India also resort to litigation to advance and safeguard their land rights. Sometimes they take individual initiatives to file cases in the court, and other times various organizations mobilize and file cases on behalf of *Adivasis* in the courts for restoring the alienated land. The *Adivasis* usually arrange financial resources required for fighting cases in cash or in-kind (crops) if the organizations are involved. Table 12.5 shows 437,173 cases covering 661,806 acres of unlawfully alienated land were filed in the courts; of these, 360,590 cases were decided, and 217,396 (60.28 percent) cases were decided in favor of *Adivasi* communities (covering 412,865 acres). However, all decided lands were not restored.

The highest number of cases were filed in Odisha (107,798), followed by Bihar (86,291) (Table 12.5). Similarly, Andhra Pradesh witnessed the highest amount of *Adivasi* land alienation (287,776 acres), followed by Odisha (106,530 acres). On September 6, 2012, the government informed the Lok Sabha that 4.37 lakh cases, covering 6.61 lakh acres of *Adivasi* land alienation had been registered, out of which 2.17 lakh cases have been legally disposed of in favor of the *Adivasis* that covered 4.12 lakh acres.[17] However, the overall progress of the restoration of alienated *Adivasi* land was unsatisfactory, with the *Committee on State Agrarian Relations and the Unfinished Task in Land Reforms* arguing the dismal progress was because the "Courts, bureaucrats and mostly public men, are often formidably interlocked against the *Adivasis*" (Government of India, 2009, p. 37).

Examining the various interim orders and judgements of *Samatha vs State of Andhra Pradesh & Ors* (Samatha Judgment), *Narmada Bachao Andolon vs Union of India & Ors* (Narmada Bachao Andolan case), *T. N. Godavaraman Thirumulpad vs Union of India and Ors* (Niyamgiri Judgment) and February 2019 judicial Order on the FRA (*FRA* case), Ambagudia (2022a) contends that the judiciary has maintained an inconsistency around *Adivasi* land rights. In the *Samatha* case,

---

[17] Lok Sabha Unstarred Question No. 4225, dated September 6, 2012, available at http://loksabhaph.nic.in/Questions.

Table 12.5 Statewise information on alienation and restoration of tribal lands (area in acres)

State	Cases Filed in Court		Cases Disposed of by the Court		Cases Decided in favor of Adivasi		Cases in which Land was Restored to Adivasis	
	Number	Area	Number	Area	Number	Area	Number	Area
Andhra Pradesh	65,875	287,776	58,212	256,452	26,475	106,225	23,383	94,312
Assam	2,042	4,211	50	19	50	19	50	19
Bihar	86,291	104,893	76,518	95,151	44,634	45,421	44,634	45,421
Chhattisgarh	49,138	NA	21,290	13,440	21,202	NA	13,364	NA
Gujarat	20,847	76,612	20,044	74,053	19,522	72,666	363	1,919
Himachal Pradesh	2	21	0	0	0	0	0	0
Jharkhand	5,382	4,002	1,362	NA	1,079	860	1,079	860
Karnataka	10,686	40,189	10,222	37,457	4,544	16,234	4,490	16,127
Madhya Pradesh	13,440	8,997	11,705	8,429	7,721	6,277	8,738	8,300
Maharashtra	45,634	NA	44,624	99,486	19,943	99,486	19,943	99,486
Odisha	107,798	106,530	107,190	105,840	62,943	57,891	61,257	57,013
Rajasthan	886	3,099	285	176	195	418	195	417
Tripura	29,152	25,476	9,088	7,368	9,088	7,368	8,994	7,318
Total	437,173	661,806	360,590	697,871	217,396	412,865	186,490	331,192

NA = No Availability Source: Lok Sabha Unstarred Question No. 6693, dated May 17, 2012, available at http://164.100.47.193/Annexture_New/lsq15/10/au6693.html.

the Supreme Court considered whether the state is a "person" under Section 3(1)(a) of the Andhra Pradesh Scheduled Areas Land Transfer Regulation 1959 (Regulation 1 of 1959) and whether it could lease out land in Scheduled Areas to mining companies. Samata, an NGO, challenged the Andhra Pradesh High Court's decision to reject the state "as a person" and uphold the mining lease in the Visakhapatnam district Scheduled Areas.[18] On appeal, the Supreme Court considered the state a person and ruled that the mining lease to non-*Adivasi* in Scheduled Areas was invalid. The federal and state governments attempted to dilute this judgment and tried to amend the Fifth Schedule to ease the legal blockade created by the *Samatha* judgment for leasing Scheduled Area lands to non-tribal entities (Ambagudia, 2022a).

Similarly, when the Supreme Court delivered the *Niyamgiri* judgement in favor of *Adivasi* communities on April 18, 2013, the Odisha Mining Corporation Limited again approached the Supreme Court in 2016 to reopen the case and reconvene the twelve Gram Sabhas that had rejected the bauxite mining in Niyamgiri in 2013 (Ambagudia, 2022a).

In the *Narmada Bachao Andolan* case, the *Narmada Bacho Andolan* launched a social movement (consisting of native *Adivasis*, farmers, environmentalists and social activists) against the Sardar Sarovar Dam Project on the Narmada River in western India, which would displace the *Adivasis* living in the region. The Supreme Court has delivered mixed judgments, with the end result being project approval and *Adivasi* displacement. In the *FRA* case, when the Supreme Court further heard the matter on February 13, 2019, the executive (central government) did not send its law officer to defend the central law, FRA, and the Supreme Court ordered the eviction of the rejected claimants of *Adivasis* and other forest dwellers from the forest land by July 24, 2019 (Ambagudia, 2022a). However, the judicial order has been put on hold due to pressure from the *Adivasis* and *Adivasi* rights activists, as due process was not followed while rejecting the claims. In short, while these institutions are expected

---

[18] Section 3(1)(a) of the Andhra Pradesh Scheduled Area Land Transfer Regulation 1959 (Regulation 1 of 1959) prohibits the transfer of tribal land to non-tribals. In 1995, the High Court of Andhra Pradesh deliberated upon the writ petition filed by Samata and considered that the "person" mentioned in Section 3(1)(a) applies to a natural person, such as tribes and non-tribes, and hence, the state cannot be considered as a person. Samata challenged the decision of the High Court in the Supreme Court (for details, see Ambagudia, 2022a).

to protect and promote *Adivasi* land rights, they have often worked to undermine *Adivasi* land rights.

Conclusions and Recommendations

Due to an implementation gap – where the executive, legislature, and courts work at odds to *Adivasi* land justice – the comprehensive constitutional and statutory measures for *Adivasi* land rights, at federal and state levels, have neither advanced nor safeguarded these rights. Indeed, what this chapter shows is that over the last decades, the *Adivasi* land base has been eroded, and landlessness and the poverty that comes with it is now a persistent problem for *Adivasis* across India.

The dispossession and deprivation of *Adivasis* have led to conflicts over land and natural resources between the *Adivasis* and other actors such as the state, MNCs, and non-*Adivasi* communities in different parts of the country. The need of the day is to take a series of robust measures to strengthen and advance *Adivasi* land rights. Six steps are critical to strengthening *Adivasi* land rights.

First, the existing legislative frameworks for *Adivasi* land rights must be implemented with sincerity and commitment across the country. In addition, existing land laws must also be independently assessed, based on their effectiveness, and any changes must be made if necessary.

Second, institutions such as the legislature, executive, and judiciary should be sensitive while dealing with the *Adivasi* land issues. Any oversight would lead to the dispossession of *Adivasi* lands. Any attempt to dilute the relationship between the *Adivasis* and land would only incite resistance on an unprecedented scale.

Third, as outlined in Table 12.5, several *Adivasi* land cases are yet to be disposed of. In this context, special courts must be set up to dispose *Adivasi* land rights cases in a timely manner.

Fourth, Sixth Schedule Areas are relatively less prone to *Adivasi* land alienation due to the legislative power of the Autonomous District Councils of *Adivasis* to make laws on land relations. On the contrary, state governments enact laws governing the *Adivasi* land in Fifth Schedule Areas with, of course, less sensitivity towards *Adivasi* land rights. In this context, enacting similar provisions of Sixth Schedule Areas in Fifth Schedule Areas would advance and safeguard the *Adivasi* land rights in India.

Fifth, building on the *Adivasi* land-based data, institutional mechanisms should be established such as independent monitoring agencies to regulate the *Adivasi* land relations with the federal and state governments and their sub-units. The monitoring agencies could collect data on various dynamics of *Adivasi* land. They could examine and (dis)approve the acquisition of *Adivasi* land. They could also examine the state governments' move to dilute the legislation to protect and promote *Adivasi* land rights.[19]

Sixth, support for *Adivasi* leaders must be enabled to build a robust *Adivasi* land movement, collaborating with civil society organizations in ways that strengthen and advance *Adivasi* land rights. The involvement of civil society organizations in the past has proved beneficial for *Adivasis*, especially in reference to PESA and FRA.

Looking ahead, further research could examine the success stories and the failures for *Adivasi* land rights – it is important to share what is working, and what is not, to guide land justice across India.

References

Ambagudia, J. (2010). Tribal rights, dispossession and the State in Orissa. *Economic and Political Weekly*, 45(33), 60–67.

(2017). Regime of marginalisation and sites of protest: Understanding the Adivasi movement in Odisha, India. In H. Devere, K. Maiharoa, & J. P. Synott (eds.), *Peacebuilding and the rights of Indigenous Peoples: Experiences and strategies for the 21st Century* (pp. 155–165), Cham: Springer.

(2019). *Adivasis, migrants and the state in India*. New York: Routledge.

(2022a). Judiciary and tribal rights in India: Shifting terrains of judicial pronouncements in India. In A. Linkenbach & V. Verma (eds.), *State, law and Adivasis: Shifting terrains of exclusion* (pp. 153–188), New Delhi: Sage.

(2024). Tribes, Covid-19 and the State in India. *Journal of Asian and African Studies* 59(2), 563–577. https://doi.org/10.1177/00219096221117073.

Bakshi, A. (2008), Social inequality in land ownership in India: A study with particular reference to West Bengal. *Social Scientist*, 36(9/10), 95–116.

Bose, P., Arts, B., & van Dijk, H. (2012). 'Forest governmentality': A genealogy of subject-making of forest dependant 'scheduled tribes' in India. *Land Use Policy*, 29, 664–673.

Buckles, D., Khedkar, R., Ghevde, B., & Patil, D. (2013). *Fighting eviction: Tribal land rights and research-in-action*. New Delhi: Cambridge University Press.

---

[19] In 2015, the Manipur Assembly passed the controversial Manipur Land Revenue and Land Reform Act (7th Amendment Bill 2015). The tribals of Manipur alleged that the Act would dilute Section 153 of the *Manipur Land Revenue and Land Reforms Act* 1960, which would lead to the transfer of tribal land to non-tribal people.

Centre for Equity Studies. (2016). *The extent and nature of individual tribal land alienation in Fifth Schedule States in India*. New Delhi: Centre for Equity Studies.

Devi, P. B. (2006). *Tribal land system of Manipur*. New Delhi: Akansha Publishing House.

Government of India. (1995–1996). *All India Report on Agricultural Census, 1995–96*. New Delhi: Ministry of Agriculture, Department of Agriculture & Cooperation.

(1998). *All India Report on Agricultural Census, 1990–91*. New Delhi: Ministry of Agriculture, Department of Agriculture and Cooperation.

(2007). *The Scheduled Tribes and other traditional forest dwellers (Recognition of Forest Rights) Act, 2006*. New Delhi: Ministry of Law and Justice.

(2009). *Report of the Committee on State Agrarian Relations and the Unfinished Task in Land Reforms*. New Delhi: Ministry of Rural Development (Department of Land Resources).

(2012). *All India Report on Agriculture Census 2005–06*. New Delhi: Ministry of Agriculture (Department of Agriculture & Cooperation).

(2013). *Statistical profile of Scheduled Tribes in India 2013*. New Delhi: Ministry of Tribal Affairs.

(2014). *Report of the high level committee on socio-economic, health and educational status of tribal Communities of India*. New Delhi: Ministry of Tribal Affairs.

(2015). *All India Report on Agriculture Census 2010–11*. New Delhi: Ministry of Agriculture & Farmers Welfare (Department of Agriculture, Cooperation, & Farmers Welfare).

(2020). *All India Report on Agriculture Census 2015–16*. New Delhi: Ministry of Agriculture & Farmers Welfare (Department of Agriculture, Cooperation, & Farmers Welfare).

(n.d.). *Land and governance under the Fifth Schedule: An overview of the law*. New Delhi: Ministry of Tribal Affairs and UNDP.

Hardiman, D. (1987). *The coming of the Devi: Adivasi assertion in Western India*. Delhi: Oxford University Press.

Housing and Land Rights Network. (2020). *Impact of COVID-19 on India's Indigenous Peoples, Submission to the Special Rapporteur on the Rights of Indigenous Peoples*. New Delhi: Housing and Land Rights Network.

Karat, B., & Rawal, V. (2014). Scheduled tribe households: A note on issues of livelihoods. *Review of Agrarian Studies*, 4(1), 135–158.

Kumar, K., & Choudhary, P. R. (2005). *A socio-economic and legal study of Scheduled Tribes' land in Orissa*. Washington: World Bank.

Land Portal. (n.d.). *India: Land governance and country narrative*. https://landportal.org/nl/library/resources/india-land-governance-country-narrative-full-report

Levien, M. (2015). From primitive accumulation to regimes of dispossession: Six theses on India's land question. *Economic and Political Weekly*, 50(22), 146–157.

Lopes, F., & Chari, M. (2021). In 12 Years, 11 states changed land ceiling laws in favour of industry over farmers. *IndiaSpend*. https://www.indiaspend.com/land-rights/in-12-years-11-states-changed-land-ceiling-laws-in-favour-of-industry-over-farmers-724650

Mohanty, B. B. (2001). Land distribution among Scheduled Castes and Scheduled Tribes. *Economic and Political Weekly*, 36(40), 3857–3868.

Murdia, R. (1975). Land allotment and land alienation: Policies and programmes for Scheduled Castes and Scheduled Tribes. *Economic and Political Weekly*, 10(32), 1204–1214.

Nikolakis, W., & Hotte, N. (2020). How law shapes collaborative forest governance: A focus on Indigenous Peoples in Canada and India. *Society & Natural Resources*, 33(1), 46–64.

Singh, D. K. (2010). *Statelessness in South Asia: The Chakmas between Bangladesh and India*. New Delhi: Sage.

Viegas, P. (1991). *Encroached and enslaved: Alienation of tribal lands and its dynamics*. New Delhi: Indian Social Institute.

Xaxa, V. (2021). Tribal politics in India: From movement to institutionalism. In J. Ambagudia & V. Xaxa (eds.), *Handbook of Tribal Politics in India* (pp. 29–42), New Delhi: Sage.

13

Legal Privileges and the Effective Recognition of Indigenous Land Rights

Lessons from Malaysia

YOGESWARAN SUBRAMANIAM

Introduction

Malaysia's Indigenous Peoples share a common experience of discrimination and a systematic dispossession of their lands. Like other jurisdictions, the predicament in Malaysia can be attributed to a persistent lack of respect, recognition, protection, and priority for Indigenous lands (SUHAKAM, 2013). Despite commonalities among Malaysia's Indigenous Peoples from a land rights perspective, their experience is somewhat distinctive due to the different rights, privileges, and treatment afforded to each under the law and derived from their local circumstances.

Exploring the nuances of the legal context in Malaysia, this chapter begins by identifying "Indigenous Peoples" and their diverse traditional land tenure systems, and then examines the constitutional categorization of, and differences between, the Peninsular Malaysia Orang Asli and the natives of Sabah and of Sarawak. After surveying their respective statutory land and resource laws and policies, this analysis examines the strategy of litigation of Indigenous customary land rights through the Malaysian courts. This chapter then explores opportunities for the inclusion of Malaysia's Indigenous Peoples in connection with international conservation commitments, followed by concluding observations on the legal protections and recognition of Indigenous land rights.

Indigenous Peoples in Malaysia

Broadly, the Federation of Malaysia comprises the peninsular land separating the Straits of Malacca from the South China Sea and most of the northern quarter of the island of Borneo. Peninsular Malaysia has eleven states and two federal territories, formerly known as the Federation of Malaya. The Borneo territories are made up of the states of Sabah and Sarawak, and a federal territory.

Prior to the formation of Malaysia in 1963, the Federation of Malaya, Sabah (previously North Borneo), and Sarawak were three separate states. The Federation of Malaya gained independence from the British in 1957, while Sabah and Sarawak remained under British rule until the Malaysia Agreement 1963, where Sabah, Sarawak, and the self-governing British colony of Singapore combined with the Federation of Malaya to form the Federation of Malaysia. Singapore left the Federation in 1965.

The 1957 Federation of Malaya Constitution, the foundation for the Malaysian Constitution, contained provisions granting distinct special privileges to two ethnic groups, namely the Malays and the Aborigines of the Malay peninsula (also known as the Orang Asli), including quota reservations and, more pertinently, rights and privileges relating to land. Ethnic Malays were granted these special privileges following a complex compromise between the interests of the major ethnic groups in Malaya immediately prior to independence from British rule. The groups mainly involved the politically and numerically stronger Malays, whose earlier settlement and kingdoms in the Malay Peninsula had been recognized by the colonial government, and the immigrant ethnic Chinese, Indians, and other groups, many of whom were vying for entrenched citizenship rights in an independent Malaya. The relatively superior political position of the Malays ensured that two important aspects of the compromise were: (i) Malay demands for the maintenance and protection of their culture, religion, and lands and (ii) their prevailing socio-economic disadvantages compared to the Chinese and the Indians (Fernando, 2002). In contrast, the Orang Asli as the "first peoples" of the Malay peninsula, who numbered less than 0.5 percent of the population and were considered "backward" and economically insignificant, played no part in this constitutional compromise (Subramaniam, 2013). As will be observed, they were nonetheless ascribed limited constitutional protections under government stewardship.

Subsequently, Annex A of the Malaysia Agreement 1963 provided for constitutional amendments to the Federation of Malaya Constitution, legally facilitating Malaysia's formation. One of the conditions of Sabah and Sarawak joining the Federation of Malaysia was the granting of special privileges to natives (*anak negeri*) of Sabah and Sarawak tailored to the local circumstances and political demands of both states.[1] The Malays,[2] natives of Sabah,[3] natives of Sarawak,[4] and Orang Asli,[5] were thus afforded varying degrees of constitutional rights and privileges due to legal arrangements for the protection of those considered as "indigenous" or "native" during the decolonization process. Ethnic Malays account for almost 58 percent of Malaysia's citizenry of 30.4 million, while the Orang Asli, natives of Sabah and natives of Sarawak collectively amount to 12.2 percent of the population (Department of Statistics Malaysia, 2023). The Malays are politically dominant at the federal level and state levels within Peninsular Malaysia, whereas the heterogenous native groups of Sabah and Sarawak have political control over their respective states. Peninsular Malaysia Orang Asli, whose eighteen official sub-ethnic groups only account for 0.7 percent of the population, are politically weak, and are among the most marginalized and impoverished groups in Malaysia (Nicholas, 2020, p. 284).

Although the term "Indigenous Peoples" is not contained in the Federal Constitution, the natives of Sabah and Sarawak and Peninsular Malaysia Orang Asli have collectively self-identified as *Orang Asal* (Indigenous Peoples) (Nicholas, 2020, p. 283) at international human rights fora and domestically. The Human Rights Commission of Malaysia (SUHAKAM, 2013) considers these groups to meet international criteria for "Indigenous Peoples" under the various international

---

[1] For commentary on constitutional federalism in Malaysia, see, for example, Fong (2008).

[2] A "Malay" under Article 160(2) of the Malaysian Constitution means a person who professes the religion of Islam, habitually speaks the Malay language, conforms to Malay custom and: (a) was born before August 31, 1957, in Malaya or Singapore, or is on that day domiciled in the Federation or in Singapore; or (b) is the issue of that person.

[3] Article 161A(6)(b) of the Malaysian Constitution provides that a native in relation to Sabah is a person who is a citizen, is the child or grandchild of a person of a race indigenous to Sabah, and was born (whether on or after Malaysia Day [September 16, 1963] or not) either in Sabah or to a father domiciled in Sabah at the time of birth. They consist of thirty-nine Indigenous ethnic groups (Nicholas, 2020, p. 283).

[4] Article 161A(6)(a) of the Malaysian Constitution provides that a native in relation to Sarawak is a person who is a citizen, is the grandchild of a person of the Bukitan, Bisayah, Dusun, Sea Dayak, Land Dayak, Kadayan, Kalabit, Kayan, Kenyah (including Subup and Sipeng), Kajang (including Sekapan, Kejaman, Lahanan, Punan, Tanjong, and Kanowit), Lugat, Lisum, Malay, Melano, Murut, Penan, Sian, Tagal, Tabun, and Ubit race or is of mixed blood deriving exclusively from these races.

[5] Orang Asli are constitutionally defined as "the Aborigines of the Malay Peninsula" (Article 160(2)) and are officially classified into eighteen sub-ethnic groups consisting of three broad groups, namely, the Negrito, Senoi, and Aboriginal Malays (Department of Orang Asli Development, 2023).

human rights documents, as they are the earliest inhabitants of their respective lands and collectively a non-dominant and marginalized group within Malaysia that has voluntarily perpetuated a cultural distinctiveness compared to the dominant sections of society. Statistically, the Malaysian government considers all three groups *and* the Peninsular Malaysia Malays as *bumiputera* (translated literally, princes of the soil) (Department of Statistics Malaysia, 2023).

Political and historical narratives consider ethnic Malays as deserving of a special legal position through constitutional privileges and government policies on the basis that their ancestors, who arrived after the Orang Asli, had established kingdoms in the Malay peninsula that were recognized as sovereign by British colonizers (Dentan et al., 1997; Idrus, 2008; Nicholas, 2000). However, the politically and socially dominant Malays have not been identified as "Indigenous Peoples" at international Indigenous rights fora, and perhaps more importantly, do not possess specific communal connections to lands, a feature common to Indigenous Peoples worldwide (Nicholas et al., 2010). In comparison, many Orang Asli and Sabah and Sarawak native communities have struggled to maintain the inextricable political, social, economic, and cultural links they possess with their respective customary territories. This connection supports their traditional livelihoods, and perhaps more critically, defines their culture, identity, and wellbeing.[6]

As such, SUHAKAM has viewed "the mainstream, not minority" Malays as not within the terms of its inquiries into Indigenous Peoples' land rights in Malaysia (SUHAKAM, 2013). This chapter adopts SUHAKAM's opinion and focuses on the customary territorial rights of the Orang Asli and the natives of Sabah and Sarawak. Nonetheless, certain Malay legal privileges are examined to highlight the disparity of rights afforded to the other Indigenous groups and, in particular, the Orang Asli.

Indigenous Land Tenure Systems in Malaysia: Diversity, Flexibility, and Susceptibility to Dispossession

Collectively, the natives of Sabah, the natives of Sarawak, and Peninsular Malaysia Orang Asli have been categorized into at least eighty-four

---

[6] The traditional livelihoods of the various Indigenous ethnic groups in Malaysia depend on their respective local customs and locations. These activities include farming, orchard cultivation, hunting, fishing, and the gathering and use of produce from forests, waters, or tidal estuaries.

different ethnic and sub-ethnic groups: thirty-nine, twenty-seven, and eighteen heterogenous groups, respectively (Nicholas, 2023, p. 238). Through oral traditions and the domestic practice of customs and usages, these groups have developed rich, complex, and diverse land and territorial customs shaped by their geographical locales and traditional connections to these spaces.

Depending on the geographical location and cultural predisposition of each group, traditional activities include farming, orchard cultivation, hunting, fishing, and the gathering and use of produce from forests, waters, or tidal estuaries. Increased encroachment and loss of traditional lands, interaction with outsiders and state intervention have modified local customs, activities, and spatial areas but customary laws continue to observed, at least for communities that still inhabit their traditional areas.

For those communities that are traditionally engaged in more settled activities and do not inhabit coastal, urban or developed areas, there are some basic commonalities in respect of areas that they consider customary territories. Broadly, a customary territory for these groups is a specific and naturally defined area that would comprise settlements, cleared and cultivated areas, orchards, old settlement and cultivated areas, cemeteries, sacred and ceremonial sites, and forested areas for hunting and the collection of produce. Within this area there would be a combination of individual, communal, and non-exclusive customary interests that are managed by the community in accordance with customary laws. Examples of such customary land arrangements can be found among the *Semai* and *Temiar* (Peninsular Malaysia), *Iban* and *Bidayuh* (Sarawak), and *Dusun* and *Murut* (Sabah) (SUHAKAM, 2013).

Less sedentary Indigenous groups also possess distinctive concepts of defined territoriality and connections in respect of their customary areas. For example, the *Seletar* Orang Asli of Peninsular Malaysia assume custodianship of sea and coastal fringes and mangroves traditionally inhabited by them and regard such areas (within their defined boundaries) as their traditional territory and resources (SUHAKAM, 2013). Groups that are regarded as semi-nomadic such as the *Batek* Orang Asli of Peninsular Malaysia and the *Penan* of Sarawak have naturally defined traditional territories marked out by landscape features and customs relating to resource use and other cultural and spiritual connections within these areas (Bulan & Maran, 2020; SUHAKAM, 2013).

These informal, decentralized, and flexible systems of territoriality provided opportunities for subsequent waves of migrants, settlers, and incoming powers to claim these lands, having viewed large portions of

Indigenous customary territories as unsettled, unutilized, and fit for domination. The most profound of these interventions was the imposition of English property law systems to regulate land and resource use by British colonisers in the nineteenth and early twentieth centuries (Bulan & Maran, 2020; Doolittle, 2005; Subramaniam & Endicott, 2020; SUHAKAM, 2013). These foreign systems facilitated the "legal" dispossession of Indigenous Peoples by ignoring Indigenous concepts of territoriality, and sanctioning the exploitation of natural resources and the expansion of commercial activities into Indigenous customary territories. These systems form the basis of prevailing domestic laws governing lands and resources in Malaysia. The following sections detail the Malaysian legal framework and the treatment of distinct Indigenous Peoples and their customary rights to lands, territories, and resources.

Constitutional Privileges for Indigenous Peoples and their Lands: State-Centric Recognition

Malaysia is a constitutional monarchy that functions through a localized Westminster parliamentary system. The Malaysian legal system incorporates elements of local customs and *Syariah* Islamic principles into its common law system that have been modified and adapted to local circumstances through written laws and judicial pronouncements. As defined in Article 160(2) of the Malaysian Constitution, "law includes written law, the common law in so far as it is in operation in the Federation or any part thereof, and any custom or usage having the force of law in the Federation or any part thereof."

Due to their dissimilar histories and circumstances prior to Malaysia's formation, the Malaysian Constitution affords differing levels of special rights and privileges to the Malays, Orang Asli, natives of Sabah, and natives of Sarawak. Article 153 of the Malaysian Constitution expressly obliges the *Yang Dipertuan Agong*[7] to safeguard the "special position of the Malays and natives of any of the States of Sabah and Sarawak." This special position includes reservations of positions in the public service, scholarships, and other educational and training privileges and licenses for the operation of any trade or business (Article 153(2)).

---

[7] This is the equivalent of the King of Malaysia who is appointed on a rotational basis every five years by the Council of Rulers of the States in Peninsular Malaysia (see Malaysian Constitution, Articles 33–8, Third and Fifth Schedules).

Malays and natives of Sabah and Sarawak (Articles 76(2) and 150(6A)) have constitutional protection against laws that may impact their own respective laws and customs.[8] In respect of land, Malay reservations created in Peninsular Malaysia immediately before independence in 1957 are protected unless a law to the contrary is passed by a two-thirds majority in the relevant state legislature and both houses of the federal parliament (Article 89(1)). Article 90 also provides for the special protection of Malay customary lands in certain states of Peninsular Malaysia.

As for native lands in Sabah and Sarawak, Article 161A(5) of the federal Constitution permits any state law for the "reservation of land . . . or for alienation" to natives of Sabah and Sarawak or "for giving them preferential treatment as regards the alienation of land by the State." Generally, land matters fall within the exclusive jurisdiction of the state governments (Ninth Schedule List II Item 1) while List IIA of the Ninth Schedule of the federal constitution provides additional juris-diction to the Sabah and Sarawak state governments over local native law and custom. In other words, the states of Sabah and Sarawak possess a high degree of legal autonomy to regulate the recognition of their respective Indigenous customary land rights. Nonetheless, these broad constitutional powers enable both state governments to subordinate the enforceability of any native customs in relation to land in favor of their respective land and resource utilization priorities.

In Peninsular Malaysia, Malays, who by constitutional definition must profess the religion of Islam,[9] have constitutional protections in respect of their religion, which is also the official religion of Malaysia (Articles 3 (1)).[10] The federal constitution has maintained the precedence and sovereignty of the Malay customary rulers of Peninsular Malay states to a considerable extent (Articles 70 and 181). The Malay language is the national language (Article 152).

In contrast, Peninsular Malaysia Orang Asli do not enjoy equivalent constitutional rights but instead are dependent on the federal govern-ment for their welfare. Item 16 of the Ninth Schedule List I of the

---

[8] There are constitutional rights for the resolution of such disputes by the *Syariah* courts (see Malaysian Constitution, Article 121(1A)) for Malays and native courts (see Malaysian Constitution, article 72(20) and Ninth Schedule, List IIA, Item 13) for Sabah and Sarawak.

[9] For a definition of 'Malay' under Article 160(2) of the Malaysian Constitution, see note 3 above.

[10] See, for example, Articles 101(4) and 76(2).

Malaysian Constitution specifically empowers the federal government to legislate for Orang Asli welfare.[11] Article 8(5)(c) permits laws "for the protection, well-being or advancement" of Orang Asli "including, the reservation of land" or the "reservation to Orang Asli of a reasonable proportion of suitable positions in the public service" without offending the constitutional equality provision contained in Article 8(1). Despite enabling positive discrimination, these constitutional provisions leave the protection of the Orang Asli and their traditional lands in the hands of the federal government and the individual state governments, the latter having jurisdiction over land matters.

The special constitutional rights and privileges afforded in Malaysia are arguably hierarchical, with the Malays possessing the strongest and widest form of protections. Broadly, natives of Sabah and Sarawak possess comparable constitutional rights and privileges in relation to their lands and customs. However, the legal power and jurisdiction over the recognition of such rights and privileges, including those relating to domestic Indigenous land customs and their enforceability, lie with the state governments of Sabah and Sarawak. In comparison, the Orang Asli possess constitutional protections that do not explicitly encompass their languages, laws, traditions, customs, and institutions, and with respect to lands and other privileges are dependent on government discretion.

There are historical reasons for the apparent constitutional anomaly between the Malays and the Orang Asli. Despite the Orang Asli being descendants of the earliest inhabitants of the Malay Peninsula and their relative independence from the Malay rulers (Carey, 1976; Clifford, 1897; Dentan et al., 1997), they were deemed non-sovereign dependents of the Malay rulers by the British colonial rulers (Noone, 1936; Sullivan, 1998). The diverse tribal lifestyles of the minority Orang Asli groups, which were considered lower on the scale of social organization compared to the Malays and backward (Nah, 2004; Wilkinson, 1923), culminated in legal protections that were paternalistic, and designed for persons incapable of self-determination and destined for integration with the dominant Malay population (Subramaniam, 2011).

Notwithstanding better levels of constitutional protection and their state governments enjoying a higher level of autonomy, local native communities in Sabah and Sarawak share a long history of dispossession

---

[11] Article 74(1) of the Malaysian Constitution empowers the federal government to legislate for matters enumerated in the federal list (Ninth Schedule List I).

of their customary territories with the Orang Asli, a dilemma exacerbated by their continued lack of security of tenure over these areas (SUHAKAM, 2013). Increased demand for lands and resources for economic growth have caused acute encroachment and appropriation of the remaining areas traditionally inhabited by Indigenous communities (Carling & Godio, 2018; Open Society Justice Initiative, 2017; SUHAKAM, 2013).

Statutory Land Rights: State Curtailment of Indigenous Territorial Space

Statutory land rights for Malaysia's Indigenous Peoples are broadly divided into two levels of legal recognition, a "lower" level and a "higher" level. At a "lower" level, Peninsular Malaysia Orang Asli have limited rights and privileges in respect of "inhabited" lands and resources "used" by them, dependent on land reservations or subsistence privileges granted by the state government. However, they do not enjoy express statutory recognition of their respective customary land arrangements. At a "higher" level, the natives of Sabah and Sarawak possess limited rights to their customary lands and resources as defined and determined by their respective state laws.

As will be observed in the ensuing subsections, both forms of statutory recognition could also be viewed as a barrier to the effective protection of Indigenous lands, territories, and resources as they have facilitated the "legal" dispossession of Indigenous traditional areas.

Lower Recognition: Peninsular Malaysia Orang Asli

The *Aboriginal Peoples Act* 1954 (*APA*) is the main statute governing Orang Asli administration and rights, including land matters. Legal commentators have described the *APA* as static and outmoded due to its paternalistic and protectionist skew that secures government control over Orang Asli and their traditional lands (Hooker, 1996; Subramaniam, 2011; Wook, 2017).

The *APA* confers extensive powers on the federal executive, including powers to: (i) determine who is an Orang Asli (section 3(3)); (ii) determine the appointment and removal of Orang Asli headmen (section 16); (iii) exclude undesirable persons from any Orang Asli inhabited areas (sections 14 and 15); and (iv) restrict the entry into or circulation of any written, printed, or photographic matter within Aboriginal inhabited areas (section 19).[12] The Department of Orang Asli Development (JAKOA), headed by the Director-General of Orang Asli Affairs, is the federal agency responsible for Orang Asli "administration, welfare and advancement" (section 4).

Orang Asli customary land tenure has not been recognized by statute. The primary legal protection of traditional Orang Asli lands is through the reservation of specific areas by the state government. In practice, JAKOA would apply to an individual state authority for the reservation of a tract of land on behalf of an Orang Asli community. Analogous to other common law jurisdictions, the state authority, essentially the state government, holds radical title over state land and possesses the power to create land interests and regulate land dealings under the *National Land Code* 1965 (*NLC*). The *NLC*, the primary statute governing land tenure, registration, and dealings in Peninsular Malaysia, does not expressly encompass Orang Asli customary land rights. However, a state authority may formally declare areas inhabited by Orang Asli as reservations under the *APA*, namely, Aboriginal reserves (section 7(1)) or Aboriginal areas (section 6(1)).[13] Despite a measure of statutory protection from the creation of land and resource interests over areas formally declared as Aboriginal reserves and Aboriginal areas (sections 7(2) and 6(2)), sections 7(3) and 6(3) respectively permit Aboriginal reserves and areas to be revoked by a notification in the state government gazette. Consequently, statutory Orang Asli reserves provide limited security of tenure as the existence of a reserve is dependent on the state government's executive fiat.[14] As for land interests, rights of occupancy to Orang Asli within an Aboriginal reserve are limited to that of a tenant at will (section 8), meaning these rights are terminable by a notification from the state authority. Section 10 permits Aboriginal communities to continue residing in areas declared as Malay reservations, forest reserves or game reserves, but upon conditions prescribed by the state authority.

Redress available under the *APA* for loss of traditional lands is far from adequate. There is no right to replacement lands for lands lost, and

---

[12] For commentary, see, for example, Subramaniam (2011).

[13] State authorities have also declared Orang Asli reserves by employing the general "public purpose" provision (section 62) in the *National Land Code* 1965. However, these reservations do not carry the protection from the creation of other land interests afforded to reserves declared under the *APA*.

[14] For commentary on how the common law has supplemented Orang Asli land rights, see notes 25–45 below and accompanying text.

statutory compensation for the loss of lands is discretionary (sections 10 (3) and 12). However, section 11 provides for the payment of mandatory compensation for the loss of Orang Asli fruit and rubber trees as a result of any alienation or disposal.

The *National Forestry Act* 1984 governs the administration of forests in Peninsular Malaysia and confers limited exemptions to Orang Asli from licensing requirements (section 40(3)) and royalty payments (section 62(2)) in respect of forest produce used for subsistence purposes. Section 51(1) of *Wildlife Conservation Act* 2010 permits Orang Asli the right to hunt limited species of protected wildlife for sustenance purposes.

The federal and state governments' broad statutory powers to protect Orang Asli and their traditional lands and resources has produced poor outcomes for land security. As of 2018, only 25 percent of officially acknowledged Orang Asli lands had been formally reserved (Bernama, 2018). The areas selected by JAKOA as "officially" inhabited by the Orang Asli is only 17 percent of the actual customary areas claimed by the Orang Asli (SUHAKAM, 2013). Further, land policies introduced through JAKOA to address Orang Asli socio-economic issues, including the 2009 Orang Asli Land Titles Policy and other agricultural development schemes, do not legally recognize a large portion of customary communal lands (*tanah adat*), lack effective community participation, and when implemented have not alleviated the economic problems of local communities (SUHAKAM, 2013). Also, Orang Asli neither possess statutory rights for customary lands within protected areas such as national parks and wildlife sanctuaries, nor are they formally recognized as co-managers or collaborative partners within such areas, despite having valuable local traditional knowledge (SUHAKAM, 2013).

The 1961 Federal Policy Regarding the Administration of the Orang Asli recognizes the "special position" of Orang Asli "in respect of land usage and land rights," and that "Orang Asli will not be moved from their traditional areas without their consent." However, these commitments are not followed by state land administrators (SUHAKAM, 2013, p. 137). Effective processes for consultations with local Indigenous communities to ascertain the extent of their "traditional areas" are also non-existent. As such, Orang Asli communal lands are often perceived as empty and unused state land that paves the way for "legal" land grabs (Mamo, 2020) and exploitative activities by others, including logging, plantations, agri-business, and commercial projects (SUHAKAM, 2013).

Natives of Sarawak

Unlike the experience of the Peninsular Malaysia Orang Asli, British rule in Sarawak acknowledged and recognized certain forms of Indigenous governance over customary lands, notwithstanding the imposition of English property rights concepts and registration systems (Porter, 1967). Despite an increasing pattern of regulation, land and resource laws during the colonial period, and beyond, have continued to recognize certain native customary rights, bridled by state powers to determine and extinguish such rights (Bulan, 2007).

Consequently, Native Customary Land (NCL) and Native Area Land (NAL) are officially categorized in the current *Sarawak Land Code* 1958 (*SLC*). NCL consists of land where native customary rights (NCR) were created prior to January 1, 1958, and still subsist; lands in a communal native reserve; and Interior Area Land (IAL) (residual areas after the excision of other classes of land, Bulan, 2012) upon which NCR has been created pursuant to a statutory state government permit (section 2). NAL comprises titled land held by natives or areas declared as such by state government (Bulan, 2012).

However, section 5(1) of the SLC limits the creation of NCR after January 1, 1958. Section 5(2) states that NCR can be created through a permit over IAL. The provision explicitly recognizes NCR land activities relating to the felling and occupation of cleared virgin jungle, the planting of fruit trees, occupation or cultivation, use for a burial ground, shrine or rights of way or any "other lawful method."[15]

Common law NCR acquired before January 1, 1958, can be established by a native or native community court through the courts. Individual natives can apply for a grant in perpetuity, where they have occupied and used any area of unalienated state land in accordance with rights acquired by customary ownership for residential and agricultural purposes (section 18). While these statutory provisions recognize some forms of NCR, they are mainly based on "occupation" (Bulan, 2012). More consistent with Western property law concepts, they focus on sedentarized and agricultural activities, and do not explicitly recognize broader native customary territories and areas used for hunting, fishing, the collection of forest produce and ceremonial purposes, such as the Iban native customs of *pemakai menoa* (a territorial domain) and *pulau galau* (a communal forest reserve). Remarkably, codified customs such as the *Adat*

---

[15] For the scope and limit of "any other lawful method," see, for example, Bulan (2012).

Iban Order 1993 also do not specifically recognize these forms of customary land use. The *SLC* does not expressly recognize the land tenure systems and territoriality of nomadic or semi-nomadic groups like the Penan and native communities claiming coastal or sea areas (SUHAKAM, 2013).

In response to the apex court decision in *TR Sandah* around the limited common law NCR to cleared, settled, and cultivated areas, the Sarawak government amended the *SLC* in 2018 to permit a native community to claim usufructuary rights enjoyed or exercised up to 1,000 hectares (section 6A). If the relevant land officer approves the claim, a native communal title would be issued describing the area as a "native territorial domain," and used for agricultural purposes or any such other purpose or conditions imposed by the state (section 6A (3)). While this amendment has recognized claims to broader sections of a native community's customary territory, the arbitrary statutory limit of 1,000 hectares for the native territorial domain has been viewed as "short-changing" natives as there exist native claims exceeding 10,000 hectares (Nicholas, 2019, p. 278). Equally, executive control over the claims process and conditions relating to the native communal title have not assuaged prevailing concerns about the government's administration of NCR matters.

Administratively, the procedures of land offices in dealing with NCR matters have been problematic for native communities due to disputes between the state and natives on the extent of lands subject to NCR. Delays and difficulties have been documented in processing applications for NCR and surveying lands, and unsatisfactory notification procedures for claims and applications, and the limitations of local state officers, have been reported (SUHAKAM, 2013). Despite 20 percent of state land being classified as NCL, only 2 percent of NCL has been formally surveyed and titled (Limbu, 2017). These problems mean the legal status of lands subject to NCR is indeterminate and open to the grant of other land interests. Further, the earlier success in taking NCR claims to the civil courts has been limited in more recent times.

Compounding matters for natives, formally recognized NCR lands are legally vulnerable to other land uses and classifications. The state government possesses wide powers to extinguish NCR subject to the payment of compensation for those natives who establish claims to NCR.[16]

---

[16] See SLC, section 5(3). For other legislation permitting the extinguishment, regulation or limitation of NCR, see for example, *Forests Ordinance* 1958; *Land Consolidation and Rehabilitation Authority Ordinance* 1976; *National Parks and Nature Reserves Ordinance* 1998.

Section 28 of the *SLC* permits a provisional lease to be granted over state land that includes native holdings where a survey of such holdings is impracticable. Registrations of Native Rights under section 7A are merely a "certification of rights" and do not constitute the indefeasible title accorded to other registered proprietors under sections 131 and 132(1) (Bulan, 2012).

Therefore, it is not uncommon for the state government to grant logging licenses and provisional leases for plantations of lands potentially subject to NCR without the local community's free prior and informed consent, often resulting in litigation by native communities. Other instances where the state has overridden the NCR interests of native communities include large infrastructure projects (Lasimbang, 2016), and the inclusion of NCR land into state-regulated protected areas including forest reserves where natives have limited rights (SUHAKAM, 2013). Complaints of violence and police action against human rights defenders in NCR land disputes suggest government inaction and implicit acquiescence (Amnesty International, 2018).

Community land development schemes initiated by the state government have not been without controversy or criticism (Bulan, 2006). For example, the joint venture arrangement between the Sarawak Land Custody Development Authority, investors and a local Indigenous community only granted a 30-percent equity share to the community, secured through its surrender of lands. Beyond the lack of community control, there have also been disputes over the consultation process with Indigenous beneficiaries, the lack of transparency in the joint-venture formation process, and non-payment of dividends (SUHAKAM, 2013).

Notwithstanding "native" autonomy and control over the recognition of NCR in Sarawak, legal power has enabled the state government and those in political power to mold the contours of the NCR recognition framework in accordance with their own primacies, which arguably do not prioritize the rights and interests of the local Indigenous communities in relation to their traditional lands.

Natives of Sabah

Analogous to Sarawak, British colonial administrators had expressly recognized native customs in Sabah. Article 9 of the 1881 Royal Charter granted by the British Crown for the administration of North

Borneo (now Sabah) obligated the British North Borneo Chartered
Company to pay careful regard to the customs and laws of the class,
tribe, or nation, especially with respect to lands.[17] As it turned out, the
colonial administration instituted a system of legal pluralism, where
selected native customary laws were supported, while those hampering
commercial land exploitation were replaced with western legal concepts
(Doolittle, 2005). After Sabah's independence and Malaysia's formation,
the Malaysia Agreement and federal constitution maintained the prevailing legal position of the natives of Sabah (Doolittle, 2005).

Section 15 of the *Sabah Land Ordinance* (*SLO*) defines NCR to include
land possessed under "customary tenure," land planted with fifty or more
fruit trees per hectare, isolated fruit trees or plants of economic value
proven to be planted or kept as personal property, grazing land stocked
with sufficient cattle or horses to control undergrowth, land cultivated or
built on within three years, burial grounds and shrines, and usual rights
of way for people or animals (Munang, 2015).

"Customary tenure" under section 66 of the *SLO* means the lawful
possession of land by natives either by continuous occupation or cultivation for more than three years, or by native title issued under written law.
Similar to Sarawak, "occupation" is central to legal recognition under the
SLO. Customary tenure confers a "permanent heritable and transferable
right of use and occupancy" of native land subject to terms prescribed by
the State Collector of Land Revenue ("Collector"), a government officer
(section 66). Additionally, the Collector possesses the power to determine
native land claims (sections 14, 81, and 82) and may deal with NCR
established under section 15 by monetary compensation rather than
issuing a title (section 16).

Although title registration is of paramount importance under the
Sabah land law system, land "still held under NCR without document
of title" is an express exception to this rule (*SLO*, section 88). However,
the Collector may require a native to take out a native title by entry in the
Native Title Register (section 67(2)). The *SLO* also provides for the
creation of individual native title (section 70(1)), native communal title
(section 76(1)), and native reserves (section 78). However, the term
"title" under section 76 is arguably a misnomer, as it is not registered
in favor of the native community as proprietor. Section 76, a legacy of
British paternalism toward the natives, provides for the land to be

---

[17] For commentary on the evolution of native land rights in Sabah, see Doolittle (2005).

registered in the name of the Collector "as trustee for the natives concerned but without the power of sale." Nevertheless, the Collector has the power to sanction the subdivision of the communal title and assign and transfer the sub-divided native titles to individual owners (section 77). It is also of note that section 76 and other provisions of the *SLO* do not explicitly recognize native customary rights to broader customary territories used for less sedentarized activities.

In addition to the obvious lack of community control over the titled communal land, a 2009 amendment to section 76 that added state power to decide the plan and purpose of a communal title has drawn criticism as being "open-ended" and, in practice, favoring joint-venture development program applications rather than NCR-based communal title applications (SUHAKAM, 2013). In 2019, the newly elected Pakatan Harapan Government abolished the communal land title policy (Dzulkifli, 2019), but sections 76 and 77 remain unamended.

Subject to subsequent modification or extinction by the state,[18] natives may also possess rights or conceded privileges that survive the creation of a forest reserve (section 12 of the *Sabah Forest Enactment* 1968 (*SFE*)). However, all other rights not expressly admitted or conceded by the state are extinguished (section 12(6)). Section 41 of the *SFE* provides limited rights to remove forest produce from state land and alienated land (with consent from the owner) for specified individual or communal subsistence purposes. The inclusion of potential NCR lands into forest reserves has adversely impacted the lives of local native communities through logging activities, complaints of harsh treatment by forest enforcement officers the statutory extinguishment, and limitation of their rights without adequate notice (SUHAKAM, 2013). Community forest management initiatives have also been said to lack "a structure to ensure effective participation in the co-management of community forest areas" (SUHAKAM, 2013, p. 97). In this respect, the Sabah Forest Policy 2018 appears to be a step forward, promising to strengthen local community participation in the implementation of forest management, protection, and tourism activities (Sabah Forestry Department, 2018).

Several other written laws for the regulation of lands and resources contain provisions that envisage protection of native rights and interests. These include the *Wildlife Conservation Enactment* 1997 (e.g., sections 7 and 32), *Biodiversity Enactment* 2000 (e.g., sections 16(b), 20(3), and 25

---

[18] *Forest Enactment* 1968, section 14.

(1)(b)), and the *Inland Fisheries and Aquaculture Enactment* 2003 (e.g., section 35). However, the power balance in relation to the recognition and exercise of such rights lies in favor of the state. The state's long-standing priority for land and resource exploitation through logging and large-scale commercial crop cultivation can be gleaned from established statutes empowering land development, such as the *Sabah Land Development Enactment* 1981, the *Sabah Forestry Development Authority Enactment* 1981, and the *Sabah Rubber Industry Board Enactment* 1981. This trend offers no assurances that written laws recognizing Indigenous rights will be implemented any differently from before. Comparable to Peninsular Malaysia and Sarawak, land interests granted to outsiders for commercial development without the knowledge or effective participation of the local native community are a relatively common phenomenon (SUHAKAM, 2013).

Procedurally, NCR in Sabah are additionally subject to extensive procedures through which native claims are asserted, determined, and protected (Nasser Hamid & Ram Singh, 2012; Wong-Adamal, 1998). Problematic land administration processes, loss of records, overlapping land applications, inadequate notification procedures and periods, poor information on third-party projects or land alienations, and delays in land survey were among the many issues raised during the SUHAKAM National Land Inquiry (Doolittle, 2011; SUHAKAM, 2013). Community land development schemes geared towards poverty eradication initiated by the state government have also been criticized for being "top-down" in terms of transparency, community participation, and consent mechanisms, and poorly implemented in terms of financial outcomes and return (SUHAKAM, 2013).

Somewhat ironically, the state's domination of NCR and the consequent loss of traditional Indigenous lands is enabled by laws aimed at protecting these lands (Doolittle, 2011). However, the state government's efforts in enabling community participation in state park areas by amending the Parks Enactment 1984 in 2011, and accommodating a traditional resource management system, *Tagal*, within its inland fishing laws and policies, are relatively laudable. Nonetheless, the lack of express legal recognition of the *Tagal* as "an Indigenous Peoples' system" has created jurisdictional conflicts between the state and native communities (SUHAKAM, 2013). While more recent developments suggest that the government appears to be working guardedly towards reinstating and strengthening Indigenous values in its administration (Nicholas, 2020), it remains to be seen whether primary state land use priorities in Sabah will be recalibrated to incorporate the effective legal recognition of NCR. Unfortunately, for local native communities in Sabah sustaining a long-term NCR agenda poses a significant challenge, exacerbated by policy priorities that fluctuate with changes in political power.

Indigenous Peoples' Rights in Malaysia and in the Courts

Indigenous rights advocacy dates from the 1980s, involving engagement with the government and broader civil society, articulation and presentation of demands, media coverage and public awareness initiatives, civil disobedience, and peaceful protests (Open Society Justice Initiative, 2017). The failure of these initiatives to yield their desired outcomes, and increased land encroachment due to rapid land clearing and development, led Malaysia's Indigenous Peoples to employ the strategy of taking their land and resource grievances to the courts. In this regard, they have enjoyed some success through a liberal judicial interpretation of the law, and the domestic application of common law principles. However, the strategy of litigating Indigenous land rights has limitations, both doctrinally and practically. This section examines the basic principles recognized by the Malaysian courts and the challenges of relying on the court process to deliver justice for indigenous land issues.

Judicial Recognition through the Common Law

From 1996, the Malaysian courts have applied international common law developments on Indigenous land rights[19] in local cases to recognize the continued enforceability of pre-existing customary land rights of the Orang Asli and the natives of Sabah and Sarawak.[20] The first case recognizing such rights was *Adong bin Kuwau v Kerajaan Negeri Johor* (*Adong HC*)[21] from Peninsular Malaysia. In affording such recognition, the court applied principles of common law native title from other

---

[19] For commentary on these developments internationally, see, for example, McHugh (2011).

[20] See, for example, *Adong bin Kuwau v Kerajaan Negeri Johor* [1997] ("*Adong HC*") 1 MLJ 418; *Kerajaan Negeri Johor v Adong bin Kuwau* ("*Adong CA*") [1998] 2 MLJ 158; *Sagong bin Tasi v Kerajaan Negeri Selangor* ("*Sagong HC*") [2002] 2 MLJ 591; *Kerajaan Negeri Selangor v Sagong bin Tasi* [2005] ("*Sagong CA*") 6 MLJ 289; *Nor Anak Nyawai v Borneo Pulp Plantation Sdn Bhd* ("*Nor Nyawai HC*") [2001] 6 MLJ 241; *Superintendent of Lands & Surveys, Bintulu v Nor Anak Nyawai* ("*Nor Nyawai CA*") [2006] 1 MLJ 256.

[21] *Adong HC* [1997] 1 MLJ 418, pp. 426–33.

common law jurisdictions, including the landmark decisions of *Mabo v Queensland [No. 2]*[22] (*Mabo [No. 2]*) and *Calder v AG of British Columbia*[23] (*Calder*) and considered the special position of the Orang Asli under the federal Constitution and the *Aboriginal Peoples Act* 1954. *Adong HC* was affirmed on appeal in 1998,[24] opening the door for Indigenous Peoples to assert their customary territorial rights in the courts beyond the literal confines of codified law. To a considerable degree, the common law recognition of pre-existing rights of Indigenous Peoples was subsequently found to be applicable to NCR in the jurisdictions of Sabah[25] and Sarawak.[26]

In *Madeli bin Salleh* (*Madeli*), the Federal Court, the highest court in Malaysia, affirmed the domestic application of *Mabo [No. 2]* and *Calder* and decided that the Malaysian common law recognizes and protects the pre-existing rights of Indigenous Peoples to their customary lands and resources.[27] The unanimous panel in *Madeli* also held that the common law formed part of the substantive law in Malaysia and that the recognition of such Indigenous rights accorded with the *Civil Law Act* 1956, the relevant legislation enabling the domestic application of the common law.[28]

According to *Madeli*, in Malaysia, the source of the recognition of Indigenous rights to lands and resources at common law, enunciated "throughout the Commonwealth" in *Mabo [No. 2]*, *Calder*, and other colonial decisions of the Privy Council, that "the courts will assume that the Crown intends that rights of property of the *(native)* inhabitants are to be fully respected" and that "[t]he Crown's right or interest is subject to any native rights over such land."[29] The domestic applicability of the doctrine of judicial precedent meant that *Madeli* would be binding upon the lower courts in subsequent similar cases.

The main characteristics of common law Indigenous land and resource rights in Malaysia are principally derived from the early "recognition" jurisprudence from Canada and Australia, but qualified by domestic constitutional and statutory provisions for the recognition,

---

[22] (1992) 175 CLR 1.
[23] [1973] SCR 313.
[24] *Adong CA* [1998] 2 MLJ 158.
[25] *Rambilin binti Ambit v Assistant Collector for Land Revenues Pitas* ("*Rambilin*") (Judicial Review K 25-02-2002).
[26] See, for example, *Nor Nyawai HC* [2001] 6 MLJ 241; *Nor Nyawai CA* [2006] 1 MLJ 256.
[27] See *Madeli* [2008] 2 MLJ 677, p. 692.
[28] Ibid.
[29] [2008] 2 MLJ 677, pp. 691–2.

regulation, and protection of such rights. The Malaysian superior courts have ruled that the radical title held by the state is subject to any pre-existing rights held by Indigenous Peoples.[30] These rights are established by way of prior and continuous occupation of the claimed areas,[31] and oral histories of the claimants relating to their customs, traditions, and connections with these areas.[32] "Occupation" does not require physical presence but evidence of continued exercise of control over the land.[33] Additionally, the federal and state governments owe a fiduciary duty to legally protect Indigenous land rights and to not act in any manner inconsistent with such rights.[34] Customary rights in common law are enforceable through the courts.[35]

However, common law land rights can be taken away through legal extinguishment by the state or, alternatively, if the local Indigenous community is demonstrated to have abandoned its lands, territories, and resources (Bulan, 2012; Subramaniam & Nicholas, 2018, p. 71). Legal extinguishment of these rights may be by way of plain and unambiguous words in legislation,[36] or an executive act authorized by such legislation.[37] If these rights are extinguished, just compensation is due in accordance with Article 13 of the Malaysian Constitution.[38]

Limitations to Recognition through the Courts

Despite these positive outcomes, recognition of Indigenous land rights solely through the judicial arm of the Malaysian government has its own issues. This section examines the limits of the judicial system in terms of the court process, substantive law, and broader observations on judicial development of the law.

---

[30] See, for example, *Sagong CA* [2005] 6 MLJ 289, pp. 301–2; *Madeli* [2008] 2 MLJ 677, p. 692.

[31] *Nor Nyawai CA* [2006] 1 MLJ 256, p. 269.

[32] *Sagong HC* [2002] 2 MLJ 591, pp. 610, 621–4.

[33] *Madeli* [2008] 2 MLJ 677, pp. 694–5.

[34] See, for example, *Sagong CA* [2005] 6 MLJ 289, p. 314.

[35] *Nor Nyawai CA* [2006] 1 MLJ 256, p. 269.

[36] *Ketua Pengarah Jabatan Hal Ehwal Ehwal Orang Asli v Mohamad bin Nohing (Batin Kampung Bukit Rok) & Ors and another appeal ("Nohing CA")* [2015] 6 MLJ 527, pp. 542–4; *Madeli* [2008] 2 MLJ 677, pp. 690, 696–7.

[37] *Madeli* [2008] 2 MLJ 677, pp. 689, 698.

[38] *Adong CA* [1998] 2 MLJ 158, pp. 163–4; *Sagong HC* [2002] 2 MLJ 591, p. 617; affirmed, *Sagong CA* [2005] 6 MLJ 289, pp. 309–10; *Madeli* [2008] 2 MLJ 677, pp. 691–2.

Many Indigenous Peoples in Malaysia cannot afford to institute and sustain the protracted trial and appeal process to defend their traditional lands (Open Society Justice Initiative, 2017). Conversely, their opponents are usually state actors and commercial enterprises that possess ample financial resources, and also importantly, the persistent will to contest claims involving Indigenous lands and resources. Also, organizing community participation, decision-making, and unity throughout the litigation process, ranging from evidence gathering to support a claim to trusteeship matters relating to the benefits from litigation, poses significant problems for communal litigants (Open Society Justice Initiative, 2017). Further, a successful case does not necessarily mean an immediate remedy. For example, the Temuan-Orang Asli claimants in the *Sagong bin Tasi* case[39] endured twelve years of litigation, including appeals, before they received compensation for the loss of their customary lands acquired for highway construction.

The formal setting and adversarial nature of court proceedings are arguably at odds with Indigenous perspectives on dispute resolution, which are relatively less formal and more participatory (Subramaniam & Nicholas, 2018, p. 72). Language barriers, cultural, and epistemological differences, and unfamiliarity with court processes put many Indigenous witnesses at a tactical disadvantage compared to other witnesses (Nah, 2008; Subramaniam & Nicholas, 2018). The issue of evidential burden defeating Indigenous land rights claims in commonwealth jurisdictions (McHugh, 2011) persists in Malaysia. While the Malaysian courts have adopted a "realistic" approach to evaluating evidence in Indigenous land rights claims, taking cognizance of the reliance on oral traditions and the impediments in producing surveyed maps and official documentation,[40] judicial circumspection towards "self-serving" testimonies of Indigenous litigants[41] suggests that proof of a case would ultimately depend on the idiosyncrasies of a particular judge. The community's lack of financial resources to engage appropriate expert witnesses to provide corroborative evidence to a claim, and the want of experienced expert witnesses, is an additional obstacle for Indigenous litigants.

The uncertainties inherent in the litigation process transcend procedural law into the substantive jurisprudence on Indigenous land rights

---

[39] *See Sagong HC* [2002] 2 MLJ 591; *Sagong CA* [2005] 6 MLJ 289.
[40] See, for example, *Abu Bakar bin Pangis v Tung Cheong Sawmill Sdn Bhd* [2014] 5 MLJ 384, pp. 407–8.
[41] *Nor Nyawai CA* [2006] 1 MLJ 256, p. 272.

(Subramaniam & Nicholas, 2018). More recently, the latter area has seen judicial limits placed on the recognition of Indigenous rights to lands and resources in Malaysia. Common law NCR land rights have been severely restricted, particularly in the states of Sarawak and Sabah.

In the 2016 decision of *Director of Forest, Sarawak v TR Sandah Tabau* (*TR Sandah FC*),[42] the Federal Court determined by a majority that the common law recognition of NCR in Sarawak or, specifically, Iban customary rights, did not extend to the broader native customary territory (*pemakai menoa*) and forest reserved for food and forest produce (*pulau*). The primary reason was that these customs were not contained in any of the legislation and executive orders in Sarawak. This ruling goes against previous decisions that common law NCR are not dependent on legislation and executive orders[43] without adequately addressing them (Subramaniam, 2018). Notwithstanding the problematic reasoning, the majority decision in *TR Sandah* has functioned to shut the door on common law claims for broader native customary territories in Sarawak as it is a legally binding precedent. Furthermore, the 2018 amendment to the *SLC* in response to *TR Sandah* has ensured that claims for these territories are regulated by statute, thereby posing new barriers and challenges for Indigenous claimants. In *TH Pelita Sadong Sdn Bhd v TR Nyutan Jami*,[44] the Federal Court decided that indefeasibility of title under the Sarawak *Land Code* 1958 overrides NCR even if such title was issued after NCR was asserted. This determination potentially allows the state government to circumvent the formal requirements of extinguishment and defeat NCR by an administrative act of alienation, reducing legal recourse to a matter of monetary compensation. Similar rulings in other jurisdictions are viewed as discriminatory since they assume that Indigenous title is "inferior and subordinate."

In 2015, the (Gilbert, 2016) Court of Appeal held that the seasonal collection of turtle eggs by Sabah natives was "not a native customary right" as it was beyond the scope of NCR defined in section 15 of the *Land Ordinance*,[45] which only encompasses sedentarized activities. In 2016, the Court of Appeal ruled that any NCR claims must be dealt with under the Sabah *Land Ordinance*.[46] Both rulings have taken a

---

[42] [2017] 3 CLJ 1.
[43] See *Nor Nyawai CA* [2006] 1 MLJ 256, pp. 269, 70.
[44] [2018] 1 CLJ 19.
[45] *The State Government of Sabah v Ab Rauf Mahajud* [2016] 9 CLJ 493, pp. 505–6.
[46] *Assistant Collector of Land Revenues v Alfeus Yahsu* [2016] 7 CLJ 848, p. 859.

narrow view of the *Land Ordinance* compared to previous rulings that land laws in Sabah do not extinguish NCR but "serve to affirm their existence."[47]

As for the domestic application of international human rights laws, the Malaysian courts have generally expressed reluctance in "sticking very closely"[48] to them, unless enacted into local laws.[49] Furthermore, Malaysia is not a party to any binding international conventions that directly concern Indigenous rights to lands, territories, and resources. In respect of the United Nations Declaration on the Rights of Indigenous Peoples (UNDRIP), the majority of the Federal Court has held that "[i]nternational treaties do not form part of our law, unless those provisions have been incorporated into our law. We should not use international norms as a guide to interpret our Federal Constitution."[50] In the same case, Chief Justice Zaki nonetheless observed the UNDRIP "must still be read in the context of our Constitution,"[51] suggesting that the issue could be open for future consideration.

There is little doubt that land rights litigation has positive impacts for Indigenous Peoples in Malaysia. Beyond the material and economic outcomes of success, litigation has also contributed to "unlocking and reframing" land rights laws and processes, increasing community and public participation in Indigenous land rights issues, and reinforcing and strengthening communal social cohesion and cultural connections to land (Open Society Justice Initiative, 2017). However, the development of substantive Indigenous rights through the Malaysian courts is subject to conservatism, regression, and a degree of judicial unpredictability.[52] Additionally, common law litigation carries high stakes as a bad judicial precedent for Indigenous claimants invariably has adverse legal, policy, and practical implications for other local Indigenous communities facing similar issues. In other jurisdictions, court judgments on Indigenous land rights are critiqued for being influenced by extra-legal and political considerations (McNeil 2004). Such occurrences could well be aggravated

---

[47] *Rambilin* (Judicial Review K 25-02-2002), p. 7.
[48] *Pathmanathan Krishnan v Indira Gandhi Mutho* [2016] 1 CLJ 911, pp. 935–7.
[49] See, for example, *Airasia Bhd v Rafizah Shima Mohamed Aris* [2015] 2 CLJ 510, p. 521.
[50] *Bato Bagi v. Kerajaan Negeri Sarawak* [2011] 6 MLJ 297, p. 338.
[51] Ibid., p. 307.
[52] This is not an altogether unfamiliar phenomenon. For the judicial curtailment of native title in Australia, see, for example, Brennan (2003).

in Malaysia, where the judiciary has not been short of controversy surrounding executive and legislative interference in its functions (Subramaniam & Nicholas, 2018; Yap, 2015). Consequently, relying excessively on the Malaysian courts to resolve Indigenous land rights issues without positive executive or legislative intervention may not necessarily be the best way forward.

International Conservation Obligations: Potential Opportunities for Inclusion

Like many other Indigenous Peoples globally, Malaysia's Indigenous peoples possess distinct customary knowledge systems and methods to conserve, protect, and regenerate their traditional territories in a sustainable manner. In this regard, international commitments towards the sustainable use of the environment and natural resources have recognized Indigenous Peoples as significant stakeholders in matters concerning their lands, territories, and resources.

For example, the *United Nations Convention on Biodiversity* 1992 (CBD), a binding international treaty to which Malaysia is a party, recognizes the need for contracting governments to respect, preserve, and maintain the traditional knowledge, innovations, and practices of Indigenous communities (Article 8(j)), and to move towards achieving its broader objectives of conserving biodiversity, sustainably using biodiversity resources, and equitably sharing benefits from the use of genetic resources (Article 1). Key to achieving these objectives is the maintenance of healthy ecosystems and a sufficient land base for Indigenous Peoples. Accordingly, the CBD's Programme of Work on Protected Areas, agreed in 2004, has called for the recognition of Indigenous Peoples and Community Conserved Territories and Areas (ICCAs) as one of the preferred governance types for protected areas (Bulan & Maran, 2020). While ICCAs are conceptually new in Malaysia and domestic frameworks for such management are still at an early stage of development (Bulan & Maran, 2020), they nonetheless provide an opportunity for Indigenous communities within protected areas to showcase the advantages of autonomous and collaborative management agreements. The successful management by Indigenous Peoples in the Bundu Tuhan Native Reserve in Sabah provides a good illustration of how arrangements like ICCAs can work to the benefit of the community and the environment (Bulan & Maran, 2020). However, it remains to be seen whether domestic legal and policy frameworks, when developed, can produce effective and equitable co-management agreements. The requirement for such areas to be regarded as protected or conservation areas by the government may also limit the general application of this alternative form of local Indigenous governance.

Pursuant to its obligation under the CBD, the federal government passed the *Access to Biological Resources and Benefit Sharing Act* 2017 (*ABSA*) that came into force in Peninsular Malaysia at the end of 2020. The *ABSA* contains extensive provisions for the protection and recognition of Indigenous communities in respect of biological resources and traditional knowledge associated with such resources and the sharing of benefits arising from their utilization (Bulan & Maran, 2020). Of note is section 23(1)(a) of the *ABSA* that provides for the requirement of free, prior, and informed consent of the relevant Indigenous community for access to biological resources on land to which the community has rights established by law.[53] Regardless of potential disputes regarding the meaning of the phrase "established by law" and its legal interpretation, the acceptance of a statutory provision on free, prior, and informed consent at the federal level constitutes a significant breakthrough toward effective engagement with Indigenous communities in matters that concern them and their customary areas.

Certification standards for sustainably harvested timber (Malaysian Timber Certification Council, 2012) and sustainable palm oil (Roundtable on Sustainable Palm Oil, 2019) consider Indigenous rights to lands and resources in their criteria. These include grievance mechanisms that may result in the cancellation of certifications for enterprises found to be in violation of these standards. In 2023, Sarawak timber giant Samling had its Ravenscourt forest management certificate revoked for not adequately engaging with local Indigenous communities (Keeton-Olsen, 2023). Despite having limited economic and reputational consequences for the transgressor, and not legally enhancing the land tenure of local Indigenous communities, these mechanisms provide an avenue for Indigenous Peoples to voice their complaints and brings attention to transgressions. Both developments suggest that international

---

[53] The *ABSA* has not come into operation in the states of Sabah and Sarawak as both states possess their own written laws governing these matters. However, Sabah has a similar provision on the free, prior, and informed consent for biological resources located on native land where the native community has a right as established by law (see section 24B (1)(a) of the *Sabah Biodiversity Enactment* 2000).

conservation efforts have had the net effect of increasing prospects for the inclusion of Indigenous Peoples in matters affecting their traditional lands and resources.

Conclusion

Notwithstanding differences in the special legal position of the natives of Sabah, natives of Sarawak and Peninsular Malaysia Orang Asli, there is little doubt that Malaysia's governments possess sufficient power to effectively recognize and accommodate land, territory, and resource rights for all Indigenous Peoples. However, a closer examination of the legal framework governing Indigenous land rights and their implementation in Malaysia in this chapter suggests that this is not a priority.

The relevant laws in Malaysia, intended in part to empower the government to protect Indigenous Peoples for their own good, have equally enabled and justified the use of traditional Indigenous areas in accordance with government plans – thereby dispossessing Indigenous Peoples of their traditional territories in practice. In Peninsular Malaysia, poor statutory and administrative protection for Orang Asli customary areas and lands has driven the Orang Asli to pursue the strategy of litigation, where they continue to enjoy a measure of success despite formidable obstacles. These victories have functioned as an added bargaining chip for Orang Asli communities and land rights advocates in their engagements with the state. However, these negotiations have yet to cause any meaningful land reform to recognize and protect Orang Asli customary territories. This legal status quo, where Orang Asli remain largely dependent on common law customary land rights for legal redress, is precarious as these rights are susceptible to judicial and legislative curtailment in the future. As observed, experiences from Sarawak, where the apex court has limited common law native customary rights, bear witness to this potential risk.

While the natives of Sabah and Sarawak can still rely on the explicit statutory recognition of their native customary rights in state laws, these rights have been legislated and administered restrictively by the legislature and executive, and more recently, interpreted narrowly by the judiciary. These actions have limited effective outcomes for the recognition and protection of native customary rights in these two states.

As such, the main impediment in Malaysia appears to be more domestically political rather than legal. The sustained lack of political will and priority for the effective recognition and protection of Indigenous lands and resources, even in states governed by a majority of Indigenous Peoples, suggest that the challenge lies in convincing the broader Malaysian polity that meaningful land rights are not only just but important to all Malaysians. It is in this regard that the increased international demand and requirements for Indigenous involvement in the sustainable conservation of lands, natural resources, and ecosystems present an opportunity to strengthen public support for Indigenous land rights in Malaysia. Towards realizing this opportunity, contextualized cross-disciplinary research on the high correlation between empowered and engaged local Indigenous land and resource management and positive conservation outcomes in Malaysia may well be crucial to rights advocacy and, perhaps more importantly, to conscientizing the populace.

References

Amnesty International. (2018). *"The forest is our heartbeat": The struggle to defend Indigenous land in Malaysia.* London: Amnesty International.

Bernama. (2018, March 5). 80% needs of Orang Asli community fulfilled: Ismail Sabri. *The Borneo Post.* https://www.pressreader.com/malaysia/the-borneo-post/20180305/282106342142597.

Brennan, S. (2003). Native title in the High Court of Australia a decade after Mabo. *Public Law Review,* 14, 209–218.

Bulan, R. (2006). Native customary land: The trust as a device for land development in Sarawak. In F. M. Cooke (ed.), *State, communities and forests in Contemporary Borneo* (pp. 45–64). Canberra: ANU E Press.

   (2007). Statutory recognition of native customary rights under the Sarawak Land Code 1958: Starting at the right place. *Journal of Malaysian and Comparative Law,* 34, 21–84.

   (2012). *The legal framework on Indigenous land rights in Malaysia: A study to contribute to the Suhakam National Inquiry into Indigenous Peoples' land rights in Malaysia.* Kuala Lumpur: SUHAKAM.

Bulan, R., & Maran, R.G. (2020). *Legal analysis to assess the impacts of laws, policies and institutional frameworks on Indigenous People and community conserved territories and areas (ICCAs) in Malaysia.* https://www.iccaconsortium.org/wp-content/uploads/2021/06/malaysia_icca_legal-analysis_2021.pdf.

Carey, I. (1976). *Orang Asli: The Aboriginal tribes of Peninsular Malaysia.* Kuala Lumpur: Oxford University Press.

Carling, J., & Godio, M. J. (2018). Association of Southeast Asian nations (ASEAN). In P. Jacquelin-Andersen (ed.), *The Indigenous World* (pp. 604–11). Copenhagen: IWGIA.

Clifford, H. (1897). A journey through the Malay states of Trengganu and Kelantan. *The Geographical Journal*, 9(1), 1–37.

Dennison, A. (2007). Evolving conceptions of Native Title in Malaysia and Australia – A cross nation comparison. *Australian Indigenous Law Review*, 11(1), 79–91.

Dentan, R. K, Endicott, K., Gomes, A. G., & Hooker, M. B. (1997). *Malaysia and the 'Original People': A case study of the impact of development on Indigenous Peoples*. Boston: Allyn and Bacon.

Department of Orang Asli Development. (2023). *The Orang Asli of Malaysia.* www .jakoa.gov.my/en/

Department of Statistics Malaysia (2023). Official Portal. dosm.gov.my.

Doolittle, A. A. (2005). *Property and politics in Sabah, Malaysia: Native struggles over land rights*. Seattle: University of Washington Press.

Doolittle, A. (2011). Native customary land rights in Sabah, Malaysia 1881–2010. In M. Colchester & S. Chao (eds.), *Diverse paths to justice: Legal pluralism and the rights of Indigenous Peoples in Southeast Asia* (pp. 81–105). Chiangmai, Thailand: Forest Peoples Programme and Asia Indigenous Peoples Pact.

Dzulkifli, H. (2019, Nov. 17). Changes in 10 key areas: CM. *Daily Express.* http:// www.dailyexpress.com.my/news/143465/changes-in-10-key-areas-cm/.

Fernando, J. (2002). *The Making of the Malayan Constitution.* Kuala Lumpur: MBRAS.

Fong, J. C. (2008). *Constitutional federalism in Malaysia.* Petaling Jaya, Malaysia: Sweet & Maxwell Asia.

Gilbert, J. (2016). *Indigenous Peoples' land rights under international law: From victims to actors* (2nd ed.). Leiden: Brill.

Hamid, N., and Singh, R. (2012). *Sabah Native Customary Rights.* Kuala Lumpur, Malaysia: Gavel Publications.

Hooker, M. B. (1996). The Orang Asli and the laws of Malaysia: With special reference to land. *Akademika*, 48, 21–50.

Idrus, R. (2008). *The politics of inclusion: Law, history and Indigenous rights in Malaysia* [Doctoral dissertation, Harvard University]. https://id.lib.harvard .edu/alma/990115821040203941/catalog.

Keeton-Olsen, D. (2023). *Small wins for Indigenous Malaysian activists in dispute with timber giant.* https://news.mongabay.com/2023/10/small-wins-for-indi genous-malaysian-activists-in-dispute-with-timber-giant/.

Lasimbang, J. (2016). Malaysia. In D. Vinding, & C. Mikkelsen (eds.), *The Indigenous world 2016* (pp. 273–279). Copenhagen: IWGIA.

Limbu, S. (2017). UNDRIP Impact in Asia: 10 Years. In K. B. Hansen, K. Jepsen, & P.L. Jacquelin (eds.), *The Indigenous World 2017* (pp. 23–32). Copenhagen: IWGIA.

Malaysian Timber Certification Council. (2012). *Malaysian criteria and indicators for forest management certification (Natural Forest)*. Kuala Lumpur: MTCC.

Mamo, D. (ed.). (2020). *The Indigenous World 2021*. IWGIA, Copenhagen.

McHugh, P. G. (2011). *The modern jurisprudence of tribal land rights*. Oxford: Oxford University Press.

McNeil, K. (2004). The vulnerability of Indigenous land rights in Australia and Canada. *Osgoode Hall Law Journal*, 42, 271–301.

Munang, M. J. (2015). Land grabs in Sabah, Malaysia: Customary Rights as legal entitlement for Indigenous Peoples – Real or illusory? In C. Carter & A. Harding (eds.), *Land grabs in Asia: What role for the law?* (pp. 137–149). New York: Routledge.

Nah, A.M. (2004). *Negotiating Orang Asli identity in postcolonial Malaysia* [Master's thesis, National University of Singapore]. https://core.ac.uk/down load/pdf/48628668.pdf.

(2008). Recognising Indigenous identity in postcolonial Malaysian law: Rights and realities for the Orang Asli (Aborigines) of Peninsular Malaysia. *Bijdragen Tot de Taal-, Land und Volkenkunde*, 164(2/3), 212–237.

Nicholas, C. (2000). *The Orang Asli and the contest for resources: Indigenous politics, development and identity in Peninsular Malaysia*. Copenhagen: IWGIA.

(2019). Malaysia. In D. N Berger (ed.), *The Indigenous world 2019* (33rd ed.) (pp. 275–282). Copenhagen: IWGIA.

(2020). Malaysia. In D. Mamo (ed.), *The Indigenous World 2020* (34th ed.) (pp. 282–290. Copenhagen: IWGIA.

(2023). Malaysia. In D. Mamo (ed.), *The Indigenous World 2020* (37th ed.) (pp. 237–245). Copenhagen: IWGIA.

Nicholas, C., Engi, J., & Teh, Y. P. (2010). *The Orang Asli and the UNDRIP: From rhetoric to recognition*. Subang Jaya, Malaysia: Center for Orang Asli Concerns.

Noone, H. D. (1936). Report on the settlements and welfare of the Ple-Temiar Senoi of the Perak-Kelantan watershed. *Journal of the Federated Malay States Museums*, 19(1), 1–85.

Open Society Justice Initiative. (2017). *Strategic litigation impacts: Indigenous Peoples' land rights*. New York: Open Society Foundations.

Porter, A. F. (1967). *Land administration in Sarawak: An account of the development of land administration in Sarawak from the rule of Rajah James Brooke to the present time (1841–1967)*. Kuching, Malaysia: Sarawak Government Printers.

Roundtable on Sustainable Palm Oil. (2019). *Malaysia National Interpretation (MYNI) 2019 of the RSPO principles and criteria 2018 for sustainable palm oil production*. Kuala Lumpur: RSPO.

Sabah Forestry Department (2018). *Sabah Forest Policy*. Sandakan, Sabah: Sabah Forestry Department.

Subramaniam, Y. (2011). Rights denied: Orang Asli and rights to participate in decision-making in Peninsular Malaysia. *Waikato Law Review*, 19(2), 44–65.

(2013). Affirmative Action and Legal Recognition of Customary Land Rights in Peninsular Malaysia: The Orang Asli Experience. *Australian Indigenous Law Review*, 17(1), 103–122.

(2018). Legal pluralism in Malaysia: The case of Iban native customary rights in Sarawak. In A. Harding, & D. A. H. Shah (eds.), *Law and society in Malaysia: Pluralism, religion and ethnicity* (pp. 123–144). New York: Routledge.

Subramaniam, Y., & Endicott K. (2020). Orang Asli Land and Resource Rights in the Malay States, 1874-1939. *Journal of the Malaysian British Royal Asiatic Society*, 93(2), 87–118.

Subramaniam, Y., & Nicholas, C. (2018). The courts and the restitution of Indigenous Territories in Malaysia. *Erasmus Law Review*, 18(1), 67–79.

SUHAKAM (Human Rights Commission of Malaysia). (2013). *Report of the National Inquiry into the Land Rights of Indigenous Peoples.* Kuala Lumpur: SUHAKAM.

Sullivan, P. (1998). Orang Asli and the Malays: Equity and native title in Malaysia. In C. J. I. Magallanes, & M. Hollick (eds.), *Land conflicts in Southeast Asia: Indigenous peoples, environment and international law* (pp. 57–79). Bangkok: White Lotus Co.

Wilkinson, R. J. (1923). *A history of the Peninsular Malays: With chapters on Perak and Selangor* (3rd rev. ed.). Kuala Lumpur: F. M. S. Government Press.

Wong-Adamal, J. (1998). Native customary law rights in Sabah. *Journal of Malaysian and Comparative Law*, 25, 233–240.

Wook, I. (2017). The Aboriginal Peoples Act 1954 and the recognition of Orang Asli land rights. *University Utara Malaysia Journal of Legal Studies*, 6, 63–83.

Yap, P. J. (2015). *Constitutional dialogue in Common Law Asia.* Oxford: Oxford University Press.

14

Indigenous Peoples and Electoral Politics in Thailand and Cambodia

One Strategy to Secure Land Rights in Contested Spaces

IAN G. BAIRD

Introduction

Over the last few decades, Indigenous Peoples' movements in both Cambodia and Thailand have expanded and received increased recognition. While the modern concept of Indigeneity is relatively new to mainland Southeast Asia, and is still not officially recognized by many governments in the region, there is no doubt that the idea of Indigeneity is gradually gaining traction (Baird, 2016, 2019c).

The Government of Thailand has so far refused to recognize Indigenous Peoples, instead adopting what has become known as the "salt-water theory" (Erni, 2008; Baird, 2011), a position that many governments in Asia have adopted, and which Ben Kingsbury (1998) has referred to as "the Asian controversy." That is, the Thai Government recognizes that there are Indigenous Peoples in the Americas, Australia, and New Zealand, but because Thailand was not colonized by large numbers of Europeans, they deny that anyone in Thailand should be considered Indigenous, since the vast majority of those living in Thailand are of Asian descent (Morton & Baird, 2019).

The concept of Indigeneity has, however, received more legal recognition in Cambodia, especially since it was legally legitimized with the passing of the Land and Forestry Laws of 2001 and 2002, respectively (Baird, 2011, 2019a), and through various other community organizing efforts in the 2000s. In particular, registered Indigenous communities are eligible to apply for communal land titles, designed to support rotational swidden agriculture (Baird, 2013, 2019a, 2023). However, recently agrarian change has led to a greater emphasis on cash crops, and the increased prevalence of microfinance loans to farmers, collateralized by private land titles, is reducing the attractiveness of communal land titles for many Indigenous communities (Baird, 2023).

Until a few years ago, the Indigenous Peoples' movements in both Thailand and Cambodia were largely centered on non-government organizations (NGOs) and other civil society groups. However, the situation is changing. This chapter considers the intersection between Indigenous movements and mainstream electoral politics, and demonstrates how, over the last few years, some Indigenous activists in both Cambodia and Thailand – including those who have advocated for Indigenous rights over land and resources – have become more involved with mainstream electoral politics. However, this shift has not always been smooth and uncontested within Indigenous movements themselves.

Methods

This chapter is based on a series of English, Thai, and Lao language key informant interviews conducted in June and July 2019 with self-identifying Indigenous activists, academics, and members of civil society in northeastern Cambodia and northern Thailand. Interviews were also completed in both countries in relation to Indigenous Peoples over the last number of years. Social media posts were also utilized – mainly from Facebook and other media from both Thailand and Cambodia – to help make sense of how ethnic minorities, and particularly people who self-identify as Indigenous, have become more involved in electoral politics in their respective countries. This change is partially a new strategy for gaining mainstream recognition and more control over land and resources, as well as more rights to protect Indigenous languages and cultures.

The following sections provide basic information about the history of the Indigenous Peoples' movements in both Thailand and Cambodia, with the goal of presenting necessary background information for framing the material that follows.

A Brief History of Indigeneity in Cambodia

In Cambodia, discrimination against upland ethnic minorities is not new. For example, they were referred to using the pejorative "*phnong*," which Indigenous Peoples dislike (Baird, 2011). Indicative of the circumstances,

Cambodia's 1993 Constitution does not explicitly mention Indigenous Peoples, instead only referring to "the Khmer people" residing in the country (Baird, 2020). However, in the 1990s the concept of Indigeneity was introduced to Cambodia via foreigners working for various NGOs. In 2001, the concept was included in Cambodia's new Land Law, specifying that only those designated as Indigenous Peoples are eligible for communal land titles. The 2002 Forestry Law also acknowledged the existence of Indigenous Peoples in Cambodia (Baird, 2011). NGOs played critical roles in getting this legislation passed. There were also NGO-organized consultations in various parts of the country in 2003 (Swift, 2019). In 2009, a sub-decree was adopted that specified the process for designating certain communities as Indigenous, thus making them eligible for communal land titles (Baird, 2013, 2019a, 2023; Milne, 2013). Historically, the Indigenous Peoples of northeastern Cambodia conducted rotational swidden on territory controlled by villages. There was no sense of private land ownership, and only members of particular villages were allowed to do swidden cultivation on village communal lands. However, these boundaries did not apply to fishing, hunting, and non-timber forest product collection, which could occur across village boundaries.

In recent years, the laws and sub-decrees related to Indigenous Peoples that have been passed in Cambodia have been crucial for increasing legitimacy of the concept of Indigeneity. For example, there are now a number of Cambodian NGOs that engage with and provide support on Indigenous issues, including the Highlanders Association (HA), the Cambodian Indigenous Youth Association (CIYA), the Conserve Indigenous Peoples Languages Organization (CIPL), the Cambodian Indigenous Peoples Organization (CIPO), the Cambodian Indigenous Women Working Group (CIWWG), the Indigenous Rights Active Members (IRAM), and others.

In recent years, some Indigenous activists from Cambodia have increased their international strategizing. This has included the annual participation of different Indigenous Peoples and their allies at the United Nations Permanent Forum on Indigenous Issues (UNPFII) in New York City. Indeed, Keating (2020) has argued that while this forum can be frustrating for activists, and does not typically lead to recognizable or immediate changes in home countries, it can serve to socialize activists in certain ways, thus contributing to the legitimatization of Indigenous struggles and potentially expanding the Indigenous movement. In 2006, the first non-Indigenous Cambodian attended the UNPFII (Swift, 2019) and in 2007 the first Indigenous person from Cambodia – an ethnic Kuy woman – presented there. Part of this transformation has involved ethnic Bunong people from Cambodia and Bunong from the United States traveling to the UNPFII to express their concerns about social and environmental issues affecting the Bunong in Cambodia and Vietnam (Keating, 2020).

Some Bunong people have also tried to increase their profiles and expand networking with Bunong people from Vietnam in the United States (Keating, 2016, 2020). Activists have started working to bring together Bunong people living in different nation-states. Recently, one ethnic Bunong activist from Cambodia argued that change is necessary, stating that, "We have been divided by nation states and associated different ideologies, and this needs to change (Indigenous Bunong activist, 2019). Indeed, the land and forest laws differ among Bunong areas in Cambodia and Vietnam.

A Brief History of Indigeneity in Thailand

Thailand has a long history of ethnic inequality and racialized Othering (Draper et al., 2019; Vandergeest, 2003; Winichakul, 2000), and those upland minorities characterized as "hill tribes" have frequently been imagined as not belonging in Thailand (Morton & Baird, 2019; Toyota, 2005, 2007; Vandergeest, 2003).

The concept of Indigeneity was first introduced to Thailand in the late 1980s by people from outside of the country, and in 1992 the Asian Indigenous Peoples' Pact (AIPP) – a regional NGO that supports Indigenous Peoples across Asia – was founded in Bangkok by an ethnic Naga man originally from an area now included in northeast India. Since the 1990s, however, the Indigenous movement has expanded considerably in Thailand, especially in the northern part of the country (Morton & Baird, 2019). While Indigeneity is not legislatively or judicially recognized in Thailand, the Thai Government cabinet did establish, in 2010, "Special Culture Zones" for the Moken (sea gypsies) and Pwakanyaw (Karen) peoples in order to protect their cultures (Morton & Baird, 2019). In addition, in 2015 the military government in Thailand seriously considered recognizing Indigenous Peoples (which they called *chon pheun muang*) in its new constitution. However, the military later changed its mind and decided to oppose the recognition of the concept of Indigeneity within the 2017 Thai Constitution (Baird et al., 2017). In addition, the military government readopted the antiquated term "hill tribes" (*chao khao* in Thai) (Indigenous Activist, 2019), after it was dropped during the Thaksin era along with the Tribal Research Center in northern Thailand (Buadaeng, 2006).

Despite the lack of legal recognition, the concept of Indigeneity has become increasingly accepted in Thai society, and some ethnic minorities have come to self-identify as Indigenous (Leepreecha, 2019). However, the meaning of "Indigenous Peoples" remains confusing and contested in the country, even amongst minorities in Chiang Mai Province, northern Thailand, a place considered to be the center of the country's Indigenous movement (Baird et al., 2017). Indeed, *chattiphan* is better known in Thailand, although it means "ethnic group" rather than Indigenous Peoples, and without any acknowledgement of self-determination as a foundational concept.

Historically, there were a number of land tenure systems in place in the uplands of Thailand. Some Austroasiatic–language-speaking ethnic groups conducted rotational swidden cultivation. However, other Tibetan-Burman and Hmong-Iu-Mien–language-speaking ethnic groups migrated into northern Thailand from China over the last few hundred years. Each had their own land tenure systems, including both rotational and pioneering forms of swidden cultivation (Leepreecha et al., 2008; Premsrirat et al., 2004). At present, the government does not issue private land titles for the uplands of Thailand. In addition, communal land titles based on ethnicity or Indigeneity do not exist in Thailand (Morton & Baird, 2019). However, in recent years, the Thai government has begun granting some non-ethnicity-based communal land titles in northern Thailand (Witthayaphak & Baird, 2018).

From Indigeneity to National Politics in Cambodia

The concept of Indigeneity has been gradually taking root in parts of Cambodia for a couple of decades now. Recently, however, some Indigenous Peoples, led by ethnic Bunong people in Mondulkiri Province, have established a political party called the Cambodia Indigenous Peoples' Democracy Party (CIPDP) (*pak prachathipitai chun cheat doem pheak dich*), which was officially registered with the Ministry of Interior on January 30, 2017. However, its office in Sen Monorom – the capital of Mondulkiri Province – was actually established in 2016, and party organizing began at least as early as mid-2015. At that time, three or four mini buses were occasionally hired to transport Indigenous activists from Ratanakiri Province to join party meetings at Sen Monorom. One of those activists was an ethnic Tampuon man named Tan Phly. He was the former leader of Indigenous People for Agriculture Development in Cambodia (IADC), an NGO based in Ratanakiri that was forced to close down a few years ago due to poor financial management. While he was originally focused on the CIPDP, he later switched over and joined the Cambodian People's Party (CPP), the ruling party. He is now a member of Yak Loam Commune's Commune Council, in Banlung District, Ratanakiri Province. Many other mainly younger Indigenous Peoples went to the CIPDP meetings in 2015, including Indigenous intellectuals, some of whom worked for the government as schoolteachers as well as in other positions. The people in Ratanakiri who initially took an interest in the CIPDP were ethnically Tampuon, Kreung, and Jarai (Hubbel, 2019). However, according to one Bunong observer, most Indigenous Peoples in Ratanakiri dared not challenge the CPP (Bunong CIPDP advisor, 2019), as Ratanakiri has long been dominated by the CPP, particularly the ethnic Tampuon/Lao former Minister of Defense, Bou Thang, who worked with the Vietnamese who ousted the Khmer Rouge from power (Baird, 2020), and retained considerable power until he passed away in 2019.

The leader of the CIPDP is a seventy-year-old ethnic Bunong man named Plang Sin. He was an activist in the royalist FUNCINPEC Party in the 1990s and 2000s. More recently, he became involved in community forestry work with NGOs in Mondulkiri Province (Bunong CIPDP advisor, 2019). As an indication of this, he was quoted in an article published in the *Phnom Penh Post* in 2016 with regard to a lawsuit that activists were pursuing against a large agri-business company, Socfin, which had grabbed a large amount of Indigenous land near Bou Sra, and converted the land into a large rubber plantation. Expressing frustration about the slow pace of progress to improve the situation, Plang Sin was quoted as saying, "We have been waiting for negotiations and justice since 2008, when our hair was black … But now our hair is gray." Indeed, the legal system in Cambodia and internationally has so far not shown any tendency to support Indigenous struggles, as affirmed in the other chapters of this book. Although the leadership of the CIPDP is mainly ethnic Bunong, including Plang Sin himself, the CIPDP has tried to expand its base of support amongst other Indigenous groups in the country, as indicated above in relation to Indigenous Peoples in Ratanakiri Province, and in Kratie Province.

The slogan of the CIPDP is "ownership, self-determination, protection and justice," and the party's flag depicts an Indigenous man from

Cambodia riding a male elephant, along with a full moon in the center on a green background.

The party is not having an easy time. First, the Indigenous movement is apparently not strong amongst all Bunong, with many not wanting to create a conflict with the government, and often many have a long history of supporting the ruling party. In addition, according to an ethnic Bunong advisor to the party, during the 2017 commune elections and 2018 national elections, the CPP and its supporters in government tried to retain Indigenous support, while watching the CIPDP carefully to see if the party was really independent, or if there was something nefarious going on behind the scenes. However, the Vietnamese and Cambodian governments have apparently been claiming that the CIPDP is linked with political dissidents aligned with the Front Uni de Lutte des Races Opprimées (Unified Front for the Struggle of the Oppressed Races) (FULRO) (Bunong CIPDP advisor, 2019) a group of upland ethnic minorities from the Central Highlands of Vietnam. It was considered pro-United States and anti-communist Vietnam, and later became allied with the Khmer Rouge after it was forced to flee Vietnam and stay in northeastern Cambodia. They fought against the communist Vietnamese after Vietnam was unified in 1975 (Baird, 2020; Branigan, 1992; Central Intelligence Agency, 1981; Duiker, 1984; Human Rights Watch, 2002, 2011; Ngon, 1983).

Whether the government truly believes that the CIPDP is somehow connected to FULRO or not, the CPP was able to use this alleged connection effectively during the 2017 commune election and the 2018 national election campaigns, causing many voters to become doubtful of the CIPDP and their true motives. According to a Bunong CIPDP advisor, the CPP used this strategy in all Bunong-populated areas during the 2017 and 2018 election campaigns (Bunong CIPDP advisor, 2019), even though FULRO is now defunct, and most of the Bunong once allied with FULRO now disavow the group (Keating, 2019).

Another obstacle that the CIPDP has faced is a lack of financial resources, which has limited its ability to campaign effectively and widely, or to attract strong candidates to run for office. The original goal of the CIPDP was to operate nationwide, but due to limitations in representation in different areas, and insufficient financial resources, the party had to focus its efforts in parts of the country where there are larger concentrations of Indigenous Peoples. There was initially some hope that the CIPDP could win some seats in the commune elections. The party managed to get 4,000 thumbprints to establish itself, but it only received 1,272 votes during the June 4, 2017, commune elections. The CPP's strategy weakened the CIPDP, resulting in support for the party wavering at the ballot box (Bunong CIPDP advisor, 2019; Swift, 2019). Later, the government offered to give the party some of the court-dissolved Cambodia National Rescue Party (CNRP) Commune seats, but the CIPDP declined the offer, as the party leadership felt that it was not right for it to fill those seats, since the people did not democratically elect the party.

During the 2018 election campaign, the party's signs were seen in Kampong Thom Province (Ashish John, 2019). However, the ruling CPP won all the seats in the National Assembly. Although the CIPDP only garnered 10,197 votes in the 2018 national elections in Cambodia, the establishment of this political party is significant for various reasons, especially because it is the first time in Cambodia that a political party has ever been established that is particularly oriented toward upland minorities. Cambodia uses a first-past-the-post electoral system, and the CPP won all 125 seats in Parliament. After the election, the CPP decided to reach out to other smaller parties, such as CIPDP, inviting them to join the National Supreme Consultative Council. Along with various other small parties, the CIPDP agreed to join this body (Bunong CIPDP advisor, 2019), although it is unclear how seriously the government is willing to take recommendations from the group.

Some Indigenous activists in Cambodia are quite concerned about the establishment of the CIPDP. They do not want their non-political efforts to become entangled in party politics, as they fear this could decrease the credibility of the movement, and levels of support for Indigenous issues. For example, one long-time Indigenous leader in Ratanakiri Province told me that she feared that politicians might claim that the CIPDP had separatist tendencies, and that this could hurt the Indigenous movement broadly in Cambodia (Indigenous leader from Ratanakiri, 2019). She also expressed some concern about efforts to bring ethnic groups divided by national borders together, fearing that could open up those groups to attacks that they are not truly loyal to the nation. As she put it, "We need to be careful about politics, as it could shut down opportunities for Indigenous Peoples." She also said, "The Bunong in the United State are FULRO, the enemies of Cambodia; they were with the Khmer Rouge. We need to be careful with them" (Indigenous leader from Ratanakiri, 2019, also for information about the links between FULRO and the Khmer Rouge, see Voice of Democratic Kampuchea, 1980; Branigan, 1992). This narrative is similar to the discourse used by the CPP in the 2017 and 2018 elections campaigns to discredit the CIPDP.

There are also other types of concerns. Some Indigenous activists fear that the CIPDP was coopted by the government through agreeing to join the National Supreme Consultative Group. Therefore, some Indigenous activists are choosing to organize and strategize behind the scenes. Some of these people have formed an informal and unnamed national network of Indigenous activists. They deal with all kinds of Indigenous issues, but due to the new NGO law that is intended to exert more control over NGOs in the country, and the generally oppressive political climate in the country, which has worsened since the CNRP was dissolved by the Cambodian courts, they have chosen to keep low profiles. The group is skeptical about what the CIPDP can do considering the present political environment in Cambodia. However, it sometimes cooperates with officially registered organizations, including NGOs (Paterson, 2019).

From Indigeneity to National Politics in Thailand

In Thailand, unlike in Cambodia, a political party specifically oriented toward supporting Indigenous Peoples has not yet been established. However, a number of Indigenous Peoples – including some who have worked with the Indigenous movement in the past – joined various political parties and ran for office during the March 24, 2019, national elections, the first election since the 2014 coup d'état and military takeover of the government. They have particularly run as party-list candidates, due to doubts that they could win seats straight up (Sirivunnabood, October 24, 2019).

In 2004–2005, Anek Laothamatas, who was the head of the Great Group Party (*phak mahachon*) at the time, tried to convince Kert Phanakamneut to join them as a key vote mobilizer. Kert was particularly attractive to them, as he was both linked to Indigenous Peoples' activism in northern Thailand, and is also closely connected with former followers of the Communist Party of Thailand (CPT), known as *phu ruam phatthana chart thai* ["those joining to develop the Thai nation"] (Baird, 2021). However, mainstream politicians' efforts to gain the minority vote did not result in much at the time (Suebsakwong, July 2019). Much more recently, party activists again tried to recruit Kert to join them when the Palang Pracharat Party (*phak palang pracharat*) was first being formed, but he decided not to join them (Suebsakwong, July 2019).

One of the first serious efforts by ethnic minorities or Indigenous Peoples in northern Thailand to gain political representation was after the Thaksin government established the Tambon Administration

Organization (TAO) in 1994. Prior to this change, the central government appointed most subdistrict leaders, or *kamnan*, who were mainly ethnic Thais. There were, however, some exceptions. For example, in 1989, Khek Noi Subdistrict was established in Khao Khor District, Phetchabun Province, and since the population was almost all Hmong, a Hmong man named Prajuab Ritnetikul (Chaw Tua Lee) was appointed as the first *kamnan* for Khek Noi (Suebsakwong, October 2019). In any case, the new TAO system gave local people a chance to vote for local leaders at the subdistrict level, which represented an important opportunity. Many Indigenous Peoples with NGO ties were elected to local government. However, several of those who stood for local elections were initially not closely linked to particular political parties. This has, however, gradually changed. For example, in 2018, Phonsupharak Sirijanthranont, a TAO elected leader in Lamphun Province, who is himself from northeastern Thailand but is married to an ethnic Yong woman, established the Thai Ethnic Party (*phak chattiphan thai*),[1] with the hope of winning a party-list seat during the national Parliamentary elections that occurred on March 24, 2019. Most of those in the party are ethnic Lue and Yong peoples, although at least one ethnic Chong person from Chanthaburi Province in eastern Thailand joined (Leepreecha, July 2019). The leader of the party did not emerge from nowhere. He was previously a member of the Assembly of Indigenous and Tribal Peoples in Thailand (AITT), where he worked with Kert Phanakamneut and Yongyuth Seubtayat, Hmong Indigenous activists. Later, however, he left the network due to disagreements over financial management. However, the party was not able to garner enough votes to win any seats in 2019 (Leepreecha, July 2019).

The author first heard of Indigenous activists becoming seriously involved with mainstream electoral politics in Thailand in June 2018, even before official party-political activities were allowed. Kert Phanakamneut and Yongyuth Seubtayat had joined the Thai Local Power Party (*phak phalang thongthin thai*), a small political party established in 2012. The party is led by Chatchewal Kong-udom, also known as Chat Taopoon, a Chinese Thai businessman and former gambling godfather. He was also previously a Bangkok Senator and because he had a relationship with Kukrit Pramoj, he was able to become the executive editor of the well-known Thai language daily newspaper, *Siam Rath*,

---

[1] *Chattiphan* refers to "ethnic group." The term differs from *chon phao phuen muang*, which specifically refers to indigeneity in Thailand (Morton & Baird 2019).

which Kukrit founded before he became prime minister of Thailand from 1975 to 1976. Crucially, Kert became deputy leader of the party, and Yongyuth was elected on June 2, 2018, as ethnic minority coordinator for the party. Notably, Yongyuth was previously the director of an NGO called the Hmong Association for Development in Thailand (MDT), with Kert as the vice-chair. Moreover, Yongyuth played a key role with regards to the Indigenous movement in Thailand, as MDT worked closely with the Association for Inter-Mountain Peoples' Education and Culture in Thailand (IMPECT), with staff moving between the two organizations, and MDT and IMPECT sometimes organizing joint activities (Suebsakwong, October 2019). Moreover, Yongyuth has defended Indigenous activists in court, and has written draft legislation in support of recognizing Indigenous rights in Thailand (Phanakamneut, 2018). Both Kert and Yongyuth were apparently sufficiently impressed with the policy of the party to decentralize power to the local level. In the Khek Noi area, the most populous ethnic Hmong community in Thailand, the Thai Local Power Party candidate was a Hmong man named Da Songsawatwong (Xiong).[2] The party-list candidate for the Thai Local Power Party in the same area was Yotying Senyakul (Chua Po Yang), who is also Hmong. A Thai retired military general in Bangkok, Sittideth Wongpratya, introduced Yongyuth and Kert to Chatchewal, and later indirectly promoted the party through his Thai language television show about ethnic minorities in Thailand.

Another important political party to consider is the Prachachart Party (*phak prachachart*), led by Wan Muhammad Noor Matha, better known as Wan Noor. He formally headed up the Wadah faction of the New Aspiration Party (*phak khwam wang mai*), led by General Chavalit Yongchaiyudh. He joined the Thaksin Shinawatra's Thai Rak Thai Party (*phak thai rak thai*) in the early 2000s. The Prachachart Party is particularly strong amongst Muslim voters in the deep south of Thailand, where it won six seats in the 2019 election. It also gained a single party-list seat, thus giving it seven seats for the 481,490 votes (1.35 percent of national vote) it gained. Crucially for this chapter, the party not only vied for the Muslim vote in the deep south, but also Indigenous Peoples' support in other parts of the country. For example, the Hmong 18 Clan Council of Thailand, which became interested in promoting Hmong candidates during the 2019 election, became particularly aligned with

---

[2] Da Songsawatwong (Xiong) was involved in Hmong transnational filmmaking in Khek Noi Subdistrict, Khao Khor District, Phetchabun Province (see Baird, 2014, 2019b).

the Prachachart Party after the party agreed to provide the 18 Clan Council with funding to support the activities of the Council. The Hmong 18 Clan Council claimed they could deliver 200,000 Hmong votes for the party, but they did not even get close to doing so. This resulted in some of the leadership of the Prachachart Party claiming that the Hmong cannot be believed, as they could not deliver the promised votes. In addition, some Hmong in Wieng Pa Pao District of Chiang Rai Province joined the Prachachart Party, but not until less than ninety days before the election, thus resulting in those Hmong not being eligible for party-list seats (Leepreecha, July 2019). The Prachachart Party also tried to create alliances with other Indigenous groups in Thailand apart from the Hmong.

In the end, the Thai Local Power Party only garnered about 800 of the many thousands of potential Hmong votes in the Khek Noi area, despite running strong Hmong candidates there, and Khek Noi is also Yongyuth's community. According to one observer, Yongyuth tried to attract support for the Party by promising to try to get the land in Khek Noi from the government and officially given to the Hmong people in Khek Noi. But this strategy only attracted interest from some elders. Some believe that he did not investigate the interests of younger people sufficiently. Younger Hmong people are apparently less likely to vote along ethnic lines than older people. The Prachachart Party chose a Hmong man named Adisak Bamrungkheeree (Hang Tsua Khang), who lives in Lao Lue Village, in Khao Khor Subdistrict, Khao Khor District to be an electoral candidate of Phetchabun Section 1, with the support of the Hmong 18 Clan Council. This caused serious disagreements between Hmong people in the Thai Local Power Party and in the Prachachart Party (Suebsakwong, October 2019). The Prachachart Party candidate only obtained about 500 votes.

The Palang Phracharat Party, with a non-Hmong candidate, ended up with the most votes in Khek Noi. They had the support of the provincial government structure, and the former Pheu Thai Member of Parliament (MP) in the area switched over to join the Palang Phracharat Party (Suebsakwong, October 2019). He is a member of the controversial Thammanat faction of the party (Sirivunnabood, October 19, 2019). The next most popular was the Future Forward Party (*phak anakhot mai*), which fielded an ethnic Thai candidate, but attracted the support of many young Hmong voters, who were attracted by the party leader. The party effectively used social media to connect with younger voters (Suebsakwong, July and October, 2019).

Nationally, the Thai Local Power Party did not do very well, gaining only 214,189 votes, or 0.60 percent of the total vote. It only ended up with three party-list seats, with none given to Hmong in the party. After the election, the party joined a coalition with the military Palang Pracharat Party, which has tarnished the party's reputation among some people.

The Hmong Thai Business Association became increasingly involved in electoral politics during the 2019 national elections, based in Chiang Mai. Two prominent leaders, Dr. Chanvit and Pho Luang Amnuay (Dou Jeng Sheng Yang in Hmong), and others, worked closely with the 18 Clan Council, and used clan leaders to mobilize votes. They worked to encourage Hmong people to run as candidates in all Hmong-populated areas (Yangcheepsujarit, 2019). However, one Hmong observer from Khek Noi believed that endorsements from the 18 Clan Council had very little impact on Hmong voters between eighteen and thirty years old, and that they did insufficient homework about what young voters were looking for (Suebsakwong, July 2019).

Yet, younger Hmong voters were attracted to the Future Forward Party, which promised to end the military draft in Thailand (Suebsakwong, July 2019). The party was also viewed as being pro-ethnic minority (Vaddhanaphuti, 2019), and has a strategy for promoting minorities (Yangcheepsujarit, 2019). Many people who were initially with the AITT, established in 1998, and later with the Network of Indigenous Peoples in Thailand (NPIT) (*kheua khai chon phao phuen muang*),[3] established in 2007, ended up campaigning in 2019 for the Future Forward Party. Initially some Indigenous leaders sided with the Thai Raksa Chart Party (*phak thai raksa chart*), led by well-known former Pheu Thai politician and student leader and CPT ally, Chaturon Chaiseng, but when the party was dissolved by the Thai Constitutional Court on March 7, 2019, many supporters switched to campaigning for the Future Forward Party. Younger Indigenous activists – and younger people more generally – ended up strongly supporting the Future Forward Party, not because they were linked to a particular ethnic group, or Indigenous Peoples more generally, but because their policies were generally more attractive (Vaddhanaphuti, 2019; Yangcheepsujarit, 2019).

Hmong voters still have a lot of interest in gaining political representation in Thailand. Za Xong Moua, the leader of the 18 Clan Council of Thailand, put it this way, "We, Hmong, have been in Thailand for almost

---

[3] This was the first time that an NGO in Thailand explicitly used the phrase Indigenous Peoples (*chon phao phuen muang*) in its name (Leepreecha, 2019).

200 years and we do not have the position to voice our rights to get support to maintain our culture and customs. If the election goes the way we planned, we will have a voice with other groups to get support to maintain our culture and customs" (Suab Hmong News, 2019). This statement articulates the key reasons motivating Hmong people to run for political office.

In 2019, the first ethnic Hmong person ever was elected to the Parliament in Thailand, winning a party-list seat in Tak Province for the Future Forward Party. Nattaphon Suebsakwong (Keng Sae Yang) is a fifty-three-year-old man born in northern Phetchabun Province, who now lives in Tak Province, where many Hmong from Phetchabun moved at the end of the Communist Party of Thailand (CPT) (*phak communit thai*) in the early 1980s (Baird, 2021). His wife is from Khek Noi, and he acted there in transnational Hmong films about the Hmong in the CPT (see Baird, 2019b), which convinced the party to take him on as a candidate (Suebsakwong, July 2019). Moreover, Nattaphon's older brother Lu Yang is also a well-known Hmong singer (Leepreecha, July 2019). Nattaphon appears committed to his people. He declared that, "I want to introduce laws that guarantee land ownership and citizenship for my people, create a body that represents ethnic minorities and establish cultural protection zones for the minorities in which, for example, we are able to freely perform our funerary rites" (Galache, 2019). He is concerned about addressing citizenship problems for some ethnic minorities in Thailand (see Toyota, 2005, 2007; Vandergeest, 2003). He is also looking for similar broad protections agreed to by the Thai Cabinet in 2010 for the Moken and Pwakanyaw peoples (Morton & Baird, 2019). However, as the first Hmong MP ever, there is apparently a lot of pressure on him from the Hmong community in Thailand (Suebsakwong, July 2019); only time will tell what he is actually able to achieve.

Nattaphon was not, however, the first Indigenous person to become an MP in Thailand. A Pwakanyaw man held a seat in Maehongson Province for one term, but he was deemed to have not been very successful as a politician, thus leading him to serve just one term in office (Vaddhanaphuti, 2019).

Another Indigenous politician, an ethnic Pwakanyaw man, Nawaphon Keereeraksakul, almost got a party-list seat with the Democrat Party in the 2019 election. He too has a strong NGO and Indigenous Peoples' activism background, having previously worked for IMPECT in Chiang Mai. In 2019, the Democrats and the Future Forward Party both campaigned for elected rather than central government–appointed governors in the province, a position that minorities might well support. However, Nawaphon missed out, as the Democrat Party generally did not perform well, and the Democrats did not list minorities high on their party-list (Sirivunnabood, October 19, 2019).

Somchart Lalaem is another ethnic Pwakanyaw TAO chief who entered politics after previously playing a big role in supporting community forestry and land titles for communities in northern Thailand. He used his network in northern Thailand to support his political career, but he was not elected in 2019. Crucially, however, he is not linked with NPIT, but rather with a different NGO network in northern Thailand, the Northern Farmers Federation (Vaddhanaphuti, 2019).

Some ethnic Pwakanyaw activists in Phetburi Province, in western Thailand, have also become involved in party politics through supporting the Green Party (*phak see khieo*) in Thailand (Leepreecha, 2019). However, the Party is new and is not well known, and thus only received 22,568 votes, which amounts to 0.06 percent of the national vote.

Other minority politicians have also moved up from being elected to Tambon Administrative Organizations (TAO). The Future Forward Party, in particular, promised to put up candidates to contest these local positions. In the past, political parties in Thailand tended to stay out of local politics, but this may be changing. Future Forward particularly strove to support politically marginalized groups, such as ethnic minorities, Indigenous Peoples, and the LGBTQ community (Vaddhanaphuti, 2019). However, the military apparently saw Future Forward as a threat, and the Constitutional Court of Thailand dissolved the party on a technicality on February 21, 2020. The former Future Forward MPs joined other parties, but the majority became MPs for a new Move Forward Party (*phak kao kai*), including the Hmong MP from Tak, Nattaphon Suebsakwong.

One of the main reasons that more ethnic minorities or Indigenous Peoples have become involved in electoral politics is that previously it was a requirement that all MPs have at least a university bachelor's degree, but the constitution in 2017 removed that requirement, thus opening up more opportunities for minorities to engage in electoral politics. In addition, in recent years Indigenous Peoples have become more knowledgeable about national politics, and social and business networking (Leepreecha, 2019). In addition, some political parties in Thailand have considered allocating a certain percentage of their candidates to ethnic minority candidates, and the Elections Council of

Thailand has expressed interest in finding ways to encourage more women and minority candidates in elections, although it remains unclear how this might be done (Sirivunnabood, October 19, 2019).

Some Indigenous leaders also moved around between different political parties. For example, a retired ethnic Lisu police general was initially aligned with Kert and the Thai Local Power Party, but later decided to change alliances and move to another party (Leepreecha, 2019).

Crucially, however, as with Cambodia, some key Indigenous movement leaders in Thailand, such as Kittisak Rattanakrajangsri (ethnic Iu-Mien) and Sakda Saenmi (ethnic Lisu), the director of IMPECT, have chosen to stay out of electoral politics. They fear that becoming engaged in party electoral politics could damage the credibility of the movement, cause division within the Indigenous community, or otherwise work against the interests of Indigenous Peoples in Thailand (Leepreecha, 2019).

Conclusion

This chapter has focused on how Indigenous activists in both Cambodia and Thailand have variously and recently become more involved with electoral politics, although not in the same ways, or with the same results. In Cambodia, a new explicitly Indigenous Peoples' political party was established, and contested the 2017 commune elections and the 2018 national elections, although with various limitations. In Thailand, however, Indigenous activists have become involved with electoral politics, but not through setting up an Indigenous political party as occurred in Cambodia. Instead, some Indigenous Peoples, both those connected with the Indigenous Peoples' movement and those connected with other activist networks, have joined various political parties not explicitly linked with the movement and stood as candidates during the 2019 national election. This has led to some disappointments but has also resulted in the first Hmong person gaining a party-list seat in the Thai Parliament.

It is noteworthy that these developments have occurred in Cambodia and Thailand as Indigenous Peoples in both countries are trying to gain more control over land and other natural resources. In Cambodia, the CIPDP was established during a time when smaller political parties were being promoted by the ethnic Khmer activist Kem Ley, a well-known member of civil society who was assassinated on July 10, 2016. He had direct contact with some Bunong leaders before he was killed, and encouraged them to set up a political party. Since then, the CNRP, the main opposition party, has been dissolved. This dissolution has resulted in increased domination of the CPP in Cambodia politics, and the general decline of democracy in Cambodia. In Thailand, however, increased involvement of Indigenous Peoples in party politics followed the coup d'état in May 2014, and a period of strong military control of the country, including the writing of a new constitution that ensured the strong role of the military in politics through Senate appointments.

Moreover, the electoral approach adopted in Thailand uses a proportional representation system that is particularly advantageous for smaller political parties. Indeed, about 100 parties tried to register in Thailand, with over seventy eventually being successful in doing so. Undoubtedly, the particular political circumstances in both Cambodia and Thailand have been important factors in the rise of Indigenous Peoples in party electoral politics in both countries.

Crucially, however, the movement of Indigenous activists into national electoral politics has been criticized by some. Certain Indigenous activists have expressed concerns that mixing of Indigenous movements with electoral politics could be detrimental to the Indigenous movements in both Cambodia and Thailand. So, do Cambodia and Thailand represent a trend in the region? This may be the case. In the Philippines an Indigenous Peoples' party, Sulong Katribu, contested the 2016 national elections. However, it failed to gain a party-list seat as hoped. This is not because of a lack of votes but because the Elections Commission and the Supreme Court refused to accredit Sulong Katribu to participate in the elections (IWGIA, 2019). There were also indications that Indigenous activists in Myanmar were considering their future involvement in electoral politics in the country (Vaddhanaphuti, 2019), but since the February 2021 coup d' état electoral politics has become less of a focus.

Does the involvement of Indigenous Peoples in electoral politics represent a step forward for the Indigenous movements in each country, and the securing of more rights over land and natural resources? Or does their direct involvement in electoral politics jeopardize the Indigenous movements? It is probably still too early to answer decisively, but the shifts that have occurred in both Cambodia and Thailand – in the latter there has not been a supportive institutional framework for Indigenous Peoples' rights – have been significant nonetheless. More attention and consideration are required, although the particular contexts in each country require particular attention.

Acknowledgements

Thanks to all those in Thailand and Cambodia who agreed to be interviewed for this study, particularly Prasit Leepreecha, Chayan Vaddhanaphuti, Urai Yangcheepsutjarit, Dave Hubbel, Neal Keating, Yutthapong Suebsakwong, Phunchada Sirivunnabood, Dam Chanty, Peter Swift, and Gordon Paterson. Thanks to others who asked me to remain anonymous. Thanks also to Neal Keating, Peter Swift, Yutthapong Suebsakwong, Urai Yangcheepsutjarit, Phunchada Sirivunnabood, John Draper, and William Nikolakis for comments on earlier drafts of this chapter. Ultimately, however, I remain responsible for the chapter's content.

References

Ashish John, personal communication, June 27, 2019.

Baird, I. G. (2011). The construction of 'Indigenous Peoples' in Cambodia. In L. Yew (ed.), *Alterities in Asia: Reflections on identity and regionalism* (pp. 155–176). Routledge, London.

(2013). 'Indigenous peoples' and land: Comparing communal land titling and its implications in Cambodia and Laos. *Asia Pacific Viewpoint*, 54(3), 269–281.

(2014). Chao Fa movies: The transnational production of Hmong American history and identity. *Hmong Studies Journal*, 15(1), 1–24.

(2016). Indigeneity in Asia: An emerging but contested concept. *Asian Ethnicity* 17(4), 501–505.

(2019a). The politics of indigeneity in Southeast Asia and Cambodia: Opportunities, challenges, and some reflections related to communal land titling in Cambodia. In N. Gombay, & M. Palomino-Schalscha (eds.), *Indigenous places and colonial spaces: The politics of intertwined relations* (pp. 176–193). New York: Routledge.

(2019b). Hollywood movies: 1.5 generation Hmong Americans and transnational film production in Thailand. *Sojourn: Journal of Social Issues in Southeast Asia*, 34(3), 366–396.

(2019c). Introduction: Indigeneity in 'Southeast Asia': Challenging identities and geographies. *Journal of Southeast Asian Studies*, 50(1), 2–6.

(2020). *Rise of the Brao: Ethnic minorities in Northeastern Cambodia during Vietnamese occupation*. Madison: University of Wisconsin Press.

(2021). The Hmong and the Communist Party of Thailand: A transnational, transcultural and gender relations-transforming experience. *TRaNS: Trans-Regional and National Studies of Southeast Asia*, 9(2), 167–184.

(2023). Indigenous communal land titling, the microfinance industry, and agrarian change in Ratanakiri Province, northeastern Cambodia. *The Journal of Peasant Studies.* 51(2): 267–293.https://doi.org/10.1080/03066150.2023.2221777

Baird, I. G., Leepreecha, P., & Yangcheepsujarit, U. (2017). Who should be considered "Indigenous"? A survey of ethnic groups in northern Thailand. *Asian Ethnicity,* 18(4), 543–562.

Branigan, W. (1992, October 11). Montagnards end fight against Hanoi. *Washington Post.*

Buadaeng, K. (2006). The rise and fall of the Tribal Research Institute (TRI): "Hill Tribe" policy and studies in Thailand. *Southeast Asian Studies,* 44(3), 359–384.

Bunong CIPDP advisor, personal communication, June 28, 2019.

Central Intelligence Agency. (1981). Antigovernment resistance in Vietnam. Langdon: National Foreign Assessment Center, Central Intelligence Agency.

Draper, J., Sobieszczyk, T., Crumpton, C.D., Lefferts, H. L., & Chachavalpongpun, P. (2019). Racial "Othering" in Thailand: Quantitative evidence, causes, and consequences. *Nationalism and Ethnic Politics,* 25(3), 251–272.

Duiker, W. J. (1984). The legacy of history in Vietnam. *Current History,* 409–412, 432–433.

Erni, C. (Ed.) (2008). *The concept of Indigenous Peoples in Asia: A resource book.* Copenhagen: International Work Group for Indigenous Affairs.

Galache, C. S. (2019, May 24). Ethnic minorities represented for 1st time in Thai parliament with Hmong MP. EPA-EPE, Madrid, Spain.

Hubbel, Dave, communication, Banlung, July 4, 2019.

Human Rights Watch. (2002). *Repression of the Montagnards: Conflicts over land and religion in Vietnam's Central Highlands.* New York: Human Rights Watch.

(2011). *Montagnard Christians in Vietnam: A Case Study on Religious Repression.* New York: Human Rights Watch.

Indigenous activist, personal communication, October 7, 2019.

Indigenous Bunong activist, personal communication, June 28, 2019.

Indigneous Leader from Ratanakiri Province, personal communication, Banlung, July 1, 2019.

International Work Group on Indigenous Affairs (IWGIA) (2019). Indigenous Peoples in Philippines. https://www.iwgia.org/en/philippines

Keating, N. B. (2016). Kites in the Highlands: Articulating Bunong Indigeneity in Cambodia, Vietnam and abroad. *Asian Ethnicity,* 17(4), 566–579.

(2020). Traversing the scales of rights: Interventions from indigenous peoples of Cambodia at the United Nations. In I. Bellier and J. Hays (eds.), *Scales of governance and Indigenous Peoples* (pp. 105–136). New York: Routledge.

personal communication, October 7, 2019.

Kingsbury, B. (1998). Indigenous Peoples in international law: A constructivist approach to the Asian controversy. *American Journal of International Law*, 92(3), 414–57.

Leepreecha, P. personal communication, Chiang Mai, July 14, 2019.

(2019). Becoming Indigenous peoples in Thailand. *Journal of Southeast Asian Studies* 50(1), 32–50.

Leepreecha, P. McCaskill, D., & Buadaeng, K. (2008). *Challenging the limits: Indigenous Peoples of the Mekong region*. Chiang Mai: Silkworm.

Milne, S. (2013). Under the leopard's skin: Land commodification and the dilemmas of Indigenous communal title in upland Cambodia. *Asia Pacific Viewpoint*, 54(3), 323–339.

Morton, M., & Baird, I.G. (2019). From Hill Tribe to Indigenous Peoples: The localization of a global movement in Thailand. *Journal of Southeast Asian Studies*, 50(1), 7–31.

Ngon V. (1983). *FULRO: Tap doan toi pham [FULRO. A criminal organization]*. Ho Chi Minh City, Vietnam: Cong An Nhan Dan.

Paterson, G. personal communication, Banlung, July 4, 2019.

Phanakamneut, Pho Luang Kert. personal communication, Khunklang Village, Chom Thong District, Chiang Mai Province, June 8, 2018.

Premsrirat, S., Dipadung, S., Suwannaket, E., Buasuang, A., Chusri, I., Srichampa, S., Thavornpat, M., Thawisak, A., & Damsa-art, P. (2004). *Ethnolinguistic maps of Thailand*. Bangkok: Office of the National Culture Commission.

Sirivunnabood, Punchada. personal communication, October 24, 2019.

personal communication, October 19, 2019.

Suab Hmong News. (2019, February 3). Hmong 18 Clan in Thailand supports candidates to get elect in public offices.

Suebsakwong, Yutthapong. personal communication, Bangkok, July 18, 2019.

personal communication, October 7, 2019.

Swift, Peter. personal communication, October 8, 2019.

Toyota, M. (2005). Subjects of the nation without citizenship: The case of 'Hill Tribes' in Thailand. In W. Kymlicka & B. He (eds.), *Multiculturalism in Asia* (pp. 110–135). Oxford: Oxford University Press.

(2007). Ambivalent categories: Hill tribes and illegal migrants in Thailand. In P. K. Rajaram & C. Grundy-Warr (eds.), *Borderscapes: Hidden geographies at territory's edge* (pp. 91–115). Minneapolis: University of Minnesota Press.

Vaddhanaphuti, Chayan. personal communication, Chiang Mai, July 14, 2019.

Vandergeest, P. (2003). Racialization and citizenship in Thai forest politics. *Society & Natural Resources*, 16(1), 19–37.

Voice of Democratic Kampuchea. (1980, February 4). FULRO appeal to DK Government. *BBC Summary of World Broadcasts*.

Winichakul, T. (2000). The others within: Travel and ethno-spatial differentiation of Siamese subjects 1885–1910. In A. Turton (ed.), *Civility and Savagery: Social Identity in Tai States*, (pp. 38–62) Curzon, London.

Witthayapak, C. & Baird, I. G. (2018). Communal Land Titling dilemmas in Northern Thailand: From community forestry to beneficial yet risky and uncertain options. *Land Use Policy* 71, 320–328.

Yangcheepsujarit, U. personal communication, Chiang Mai, July 16, 2019.

15

Conclusion

Reclaiming Land Rights under the Pressure of Nation-States – Insights and Future Directions from Sápmi

OULA-ANTTI LABBA

Dispossession and Resistance: The Pathway to Recognition and Reclamation

The Sámi are an Arctic Indigenous Peoples. The Sámi lands, what we call Sápmi, are in the northern part of Scandinavia and across Russia's Kola peninsula. Sápmi and the Sámi people have been divided up over the course of history by the nation-states of Sweden, Norway, Finland, and Russia. Like the experiences of the Indigenous Peoples shared across this book, those of the Sámi indicate that they too have been dispossessed. Likewise, the Sámi have also fought back against this dispossession. It is through ongoing resistance and persistence that positive changes take root.

The Alta conflict, for example, involved a series of protests in Norway during the late 1970s and early 1980s against the construction of a hydro-electric power plant in the Alta-Kautokeino River (in Northern Sámi language, *Álta-Guovdageaineatnu*) in Sámi area, northern Norway. For the first time in history, Sámi organizations and activists, together with environmental activists, rallied against the Norwegian Government. Despite major demonstrations, eventually the hydroelectric power plant was built. But the resistance led to the recognition of Sámi rights on many levels.

For instance, after the conflict the Sámi Rights Commission was established. This Commission wrote a report resulting in the Norwegian Constitution recognizing Sámi culture and society. The Sámi Rights Commission also proposed the establishment of a Sámi Parliament, which had its first elections in 1989 (Somby, n.d.). Later on, through the courts, came a recognition of Sámi customary and collective rights to their lands in Norway, and their constitutional right to fishing in Finland.

We see this pattern above throughout this edited collection – dispos-session followed by resistance and then some recognition by the state. It is an unfortunate fact, however, that for many Indigenous Peoples their lands have not been reclaimed. They do not even have access to their lands, let alone any secure land title to them.

This concluding chapter weaves the themes from this book with the Sámi experience, and offers future directions for thinking about land rights in the context of the pressure of nation-states.

Insights from the Sámi and their Resistance

The official colonization of Sápmi commenced in the seventeenth and eighteenth centuries by the Swedish Crown (Kingdom).[1] The official settlement politics by these nation-states have since then gradually dis-placed the Sámi as a majority in Sápmi. Today, Sámi are a majority in only a few municipalities.

Sámi Governance

The ancient Sámi were governed by the *siida* (Sámi Village) system. In each *siida*, families formed their own economic entities for the annual fishing, hunting, and reindeer cycle, which are important livelihoods for Sámi (Hyvärinen 2010, p. 126). It is possible to demonstrate the existence of legal concepts comparable to land ownership in the *siida* society. There were boundaries to land and water in *siidas* that were exclusive, and smaller inherited tax lands for private families, or the Sámi tax lands (Korpijaakko, 1986). Legal history research shows that members of the *siidas* owned their taxlands, and *siidas* had a collective responsibility to pay taxes to the kingdoms in which the *siidas* were located. The ancient *siidas* disappeared from Finland when it became part of Russia in the nineteenth century, even though *siida* members continued to pay taxes for their lands until the 1920s (Korpijaakko-Labba, 2000). Also, in other parts of Sápmi, the ancient *siidas* disappeared as state borders were fixed, reindeer herding changed, and land-use decisions became centered in the state (Aikio, 1992; Päiviö, 2011).

---

[1] However, the non-state-based colonization of Sápmi and exploitation of its natural resources began at the dawn of Middle Ages, and expanded during the thirteenth and fourteenth centuries when trade with Sámi flourished, and taxes were levied on them (Baer, 1982).

In Sweden, the *siida*-based reindeer herding, hunting, and fishing rights have survived, albeit with reduced legal protection, as part of reindeer herding communities (*sameby*) (Korpijaakko-Labba, 2000). The reindeer herding *siida* system, still in existence today, is an adaptation of ancient *siida* principles for large-scale nomadic reindeer herding (Sara, 2009).

Sámi Resistance

For as long as we remember and know, we the Sámi have had to fight for our rights. For a long time, this fight was mostly at the local level. For example, in the year 1584, local Sámi complained to the King of Sweden, John III, that farmers from the south had caused them harm by invading their lands. The king drew up a letter of protection for the Sámi, forbidding the farmers from trespassing on Sámi lands. The members of the Sámi village kept this letter carefully and appealed to it to secure their rights in the courts in the year 1727, showing a continuous resistance against dispossession (Fellman, 1912).

In the modern era, the Sámi Elsa Laula-Renberg gathered Sámi for their first joint cross-border meeting in Trondheim, Norway's Sámi region, on February 6, 1917. The goal of the meeting was to strengthen the legal status of the Sámi people and to end discrimination against them (Labba, 2021). Since then, the Sámi's rights as an Indigenous Peoples have been recognized in the constitutions of Finland, Norway,[2] and Sweden.[3] These are individual and collective rights based on international law. Only Norway has ratified the International Labour Organization (ILO) Convention 169 on Indigenous and Tribal Peoples. As part of the ILO 169 implementation process, the so-called state land in Finnmark was transferred to the Sámi inhabitants of Finnmark through an organization called FeFo (Finnmark Commission) in July 2006, enabled by the Finnmark Act of 2005 (Saami Council et al., 2022).[4] In Russia, Sámi rights

---

[2] Amendment (FOR-2023-05-26-739) to the constitution of Norway in 2023 recognized Sámi as an Indigenous Peoples.

[3] In the constitution of Sweden, the Sámis are recognized as people. The Instrument of Government (1974, p. 152) Section 2 Subsection 6: "*The opportunities of the Sami people, and ethnic, linguistic and religious minorities to preserve and develop a cultural and social life of their own shall be promoted.*"

[4] Many Sámi think argued the Finnmark Act is deficient, and have also criticized FeFo's actions, which are seen as restricting the Sámi right to self-determination. It is also worth mentioning that the area that is defined in the Finnmark Act is only a part of the traditional Sámi lands on the Norwegian side (Saami Council et al., 2022).

activists have been facing increasingly difficult, almost impossible circumstances in recent years (Labba, 2022).

Litigation

There have been a number of significant legal cases on Sámi rights. In the 1981 Tax Mountain case[5] (Skattefjällsmålet), the Supreme Court of Sweden found that nomadic people, like the Sámi, can acquire ownership rights to land and water through long-term use (claimed from time immemorial) and occupation of derelict land (Samiskt informationscentrum, n.d.). In the January 2020 *Girjás* case, drawing from historical evidence, Sweden's Supreme Court found that the Girjás Sámi had established exclusive rights to small game hunting and fishing on their lands. Thus, the Sámi reindeer herding community had an exclusive legal right to manage hunting and fishing in the Girjás area (Saami Council, 2021).

In the 2001 *Svarskog case*, the Norwegian Supreme Court ruled that the Olmmáivággi Sámi community had acquired collective ownership to a parcel of land through communal utilization since time immemorial. This ruling was found to conform with Article 14 (1) of the ILO Convention No. 169 (Environmental Law Alliance, n.d.). The decision followed a century of resistance by the Sámi (Senter for nordlige folk, n.d.).

Finland's Constitution provides the Sámi with the right to maintain and develop their own language and culture (section 17 (3)). Culture is understood broadly, and extends to protecting traditional Sámi livelihoods, such as reindeer husbandry, fishing, and hunting (Government proposal HE 309/1993 vp). Constitutional fishing rights have prevailed for Sámi fishers where these have come into conflict with state fishing legislation and regulations (Labba, 2023).

Norway's Supreme Court has also upheld a right to cross-border reindeer herding, a right confirmed as early as 1751 in the Lappekodisil Protocol. Norway's Supreme Court held that Sámi from the neighboring Saarivuoma reindeer herding community from Sweden "have a right to herd reindeer in the disputed area in Norway, independent of provisions

---

[5] The case mostly dealt with the ownership of certain areas known as tax mountains covering an area of about 4,000 square kilometers in the parishes of Frostviken and Hotagen in the northern parts of Jämtland province in Sweden (Bengtsson, 1982a). The main claims of the Sámi parties were dismissed by the Supreme Court, but the Court disclaimed the statement made elsewhere that nomads cannot acquire ownership rights (Bengtsson, 1982b).

found in the *Cross-border Reindeer Herding Act,* including its regulations" (Hofveberg, 2021). However, the court also held that the
Norwegian state does not need to financially compensate the
Saarivuoma for past infringements of that right, and that the parties
must bear their own litigation costs before the court. On the costs issue,
the Saarivuoma reindeer herding community is appealing to the
European Court of Human Rights (Skoglund, 2022).

Norway's Supreme Court ruled in 2021 that a license to construct a
large wind power plant in the South Sámi reindeer herding area violated
the Convention of Civil and Political Rights, Article 27. The implementation of the verdict is still an ongoing process, and the slow progress has
caused large protests in Norway by the Sámi and human rights activists
(Rasmussen, 2023).

It is also worth mentioning that international treaty bodies such as the
Human Rights Committee and the Committee on the Elimination of Racial
Discrimination (CERD) have implemented the United Nations Declaration
on the Rights of Indigenous Peoples (UNDRIP) in recent decisions on the
rights of the Sámi.[6] This can be seen as a clear signal that UNDRIP is a core
instrument of international law for Indigenous Peoples' rights.

Strategies for Securing Land Rights, and Overcoming the Barriers: Insights from the Collection

The chapters in this book show the diverse strategies used by Indigenous
Peoples to have their rights recognized by the state, and to reclaim their
lands. These strategies include direct action, where Indigenous Peoples
physically resist dispossession, political activism, and litigation like that
pursued by the Sámi. The opening chapter by William Nikolakis
described the activism and litigation used by Yolŋu people in northern
Australia to safeguard their land rights. Litigation has been an important
strategy in Australia, Botswana, Brazil, Canada, Chile, and Malaysia.
However, Fernanda Frizzo Bragato and Jocelyn Getgen Kestenbaum
documented in Brazil that the state applied the "temporal framework
doctrine" (*tese do marco temporal*) to contest Indigenous land claims –
though with a change in government, there appears to be more political

---

[6] CCPR/C/124/D/2668/2015 (*Sanila-Aikio v. Finland*), CCPR/C/124/D/2950/2017
(*Näkkäläjärvi et. al v. Finland*), *Ågren et al. v. Sweden* (CERD/C/102/D/54/2013), and
Nuorgam et al. v. Finland (CERD/C/106/D/59/2016). Three of the cases mostly deal with
the political participation rights of the Sámi.

support for Indigenous land rights. In many countries the courts have simply ignored or avoided the land rights and title of Indigenous Peoples. In the chapter on the Democratic Republic of Congo (DRC), Lassana Koné writes that the Baka, Bambuti, and Batwa peoples have pursued community forestry concessions as an intermediary strategy to secure some jurisdiction over their lands, where the courts and state ignore their customary land titles. This approach by the Baka, Bambuti, and Batwa peoples is fraught with administrative hurdles, and they remain vulnerable to encroachment without secure title. The recent Indigenous Peoples' rights legislation in the DRC may be helpful to address this problem.

The chapters show that the process toward recognition and reclamation is non-linear. In Paraguay, Correia, Villagra-Carron, and Glauser documented a pattern of "pendulum policies" starting with the violation and transgression of Indigenous land rights, moving towards justice and then back again to transgression. In Canada, where First Nations peoples have constitutionally backed rights, Diamond and Sanderson illustrated how the Torrens land titling system in Western Canada remains a major barrier to land reclamation, and brings into question the settler land titles. In New Zealand, Jones and Acosta concluded that the statutory approach to land rights has reduced the potential scope for change and treating land as *tāonga tuku iho* (a treasure that connects current generations with their ancestors and future generations). In India, Ambagudia showed that despite the focus on restoring lands to *Adivasi* peoples through statutory measures, there has been an overall decline in formal-titled *Adivasi* land holdings. In India, federalism and power to sub-national governments are frustrating land rights policies. While Indigenous Peoples may have constitutional recognition and land rights frameworks, as exemplified in Malaysia by Subramaniam, without secure and binding commitments that are coupled with social change there will always remain an "implementation gap" in land rights laws. Efforts to address the implementation gap, like the failed constitutional reforms in Chile, analyzed by Tomaselli, and the Peace Accord in Colombia in the chapter by Bolaños and Camilo Niño, illustrate the contested and highly politicized contexts in which Indigenous land rights exists.

In several of the chapters, Indigenous Peoples are not recognized for their rights. In Botswana, Hitchcock, Sapignoli, and Smith Moeti wrote that the country does not recognize the San as Indigenous Peoples, and High Court judgments supporting land and water rights are simply ignored, leaving San in a precarious tenure position. In Morocco, Bendella and colleagues documented the forces of a Pan-Moroccan

Islamic identity that is subsuming the *Amazigh* (the country's Indigenous Peoples). However, Amazigh's *agdal* land rights system and the *j'maa* (local community assemblies) have survived in the High Atlas, and create a socio-ecological balance in this fragile region. Finally, Baird shows how, in Cambodia and Thailand, Indigenous Peoples are pursuing political strategies, seeking to build support in the electoral system to influence change and land rights.

These strategies used by Indigenous Peoples show their ingenuity and resilience for reclaiming their lands, often in the face of severe discrimination and violence.

Opportunities and Future Directions

Governments have made commitments to addressing land justice for Indigenous Peoples, yet in many instances, there are significant barriers to delivering on these promises. Processes like the Peace Accord in Colombia and new legislation in the DRC herald national commitments to land rights – but the pathways are unclear and there will always be resistance, like that to the recent failed constitutional reforms in Chile that aimed to strengthen Indigenous land rights, and the rejection of the Indigenous Voice to the Australian Parliament in late 2023.

Amongst all of this, there are customary systems and institutions that have been maintained in the face of severe assimilative pressures, like the Moroccan *agdal* system and the reindeer herding *siida* system across Sápmi, which offer critical lessons for creating robust and resilient institutions and land rights. These examples point to the need for Indigenous Peoples to look inwards and build on their own governance moving forward. However, there is a critical need to secure land for the collective survival of Indigenous Peoples all over the world. If this is reached, the benefits to people, the planet, and biodiversity will all be considerable since Indigenous Peoples are also the custodians of much of the world's biodiversity and forests.

Concluding Thoughts

A longtime Sámi rights advocate Lars-Anders Baer summarized the land rights issue well from the Sámi perspective:

> The future of the Sámi as a people and of the Sámi Way of life and culture is inseparable from the question of our right to land and water. . ..
> Our Sámi land is literally speaking the foundation for our existence as a

people and an absolute requirement for our survival as such. It is the source of natural development for the Sámi economy and culture and guarantee for future generations of the Sámi in freedom to choose Sámi alternative (1982, p. 11).

The Sámi fight for the recognition of their land rights is part of the international Indigenous movement. It has led to a development in recognizing the Indigenous rights at the local, state and international levels. The ILO 169 Convention and UNDRIP are the best examples of the legal instruments that have been the outcome of the movement. However, these instruments have neither been fully implemented by nation states, nor have the judgments on Indigenous land rights by the highest courts been followed. Thus, land rights, to a large extent, remain unfulfilled. What is required in general is respecting, recognizing and safeguarding Indigenous Peoples' land rights and rights to use their natural resources. Indigenous Peoples have had, since time immemorial, a strong connection to their own lands and the core of their culture is related to these regions and the natural resources within. A first but major step is for all nation-states with Indigenous Peoples to create appropriate legislation to protect land rights in ways that are designed by Indigenous Peoples themselves and reflect their institutions, values, and goals. A non-negotiable requirement is for any legislation to be dependent on the free, prior, and informed consent of Indigenous Peoples themselves. Drawing from the insights from this book, the next step is for the state to support a comprehensive and good faith implementation of these land rights. Without this commitment, the reclamation of Indigenous Peoples' lands will remain just that – an elusive promise.

References

Aikio, S. (1992). *Olbmot ovdal min*. Girjegiisá Oy: Ohcejohka.

Baer, L. (1982). The Sami: An Indigenous People in their own land. In B. Jahreskog (ed.), *The Sami national minority in Sweden* (pp. 11–22). Stockholm: Rättsfonden.

Bengtsson Bertil (1982a). Introduction. In B. Jahreskog (ed.), *The Sami national minority in Sweden* (pp. 143–145). Stockholm: Rättsfonden.

(1982b). Afterword. In B. Jahreskog (ed.), *The Sami national minority in Sweden* (pp. 249–250). Stockholm: Rättsfonden.

Environmental Law Alliance. (n.d.). The Supreme Court of Norway's judgement in 2001: Landowners and right-holders in Manndalen, under cadastral

Nos. 29 – 35 in the Municipal Area of Kåfjord. https://www.elaw.org/system/files/svartskogdommen.pdf

Fellman, I. (1912): *Handlingar och uppsatser angående Finska Lappmarken och lapparne (III)*. Helsinki: Finska litteratursällskape.

Hofverberg, E. (2021). *Norway: Supreme Court defines extent of Swedish Sami reindeer herder rights.* www.loc.gov/item/global-legal-monitor/2021-07-28/norway-supreme-court-defines-extent-of-swedish-sami-reindeer-herder-rights/

Hyvärinen, H. J. (2010). Saamelaisten kulttuurin ja elinkeinojen sääntely. In K. Kokko (ed.), *Kysymyksiä saamelaisten oikeusasemasta* (pp. 120–148). Rovaniemi: Lapin yliopisto.

Korpijaakko, K. (1986). Is a nomad a landowner after all? In T. Utriainen, H. Vento, & R. Foley (eds.), *Lapin korkeakoulun oikeustieteiden osaston juhlakirja, Juridica Lapponica no. 1. 1986* (pp. 158–183). Rovaniemi: Lapin korkeakoulu.

Korpijaakko-Labba, K. (2000). *Saamelaisten oikeusasemasta Suomessa kehityksen pääpiirteet Ruotsin vallan lopulta itsenäisyyden ajan alkuun.* Guovdageaidnu: Sámi Instituhta.

Labba, O. (2021). *Vihapuhe nostaa ikävästi päätään saamelaisten kansallispäivän alla.* https://www.suomenpen.fi/oula-antti-labba-vihapuhe-nostaa-ikavasti-paataan-saamelaisten-kansallispaivan-alla/

(2022). *Russia: Sámi livelihoods under threat as mining in the Arctic gathers pace.* https://minorityrights.org/wp-content/uploads/2022/06/2022_MR_Report_170x240_v7-1.pdf

(2023). Finland: Fishing restrictions may lead to the disappearance of an ancestral way of life. https://minorityrights.org/wp-content/uploads/2023/06/Minority-and-Indigenous-Trends-2023-Focus-on-water.pdf.

Päiviö, N. (2011). *Från skattemannarätt till nyttjanderätt: en rättshistorisk studie av utvecklingen av samernas rättigheter från slutet 1500-talet till 1886 års renbeteslag.* Uppsala: Uppsala universitet.

Rasmussen, E. (2023). *Norway to pay Sámi reindeer herders millions for violating their human rights.* https://grist.org/global-indigenous-affairs-desk/norway-to-pay-sami-reindeer-herders-millions-for-violating-their-human-rights/.

The Saami Council. (2021). *Statement on the Draft General Comment No. 26 (2021) by the Committee on Economic, Social and Cultural Rights on land and economic, social and cultural rights (CESCR).*

The Saami Council, Saami University of Applied Sciences (Sámi allaskuvla) and International Work Group for Indigenous Affairs. (2022). *Indigenous Navigator in Sápmi. The national survey Norway.* https://indigenousnavigator.org/data-explorer/2.

Samiskt informationscentrum. (n.d.). *Domstolsprocesser om rätten till land och vatten.* https://www.samer.se/3605.

Sara, M. N. (2009). Siida and traditional Sámi reindeer herding knowledge. In C. Southcott (ed.), *The Northern Review no. 30* (pp. 153–177). Yukon: Yukon University.

Senter for nordlige folk. (n.d.). *Kampen om Svartskogen.* https://nordligefolk.no/sjosamene/historie-religion/kampen-om-svartskogen/.

Skoglund, J. (2022). *Europadomstolen tar upp Saarivuoma samebyns överklagan.* https://sverigesradio.se/artikel/saarivuoma-sameby-och-norska-staten-mots-i-europadomstolen.

Somby, Á. (n.d.). *The Saami hungerstrike in 1979.* http://www.jus.uit.no/ansatte/somby/hunger.html.

INDEX

For EU product safety concerns, contact us at Calle de José Abascal, 56–1°,
28003 Madrid, Spain or eugpsr@cambridge.org.

www.ingramcontent.com/pod-product-compliance
Ingram Content Group UK Ltd.
Pitfield, Milton Keynes, MK11 3LW, UK
UKHW022113170925
463025UK00008B/304